INDIAN INDEPENDENCE MOVEMENT IN EAST ASIA

INDIAN INDEPENDENCE MOVEMENT IN EAST ASIA

KESAR SINGH GIANI

GYAN

Published by

Gyan Publishing House
5, Ansari Road
Daryaganj, New Delhi-110002
Phone: 011-47034999, 9811692060
E-mail: books@gyanbooks.com

Distribution Network
gyanbooks.com
India, USA, Canada, UK, Australia

ISBN: 978-93-7169-354-7 (HB)
First Published, 1947

2nd Impression 2025

Printed at: Gyan Press, Delhi.

INDIAN INDEPENDENCE MOVEMENT IN EAST ASIA
Author: KESAR SINGH GIANI

Unity **Sacrifice** **Faith**

INDIAN INDEPENDENCE MOVEMENT IN EAST ASIA

The Most Authentic Account

of

The I. N. A. and The Azad Hind Government

Compiled from the original official records

BY

KESAR SINGH GIANI

Civil Administrator

Provisional Government of Free India

WITH A FOREWORD

BY

SRIYUT SARAT CHANDRA BOSE

DEDICATED

TO THE MEMORY

of

Countless Martyrs
who laid down their lives
in the cause of India's Battle of Freedom
in East Asia

Memorial to unknown Azad Hind Martyrs
at Singapore
The foundation stone was laid down by
Netaji Subhash Chandra Bose on July 8, 1945

CONTENTS

PART II

1 Woodburn Park

Calcutta

15th January, 1947

FOREWORD

In this book entitled "Indian Independence Movement in East Asia", Sardar Kesar Singh Giani has given a historical narrative of that Movement. His narrative starts from the beginning of this century and ends with the end of the last World War. Sardar Kesar Singh has done me the courtesy of handing over to me a pre-publication copy of his book and I have glanced over its pages with interest and profit.

Unfortunately, very little is known to the younger generation about the great Indian revolutionaries, who left India in the early years of this century and went to Japan, China, Siam, Malaya and other lands and started their revolutionary activities there with the object of liberating India from foreign yoke. Sardar Kesar Singh has done well in giving to Young India a short account of the activities of those great revolutionaries who dreamt dreams of Indian Freedom and worked for the realisation of their dreams. I hope in the next edition of his book, Sardar Kesar Singh will give a fuller account of their lives and activities.

The greater part of his book is devoted to the Indian National Army—its formation, its dissolution, its re-formation under the leadership of its Supreme Commander NETAJI SUBHAS CHANDRA BOSE and the fight it launched for the achievement of Indian Independence. I am sure that the pages which deal with the Indian National Army and its achievements will be read with very great interest by those who are interested in the study of Indian history and in the movement for Indian Independence.

The last World War was a war between rival Fascisms—Anglo-American Fascism on the one-hand and Axis Fascism on the other. When it was in progress, British old school ties and their Indian counterparts went the length of describing the Supreme Commander and Officers and men of the Indian National Army as Quislings, traitors and puppets. But the facts that have come out since, have proved disconcerting to those who let loose the tongue of calamony. History has already pronounced its verdict upon the Indian National Army and its Supreme Commander and that verdict is, that if there was any army which and any commander who, during the last War fought for freedom and democracy, it was the Indian National Army and its Supreme Commander.

The Indian National Army, it is true failed to achieve independence for India during the last World War. But the record of its great achievements will always remain inscribed in the pages of history. The movement for Indian Independence may suffer defeats, it may seem to languish for a while, it may even retreat for a moment; but, even in its retreat it will continue to mature and will eventually win because the conditions which gave it birth have given it the dynamism necessary for its triumph. The spirit of the Indian National Army has permeated into the soil and soul of Indians and nothing can kill it.

I commend Sardar Kesar Singh's book to the reading public of India

Sarat Chandra Bose

INTRODUCTION

The writer needs no apology for bringing out the present volume. The achievements of the Indian National Army and the story of the bold bid made for the Independence of India by the Indian patriots in East Asia, are so fascinating and soul-stirring that they have created a deep interest and desire in the minds of Indian public to know more and more about them. The Indians in East Asia, first under the able guidance of that verteran revolutionary-Sri Rash Behari Bose-and General Mohan Singh and then under the dynamic personality of Netaji Subhash Chandra Bose made a novel experience of winning the Freedom India from without. The movement was so wonderfully organized and its achievements, were so glorious that even the worst enemies of of India had to acknowledge its force and potentialities. The Indians of all nationalities in East-Asia gave their whole-hearted and willing co-operation and support to the movement. With an unrivalled fervour and zeal, they gladly sacrificed their all, including their lives at the Altar of their country's freedom. When Netaji asked them for the 'total mobilization' of their resources to fight the enemy, the response was magnificient. Millions of dollers were collected in no time, thousands of youngmen offered themselves for national service and not a few families dedicated their all for the cause of their motherland. Never before in our history was so much spirit, enthusiasm or unquenchable thirst for freedom infused in our hearts.

The Indian Independence Movement in East Asia, has made an immense contribution to our struggle for freedom. The political achievements of those three years and eight months (Dec. 1941-Aug. 1945) have enabled the Indians to raise their heads with pride and dignity before the world. For the first time in modern history a Government of Free India was formed and recognized by nine friendly powers. A National Army several thousands strong, armed with modern weapons and trained and officered entirely by Indians was formed and recognized as an Army of Free India. This Army fired by boundless enthusiasm and a desire to 'Do or Die' for India's emanicipation, went to battle with slogans of 'Chalo Delhi' and 'Blood, Blood and Blood' on their lips. They proved their mettle on the battle-field and by their personal disregard of dangers and hardships and by their enormous sacrifices left an impress on India's history, which can never be effaced.

The desire to serve in the cause of India's liberation, became such a burning passion with the East-Asia Indians, that even the womenfolk came forward and asked to be enlisted as soldiers in the Army of Liberation. So a special regiment known as Rani of Jhansi Reginment was formed, The members of this corps underwent full military training and gave as good an account of themselves as their brothers-in-arms. They gave a practical proof of the magnificient part, which the Indian women can play in India's battle of Freedom and became a living example to Indian womanhood in future for patriotism and heroism,

The Azad Hind Fauj had another subsidiary organization called the 'Balak Saina.' Thousands of boys and girls from eight years upwards joined this body and received national training. They were brought up in an atmosphere of patriotism and independence and showed a wonderful spirit of sacrifice, comradeship and enthusiasm in the great cause.

But Nataji did not give his attention to military matters only. With a peculiar organizing capacity, penetrating insight and far-sightedness, he set up an elaborate Government machinery to run the movement. The 'Azad Hind Bank', the Civilian Training Centres to train civilians as administrators in liberated areas, the 'Azad Hind Dal' and various other departments under the Indian Independence League were efficiently organized and bore an eloquent testimony to the remarkable resourcefulness and the magnificient administrative and organizing capacity of the Indians.

The marvellous sacrifices of the East-Asia Indians and the Azad Hind Fauj have not gone in vain. They have left many lessons for us and have instilled in us full faith and confidence in our mission as well as in our capabilities. No doubt, the movement failed to achieve its immediate object but the bold struggle and innumberal sacrifices form a glorious chapter of the Indian Independence Movement and deserve to be written in letters of gold. Their amazing sacrifices would serve as a beacon-light to inspire and guide the nationalist India in its fight for freedom.

A true, authentic and comprehensive account of the whole movement was, therefore, a hard necessity. During the days of the struggle itself, true facts did not come to light due to the strict censorship by the Indian Government. No doubt, there were regular broadcasts from the Azad-Hind Radio Stations at Saigaon, Singapur and Bangkok, but very little was known about these to the general Indian public. Instead incorrect and distorted accounts of the movement were given out by the British Broadcasting stations and All India Radio, in which it was stressed that the Indian National Army was Japanese-sponsored Army and a puppet in their hands. No stone was left unturned to discredit the movement and lower the liberators of India in the eyes of the Indian public.

The cessation of war has brought to light the true and bright side of the Indian Independence Movement in East Asia to some extent. The personal contact of the leaders of the movement with the Indian public and the facts placed before the Court-Martial in the first trial of the officers of the Indian National Army, have helped to dispel many a doubt and suspicions. Quite a large number of books have been published on this subject, but due to their zeal to be first in the market or to their ignorance of facts, most of the writers have indulged in half-truths and have produced readiug matter, which gives very meagre and scanty knowledge and mostly incorrect and incomplete information about the movement. An all-comprehensive and exhaustive account of the whole movement was urgently needed in order to appease the thirst of the Indian public for a true and fuller information about this glorious movement. It is with this object in view that I have made this humble attempt to set forth, the history of the movement in detail.

I went to Malaya in 1936 and from the very beginning associated myself with the Indian patriots there and began to work for the movement in my own humble way. Just after the attack of the Japanese on Malaya I along with some other friends, started a paper called 'Azad Hind' and we began to do active propaganda in the British Indian Army and Malai Indians to fight for the freedom of India. The paper was made over to the Indian Independence League, after the fall of Singapore and later on became its official organ. I was all along actively connected with the movement and had therefore had the opportunity of having first-hand and inner knowledge about it. In the later stages, I was selected as a member of the Azad Hind Sewak Dal, which was trained for the civil administration of the liberated areas In that capacity, I had the privilege of marching along with the Azad Hind Fauj upto the Arakan and Imphal Fronts and work in the liberated areas of Manipur. I returned to Malaya with Netaji Subhas Chandra Bose, when he left Burma on the 24th April, 1945.

Much of the account of the Indian Independence Movement was available to the general public in East Asia in the form of official reports, statements, speeches and Govt. documents, newspapers, pamphlets, books and propaganda leaflets, published on a large scale, during the period of active operations. But I had also the benefit of have personal knowledge and the rare privilege of having access to some of the private and secret documents of the Indian Independence League. After the surrender of the Japanese, I had to go underground for about one year. During this period the available material was sifted and sorted and it is with this authentic material that the present volume has heen compiled.

I have set forth the bare facts about the movement in a choronological order and have purposely refrained from giving any colour to these or commenting upon controvertial matters. I do not claim to have any degree of command over English language or to have psesented the reader with a literary treaties. But I hope the book would give the reader a true picture of the eventful four years of Indian Independence Movement in East Asia.

About the disruptions and ruptures between the Indian leaders during the first stages of the movement, my personal view is that they were due to honest differences of opinion and so I have refrained from apportioning the blame.

India is passing through the most critical stage in her Independence struggle. The stage is being set for the final battle to free India. The pious hope of Netaji Subhas Chandra Bose. " India would be free and before long " is going to materialize and more than ever India needs now the soul-stirring story of Netaji's achievements. I hope, this book will be read with deep interest by all the patriotic Indians,

In the end, I have to thank my numerous friends for helping me to collect and preserve the records, more especially Mr. Ranbir Singh and S. Tarjit Singh of Messrs Boor Singh Inder Singh Bangkok for making available to me numerous valuable and rare photographs. I have also to thank Giani Lal Singh B. A. of Gujranwala, without whose active help and indefatigable efforts, this book would not have seen the light of the day. He kindly undertook to help me in sifting and arranging the matter and go through the proofs. My special thanks are due to Sriyut Sarat Chandara Bose, who very kindly spared time from his multifarious engagements to go through the book and write a foreword to it.

Mohini Road
Lahore
Jan. 18, 1947.

K. S. Giani.

Sri Rash Behari Bose

President Council of Action
Indian Independence League

General Mohan Singh

General Officer Commanding
Indian National Army

Indian Independence Movement in East Asia

PART I

National Anthem

I

Subh sukh chain ki barkha barse Bharat bhag hai jaga.
Punjab, Sind, Gujrat, Maratha, Dravid, Utkal, Banga.
Chanchal sagar Vindh Himala, Nila Jamna Ganga.
Tere nit gun gayen, Tujh se jiwan payen, sabh tan paye asha.
Suraj ban kar jag par chamke, Bharat nam subhaga.
Jai ho, Jai ho, Jai ho ; Jai, Jai, Jai, Jai ho Bharat nam subhaga.

II

Sab ke dil men prit basae, teri mithi bani.
Har sube ke rahne wale, har mazhab ke prani.
Sabh bhed aur fark mita ke, Sabh god men teri a ke
Gunden prem ki mala.
Suraj ban kar jag par chamke, Bharat nam subhaga
Jai ho, Jai ho, Jai ho, Jai, Jai, Jai, Jai, ho Bharat nam subhaga

III

Subah sawere pankh pankheru, tere hi gun gayen.
Bas bhari bharpur hawaen, Jiwan men ru t layen.
Sab mil kar Hind pukaren, Jai Azad Hind ke nare,
Piara desh hamara
Suraj ban kar jag par chamke Bharat nam subhaga
Jai ho, Jai ho, Jai ho, Jai, Jai, Jai, Jai ho Bharat nam subhaga

CHAPTER I

INDIAN REVOLUTIONARIES IN THE FAR EAST

It was in the beginning of this century that some Indians connected with the terrorist movement in India went to Japan, China, Siam and Malaya and started revolutionary activities, with the object of liberating India from foreign yoke. Realizing that there was no scope in India of an armed revolution or secret subversive activities, they shifted the sphere of their work to foreign lands. Their intention was to profit by the rivalries of the Great World Powers and oust the British from India with the help of a foreign country.

The foremost of these revolutionaries was Sri Rash Behari Bose, who had escaped to Japan in 1911, after throwing a bomb on Lord Hardinge. The Government of India had offered a reward of twelve thousand rupees for his arrest. In Japan he organised the struggle for India's Independence. He wielded considerable influence among the higher Japanese political circles and his activities were indirectly supported by the Japanese Government.

The movement was carried on by Mr. R.B. Bose during the First Great War. His main work consisted in doing strong anti-British propaganda and in creating bitter feelings against the British among Indians in these countries. About the same time, another great Indian patriot Raja Mahendra Partap was exiled from India and he also took shelter in Japan. He started a paper named " World Federation " and preached universal love and world peace.

At this time about three million Indians were living in various parts of East Asia. A vast majority of them worked as labourers or watchmen in Malaya and their economic condition was far from being satisfactory. They had played a great part in the development of this country, but the British Malayan Government had not made any attempt to improve their lot. There was no proper provision with regard to health, medical treatment and education of their children. The labourers also demanded standard minimum rates of wages, with provision for full wages during sickness, periodical bonus and gratuity for long service. There was great resentment among Indians of all classes as these demands were not complied with. They felt that the cause of all their sufferings was their slavery. So in Malaya also an Indian Association was formed and Mr. Nilkhanda Ayyar and Mr. Raghavan carried on an intensive propaganda for the Independence of India. The visit of Pandit Jawahar Lal Nehru to Malaya in May 1937 and his stirring addresses to his countrymen there, kindled their patriotic fervour and devotion towards India. He infused a new spirit in them. A conference of Indian nationalists was held at Tokyo, where in all leading workers participated and decided to intensify propaganda for Indian Independence in Thailand, Malaya and Burma. After the outbreak of hostilities in Europe in Sep. 1939, the activities of the Indian revolutionaries took a new turn. They secretly circulated anti-British literature in the British Indian Forces in Malaya and incited them for a revolt. They also sent a party to infiltrate India and do anti-British propaganda.

A *gadar* (revolutionary) party had been formed in Shanghai under the leadership of Baba Osman Khan. This party published a newspaper called *gadar*. It was circulated in all the principal towns of China, Japan, Java, Sumatra, Indonesia and even in Burma, Malaya and India. When Shanghai fell into the hands of Japanese, Baba Osman, in collaboration with the Japanese Navy sent some of his men to India *via* Thailand and some other youngmen to Malaya to do anti-British propaganda in the British Indian Forces.

The members of the Shanghai Revolutionary party used to visit Hongkong. As a result of their secret visits and subversive activities, three *granthis* (priests) of a Sikh Infantry battalion were arrested and deported to India, on the alleged charge of hatching a conspiracy. This created a good deal of stir in Hongkong.

Reverting to Thailand, we find that it was the centre of Indian revolutionary activities. The most prominent institution of Indians in Bangkok was Thai Baharat Culture Lodge. It had been opened by a great Indian scholar and philosopher named Swami Satya Nanda Puri. This gentleman was a disciple of Sri Rabindara Nath Tagore and had intimate connections with some of the arch revolutionaries of India. He was the first to hoist the Indian National tricolour in Thailand, the ceremony being performed by H. R. H, Prince Wan Waithiyakon of Thailand. This institution imparted cultural, physical and spiritual education to the Indian Youths. Swamiji was mainly concerned with literary activities. By a comparative study of Indian and Thai culture, he tried to cement the bond of friendship between the Thai and the Indian people. But side by side, he carried on political propaganda for the liberation of India in his institution. He wielded great influence among the Indians of Thailand and just after the outbreak of Japanese War, started an Indian National Council in Bangkok and began to work for the Indian Independence.

Another veteran revolutionary in Bangkok was Baba Amar Singh—a symbol of love, devotion and sacrifice. He had been arrested during the first Great War along with Pandit Sohan Lal and S. Budha Singh. He underwent rigorous imprisonment for 22 years. For some time in 1927 he was kept in Rangoon Jail along with Sri Subhas Chandra Bose. After his release, he managed to escape to Thailand and began his revolutionary activities again. He had grown too old for hard work but fortunately he found a worthy and helpful companion in the person of Giani Pritam Singh*—a Sikh missionary of Bangkok. This young patriot had devoted his life for the freedom of his motherland and under the guidance of Baba Amar Singh, he did considerable underground work before the outbreak of war. He used to address letters to the British Indian Army in Malaya and Burma and these letters were secretely circulated in the Indian Forces. A facsimile of one of these letters has been given on opposite page.

---

*S. Pritam Singh (born Nov. 1910) came of a noble Sikh family of Nagoke Sarli in the district of Lyallpur (Punjab). After matriculating, he joined the Lyallpur Agricultural College. But he left the college without completing his studies, as he had taken a liking for religious and political studies. He then joined the Shahid Sikh Missionary College Amritsar, where he topped the list of successful candidates in the annual examination. He became one of the active workers in the Sikh political circles. During the Kashmir disturbances of 1928, he was

See page 18

PRITAMSINGH SIKH MISSIONARY

GURDWARA SINGH SABHA

written in simple words for Indian soldiers

(Copy)

Bangkok 5 — 9 — 1941

Dear Indian Soldiers in Malaya & Burma! We advise you to follow the programme of the Indian National Congress under the direct leadership of our great Saint Mahatma Gandhi & the programme instructed by our Indian patriots abroad. The programme for you is that you should never obey the orders of your English Commanders when they would order to attack Thailand. Thailand is connected with India through Religion of Lord Buddha, Culture & Sanskrit literature. Therefore Thailand is a brother Country to India. So you should not fight them in any case. And you should never fight Japan, Germany or any country who is enemy of British, because all such countries are our indirect friends. So to come to the Conclusion you should never help England in this war. If English loose this war there would be an ample chance for India's freedom. Some deceiving English propagandists would cheat you and the writer has heard that English dogs bark before the innocent Indians to show that they (English) are saving India from Germany, Japan or some other enemy countries of England who want to govern India, but it is wrong. No country has ever done any wrong to India, except these English pirates & thieves in disguise of democratic devils as they call themselves. Congress & patriotic Indians like Independent League of India prohibit you to follow English.

(Pritamsingh ...)

Bhai Chanda Singh was another revolutionary working in Southern Thailand. He was a simple man, kind of heart and a source of consolation to the poor, destitute and orphans. An arch enemy of Imperialism and Capitalism, he was known to rob the rich to feed the poor. You could always find him in the midst of poor labourers in their cottages, chatting and laughing with them and consoling them in their sorrows and miseries. Later on he became the personal informer of Sri Subhas Chandra Bose.

The Shanghai branch of revolutionary party, later on got direct contact with the revolutionaries of Thailand. We find the address of Baba Osman Khan in S. Pritam Singh's diary. The revolutionaries for doing anti-British propaganda in British Indian Forces in Malaya were sent through Bhai Chanda Singh. Once two revolutionaries named, Bh. Harnam Singh and Bhai Kartar Singh came to Bhai Chanda Singh. He deputed Bh. Sadhu Singh of Sungli Golok (on the border of Thailand and Malaya) for infiltrating them into Malaya. They crossed the Malayan-Thai border without any mishap and reached safely at Kota Bharu (Kelantan) In those days the C.I.D. of the British were very vigilant and all these gentlemen were arrested at Kuala Krai. Though there was no legal proof of their guilt, they were sentenced to rigorous imprisonment of ten years each. They underwent their sentence in Kota Bharu jail, till the surrender of the British in Malaya. After their release by the Japanese they joined the Indian National Army. But while in Jail, Bhai Sadhu Singh lost one of his legs by the bombardment of the Japanese and was confined in hospital for several months afterwards.

Baba Osman Khan sent S. Tara Singh and some other men to infiltrate into India through Burma, before the East Asia war, to contact the revolutionaries in India. They were successful in their attempt and returned to Burma after one year with some more men when the war had broken out. The Head Quarters of the Provincial Government of Free India had been, by then, transferred to Burma and S. Tara Singh was again sent to India by Netaji Subhash Chandra Bose, with some other men. But he betrayed the cause and all his companions were arrested and either executed or sentenced to life imprisonments.

Foot note continued

despatched there at the head of volunteer corps. Again in 1930, he led a group of 300 Akalis to Peshawar to protest against high-handedness of the Government in suppressing the Red Shirt (or Khudai Khidmetgar) Movement. He was arressted at Gujrat, while still on the way and was sentenced to rigorous imprisonment for a year and half. The contact of many nationalist leaders in jail made him a confirmed nationalist. On the 11th April 1933 he went to Bangkok (Thailand) as a missionary of the Singh Sabha Bangkok. His vast learning, simple living, bold and fearless character, broad mindedness, love and sympathy for the poor and patriotic fervour for his motherland, won for him the respect of all Indians.

He came in contact with the Indian revolutionaries in the Far East like Raja Mahendra Partap and Baba Amar Singh and joined the secret anti-British movement for liberating India. He saw a chance of the freedom of India in the war of East Asia and started the Independence Movement.

Baba Chanda Singh (Shaheed)

Baba Osman Khan

Bh. Mohindar Singh (Martyr)

S. Harnam Singh

Baba Amar Singh

S. Kartar Singh

These revolutionaries had secret connections with Japanese and German Consulates at Bangkok and looked forward to their moral sympathy and active support at the opportune time.

As Malaya was under the British rule underground work could not be started here to any appreciable extent. But after the Kota Bharu incident (arrest of three revolutionaries) many youngmen volunteered to do anti-British Propaganda in British Indian Forces. Much hatred of British germinated in Indian Civil as well as Military circles of Malaya. The British Officers and the Intelligence Branch was very vigilant, but somehow the printed literature was circulated in the Army. The C.I.D. tried its level best to get hold of the revolutionaries, responsible for circulating anti-British leaflets in Jitra Camp, at the Malaya-Thai border, but to no purpose. In the middle of 1940, Bhai Munsha Singh "Dukhi" Editor "Dukhi Dunya" Jullundur came to Malaya for propaganda work. The police came to know of his arrival beforehand. Warrants for his arrest had been issued and the police was after him but the clever ruse of Shaheed Bh. Mohindar Singh of Hoshiarpur Distt. outwitted the police and he escaped arrest.

Apart from the underground activities, the Malayan Indians were vigorously carrying on their activities for the economic, political and social uplift of Indians. The Central Indian Association of Malaya, Kuala Lampur had Championed the cause of Indian labourer. There were strikes in various Rubber Estates and as most of the big Estates belonged to the British, there was a great friction between the British, capitalists and Indian labourers. The activities of the Indian Youth League Singapore and the Youngmen Sikh Association Penang were also being watched with suspicion by the Malayan Govt. and The Editor of "Tamil Morasu" Kuala Lampur had been deported from Malaya in connection with the Rubber Estates' strike.

It is clearly manifest from the above-mentioned incidents that emboldened by the continuous defeats of the British in the Western theatres of War, the Indian revolutionaries in East Asia, had become active and begun to defy the mighty British Empire and there was much hatred and ill will against the British in the minds of Indians. An interesting incident happened in Nov. 1941, when early one morning a Tamil youth stole to the Singapore harbour, with the Indian National tricolour under his arm. He crept up to the high pole, on which the Union Jack was flying and tore and stripped it off. But in so doing, the National Flag fell down and he could not accomplish his design of hoisting it on the pole. Rather than get down, he waited there for more than two hours, in the hope, that some Indian might come and hand him over the National flag. At day-break, he was forcibly brought down the pole by the guard and was tried and sentenced.

No doubt, the Japanese Government was secretly at the back of this movement. With its secret intentions of dominating the East Asia, it tried to encourage and win over Indians, who happened to be the subjects of their enemies. "For twenty years," writes Mr. John Goette, Japanese have been grooming every diffident Indian, they could "encourage to come into their territory. They openly sponsored annual conventions of Indians elements under some fancy name of Pan-Asiatic solidarity. These were held in Dairen in Japanese-leased Manchuria long before the 1931 occupation." In their own interest, the Japanese helped the Indian revolutionaries in the Indian Independence Movement, because so long as the British were not ousted from India, they could not dominate East Asia.

The effect of anti-British propaganda in the Indian Army in Malaya had begun to manifest itself. They had begun to realize that they were slaves fighting for the preservation of British Empire. The discriminatory treatment meted out to them and difference in pay of British and Indian soldiers was a cause of further discontentment and indignation. Indian Commissioned Officers in particular, bitterly resented the inferiority of status, pay and allowances as compared with the British Officers of the Indian Army in the same ranks. Besides this the Indians Officers were not allowed to become members of a large number of clubs in Malaya and could not travel in the same compartment as Europeans. This inferior treatment led them to believe that their slavery was the root-cause of all their ills and that they should better fight for the freedom and independence of their motherland.

Thus the reader will understand, that the Indian National Army and the Indian Independence League had not been formed over night or sprung up suddenly at the out-break of the East-Asia war, but long before the war, the Indian revolutionaries were busy in setting the stage and making strenuous efforts for preparing the ground, essential for launching and promoting the Indian Independence Movement at the opportune time. The East Asia war afforded them the real opportunity for which they had waited so long. Much of the credit, therefore, goes to those pioneers of the movement—Sri Rash Behari Bose, Swami Satyananda Puri, Giani Pritam Singh and hundreds of their companions —who by their indefatigable work and sacrifices had prepared the ground and every Indian should be grateful to these first martyrs of the movement.

CHAPTER II

The War in East Asia

With the out break of War in Europe between Britain and Germany in 1939, the relations between Germany and Japan became more close and intimate. Japan had long intended to dominate Asia and now she saw her chance. The war-clouds hovered over East Asia in 1941. Japan was making full preparations for a bloody war. She was striving hard to make her Navy and Air Force the strongest in the world. All her activities in the Far East indicated that a war was imminent. General Tojo became the Premier of Japan in the beginning of 1941. He had all along advocated a war with the British. So his Premiership was a sure indication that the war would soon break out.

The British began preparations for the defence of Malaya. They brought there a large number of British Indian Forces, but their equipment was far from being adequate. They could not spare sufficient number of ships and aeroplanes, as they were urgently needed in more important theatres of the European war. These half heart d efforts did not go unnoticed by the Japanese. In every importa t centre of Malaya, trained Japanese spies were at work in the garb of photographers and dentists and through these expert workers, the Japanese Government had an easy access to the war-secrets of the British. The occupation of Northern Indo-China by the Japanese troops after the collapse of France had opened the back-door to Singapore. The Japanese had also influenced the Thai Government to open the land frontiers of Malaya for her. General Tojo resolved to strike the British, when they were still unprepared.

Early in Dec. 1941, the newspapers in Malaya, splashed the news that the Japanese Navy had left the coast of Japan for an unknown destination. Some thought that it was bound for Australia. In the opinion of others its destination was Malaya. During the first week of December great activity was noticed in the Japanese business circles all over Malaya. On the morning of 4th Dec. a number of Japanese left Malaya for Thailand. Japanese businessmen were seen making hurried preparations to leave the country. All these were sure indications of an early war, but no one imagined that it would come so soon.

After concentrating her forces and consolidating her position for the campaign, Japan declared war on America and Britain on Dec. 8, 1941, while the Japanese Consul at Washington was still discussing terms for maintaining peace in the Pacific. With almost lightning speed, she attacked Pearl Harbour on the 7th Dec. even before the declaration of war and sank five of the heaviest battle-ships of American Navy. On the midnight of Dec. 7/8, the Japanese Navy stole to the shores of North-eastern Malaya and Thailand. In spite of the heavy fire from the British Artillery, they were able to land their forces at three different places—Kalantan (Malaya) and Sanghora and Pathani (Thailand). The day-break saw them advancing rapidly towards Kotah Bharu. The resistance of the land forces of the British was very poor. They had no armoured units and the Japanese tanks invariably broke through their defences. They had no training in the jungle warfare. The Japanese, on the other hand, were masters in jungle craft and always managed to out-manoeuvre the British forces through jungles which were impossible to the British troops.

The result was that within a month the Japanese swept over the whole of Malaya. The Aerodrome of Kotah Bharu (Kalandan) was captured by them on the 10th Dec. The Japanese forces launched their attack on Malaya from three different directions. One unit marched towards the west coast, the second unit made its way through the jungles of Kalantan and Pahang, while the third advanced from Kotah Bharu towards the Eastern Coast. The first battalion of the 14th Punjab Regiment stationed at Jitra in North Malaya, just on the Malaya-Thai border fought gallantly for three days, but had to give way before the superior Japanese forces on the 11th Dec. 1941. Two capital ships of the British Navy—Prince of Wales' (3.000 tons) and 'Repulse' (32000 tons) were sunk on Dec. 10 and the Navy was rendered completely useless. The South Pacific came under the control of the Japanese Navy. Most of the British air planes were put out of action in the earlier days of the war and the rest were forced by the Japanese to remain on the ground. So, owing to the inactivity of the air and naval forces, througout the campaign, the Japanese were able to land troops wherever and whenever they wanted and were thus able to outflank the retreating British forces.

The rest of the sorrowful tale of the collapse and disaster of Malaya is simply told. It is a tale of the inefficiency and inactivity of the British officers and the shattered morale of the soldiers. Also Star and Sungri Patani fell on Dec. 15. On the 19th Dec. one unit of the Japanese forces captured Penang and Paru Buntar and the second unit seized Kuala Krai and Trengana. The Japanese forces entered Taiping on the 23rd Dec. and Kuala Kangsar on the 24th. They reached the Perak river on the 25th and fought the British Army. Crossing the Perak river on the 26th Dec. they captured Epoh on the 28th Dec. and Tanjong Malim on Jan. 8, 1942. The battle of Slim River was lost by the British on the 10th Jan. and the Japanese forces entered triumphantly in Kuala Lampur, the capital of federated Malaya States, on the following day. The rest of the Malayan States-Seping, Gemas, Malacea, Batu Pahat, Segamat, Batu Annam, Endau and Kulwang fell into their hands before the end of January. The British, withdrew all their available forces into the island of Singapore and destroyed the Johore Cawsway (bridge), that connected Singapore with the mainland, on the morning of the 31st Jan. 1942.

The majority of the Indian troops in Singapore had already fought on the mainland and were thoroughly exhausted mentally and physically. The general morale of the army as well as the civilians was very low. The Japanese forces reached Johore Bharu on Feb. 4 and bombarded and machine-gunned Singapore for four days. Crossing the Johore Bharu Bridge they made their initial landing on Singapore on the 8th Feb. After bitter fighting for a week the British forces unconditionally surrendered to the Imperial Japanese Army on the 15th. Feb. 1942.

It would be idle to trace the causes of the general rout of the British in Malaya, we are mainly concerned with the British Indian Army, about which one or two casual observations must be made. Throughout the Malayan Campaign the Indian troops fought courageously against the heavy odds. Time and again they were made victims of blunders committed by their British Commanders, but they patiently and loyally continued to fight, while their British Commanders were being taken to safety on the island-fortress of Singapore. When the troops saw the officers in such a state, their morale was naturally shattered. No wonder then that the resistence of the Indian troops in the later stages was not strong enough. So they were suspected of being in league with the Japanese forces by the British. It is said that under this suspicion, a unit of the Indian Army was fired at by the British and Subedar Major Arjan Singh of 1/8 Punjab Regiment was killed. This incident caused a great resentment among the Indian soldiers and proved to be one of the factors in their joining the Indian National Army.

The ease and speed with which the Japanese defeated the British forces in the Far East, convinced the Indian soldiers and the civilians that the Japanese would ultimately succeed in defeating the British quite easily.

The British had not only made good their promises of protecting the Ind.an Civilians in Malaya, but had left them in the lurch. This naturally created a feeling of disgust in their minds for their erstwhile masters and every Indian in the Far East was up against the British.

CHAPTER III

Indian Independence Movement

It has been mentioned already, that the Indian patriots and revolutionaries in the Far East were waiting for an opportunity to accelerate the Independence Movement. The war afforded them that opportunity and they were not slow in catching it. The very day, when the Japanese declared war on Britain and America, the Indians in Tokyo met at the Rainbow Grill and decided upon a programme of action to foster the movement. They formed a committee under the Presidentship of Sri Rash Behari Bose to arouse Indian opinion in East Asia in favour of armed fight against the British. This Committee, later on, resolved to hold a conference of the Indian leaders of East Asia at Tokyo.

The Indians in Thailand proved more practical in this respect. They hailed this opportunity as God-sent and forthwith sought the help and co-operation of Japanese in their struggle for the liberation of their motherland. With a dramatic promptness, the Independence 'League of India' was formed at Bangkok, under the leadership of Baba Amar Singh on the 9th December, 1941—the day following the landing of Japanese forces on Thailand. Swami Satyananda Puri thanked his Thai Bharat Culture Lodge into Indian National Council and joined hands with the League. He enlisted many thousand volunteers for active work in the movement. The late Mr. P. D. Narula was put in charge of the training department. But, by far the most zealous worker was Giani Pritam Singh. He contacted the Japanese high officials in the very beginning and set to work in right earnest. The Japanese were equally anxious to enlist the help and co-operation of the Indians and they formed a laison department to deal with the Indian matters. This department was called 'Fujiwara Kikan'—Major Fujiwara being its head and Kikan meaning department.

It will not be out of place here to mention, that though the main object of the Indian patriots of East Asia was to achieve the freedom of their motherland by the help of the Japanese, many other immediate factors also prompted them for the cause of action, which they took. One of these was to safeguard the lives and properties of the Indians in Thailand and Malaya. They had known the Japanese too well to form the opinion that they were a ruthless people. Their treatment with the enemy nationals was most brutal and barbaric. The Japanese soldiers indulged freely in raping and looting wherever they went. The Indians in Malaya in the event of their remaining aloof, would have been treated as "enemy nationals" and put to incalculable hardships and sufferings. By starting the Indian Independence Movement, the Indian leaders were able to protect life, property and honour of the Indians residing in the Far East. To quote the words of Major General Shah Niwaz, "Brutal as the Japanese soldiers were, I will say this much for them that they never molested any Indian woman. In fact many a Eurasian and Chinese woman escaped molestation by putting on sarees or dupattas and telling the Japanese that they were Indians.........It was a very common sight to see Japanese soldiers approaching Indian houses and trying to talk to the inmates. Most of them knew no other language than their own. They would go up to an Indian and say, 'Gandhi Ka' ?...meaning are you a follower of Mahatma Gandhi ? If the reply was the affirmative, they would say 'Ha', shake hands or bow and push off."

Equally hazardous was the case of Indian prisoners-of-war. The Japanese knew no canons of civilized law and it was unthinkable to expect a fair and reasonable treatment from them. By forming the Indian National Army, it was made possible to a certain extent to provide some relief to the Indian prisoners-of-war. The Japanese had their own motives for driving the British out of India and they were fortunate in having the Indians making common cause with them. In return they undertook to afford all possible facilities to the Indian Civilians and prisoners-of-war in the Far East.

On occasion of the opening of the Independence League of India in Bangkok on December 9, 1948 S. Pritam Singh put before the public the policy of the League, as embodied in the following declaration of the League :—

"The whole of Japanese nation unanimously in a single voice has taken a pledge to stake her fate for the fulfillment of her incomprehensible spiritual aim of liberating the whole of Asia from the British yoke. We welcome this God-given opportunity that the Indians have been waiting for since 1904. By the grace of God we are starting on a non-stop voyage to reach India's goal of Complete Independenoe. The members of the Independence League of India either in India or abroad firmly believe that all the Independence movements started by the patriotic Indians in India or outside can only prosper, when they receive world-wide sympathy and solid help, along with their heroic struggles against the British.

In the past, Indian national leaders repeatedly urged the British to reconsider to abandon their bloodsucking policy towards India for which the English never cared in the least, British Jingoism is incorrgible now. The day of decision has now come when the God's curse is inflicted upon the British for their wicked and treacherous deeds.

England is gasping for breath on the verge of death, having tasted the result of her incendiary declaration of war against Germany, and now she has to face the indestructible armed forces of Japan.

Nations in the world have stood up in increasing numbers, declaring England as the common enemy of humanity, and this combined power, still increasing in number, directly and indirectly help the achievement of Indian Freedom. The liberation of India would also emancipate the whole of Asia from British Imperialistic suppression and rule, and the emancipated Asiatic countries would not then be called the Colonies of any Empire. Thus the Asiatics would no more be the black coolies of the white Anglo-Saxon.

Every attempt made by the Indians to achieve freedom of India has always been called "a revolt" by the English, perhaps because other nations were not in a position, under the circumstances then prevailing, to openly sympathise towards it. From now on we wish and surely hope that all the freedom loving nations in this world would whole-heartedly and openly sympathise with Indian patriotic movements and would officially recognize the Indian People's legitimate right of Complete Independence of India.

We appeal to all our Indian, brethren, wherever they are, to refrain from helping the British war efforts, and to stand up together to attain the glorious Indian Freedom. All Indians should fight to eliminate the Anglo-Saxon from the whole of Asia whatever energetic endeavours and sacrifices they have to make.

Immortal Prophets and Martyrs of India call upon you to serve your Motherland Bharta.

The Bangkok branch of the Independence League of India. The League decided to send its representatives with the Japanese forces, as they advanced into Malaya, to infiltrate into the British defence-lines and prevail upon the Indian soldiers not to fight the Japanese. Giani Pritam Singh was put in charge of this work. His other objects in accompanying the Japanese forces were to save the Indian people from the aggression of the Japanese soldiers and set up the branches of the Independence League of India all over Malaya, with the help of the local Indians. Giani Pritam Singh and his companions had to labour hard day and night for several days continuously to save the Indians in East Asia from the impending disaster. Gianiji wrote, printed and circulated the propaganda leaflets among Indians. He arranged public meetings in every big town and organized Peace Committees. He made appeals for funds and volunteers in the public meetings. These volunteers were sent along with the Japanese forces to search out and collect the Indian soldiers, and bring back the wounded, left behind in the jungles. The funds were used to provide board and lodging to these soldiers and in giving aid to the sick and wounded. The Indian civilians were also brought back from the jungles and provided with rations. In short every possible relief was given to the needy and desolate. Giani Pritam Singh deserves a high tribute for giving consolation to thousands of terrified souls-civilians as well as soldiers.

After the formation of the Indian National Army by Captain Mohan Singh, the members of this Army took an active part in the fighting in Malaya against the British. This group was commanded by Captain Allah Ditta Khan, 22 Mt. Regt. and was among the very first troops to land on the island of Singapore.

We now reproduce some relevant extracts from Giani Pritam Singh's diary to show the course of events connected with the Indian Independence Movement :—

Dec. 10, 1941—Left Bangkok by air at 9.05—reached Sanghora at 12.05, collected Indians, hoisted Indian National Tri-colour and formed the

League branch. Went to Haddyi (Thailand) by car and formed the League branch-distributed declaration of the Bangkok League at both the places. S. Kishan Singh, Anrodh Ujhaji and Raghunandan Pasiji were with me.

Dec. 11.—Early in the morning at 6-30, I went to Sada,—(just on the Thai-Malaya Border along with Major Fujiwara, interpretor Ottaguru and Lt. Nakamia. We found only one person S. Sadhu Singh in the city. I sent him, along with two others to accompany Lt. Nakamia on the front.—Came by a special lorry to Yale (Siam). Many Indians gathered there. S. Sher Singh and Ram Singh had been sentenced to death for not supplying lorries to the Japanese. I got this sentence set aside. I advised the Mayor and Police Officers to bring the civilians back.

Dec. 12.—S. Teja Singh went to Kotah Bharu front. S. Kishan Singh, B. Sudarshan Ujhaji and S. Hazara Singh went to Betong. I returned to Haddyai at 11-30.

Dec. 13.—Master Bhagwan Singh,Dehati Dunya and Tirlochan Singh came from Bangkok to Hadyai early in the morning.

Dec. 14—I reached Alor Star along with S, Gopal Singh and eight others from Haddyai at 7-20 in the morning. Five brave young men, Jamadar Puran Singh, Subedar Raman, S. Gopal Singh, S. Bhagat Singh and Dehati Dunya went to the front (Bravo!) Two Tamils refused to go, though they had offered themselves.

Dec. 15—British Indian officers, soldiers and others were rounded up from the jungles and brought to the Japanese from the early morning at Alor Star. The first to arrive were Lt. Col. Fitzpatrick and his companions. (Captain Mohan Singh and Captain Mohd. Akbar Khan of the 14th Punjab Regiment). By the evening the number of these captured soldiers went up to 200. General Terauchi (C.I.C.) came to see me. Gopal Singh went to the front. From Chamida two Britishers and a lorry were brought. The Japanese M.P. patrolled the city for peace and order.

It was in the jungles near Jitra Cantonment that Pritam Singh met Captain Mohan Singh, who was the senior-most Indian Officer in the 14th Punjab Regiment stationed at Jitra. Captain Mohan Singh had already been thinking of raising an Indian National Army to oust Britishers from India. Seeing the Indian National Tri-Colour on one of the cars accompanying the Japanese forces, he had resolved to approach the Japanese. He explained to him aims and objects of the Indian Independence League and persuaded him to join the League and form the Indian National Army. After prolonged discussions, in which Major also participitated, Captain Mohan Singh agreed to join the Indian Independence Movement and fight against the British. It was here that Captain Mohan Singh, and 54 of his companions pledged their lives for the freedom of India and the service of Indian Independerce Movement. The Azad Hind Fauj (Indian National Army) was formed at Jitra and Captain Mohan Singh was styled General Officer Commanding G.O.C.)

of that Army. For the first time in his history the sky rent with the shouts of 'Azad Hindustan Zindabad' and 'Azad Hind Fauj Zindabad.' Captain Mohd. Akram Khan and Jamadar Sadhu Singh were the first to join the I.N.A. They came to Alor Star on the 15th Jan. 1942.

It is evident that Giani Pritam Singh and his party were infusing a new spirit and national awakening in the hearts of Indian Civilians and British Indian forces. The following lines in his diary under the date Dec. 16, 1941 would show that the horrors of war had begun to manifest themselves in Malaya and Thailand. He seems to feel the troubles and hardship to which his countrymen were being subjected to. He writes :—

S. Labh Singh and Mr. Ram Swarup Chobe came from Bangkok. They have brought some dreadful news from there. Well! The Almighty God knows what is right and what is wrong! About 100 armed soldiers have been brought to Alor Star from different places. Due to the availability of arms, many dacoities and thefts have taken place. The disposal of dead bodies and sanitation and water works arrangement have started.

Jan. 1, 1942—I reached Epoh from Taiping with my companions. Under the leadership of Col. Taimura the Japanese celebrated the new year (2485 Buddhist year) by bowing in front of the sun. In Taiping S. Dalip Singh, Mr. Jalmanikshah, Mr. Nathu Ram etc. are very energetic and honest workers. In Epoh S. Sucha Singh, Saudagar Singh, Uttam Singh, Rab etc. are very hard working.

Jan. 2—Remained busy for the day in printing propaganda leaflets. The British had set the rations and big shops like Whiteways on fire.

They had also taken all the public cars and lorries forcibly. The people have fled to the jungles. A very small number returned. The people are not to blame! Who can dare to come in the city in such like unsettled and uncertain conditions (bloodshed, looting and raping)! Those with large families have left for far off places.

Jan. 3—Remained busy in propaganda leaflets without any rations. Printed 20,000 of four varieties! In the evening Gopal Singh, Jagat Singh, H.A. Connard, Bali Chand 4/19, Hanuman Singh 4/19, Bhagwan Singh 4/19, Hazari 2/19 and two Tamils were sent to the Front. I also accompanied them.

Jan. 4—Came back at 9-20 A. M. At 9-30 came to know of the horrible incident of 80 Indian soldiers being killed at Kantang. Spoke for about 25 minutes in the public meeting of Indians. More than 4,000 Indians, were present. Major Fujiwara also spoke. A Peace Committee of ten members with Mr. B.K. Das as leader was formed. Donations for Indian National Army were collected. Dehati Dunya, Ram Swarup Chobe, Tirlochan Singh and others were sent to the front. 30 Indian soldiers were collected. Sent letters to Penang. The Indian Independence League was formed under the Presidentship of Mr. B.K. Dass and a relief camp for civilians and Indian soliders was started.

Jan. 5—Introduced the members of Peace Committee with Khojima Department. Hav. (M. T.) Bachittar Singh of 5/14 along with six soldiers returned and immediately left for the front again. Sepoy Dhan Singh No. 16047 of 5/14 Regiment got wounded seriously and was burried under dead bodies. He was saved, returned and told his tale.

Jan. 6—Captain Mohan Singh, Captain Mohd. Akram and 25 soldiers went to the front. The Chinese British Fifth Columnists set fire at two or three places and supplied information and rations to the British. The curfew order was, therefore, imposed. Captain Mohan Singh saw Lt. Kunizuka.

The inangural meeting of the Kuala Lampur branch of the Independence League was held on Jan. 16, 1942, at the Police Depot Padang Kuala Lumpur. It was attended by a large gathering of Indians from all parts of Selangar. Col. Fujiyama, the first Governor of Selangor and Major Fujiwara were also present and addressed the gathering. They explained the objects of the East Asia war waged by Japan and assured the Indians that the Japanese Government would give them every possible assistance in their attempt to achieve liberty from the 'Anglo-Sexon Yoke. With the shouts of 'Bande Matram' and 'Azad Hindostan Zindabad' renting the sky, S. Pritam Singh rose to address the gathering and appealed to them to form the Independence League of India and not to lose this chance of liberating their motherland. He said that he had conferred with the Japanese and discussed the matters relating to India with them. They were prepared to offer every assistance to Indians in their struggle for obtaining India's freedom.

The leaders of the Indians in Selangor forthwith formed the Independence League of India at Kuala Lumpur under the Presidentship of Dr. Lakhshmyah. Centres for enrolling members were opened at various places in Kuala Lumpur and outstaions and 20,000 members had been enrolled within a fortnight of the inaugural meeting.

At this time the number of Indian Prisoners-of-war at the main camp at Kuala Lumpur had risen to 5,000. After the formation of the Independence League of India on Jan. 16, Captain Mohan Singh addressed these soldiers and appealed to them to join the I. N. A. to fight the British in Malaya and elsewhere. He said that the object of the I.N.A., was to drive the British out of India and that the Japanese had promised to help them in the achievement of their liberation from the British. Captain Mohan Singh had become very popular with the great majority of Indian soldiers and met with a ready response. About 4,000 of them joined the I.N.A.

Captain Mohan Singh and Captain Mohd. Akram opened a camp for these soldiers in a spacious building at Batu Road, with the help of Giani Pritam Singh and Major Fujiwara. Subedar Onkar Singh of the 5/14 Punjab Regiment was temporarily put in charge of this military camp. Arrangements were made for their feeding by the civilians of Kuala Lampur. The lot of the Indian soldiers at various camps in

Malaya was not a happy one. The Japanese did not give them any help with regard to rations, medicines and clothing etc. There was a serious shortage of these things at every place. The branches of the Independence League took upon themselves the duty of providing these soldiers with their needs as best as they could. In this connection the services of S. Budh Singh and Hakim Anwar Ali Shah of Kuala Lumpur and S. Bhagwan Singh of Epoh and his dutiful wife Bibi Sundar Kaur need be mentioned with gratitude. They devoted all their time and energy for the relief and assistance of Indian soldiers and went from door to door collecting rations, medicines, clothing and other materials. Hakim Anwar Ali Shah saved the lives of many wounded and sick Indian soldiers, for whom a hospital was also opened. These kind-hearted gentlemen not only helped the Indian prisoners-of-war, but also opened relief centres to assist the desolate and poor Indian civilians of Malaya, who had suffered the horrors of war.

By the end of January, a net work of the branches of Independence League had been formed throughout Malaya and they had begun to work in the right earnest for the amelioration of the lot of Indians in Malaya. The main objects of the League were to save the Indian civilians from being molested by the Japanese and to help the Indian Prisoners-of-war.

The fall of Singapore and the unconditional surrender of the British brought new problems before the Indian Independence League and the Indian National Army. Contrary to International law, the Japanese treated the British and Indian Prisoners of war on entirely different lines. They generally meted out good treatment to the Indian soldiers and told them that they regarded them as brothers and not as enemies. They asserted that they were fighting the war to help India to win her independence from the British. This technique proved effective and appealed to the Indian solidiers to join the Indian National Army.

Singapore fell on 15th Feb. On the night of Feb. 15/16, the Indian Army received orders to concentrate in the Farrer Park on the following morning. Subsequently the Indian Army (Prisoners-of-war) assembled at Farrer Park Singapore on Feb. 16, 1942 at about 2, P.M. Lt. Col-Hunt a staff officer of the British Military Headquarters at Malaya, Major Fujiwara, Captain Mohan Singh, prominent members of the Independence League of India and some Japanese and Indian Officers appeared before the Indian Army. Lt. Col. Hunt made a brief speech on the microphone, in which he said, "Today, I, on behalf of the British Government, hand you over to the Japanese Government, whose orders you will obey, as you have done ours." After this the Japanese representative Major Fujiwara came to the microphone and said, "I, on behalf of the Japanese Govt., take you over under our command and hand you over to G. O. C. Captain Mohan Singh." He went on to say, "As the British Empire is coming to an end, the Indians have a unique opportunity to attain freedom. It is an ideal time for you to rise and strike for your country's cause. Japan is prepared to help Indians in every way, even though Indians are British subjects and thus technically enemy nationals. We know that Indians are not British subjects from choice. The Japanese army would not treat you as enemies, but is prepared to treat you as friends if you repudiate British nationality." He appealed to the Indian soliders to join the Indian National Army and assured them that Japan would give them every possible help for the liberation of their mother-land.

After this Captain Mohan Singh came to the microphone and delivered a speech in Hindustani. He said, "The days of British oppression in the East are numbered and their hated rule must soon come to an end. The Japanese armed forces have driven them from Malaya and Singapore and they are beating a hasty retreat in Burma. India stands on the threshold of freedom and it is incumbent on every Indian to fight and drive away those demons, who have been for so many decades sucking the life-blood of Indians. The Japanese have promised as their all-out help in the realization of our coveted dreams and it is up to us now to organize ourselves and fight for the freedom of 400 millons of our countrymen and women. For this purpose, we have organized an Indian National Army from amongst the Indian soldiers and civilians in the Far East and I appeal to you all to join this Army."

The speech of Captain Mohan Singh was generally well received by the Indian soldiers. They acclaimed it with shouts of "Inqilab Zindabad", and "Azad Hindostan Zindabad" and raised their hands to show their willingness to join the I.N.A. Immediately after the handing over ceremony, Captain Mohan Singh organized propaganda lectures for the Indian Prisoners-of-war with the object of infusing a national spirit in them and inducing them to join the I.N.A. He received active help from Col. Gill, Col. Chatterje and Captain Mohd. Akram Khan in this work. More than 30,000 Prisoners-of-war volunteered to join the I.N.A.

On reaching Singapore, Giani Pritam Singh immediately called a meeting of Indian civilian leaders and formed a Peace Committee and Independence League at Singapore with Mr. S.C. Goho as President. The Indian patriots suspected the motives of the Japanese and were, therefore, very cautious in co-operating with the Japanese. But by and by, they realized that it was worth while to try the chance. Some days after the surrender of Singapore a meeting of the Presidents and other leading members of all the Malaya branches of the Independence League was held at Singapore and Giani Pritam Singh handed over the task of organizing the League work in Malaya to the Malayan Indians. A Central organization—The Independence League of India—for Malaya, was formed with its Headquarters at Singapore. Sri N. Raghawan was elected the President and Sri B.K. Das, the secretary of League. Thus, the League got a firm footing in Thailand and Malaya. The following figures showing the number of I.I.L branches, its members, and the strength of the Indian National Army up to 28.2.42, speaks volumes for the indefatigable work, put in by Giani Pritam Singh and other pioneers of the movement :—

The Central Committee of the League of India, Malaya, Singapore consisted of 14 members, the Financial Committee of 3 members and the Military Committee of 3 members. The position of various branches was as follows :—

State	Branch.	President.	No. of Com-mittee members	Total membership
1. Kedah	(*a*) Alor Star	Bhagwan Singh	10	1,000
	(*b*) Sungei Pattani	V. M. Kader	5	200
	(*c*) Kulim	Wazir Singh	10	500
2. Perak	(*a*) Taiping	Jalmanekshah	12	1,000
	(*b*) Kuala Kang-sar	Lal Singh	11	1,000
	(*c*) Ipoh	B. K. Das	13	5,000
3. Selanger	(*a*) Kuala Lumpur	Dr. Lakshmiaya	17	4,000
	(*b*) Kajang	Zakariah	11	2,000
	(*c*) Kalang	Lachman Chet-tiar	10	14,000
4. Negri Sembi-	Seramban	Dr. Majumdar	10	800
5. Mallaca		Shanmugham Pillai	12	No report
6. Penang		N. Raghwan	11	7,000
7. Singapore		S. C. Goho	41	50.000

The strength of the Indian National Army up to the fall of Singapore was 9,100, distributed as follows :—Allor Star 800 ; Sungi Pattani 600 ; Ipoh 1,000 ; Kuala Lumpur 4,200 ; Muar 1,100 ; volunteers in Singapore before the surrender 1,400.

Here, it will be worth while to mention, that though Captain Mohan Singh, received a ready response from the rank and file of the Indian Army, he was not successful in enlisting the support of the senior officers of the Army. It is difficult to enumerate all the obstacles he had to contend with. On the one hand some senior officers vehementally resisted the formation of the I.N.A. and advised the soldiers under them to keep out of it. On the other hand the treatment of the Japanese with the Prisoners-of-war was not wholly satisfactory. They did not supply enough rations, clothing and medicines for them and it became increasingly difficult for captain Mohan Singh and the Indian Independence League to supply their needs. The Japanese also began to issue arbitrary orders to the I.N.A. and Indian Prisoners-of-war. Added to this there were cases of indiscipline in some of the Prisoner-of-war camps. Cases of loot and rape by them were also reported. Some mischievous persons tried to create Hindu-Muslim disturbances. Of course British Fifth Columnists were there and tried to impede the progress of the Indian National Army. There were others who had honest differences of opinion. Many of the V. C. O's and K. C. O's believed that the Japanese were raising the I. N. A. to utilize it for their own selfish ends. There were others, who did not want to work under Captain Mohan Singh, because they were senior to him in the British Indian Army. Captain Mohan Singh tried to steer through these difficulties as best as he could and was in the end able to convince most of them of his sincerity of purpose.

Captain Mohan Singh set up his Headquarters at Mount Pleasant in Singapore. A prisoner-of-war Headquarters was set up under Col. N.S. Gill with Col. J.K. Bhonsle as the Adjutant and Quarter Master General and Col. A.C. Chatterji as the Director of Medical Service. Vigorous propaganda was done in the Army as well as the civilians asking them to co-operate with the Indian Independence Movement. Propaganda leaflets were prepared and distributed. Interesting programmes of Indian Independence propaganda were broadcasted from Singapore, Saigaon and Bangkok Radio Stations. A paper called 'Azad Hind' was published daily from Singapore under the control of the Indian Independence League. This paper was first published on the 10th Dec. 1941 at Ranjit Estate of S. Bahadur Singh at Ulukanas on a cyclostyle machine. It remained in the hands of its original publishers up to the fall of Singapore, when Giani Pritam Singh, handed it over to the Independence League of India.

Stress was laid on developing the national spirit among the Indians in Malaya. Strenuous efforts were made to develop a high sense of honour and responsibility in all ranks of the army. They were taught to be Indians first irrespective of caste and creed. Gradually separate kitchens and other religious barriers were done away with. Every sepoy and officer lived, ate and worked together. The Congress Tricolour was adopted as the National Flag of the I.N.A.

The Independence League of India particularly looked after the interests of Indians in Malaya, saved them from the aggression of Japanese and rendered active help to those, who were in need of it. It was high time to take a forward step and for this purpose the Indian leaders of Malaya and Thailand met at a Conference in Singapore to decide upon the future course of action.

(Standing I row) Lt. Kunizuka, K A. Nilakhanda Ayyar, Sucha Singh, K.P K. Menon, General Mohan Singh, Giani Pritam Singh, Major Fujiwara, Col. N. S. Gill, S. C. Goho, Col. M. Z. Kiani, Captain Mohd. Akram Khan
(Standing II row) B.K. Das, N. Raghavan
(Sitting) Ottaguru (Jap.) Lt. Mohd. Iqbal, Lt. Rattan

Presidents of the I. I. L. Branches of Malaya (28-2-42)

(Sitting) , C. L. Chopra, K. P. K. Menon, Major Fujiwara, N. Raghavan,

CHAPTER IV
TOKYO CONFERENCE.

I

Preliminary Meeting at Singapore.

Indian Independence Movement had now started all over the Far East in right earnest and the Indian leaders and patriots at Tokyo had decided to hold a Conference of the representatives of Indian community at Tokyo from Shanghai, Malaya, Hongkong and Thailand to decide upon the future course of action and act jointly. S. Pritam Singh and Swami Satyananda Puri were in constant touch with the Japanese authorities and Indian nationalist leaders at Tokyo. Before proceeding to Tokyo S. Pritam Singh convened a joint meeting of the representatives of various national elements of Malaya and Thailand to take stock of the whole situation, to exchange views on different problems and to select delegates for the Tokyo Conference. It was held at Singapore at the residence of Sri S. C. Goho at 3-30 p. m. Tokyo time on Monday, the 9th March 1942.

Before the proceedings of the conference began a group photograph of the representatives present, with Major Fujiwara, was taken.

The following gentlemen were present.

The Indian Independence League, Malaya :

1. Sri N. Raghavan ... Penang.
2. ,, B. K. Das } ... Ipoh
3. ,, Sucha Singh }
4. ,, K. A. N. Iyer. ... Kuala Lumpur.
5. Dr. Majumdar ... Seremban
6. Sri S. C. Goho } ... Singapore
7. ,, K. P. K. Menon }

The Indian Independence League, Thailand :

8. Sirdar Pritam Singh.
9. ,, Amar Singh.
10. Doctor Onkar Singh.

The Indian National Council, Thailand :

11. Swami Satyanand Puri.

Indian National Army :

12. Captain Mohan Singh
13. Captain Mohammad Akram

Indian Prisoners of War :

14. Lt. Col. N. S. Gill
15. Major M. Z. Kiani.

Mr. Otaguro of the Fujiwara Department attended the meeting as observer.

Sri N. Raghavan presided. He requested Major Fujiwara to open the Conference. Major Fujiwara expressed very great pleasure at having had the opportunity of meeting the representatives of the Indian Independence League of Thailand and Malaya. The meeting was of particular significance in that it was being held in the citadel of British Imperialism in Asia, namely Singapore. He wished the Conference every success and earnestly hoped that their endeavours to liberate India would be crowned with success. He regretted that he could not remain longer with them owing to other engagements.

Sri Raghavan thanked Major Fujiwara for his very encouraging words. Major Fujiwara then left the meeting.

The Chairman then requested Sirdar Pritam Singh to address the meeting. Sirdar Pritam Singh explained how the Indian Independence League was formed in Thailand at Bangkok. He thanked the Indians in Malaya for their ready co-operation in having organised branches of the League in all centres of Malaya.

The Chairman proposed a resolution appreciating the patriotic work of Sirdar Pritam Singh and thanking him on behalf of the Indian community in Malaya for his self-less work in the cause of the liberation of their mother-land. The resolution was acclaimed unanimously by the Conference.

The Chairman then pointed out that two points were to be considered by the Conference :—

1. Whether the present time was the proper occasion for the Indians in the Far East to take action for the attainment of Indian Independence.
2. If that was the proper occasion, how should they proceed towards the attainment of their goal.

Captain Mohan Singh said that he got into conact with Sirdar Pritam Singh at a place near Jitra on 15th December 1941, and learnt about the Indian Independence League. Subsequently he met Major Fujiwara, and after that he had been in constant touch with them. At first he was doubtful of the Major's purpose, but now he was fully convinced of his sincerity in desiring to assist us in the liberation of India from British control. The situation that all of them visualised at that time, was completely changed with the fall of Singapore. They did not expect to find in Singapore such a large number of Indian soldiers—nearly 50,000. The total strength of the Indian Army now in Malaya was near 60,000. To feed them, to equip them and look after their other requirements would be a big problem, and the Indian Independence League must give immediate consideration to it.

Lieut. Col. Gill spoke about the 50,000 Indian prisoners of war in Singapore and wished to know what was to become of them.

Swami Satyananda Puri explained the formation and objects of his organisation, the Indian National Council of Thailand. The objects were mainly (1) to work in co-operation with the political activities in India, (2) to win the sympathy of the Indian National Congress, (3) to secure an All-India leader as president of the organisation. Explaining the third object, he told the meeting, that Pandit Jawaharlal Nehru was reported to have stated that Indians residing outside India would not interfere in Indian politics, and that those who do so would be considered as traitors. His organisation was therefore afraid that it might be treated as a body of Quislings in the pay of the Japanese. Unless all possibilities of such a stigma were removed, nothing could be achieved. He therefore suggested that contact should be established with Sri Subhas Chandra Bose and that he be requested to lead them. Swami Satyananda Puri further said that he had sent a telegram to Sri Bose from Bangkok on 2nd Feb. 1942, to that effect, and had received a reply over the radio agreeing to accept the presidentship of the Indian organisation in the Far East working for Indian Independence.

Sri S. C. Goho requested Sirdar Pritam Singh to explain to the Conference the purpose of the proposed delegation to Tokyo.

The Sirdar said that the delegation was proposed for two purposes; (1) to meet in an informal conference at Tokyo Indian representatives in Asia outside India and discuss the problem of Indian Independence, (2) to negotiate with Japanese authorities terms of co-operation with Japan for achieving the independence of India.

Lt. Col. Gill stressed the importance of carrying out effective propaganda in India to prepare the necessary atmosphere so that the Indian Army overseas would receive the willing co-operation and help of all Indians when it would march into India. The Indian Army had been till now fighting under certain pledges. Before they could break those pledges, they should be convinced that their former pledges were really not in keeping with the honour and self-respect of free Indians, and that by breaking them they would not be doing anything unsoldierly or dishonourable. For that too, propaganda among them was essential.

Sirdar Pritam Singh said that some propaganda was being carried on among the troops and that more would be done in that line.

Sri K. P. K. Menon discussed at length the policy followed by the Indian National Congress till then. Two years ago the Working Committee of the Congress asserted complete Independence as the goal of India. In the past the Congress had followed two methods, both without success. It had first tried to appeal to the good sense and democratic sentiments of the British to grant freedom to the Indians. Later on, on the outbreak of the present War, Mahatma Gandhi started the "No-War Campaign" which, however, did not ask the country to desist from helping in the war-efforts by positively refusing men, money and material for the prosecution of the War. The result had been a watchful inactivity on the part of the Congress. There was another course remaining, namely the application of force. India was not prepared for that, but now that Japan was willing to offer them help, they should accept it. Efficient propaganda should also be carried on both inside and outside India.

Sri S. C. Goho spoke on the necessity of creating in India confidence in the intentions of Japan regarding India.

Swami Satyananda Puri suggested that Japan should make a declaration assuring Indian Independence. He mentioned that he had heard over the radio that the Working Committee of the Congress had removed on the 13th January, 1942 the "non-violence" from the creed of the Congress.

Sri Sucha Singh stressed the necessity of immediate action, as delay would be detrimental to the cause. India was ready for action.

Lt. Col. Gill agreed with Sri Sucha Singh. He said that if the British were to know of the intentions of the Indians Overseas, they might remove the Indian units from India to the Middle East and replace them with British units. Moreover, delay would make the strength of the British in India greater as they would be able to produce more ammunition and war materials. Hence delay would be suicidal to the cause. .

In conclusion it was decided that :—

(1) That was the time when all Indians in East Asia should unite for India's freedom. The psychological moment had come to strike for India's freedom.

(2) The first thing to do was to carry on propaganda both in and outside India among the Military forces and civilians.

(3) Sri Subhas Chandra Bose should be requested to come to Tokyo and accept the leadership.

The meeting was adjourned till 10. 30 a.m. Tokyo time, Tuesday, 10th March, 1942.

The second sitting of the conference was held at the same place the next day—Tuesday, 10th March, 1942 at 10-30 a. m. Sri Raghawan presided.

The Chairman summed up the conclusions arrived at the last sitting of the Conference. One of the question discussed at that meeting was whether the present time was opportune for taking action. The news of the fall of Rangoon and the surrender of the N. E. I. gave strength to the conclusion arrived at by the Conference that the time was opportune. He stated that the Conference should now discuss the broad outlines of the methods to be adopted to achieve the freedom of India. His own personal view was that no method which did not get the approval of the Indian National Congress would succeed. If the Indians in the Far East went against the opinion of the Congress, they would run the risk of being taken to have gone against the wishes of the people of India. At present it was difficult to know the views of either the people of India or the Congress. The presence of the British in India made it particularly hard for the people to give free expression to their opinions.

Sri S. C. Goho asked whether it was proposed to give the public in India previous information of their intentions to act for the liberation of India. If such information were given, it would help the British.

The Chairman said that an expert committee would have to be appointed to go into the details of propaganda to be made to India.

Sri K. P. K. Menon said that the history of the Congress showed that when there was a strong public feeling in favour of any particular course of action, the Congress had always yielded to it. He believed that by strong propaganda, it would be possible to create such a public opinion in India in favour of their course of action. In their propaganda they must emphasise the following :—(1) There is no other course left except force for achieving the independence of India, and for that the help of Japan is essential. (2) The British as well as a certain sections of Indians have been carrying on propaganda against Japan. As a result there is in

India a very wrong impression of Japan's intentions. We must clear this misconception. (3) We must tell India of the might of Japan. (4) We must, in the light of our own experience in Malaya, advise Indians regarding the safeguards to be adopted in the period of transition. (5) The British may promise some sort of concession to India and a section of Indians may be deceived by such a promise. We must counter-act such a move. (6) The Indian leaders must be induced to declare the independence of India at the psychological moment.

The propaganda could be by means of broadcasts, leaflets and pamphlets. They must also carry on propaganda among the men in the Army, in order to convince them of the justice of their cause.

The Chairman suggested that the representatives attending the Conference should not themselves broadcast in the initial stage. If they were to do so, they would be committing themselves, and later on they would find their intentions doubted by the leaders in India. He said that the delegates attending the Tokyo Conference should not broadcast from Tokyo on the question of the Independence of India.

The conference accepted the view of the Chairman.

The Chairman doubted whether the creation of a strong public opinion which could change the attitude of the Congress leaders, would not take time.

Sri K. P. K. Menon was of opinion that in these times persistent propaganda would be effective in a short time.

Sri S. C. Goho asked whether it would be possible for some responsible person from there to go and see the Congress leaders and try to convince them of the sincerity of their aims and the practicability of their methods.

Captain Mohan Singh said that it would be possible, and that it must be done. Such a course would be more effective than anything else. Hence the importance of the decision that the leaders there should not broadcast at this stage.

Swami Satyanand Puri stated that infiltration into India was possible, but that it would take about two months for a person to get into India.

The Chairman said that time was an essential factor and wanted to know what the cost would be of maintaining an army of 60,000 men.

Capt. Mohan Singh promised to give the information later on.

Sri K.A. N. Iyer said that it would be difficult for them to know that a strong public opinion had been created in India. Hence they should concentrate on other methods to convince and convert the leaders of the Congress directly. He wanted it to be made clear whether they were to act only after the Congress had been won over, and whether in case they failed to convert the Congress, they were to act inspite of the Congress.

Sri K. P. K. Menon said that they should act with the consent and co-operation of the Congress, if that should be possible, but if necessary, without the Congress. He, however, believed that the Congress could be won over.

Lt. Col. Gill said that all the men in the Indian Army in Malaya were not educated men. It would take time to convince them of the justice of the cause, they would be asked to fight for. He asked the conference whether they liked to have a few thousand sincere men immediately or a larger number after some time. He also reminded the conference that in a modern Army the proportion of fighting men to non-combatants was one to one, and that therefore, though they had an army of 60,000 they had only 30,000 combatants. To educate all of them into a sincere faith in their cause would take at least six months.

Asked as to how many could be got in three months, Lt. Col. Gill said that it would be possible to get about 10,000.

The chairman then raised the question, whether they should receive assistance of Nippon (Japan) in their independence fight. The conference decided that in the attainment of independence, full support and co-operation of Nippon may be received.

Lt. Col. Gill said that propaganda should be carried on by all possible means.

Sri K. P. K. Menon said, that apart from broadcasting and dropping leaflets and pamphlets, they should also try infiltration; but that it would have to be left to experts.

Sri K. M. Kannampillay said that in the last civil disobedience movement in India, it was possible to circulate News-sheets secretly, and that they could have recourse to such a method of propaganda also.

Sri Sucha Singh remarked that since the Congress was bound to a policy of non-violence, which was different from their policy, there was a possibility of its not agreeing to act with them. He wanted a definite decision to be arrived at by the conference, as to what their policy would be in such an eventuality.

Swami Satyanand Puri pointed out that the Congress had eschewed non-violence from its cread. He was of opinion that if the Congress did not agree to assist them, they should form a Council of Action in the Far East to liberate India. Any territory taken by their Army (I. N. A.) should be immediately handed over to the Congress as a token of their sincerity of purpose.

The conference then unanimously decided that if they would be convinced that the action they were going to take, would be in the best interests of India, they shall act with or without the Congress, preferably with.

The next point taken up for decision was the proposed delegation to Tokyo.

The chairman requested Mr. Otaguro to give the conference any information he could on the point.

Mr. Otaguro said that the calling of the delegation for the Tokyo meeting had come as a surprise to Major Fujiwara himself. Mr. Otaguro, however, thought that the Indians in Japan must have been inspired by the statement of the Prime Minister of Japan promising all *assistance* to India in their fight for independence. They might have approached the authorities to arrange for a meeting at Tokyo of the representatives of

Indians in all parts of the Far East. The Tokyo conference would be quite informal. An official conference would be mainly to provide an opportunity for Indian *patriots* to meet and exchange views, in order to remove all differences of opinions among them. The Indians in Tokyo were out of touch with India and would like to hear from the Indians in Malaya and Thailand about present conditions.

The chairman wanted to know whether the Malayan delegation would be considered as the representative of a free people, and given the right and facilities of free speech and ventilation of opinion.

Mr. Otaguro assured the conference that there would be no doubt about that.

Swami Satyananda Puri stated that the Indian National Council in Bangkok had got into telephonic communication with Sri Sahaye of the Indian National Council, Japan and asked for an opportunity to clarify the policy. Sri Sahaye said that he had approached the authorities and arranged for the meeting at Tokyo. Swami Satyananda Puri, however, stressed that the conference at Tokyo should be an informal one.

Sri B. K. Das said that the discussions of the conference, though informal, would bound to be of an extensive nature, and that therefore it was essential that the civilians and the Army should be given as large representation as possible.

Mr. Otaguro said that Major Fujiwara had suggested four civilian representatives from Malaya and Two from Thailand, and two representatives of the Army.

Captain Mohan Singh said that he had asked that there should be at least three Army representatives. He was expecting the reply of Major Fujiwara that day.

The following four were nominated as the Malayan delegate by the conference : Sri N. Raghavan, Sri K. A. N. Iyer, Sri S. C. Goho and Sri K. P. K. Menon The representatives from Thailand would be Sirdar Pritam Singh and Swami Satyananda Puri. The delegates from Indian Army were to be decided later on.

The leader of the delegation was left to be elected by the delegates themselves at a seperate meeting.

The chairman asked the conference to decide on the instructions to the delegation. After discussion it was unanimously decided that " the delegation could at that stage (at the Tokyo Conference) commit themselves to not more than inducing the Indian National Leaders to the view, that may be adopted by the delegates at the conference at Tokyo."

The question of Indian Prisoners of War was taken for discussion next.

Sri B. K. Dass said that he was painfully surprised to hear that the Indian soldiers in Singapore were Prisoners-Of-War, while those in other parts of Malaya were not. He wanted the conference to impress upon the Nipponese authorities that the soldiers in Singapore should be treated on the same basis as those elsewhere in Malaya.

Captain Mohan Singh explained that there was not much practical difference in the treatment of both, apart from a few restrictions placed on the soldiers in Singapore. He reminded the conference that the Indian Army outside Singapore had not yet been recognised officially as the Indian National Army. Indian soldiers in Singapore had surrendered on the order of the British authorities and as such were technically considered as Prisoners of War.

The chairman wanted to make it quite clear that the protest did not at all come from the soldiers themselves, but from the civilians. He proposed the following resolution to be adopted by the civilian members of the conference and forwarded to Major Fujiwara and anyone else he might suggest : "Considering the present atmosphere and gratefully considering the attitude of Nipponese Military authorities, the civilian delegates of this conference make a strong appeal that, if possible, before the Tokyo delegation leaves, as a gesture of Nippon's goodwill, the Indian Prisoners-of-War in Singapore be placed on a par with the proposed Indian National Army, even though such soldiers became Prisoners owing to the cease-fire order of the British Military authorities ".

The resolution was unanimously adopted by the conference.

Mr. Otaguro told the conference that Major Fujiwara was doing his level best in the matter.

The conference was adjourned sine die.

CHAPTER V

TOKYO CONFERENCE.

II

The Fateful Air Disaster—The First Sacrifice.

The joint conference at Singapore after due deliberations had decided to send nine delegates to the Tokyo Conference. But, as ill-luck would have it, the delegation was destined to meet with a fatal accident. The delegation was to leave in two batches. The first batch consisting of four most zealous workers left for Japan via Saigaon on the early morning of 11th March 1942. They were Swami Satyananda Puri—the organiser of the Indian National Council of Thailand, Sirdar Pritam Singh—the originator of Indian Independence League, Captain Mohammad Akram—the right-hand man of General Mohan Singh in the Indian National Army and Mr. Nilkanth Ayre, the trusted assistant of Sri Raghwan. Mr. Ottaguru of the Fujiwara Department along with six other Japanese also accompanied them. They were reported to have left Saigaon on the 13th March 1942, and after that nothing was heard of them.

The second group comprising of General Mohan Singh and Col. Niranjan Singh Gill of the Indian National Army, Sri Raghavan, Sri S. C. Goho and Sri K. P. K. Menon left Singapore on March 15, and reached Tokyo on the 18th March. They were anxiously awaiting the arrival of their comrades, but they waited in vain. It was reported that the plane was nearing Tokyo on the 24th March, but thereafter it seemed to have disappeared into the unknown ! That bleak, stormy afternoon of the 24th March 1942, had led the plane astray. Months later, their remains were discovered on a mountain top in the Imperial Forests at Mount Shirakura in Shizuoka Perfecture.

The news of the tragedy came as a sudden shock and severe blow to all the patriots in the Far East. Four of their sincerest workers and comrades had departed at a time, when their services were needed most. It also stunned the public of Japan and cast a shadow over the conference at Tokyo. The absence of those leaders, who were going across with great enthusiasm to serve the cause of India, was felt by one and all alike. The National Memorial Service held at Hongenji Temple Tokyo was one of the biggest of its kind—a most solemn, heartfelt and dignified function. General Tojo expressed sympathy over the loss of four heroic souls, pledged to extend all possible aid for the complete Independence of India and hoped that the cause for which they gave up their lives would not go in vain.

Malaya and Thailand celebrated the memory of these martyrs in a befitting manner. When the delegates returned from the Tokyo conference, a Memorial meeting was held at Syonan-to (Singapore) on the 24th April, 1942. High tributes were paid to the spirit of service and sacrifice of the departed patriots. It is worthwhile to reproduce here two of the most important speeches—one by Major Fujiwara and the other by Sri N. Raghawan.

Major Fujiwara addressed the spirits of the four Indian patriots in these words :—

It was on the early morning of 11th March when you, four comrades of mine started, from Singapore Civil Aerodrome in high spirits with burning passion for your mother country and with the noble aim of India's Independence.

You, the spirits of the glorious dead, it is tragic you cannot speak, but I remember you departing in high spirits so vividly as if it took place yesterday. I have no words to express my heart-felt praise for you, when I think of your manly resolution to fly in bad weather to attend the Tokyo Conference, which decided the very big problem of helping India to free herself from the yoke of British rule. I have no words to express your mental anguish, when at the last moment, when Tokyo was only a stone's throw away from you, the aeroplane crashed into the sea with your comrade Otaguro—the Nippon English interpreter. We deeply grieve and mourn this destiny of God. 400 millions in India mourn your loss with deep regret.

I look back with pride on my association with S. Pritam Singh and Mr. Swami in Bangkok when the war clouds were hanging so low over ASIA, and with Mr. Aiyer and Captain Mohd. Akram, when the whole of Malaya was covered with strife and bloodshed ; our belief, knowledge, and ambition to help 400 million Indian Masses to attain complete Independence ; our complete faith in the strong union of Nippon and Hindustan. We vowed to each other that it would give us the greatest satisfaction to sacrifice our lives for the sake of this noble mission. Hence we helped each other and ran about here and there under the enemy's fire. Inspired by this great idea we found "Light ". These numerous people, who are in your presence, are the very people, who had been saved by your ardent courage and great mercy. These people will carry on your noble ideal. There are many comrades scattered all over Malaya, who cannot participate in this service to-day. They have the same feelings and are offering the same prayers. They appreciate whole-heartedly that your efforts to rouse feelings of sympathy in GREATER EAST ASIA for Indian Independence are bearing fruit. I recall to my memory your sublime activities, grand merits, deep friendship and trust shown to me and my staff. I recall to my memory countless impressions given to me in your private and public lives.

I cannot help feeling again in great sorrow and restlessness that I lost my most intimate and great comrades. Your sacrifices created a great and everlasting impression both in India and Nippon. They achieved great success for the Tokyo Conference. The Indian Independence Movement initiated by you, and supported by general public opinion both in Japan and Hindustan, is about to make a glorious start. You will be satisfied to see that your mother country rejected unanimously the ridiculous proposals of the British Government and is going to spring forward to uphold honourable aims. I take consolence in the thought that your heroic deaths and sacrifices during your life contributed so much to the freedom of your motherland and stimulating the hearts of your countrymen. I am sure that your glorious deaths will be written in golden letters in the history of the Indian Independence Movement. They will remain an everlasting beacon light in the memory of your countrymen, spurring them on in the achievement of your noble ideals. I pay my highest respects to your spirits. I have full confidence, that in the near future we shall perform what you undertook with your comrades. I offer in front of your spirits the gorgeous wreath "India for Indians." "Complete Independence of India."

I close my message of condolence with the prayers of my staff so intimately associated with you, that your spirit may rest in Paradise and that you will protect the Indian Race for ever. I invoke you will come and receive my message.

Tributes by Sri N. Raghavan, Chairman, at Syonan Memorial Meeting.

Little did we think when we left Syonan-to on the 15th of last month that on our return we might have to assemble here to mourn the loss of four of our valued colleagues and one of our sincere friends. They were themselves on their way to Nippon, full of burning enthusiam for the noble cause that they have expoused on behalf of their country and countrymen. They might not have cared one way or the other, whether they lived or died in the achievement of their purpose. But heroes do not die; they live for ever.

We are here to-day to pay homage, not to persons who are dead but to those who live for ever. We mourn, but we do so, not for the death of anyone, but for our own loss, the loss of Patriots, a loss which we could ill-afford at this time of our destiny. It is true that they will live in human hearts cherished and honoured by those grateful countrymen of theirs, until human memory can last. They shall live, indeed, in the undying affection of those for whom they made their supreme sacrifice.

The details of how they came to their unexpected end, the culmination of their terrestrial career, are now common knowledge to all of you. If, as I said the other day, they had been a day earlier or a day later, for their arrival in Japan, any day other than that stormy afternoon on the 24th of last month they might have escaped the accident completely. But

The first four Martyrs

Mr. K. A Nilakhanda Ayyar

General Secretary
Central Indian Association
Malaya

Capt. Mohd. Akram

Right hand man of
Gen. Mahan Singh

The Great Scholar

Swami Satya Nanda Puri

The Veteran Revolutionary

Giani Pritam Singh

Those who served the Prisoners of War

S. Bhagwan Singh of Ipoh

S. Budh Singh of Kuala Lumpur

S. Bahadur Singh
Owner of Ranjit Estate Upakanas

S. Sucha Singh of Ipoh

it is difficult to say. The ways of Fate are inscrutable and mysterious, but it may be that Providence had assigned to them the privilege of ending their worldly existence as Martyrs in the cause of India. Our beloved colleagues, Neelakandha Aiyer and Mohamed Akram, Satyanand Puri and Pritam Singh and our friend Ottaguro are not here in person to-day, but it is the firm belief of most of us, that they are here in spirit and shall continue to hover around us, inspire us and guide us in the work that we have set out to perform.

The loss, I am sure, must have come to you with as sudden a shock as it came to us. Not only to us, but to the whole of the people of Japan it came as a bolt from the blue, least expected, and most grieved about. Never had we witnessed a whole nation mourning so much the loss of Four Heroes who were not their own nationals. If our sorrow was keen and acute, the sorrow of the people of Japan was none the less severe. Thus, mourned by two nations, one their own kith and kin and the other their hosts and friends, the noble souls passed into the Great Beyond.

I may be excused in mentioning first my friend and brother Neelakandha Aiyer. To an audience of Malayan Indians, Mr. Aiyer's face must be very familiar. He served them for nearly thirty years with all his indefatigable energy, and indomitable spirit, he served them to the utmost of his ability, which was considerable indeed, without fear or any desire for any favour. He was one of those whom any country would have regarded as a national asset, whom any person would have cherished and loved as a most valuable friend. A man genial, sincere, affectionate, loyal, one who was fired with noble ambitions, one who was inspired and could inspire. Let me not dwell upon him for long as you, those assembled here, know fully well his past record. To me his loss was a personal as well as a national one.

Mohamed Akram who passed away, I knew only for a short time But the little that I knew of him was enough to convince me that here was a Patriot whose one end and aim was to liberate his Motherland. He was actuated by the noblest of motives and had he lived, he would have been an inspiration to his colleagues and men in the Indian National Army. Shorn of prejudices, a thorough nationalist at heart and in convictions, in words as well as in action, Captain Mohamed Akram was an invaluable asset to the cause of Indian Nationalism at this juncture. The sense of this loss is perhaps felt greater in the Indian Army. But believe me, the whole of the Indian people to-day are one in their sorrow at the passing away of this heroic soul.

Swami Satyanand Puri was a flower of Indian Culture. Those who lived with him, those who were associated with him, those who knew him in Thailand, came to realise the fragrance of that flower. He was not only a leader of thought, but he was a leader of men. The wonderful manner in which Thailand Indians rallied round the banner of Indian Independence which Swamiji unfurled, the quick manner in which he carried the Torch of Indian Independence from heart to heart amongst those who came into contact with him, where-ever he went, these were indeed the signs of a Hero committed not only to self-abnegation, but to an active programme of Indian liberation. His loss has created a void in Thailand which it is almost impossible at the present to fill. Before he passed away, I was particularly fortunate in having had a series of discussions with him both here and at Saigon in which he expounded to meet his political philosophy and ideals which guided us, the members of the Malayan Delegation to Japan in various different ways.

Our friend Pritam Singh came into his country, went from place to place, organised his countrymen for the Independence of India, did everything that he possibly could do for cementing the friendship that existed between his countrymen and the people of Nippon. He was a simple man. He was a kind soul. He was a good spirit, and the unaustentatious way in which he went about, the true sincerity that he evinced in the cause of his people the fervant manner in which he wanted to serve his Country became evident to us soon after his arrival in this country from Thailand. Many a centre in Malai is indebted to him for his words of advice, and guidance. The whole of the Independence Movement in its present form in this country was to a very great extent his creation. At the last Malayan Conference that we had at Syonan-to prior to our departure for Tokyo, Pritam Singh told us in words the full significance of which he could not then be conscious of, words which unfortunately became too true, he told us, addressing me in the Chair, "Mr. Chairman, My task now is finished. I hand over to you all whatever I have done. It is for all of you now to carry on the work." He meant of course that he was going to return to Thailand and hand over Malayan Organizations to Malayan Indians themselves. But the words as I said happened to be true, in more ways than one. Little did we realize when we passed a resolution of grateful appreciation and thanks that we had put the lid on the work of one of the most enthusiastic servants of India.

Ottoguro san, our Nipponese friend who accompanied them on their last voyage was one as you know who made India's cause his own. His charming personality affected all those who came into contact with him. As the right-hand man of Major Fujiwara, that friend of India, his contribution in the short space of three months to the cause of Indian Nationalism and Independence was such as any man could be proud of. We Indians assembled here are grateful to him, and those who are not here but who would come to hear the story would remember him with affectionate regard.

May the souls of these heroes and patriots rest in peace! Bande Mataram.

CHAPTER VI

TOKYO CONFERENCE

III

The Proceedings.

The Indian Independence Conference was held under the chairmanship of Mr. Rash Behari Bose, at Sanno Hotel, Tokyo, Japan from

Saturday, the 28th March, 1942 to Monday, the 30th March, 1942. The following representatives were present.

1.	Mr. Rash Behari Bose	... Chairman.
2.	Mr. N. Raghavan	... Delegates from Malaya.
3.	Mr. K. P. K. Menon	
4.	Mr. S. C. Goho	
5.	Captain Mohan Singh	
6.	Col. N. S. Gill	
7.	Mr. D. N. Khan	... Delegates from Hongkong.
8.	Mr. M. R. Mallick	
9.	Mr. O. Asman	... Delegates from Shanghai.
10.	Mr. Piara Singh	
11.	Mr. D. S. Deshpande	... Representatives from Japan.
12.	Mr. A. M. Nair	
13.	Mr. C. Lingham	
14.	Mr. B. D. Gupta	
15.	Mr. S. N. Sen	
16.	Mr. Rajah Sherman	
17.	Mr. L. R. Miglani	
18.	Mr. K. V. Narain	

1st Day, Saturday, the 28th March, 1942.

General Tojo, the Premier of Japan, sent the following message to the Conference :—

" I wish to express my great pleasure at this opportunity to great Indians in Japan as well as Indians who have come to this country from Shanghai, Hongkong, Thailand and Malaya. At the same time I cannot but express my deep sorrow over the unfortunate accident involving the death of some of the representatives, the lack of whose presence we regret on this occasion.

" I believe, you are quite aware of the fact that the British Empire is fast heading towards its downfall and the world situation is going through events, which are hard to foresee. The Japanese Empire is determined to go ahead with its mission of destruction of the Anglo-Saxon power, and will not rest until that mission is fulfilled. Here I want to state frankly that the Japanese Government cannot remain indifferent to the fact that the Britain is going to make India, the base of its Eastern defence. In view of this fact, the Japanese Govt. sincerely expects that the Indians would throw away the British Yoke by themselves and create an Independent India. I hope, when you go back to your respective places, you would make this feeling of ours clear to your country-men and work unitedly to exterminate the British Yoke and create an India for Indians. As has been repeatedly stressed by me the Japanese Government is fully sympathetic towards your efforts and will not hesitate to render all possible help in this respect. The true intentions of the Japanese Government in connection with the bombing of British military bases in Ceylon has been clarified by me in my statement issued yesterday.

" In conclusion, I pray that you may have a safe return journey and that your move may bear full fruit in the near future."

Mr. Rash Behari Bose, the chairman, opened the conference at 2 p. m., with a welcome address to the delegates and other gentlemen and requested their whole-hearted co-operation in the attainment of the common object, *viz.*, the complete independence of India.

At the outset the chairman expressed heart-felt condolence on the sad demise of their colleagues, namely, Sirdar Pritam Singh and Swami Satyananda Puri from Thailand and Mr. K. A. N. Iyer and Mohd Akram Khan from Malaya who were to attend the conference and who met a fatal air accident while on their way to Tokyo.

All stood up and offered profound prayer in silence for the repose of the souls of the departed patriots.

The conference resolved to send letters of condolence to the bereaved families and Mr. Raghavan kindly undertook the responsibility of conveying the letters.

Resolved :

1. (*a*) That this conference is shocked and grieved at the news of the air disaster in which four Indian representatives *viz.*, Messrs Iyer and Mohd Akram Khan from Malaya, and S. Pritam Singh and Swami Satyananda Puri from Thailand, who were travelling to Tokyo lost their lives ; and while expressing its deep sense of sorrow, place on record the great loss to the movement and to Indians generally caused by their untimely deaths.

(*b*) That a copy of this resolution be sent with the condolence of this conference to the members of the bereaved families.

2. That this Conference sends its sincerest condolences and sympathies to the members of the bereaved families of Mr. Ottoguro and six other Japanese gentlemen, who lost their lives while travelling by plane to Tokyo.

At this stage Colonel Iwaguro, who attended as the representative of the Govt. of Japan, very kindly gave the following address of welcome to the members of the conference. On behalf of the Imperial Government of Japan, he expressed whole-hearted support to this conference in its noble efforts to achieve Independence of India.

" It is my great pleasure to greet you at this conference, which would make the birth of New India. To-day your dual ideology of " Independence, of India " and " India for the Indians!', over which you have been most concerned, is going to be realised before long, because it it my belief that the outbreak of this war has created an opportunity, which is most favourable for its realisation. If you lose this golden opportunity by being cowardly, lazy or too much involved in natural antagonism, you and your descendants would remain as slaves for, nobody knows, how long. The objective world situation is rapidly changing, It is your mission to prepare fully and immediately so as to adjust yourselves for the fast changing times and to liberate India from the British yoke. We, the Japanese, are prepare to give the spiritual and natural aid to your revolutionary task, without any compensation or condition. It is needless to say that our common enemy, Britain, will employ every means, such as deceipt, bribery, " divide and rule" policy " and threats. On these points we must be very cautious. " Heaven helps those who help themselves". Indian Independence cannot be a gift from anybody far less from India's enemy, England, from whom you can only expect oppression. India's able leaders must make good use of the surrounding international conditions, in order to lessen the amount of sacrifices involved. On her part, what Japan expects from India is that she should do away with all the retarding ideas of religious and class antagonisms and the various rivalries between political and military ways of thought and become a united body of 400,000,000 to proceed along the way of independence, that she should realize that the realization of Indian Independence in itself is a great revolution to be led to succeed ony on the strength of her leaders' firm determination and of the fiery patriotism of all the Indians and that realizing that one action is superior to hundreds of arguments, she should make use of conditions surrounding her and advance for the attainment of independence. And we wish to assure you that Japan has not the slightest territorial or political ambition on India, and that she will not hesitate to extend any help to the Indians in their fight and that without any ulterior motives.

Please take your own time and engage yourselves in calm deliberations so that you may arrive at a plan of action which may be beneficial on all parts for future India as well as future East Asia. This is my request to you all, and it comes from the bottom of my heart."

Mr. Raghavan, on behalf of the conference thanked suitably Col. Iwaguro and through him the Imperial Japanese Govt. and the Japanese people for their kind encouragement.

Agenda No. I. Attitude of the Indians regarding this war was then taken up and the following resolution was read and unanimously passed :—

Whereas we believe that this war of greater East Asia is sure to destroy British Influence and power in Asia and whereas we believe that this is a golden opportunity for the realization of India's National Goal, which is nothing but complete Independence and whereas depending upon the self consious efforts of various Asiatic Nations a new Asia is sure to arise as a result of this war, we hereby resolve that we must join hands with Japan in accordance with the declared policy of the Imperial Japanese Government made through Premier Tojo on the occasion of the fall of Singapore.

Agenda No. II. Complete Independence of India.

1. *Ideology of Independence.*

After discussions, which all members participated, it was resolved that, **unity, faith, sacrifice,** shall be the motto of the Independence movement.

2. *Nature and time of Independence.*

The meeting of the Complete Independence of India was fully clarified and the following resolution was unanimously passed. "That Independence complete and free from foreign domination, interference and/or control of whatever nature, shall be the object of the Movement and in the opinion of the Conference now is the right time to achieve the object and secure such independemce."

Agenda No. III. To spread the Independence Movement in East Asia and India, it was unanimously decided to carry on propaganda work in the following manner :—

East Asia.—By broadcast, Leaflets, Pamphlets, Newspaper Articles, Lecturers, Demonstrations, Music, etc.

India.—By broadcast, Leaflets, Pamphlets, Infiltration, Establishment of contacts with Indian Leaders and organizations etc., etc.

Organizations. (*a*) Formation of Local branches of the League. For the duration of war the President to be elected by the committee formed at a meeting of the representatives of the place. Vacancy in the committee to be filled by the majority of votes of the committee. President, not removable without the vote of three-forths of the members of the committee.

(*b*) *Central* : The Presidents of the various local bodies together with the representatives of the Indian Army in East Asia, which representation shall not exceed the total number of civilian members ot the committee, will form a committee of Representatives, who will lay down general policy of action and elect a Council of Action consisting of a President and four staff members, of whom at least two shall be from the Military.

The Council of Action shall be responsible for the working out of the General Policy and in such working out they shall appoint departmental officers for the purpose of administration.

Departments.

Civil : (*a*) Foreign Department or Liaison Department.

(*b*) Finance Department.

(*c*) Legal Department.

(*d*) Propaganda Department.

(*e*) Administration of Branches.

(*f*) Relief Department

(*g*) Civil Police and Intelligence Department.

(*h*) Civil volunteers Department.

Indian National Army Headquarters.

Military : (*a*) War Department.

(*b*) Recruit Department.

(*c*) Military Intelligence and Military Police Department.

(*d*) Prisoners of War Department.

1. It is resolved that, if in the descretion of the Council of Action it is feasible to summon a meeting of the representatives and take their advice on the matter of general policy, the Council shall do so.

2. It is resolved that, before taking any military action against India, including Ceylon, contrary to the wishes, policy or opinion of the Indian National Congress, the Council of Action shall first get the approval of the Committee of the Representatives and act as directed.

3. Resolved that Japan Government be requested that military action against India should be taken only by the Indian National Army and under the Command of Indians, together with such military, naval and air co-operation and assistance as may be requested from the Japanese Authorities by the Council of Action.

Request to Imperial Government.

1. It is resolved that, in further clarification of the attitude of Japan towards India, the Imperial Govt. of Japan be requsted to make a formal declaration to the effect :—

(*a*) That Japan is ready and willing to give all possible help to India to sever its connection with the British Empire to attain complete Independence.

(*b*) That on such severance of India from the British Empire, Japan would recognise the full sovereignity of India on attaining independence.

(*c*) The absolute independence of India would be guaranteed by the Imperial Government of Japan.

(*d*) That the Imperial Government of Japan would exercise its influence with other powers and induce them to recognise the independence and sovereignity of India.

(*e*) That the framing of the future constitution of India will be left entirely to the representatives of the people of India.

2. It was also resolved to request the Imperial Government of Japan :—

(*a*) To render such financial help for the successful carrying out of our object as may be required from time to time, on the distinct understanding that such help is to be treated as a loan to be repaid to Japan by the National Government of India, when it comes into being.

(*b*) To give all facilities for propaganda, travel, transport and communications, within the regions that are under the control of the Imperial Japanese Government in the manner and to the extent requested by the Council of Action and also all facilities to come into contact with the National Leaders, workers and organisations in India.

(*c*) To clarify the position of the Indian Troops now under control in occupied territories.

(*d*) To recognize and facilitate the use of the present National Flag of India in all territories under the Imperial Government of Japan.

(*e*) To consult in all matters of administration affecting the Indian community, the Indian Independence League of the respective places, and in places where there are no leagues, recognized leaders of the community, approved by the league branch nearest to such place.

Resolution of Interim Constitution.

(*a*) This Conference resolves that in order to obtain full support and co-operation of Indians in various parts of Greater East Asia, a fuller conference of Indian representatives should be called at Rangoon or any other suitable place at the earliest opportunity and that Mr. Rash Bihari Bose is hereby authorised to take the necessary steps to give effect to the various decisions made by this conference pending their ratification at a later conference as stated above.

(*b*) This conference hereby appoints Mr. Rash Bihari Bose as interim President of the Council of Action.

(*c*) Resolved that the next conference shall be held before the 1st of June, 1942, if possible and in any case not later than the 1st of July, 1942 and the interim President shall make the necessary arrangements.

(*d*) Resolved that at the next conference besides the Presidents and/or representatives of various Indian Independence Leagues as hereinafter limited (in person or proxy) and military representatives of Indian Army in East Asia, all the members attending this conference should also be invited to attend.

The Conference to ratify the decisions herein, shall be held at Bangkok in the 3rd week of May, 1942, and representatives and/or presidents not exceeding the number indicated here below may attend the said conference.

Japan	8	Hongkong	8	Thailand	9
Malaya	20	Macao and Manila	2	Indo China	5
Shanghai	8	Burma	20	East India	8
Port Blair	2			(Java, Sumatra, Borneo, Celebes).	

Total 90

Representatives of the Indian Army in East Asia will also attend as previously agreed to under Agenda III, 2, b.

GENERAL

(*a*) That this conference is committed to a definite policy of the closest co-operation with Japan and it shall, on eliciting an official definition of the term "Greater East Asia Co-prosperity Sphere" and its implications, endeavour by every possible means at the command of this movement :—

1. To persuade Independent India to be member of the Sphere on a footing of equality with Japan.

2. To confer on Japan the Most-Favoured-Nation treatment on a reciprocal basis.

(*b*) This conference places on record its profound gratitude to the Imperial Government of Japan for their active sympathy for the cause of Indian Independence and expresses its thanks for their generous hospitality and for the ample facilities provided for their successful termination of this conference.

(*c*) This conference places on record its profound thanks to Mr. Rash Bihari Bose who by tact, patience and geniality as Chairman contributed not a little to the success of this conference.

(*d*) While they individually find themselves in perfect agreement with the decisions of this conference, the members of the Goodwill Mission of Malaya, hereby make their position clear in taking part in this conference that they do not commit the Indians in Malaya to the decisions of this conference, but will try their best to induce them to the views of the conference.

The following suggestions of Mr. Asman on education and other matters were noted for action at the opportune time :—

1. Specific instructions should be given to any troops attacking India to refrain themselves and to stop others from destroying or

damaging places of worship belonging to the various religious bodies in order to avoid any sort of friction liable to be caused by such sabotage acts.

2. As soon as possible the property of the Indian Government and other rich Indians considered pro-British including the Indian Princes should be placed under the joint control and custody of the occupying Indian troops to avoid embezzlement or looting, etc., so that on the expiration of the war the Indian Government may be in a position to cover up the expenses.

3. In all kinds of Government affairs, external or internal, the Indian religious leaders should not be consulted and their membership should never be taken in various state councils.

4. Compulsory education, irrespective of male and female sect should be started as soon as possible on realization of the independence of India.

5. Various societies opened in different cities found not in favour of achieving complete independence of India and not co-operating with the main body, should be dissolved as soon as possible.

6. Able and patriotic volunteers should be enlisted from each and every part of East Asia including Shanghai, Hongkong, Java, Sumatra, etc., so that they can enjoy equal privileges in order that they may also partake in serving their motherland.

7. All Indian nationals, irrespective of their financial standing class or religion, should be treated on an equal footing in the matter of State affairs.

8. In war time just as women in all countries of the world are allowed to take full share in rendering their best services for the freedom of their respective countries, similarly Indian women are also anxious to fulfill their duty, in every possible way, for the freedom of the country. But during the British reign, the women of India have not been given the same power and freedom which the men have been enjoying so far, as a result of which women in India have not been allowed to take part in Government affairs. In order to raise them to the same standard of freedom as the men, should allow them the discretion of taking active part in serving our motherland, even against the wishes of their parents, husbands and other relatives, supposed to be pro-British.

9. Military training should be condsidered as a compulsory part of education.

Sd. RAS BEHARI BOSE,

TOKYO — Chairman,

April 8, 1942. — Indian Independence Conference.

AFTER THE TOKYO CONFERENCE.

Interim period between Tokyo Conference and Bangkok Conference.

The delegation from Tokyo had returned with new hopes and expectations of bright future for India's independence. It had been entrusted with specific responsibilites, and duties and the members of the delegation immediately took to their task in right earnest. They knew they had taken a heavy and onerous burdens on their shoulders—the liberation of India, their mother-land. They had to educate public opinion in Malaya and Thailand, to tell their people—the Indians—the true significance and implication of the resolution passed at the Tokyo Conference. They had to reassure themselves and also to assure all the Indians in the Far East—Civilians as well as Military—that they were not going to be exploited by the Japanese, but move only where furtherence of India's liberty was concerned.

To achieve these ends, it was necessary to bring the Indian Independence League on a firm footing to reorganize it, to prepare its constitution, to organize League branches in all the Malayan States and in all the important towns and finally to raise funds for it. For this purpose a conference of delegates from the Independence Leagues of India of Malayan States was held at Broadrick Road Syonan-to (Singapore) from the 22nd April to 26th April 1942. The scene of activity had now shifted from Thailand to Malaya, firstly because Singpore was the most important headquarter of the Japanese Government and the Department dealing with the Indian problems was stationed here and secondly because both the delegates of the Tokyo conference from Thailand—Swami Satyanda Puri and Sirdar Pritam Singh had died in the air disaster. The Malaya League under the able leadership of Sri N. Raghawan started the work. Besides holding the Conference, they also convened public meetings and met the Fujiware Department to seek help and give suggestions for the furtherence of Indian Independence movement. Through this department, they requested the Japan Government to make her War-aims clear and make a formal declaration about the acceptance of Tokyo resolutions. But their main concern was to safegurd the interests of Indian Civil population and to better the lot of Indian prisoners of war. They asked the Fujiwara Department to recognize the Indian Independence League as the sole representative of Indians and to consult its branches, in local matters affecting Indians. The League could justify its existence and win the confidence, love and reverence of its people only by looking after the social and economic welfare of the Indian community in Malaya and other parts of Far East. It looked upon the Fujiwara department and subsequently the Iwaguro Department (The department attached to the Indian Independence Movement to assist it) as a link between the Japanese Government and the Indian people for solving all the problems of the community. But to the great disappointment of the League the policy of the department left much to be desired in this respect and though not saying in so many words it made it clear through its actions that the League could not expect the department for any intervention with the administeration in the matters affecting local interests.

Below we give a summary of the proceedings of the conference of the Indian Independence Leagues of Malaya, speeches of Mr. Fujiwara and Mr. Raghawan at a public meeting held at Singapore on the 24th April 1942 and a summary of the relations of the Indian Department of the Japanese Government with the Indian Independence League. The proceedings speak for themselves and the reader will clearly see that all was not well.

The Conference of Malayan delegates of the Indian Independence Leagues was held from the 22nd April to 26th April 1942. In all it held six sittings.

The following were present :—

1.	Sri N. Raghavan	Penang
2.	,, S. C. Goho	Syonan
3.	,, K. P. K. Menon	,,
4.	,, S. Shanmugam	Malacca
5.	,, Gurdial Singh	Segamat
6.	,, S. N. Chopra	Batu Pahat
7.	,, Budh Singh	Kuala Lumpur
8.	,, Govindasamy	,
9.	Dr. Luskhumeyah	,,
10.	Sri P. M. Dalal	,,
11.	,, Lal Singh	Kuala Kangsar
12.	,, Nagappa Chettiar	Alor Star
13.	,, J. Maneckshа	Taiping
14.	Dr. Majumdar	Seremban
15.	Bri B. K. Das	Ipoh
16.	,, Sucha Singh	,,

Some representatives of the Indian Military were also present.

Sri K. M. Kannampillay acted as Secretary.

Sri N. Raghavan presided.

Sri Sucha Singh reported that he had gone to Johore Bahru to fetch the delegates from there but that the President was indisposed and could not come.

The President read out the minutes of the Conference at Tokyo. With regard to the requests made by the Conference to the Japanese Government no official reply had as yet been received. The delegates met the Japanese Premier, who on two occasions stated that the intention of Japan was to liberate India with no ulterior motives at all. Sri N. Raghavan also read out the report signed by the delegates from Hongkong and Malaya regarding their impressions and programme. The Conference thanked all the delegates, who had gone to Tokyo for the splendid work they had done in the cause of Indian Independence.

It was suggested that it would be better to proceed in the movement after an official declaration is received agreeing to the proposals made by the Conference at Tokyo preferably from the Emperor of Japan, since a policy accepted by the present Government might be altered by another Government. Sri N. Raghavan replied that it would be impossible to receive an assurance from the Emperor in view of the peculiar position of His Imperial Majesty in Japan. He said that General Tojo's policy with regard to India is supported by all other parties and leaders including ex-premiers. Even the ordinary man in the street seemed to be in full support of that policy.

The opinion of the Conference was that an official and formal Declaration by the Government of Japan accepting the proposals should be had before they proceeded.

In its deliberation extending over five days, the conference discussed and decided the following problems :—

1. The Conference thanked the delegation to Tokyo for their splendid work in the cause of Indian Independence.

2. The report of the Toyo Conference was accepted, with minor modifications.

3. The position of the Indian troops in Malaya was discussed. Sri Raghavan read out the resolution passed at the Conference of Malayan delegation on 10th March 1942 regarding the Indian prisoners of war and also the reply from Major Fujiwara to that. It was suggested that the original request to have the Indian soldiers in Syonan-to placed on an equal footing with the soldiers in other parts of Malaya should be repeated. This was seconded. Sri Das proposed that this conference authorises the President in consultation with Capt. Nohan Singh to speak to Major Fujiwara regarding this point. The proposal was agreed to by the Conference.

It was stated that difficulties were being experienced regarding the ration supplied to the Indian National Army. The President replied that the matter was already under consideration of the Fujiwara Department and that the main difficulty might be in getting stocks. It was stated that stocks could be got from Burma, China and Java. It was decided that at the joint conference with the military representatives, we should discuss the needs of the army and decide on our course of action after that.

4. It was agreed to present a purse of 10,000 to the bereaved family of Mr. Otaguro through Major Fujiwara.

5. It was decided to make representation to the authorities to have transport facilities at the disposal of the Independence Movement, such facilities to be under the control of the Secretaries.

6. A Central Body of Representatives totalling 22 distributed as follows was formed :—

Perlis 1, Kelanthan 1, Trengganu 1, Pahang 1, Johore 2, Malacca 2, Negri Sombilan 2, Perak 2, Penang (including Province Wellesley) 2, Kedah 2, Selangor 3, Syonan 3.

7. The following Leagues were accepted as State Leagues :—

Syonan, Batu Pahat, Malacca, Seremban, Kuala Lumpur, Ipoh, Penang, Alor Star, Kangar Koto Bahru, Kuala Trenggenu, Raub.

8. The office of the Central Body was fixed to be at Syonan.

9. A Supreme Council for Malaya made up of a President and 4 others was elected as follows :—

Sri N. Raghavan
,, K. P. K. Menon
,, S. C. Goho
,, S. N. Chopra
Dr. Lukshumeyah

The Commander of the Indian National Army, Malaya, would be as ex-officio member of the Council as Military Advisor. Sri B. K. Das was elected as Secretary to the Supreme Council. Whole time workers may be paid honoraria according to the discretion of the Supreme Council.

10. All State Leagues should submit to the Central Body before the 10th of every month a monthly report and statement of accounts and finances.

11. Each State League should transfer 25% of its income to the Central Body. The Central Body can always draw on any funds belonging to the State Leagues. Any League in needs of financial assistance would be according to the discretion of the Central Body.

12. All Leagues in Malaya, including those in existence now, must be registered with the Central Body.

13. The Military Administration should be approached to have the Independence League of India, Malaya Branch, recognised by the various military administrative departments in Malaya as the only legal Indian political body throughout Malaya.

14. A letter should be written to Major Fujiwara to abolish the liason department between the Fujiwara Kikan and the Independence League and to see that Sri Rathore and other similar persons will not interfere with the community in any form, giving examples of difficulties experienced by such interferences. In case the Fujiwara Kikan wants an Indian attached to it, the Independence League shall nominate a person satisfactory to major Fujiwara.

15. It was desired to ask that the Independence League of India be recognised both for the Independence of India as well as for tackling local Indian problems and to request the Government that the League be consulted on all matters connected with Indians in Malaya.

16. It was resolved to make official representation that toddy should be abolished in Malaya and that non-intoxicating drinks shold be sold to Indian labourers unless on medical grounds.

17. To enable the supreme Council to study the situation and take necessary steps, each State League should submit to the Head Office a report about unemployment, food distribution and distress relief in its area before 10th May, 2602.

Indo-Japanese Relations

The Japanese foreign ministry created a separate department to help and guide the Indian Independence Movement. The chief officer attached to this department was major Fujiwara and his department was known as Fujiwara Department. The major had intimate association with the first and foremost organisers of the movement in Thailand and Malaya The part played by him in organising the independence movement in Malaya and in rendering the movement every help was great indeed.H is presence at almost all the conferences and meetings of the independece league of India gave the workers encouragement by his sympathetic attitude. He also convened joint meetings of the members of his department and the representatives of Indian Independence League and also addressed the mass meetings of Indians.

A report of the meetings at Fujiwara place held on 26th April, 1942, is reproduced below. Major Fujiwara, Lt. Kuniska, Sri Raghavan, Sri Goho, Sri Menon, Dr: Lakohmyah, Sri Chopra and Sri Das (Secretary) were present :—

Major Fujiwara suggests that the office of the Central Committee be near Fujiwara Kikan at Bukit Timah. Two houses will be allotted, one for office and the other for residential purposes. Sri Raghavan informed the Major that all Tokyo resolutions-some with verbal alterations only-were accepted in the Conference. The work of the League will be started after formal acceptance of the resolutions by the Imperial Government. Major says that he will obtain formal confirmation of the acceptance of the resolutions as soon as possible.

Raghavan says that the authorities should recognise the League as representing Indians in Malaya in matters of local importance. The League will have a department in each centre dealing with local affairs and this may be termed as "Consultative Committee." The Major says that there will be no political parties for Chinese, Malays or Indians in Malaya but the administration will have departments dealing with the welfare of each community. He agrees to the League having a local affairs department to deal with local problems but such department should not work in the name of the League. For purposes of consultation or dealing in local affairs the Government will deal with persons chosen by the League. There will be mutual understanding that the League can (through its special department) deal with the administration but there will be no official recognition of this department of the League. The main function of the League will nevertheless be the attainment of Independece of India.

Major further intimates that while in his tour in the Mainland he will tell the administration that the League will give such advice and assistance as may be needed and that the administration on their part should extend their co-operation to the League.

Facilities for Transportation and Communications.

Major says that details are being worked out and will be made known later.

Propaganda.

Major promises all assistance in this connection.

Re Laison Department.

Major agrees to abolish this department but wishes that the two people connected therewith, *viz.*, Sucha Singh and Rathore, should be given their proper place in the Movement. Raghavan says that Sucha Singh will get his proper place in the Movement (Das informs that he is already a member of the Ipoh Committee) but he cannot promise the same with regard to Rathore. In his opinion Rathore's presence will be harmful to Fujiwara Kikan and the Movement. Major suggests that Rathore be employed at Bangkok in a minor position such as a clerk. He knows of Rathore's movements in Singapore and is very annoyed at his attitude.

Toddy.

Major says that he will discuss this question with the chief of the administration.

Indian Prisoners of War.

Preparations are already being made to place these persons on the same footing as the members of the I. N. A. Tokyo Government has decided that they should no longer remain prisoners of war.

Indian National Army.

Major says that it will take some time to infuse a new spirit in the Indian Army. Therefore a nucleus of the Indian National Army will be formed with 500 commissioned officers, 1,000 non-commissioned officers and 1,000 privates who will be given special training. The rest will be split up into different groups and assigned for garrisoning work, labour, technical training, etc., and will be attached to the Japanese Army. These troops will be paid pocket money almost, but not the same amount, as the Japanese troops. Contributions will be asked for from these troops to the National Army. The strength of the National Army will be decided upon by the Indian Officers. The Japanese authorities wish to nominate Capt. Mohan Singh as Supreme Commander of the Indian National Army but if Indian civilians have any other opinion, the Major would like to know. Raghavan says that Indian civilians wish Capt. Mohan Singh to be the Commander-in-Chief.

Major is very pleased with the attitude of the civilian Indians towards the movement. With regard to the Army Officers he regrets that some of them are too much affected by materialistic considerations and that their conduct is not conducive to the welfare of the movement. Capt. Mohan Singh may have to take strong measures against such elements in the Army.

If all prisoners are told that they are free they may make demands on the Japanese authorities which they may not be able to meet. There have been innumerable complaints against Indian troops as to their conduct—cases of looting, etc., have been reported, some have deserted their camps. Indian soldiers should realise that even if they are free they cannot expect to enjoy full liberty.

Raghavan suggests that propaganda be carried on in the Army and the number of men to be taken in to form the nucleus be much larger than that suggested by the Major. Major says all soldiers will be taken together but they will be split up into different batches. He says that the fighting qualities of the Indian soldiers are very good but their revolutionary spirit is nil. He refers to the 100,000 men limited to Germany by the Versailles Treaty who form the backbone of the present German Army. A large army can be created in a very short time—a month or so—if the nucleus is properly trained and is imbued with the real revolutionary spirit. Major wishes to have Civilian Volunteers as well. The Headquarters of the Indian National Army will be at Nee Soon Camp and a department will be set apart to deal with this question. He wishes to train 300 or 400 civilians as officers to form the nucleus of the civilian volunteers.

Re Army.

He wishes to utilise as many as possible for special work such as Military Transport, Aeroplane Engineering party, Pioneers, etc., but those who have no technical qualifications to fatigue duty. Political and Spiritual training will be left to the Indian National Army Supreme Command.

Other training will be under the control of the Japanese Army authorities and the troops attached to the Japanese Army will be considered as part of the Japanese Army. For the present only the nucleus will be called the "Indian National Army", the others after training will become members of the Indian National Army. Prisoners will be freed in the course of two or three weeks.

Re Salute

Indian National Army Officers would salute all Japanese Officers. Indian non-commissioned officers and privates should salute all Japanese soldiers. Major says that in view of the present mental condition of the Japanese Army a change in this cannot be effected very soon. Gradually the position will be improved.

Major Fujiwara was succeeded by Col. Iwaguro as the head of the Indian department of the Japanese. He arrived at Singapore on the 20th May, 1942. The members of the Central Executive of the Indian Independence League Malaya Branch and the Presidents of most of the State Branches were in Singapore awaiting the Col's. arrival Sri N. Raghavan representing the League and Capt. Mohan Singh representing the Indian National Army welcomed the Colonel at Singapore Civil Aerodrome.

The following day a Conference of the Representatives of the League and Col. Iwaguro and his colleagues was held at the office of the Malaya branch of the League, No. 31, Malcolm Road, Syonan. In the discussions which ensued the Col. emphasised the two-fold duties of the Indians in Malaya, namely (i) to organise and promote the Independence Movement and (ii) to co-operate with the Nipponese Administration in Malaya. He assured the representatives of the League that his Kikan would, in every possible way, assist the Independence Movement.

The Government Recognised the Independence League of India as the only Political Organisation for Indians in Malaya and would not allow any Sectional Organisationto Function as a Political Institution.

Col. Iwaguro entertained the reprentatives of the League and some officers of the Indian National Army at the Raffles Hotel the same evening. In after dinner speech the Col. dwelt at length on the attitude of Japan towards the Indian question. He reiterated the assurance given to the delegates to the Tokyo Conference that Japan has no Political or Territorial ambition in India. She is only anxious to see a free and independent India and is prepared to give all such assistance and co-operation as the Indians may need to free their country from the yoke of British Imperialism. The Col's duty is not to lead the Independence Movement but to give it a helping hand. He referred to the centuries old cultural link between India and Japan. Japan was indebted to a very great extent to India for her culture and civilisation and today, she on her part is prepared for everything that is necessary to assist in the liberation of four hundred million Indians. Sri N. Raghavan thanked the Col. for the very encouraging words he had uttered. He referred to the visit of the Indian goodwill Mission to Tokyo and said that whomsoever they met in Japan, whatever might be his or her station in life, every man and every woman showed a sincere desire to assist India in attaining her freedom. Such a feeling of enthusiasm for another country would hardly be imagined, and, to add to all that, the Japanese Government through its spokesman, Col. Iwaguro, pledged its support to the cause for which the Indians had been fighting so long, and this, without in any way asking for anything in return. Such a gesture was unique in the history of the world.

Mr. Senda, Chief adviser of the Iwaguro Kikan, said that he had lived for a number of years in India. What he was today was due to what he had learned in India and from Indians. He had been a businessman there and in his characteristic commercial language he said that he went to India as raw material from Japan and became a finished product in India. He could truly be labelled as "Made in India". He said that the problem of the four hundred million inhabitants of India was a world problem. Japan, which is fighting for the establishment of a new order in the world, is determined to see that that problem is also solved.

The Representatives of the League had the advantage of having a full and a frank discussion with the Chief of the Military Administration in Malaya when the latter, Col. Watanabe, invited them to luncheon party at the old cricket club, Syonan, on 23rd May. In a true spirit of friendship Col. Watanabe gave an Indian lunch to the representatives of the League and thereafter discussed local problems. Sri N. Raghavan pointed out that about 75% of the Indian labourers in Malaya, most of them until lately employed in rubber estates, were still unemployed. Both in the rubber estates and in the urban areas there was a large number of labourers who were without work and without food. He also raised the question of the re-employment of people who had been in Government service until the occupation of this place by the Nipponese Army. Col. Watanabe dealt generally with the present economic problem. He emphasised the necessity for enduring hardships under present conditions; the administration would be prepared to pay in kind to those who worked. He said that rubber estates were being opened from north to south but that Johore Bahru area, due to too much devastation caused by the War, could not be opened immediately. Dealing with the rice position he informed the representatives of League that arrangements had been made for the importation of 40 thousand tons of rice from Burma and Thailand every month. This, in his opinion, should be sufficient to meet the normal requirements of Malaya. Already three shiploads of rice were coming from Burma and one from Thailand. The policy of the Government is to make Malaya self-sufficient in the matter of food. He stated that the Japanese Government have no intention to squeeze Malaya to satisfy their Military needs.

Sri N. Raghavan then raised the question of the recognition of the Indian National Flag. Col. Watanabe informed the representatives that he was giving favourable consideration to this question and that orders would be issued soon.

In conclusion Col. Watanabe clarified the administration's policy with regard to various communities in Malaya. He said that when the Japanese first occupied this country they considered all the inhabitants of Malaya as enemy nationals but as soon as people showed their sincerity and their spirit of co-operation they would be treated as loyal citizens. Before the party broke up Col. Iwaguro said that the war must be won at any cost and that people in Malaya should be prepared to endure hardships until this goal was attained.

CHAPTER VII
BANGKOK CONFERENCE
15th—23rd June, 1942

In pursuance of the decision arrived at the Tokyo Conference to hold a larger and more representative assembly, Indian delegates from various parts of East Asia assembled at the Thai capital for a nine-day conference commencing on June 15, 1942. The Silapakorn Theatre, Bangkok, was packed to overflowing. There was no standing room anywhere and even the spacious ground itself was packed to capacity, while the roads leading to it were crowded with people who were eager to get a glimpse of the distinguished visitors. The Hall was decorated with portraits of Mahatma Gandhi, Pandit Nehru and Maulana Azad, and mottos snch as " Freedom is our Birth-right." A large number of representatives of Japan, Thailand and the Axis countries were also present.

The following Indian delegates attended the conference :—

From Japan.—Messrs. Rash Behari Bose, A. M. Sahay, D. S. Deshpande. S. N. Sen, Rajah Sherman, V. Choklingam, J. K. Parekh, Ramsingh Rawal, B. D. Gupta, and V. S. Supanekar.

From Manchukuo.—Mr. A. M. Nair.

From Hong Kong.—(Civil) Messrs. D. M. Khan, P. A. Krishna, and H. M. Parwani. (Military) Major Hakim Khan, Capt. Mohd. Iqbal, Capt. Tara Singh and Capt. Aya Singh.

From Burma.—Messrs. L. B. Lathia, N.K. Bannerji, J. G. Buckle Balan, S. K. Chakravarty, T. G. Desai, C. P. Mehta, Mohd. Jaffer, Prof. E. Now, Messrs. M. Randeri, Mohamed Yakoob Khan, E. P. Pillay, Mohamed Shaffee, Latchman Singh, Ahmad S. Ginwala, Mohamed Sheriff Khan, Abdul Satar, and Sultan Mohamed.

From Borneo.—Messrs. J.Lalchand, Kranal Singh, V. N. K. Pillai, K. K. Thangavelu Pillai, and Joginder Singh Greval.

From Java.—Messrs. S. Haque, J. L. Gandhi, D. T. Assoomall, Yusaf Akbani, and Narain Das Chobarmal.

From Malaya.—(Civil) Messrs. N. Raghavan, K. P. K. Menon, S. N. Chopra, Dr. M. K. Lukshumeyah, Janab B. Mallal, Sardar Hardit Singh, Janab Amir Khan, Dr. D. K. Majumdar, Sardar Budh Singh, Messrs. S. Shanmugam, M. K. Ramachandram, P. M. Dalal, J. A. Thivy, Kundan Lall, P. N. Pillai, Janab H. H. Abdul Kader, Dr. Jagat Singh, Messrs. S. N. K. Nagappa Chettiar, B.K. Das, K. A. Narayan L. Xavier, Dharam Singh, Mukum Singh, Kehar Singh, Sucha Singh & S.C. Goho. (Military) Capt. Mohan Singh, (organiser, Indian National Army), Lt. Col. G. Q. Gillani, Lt. Col. A. C.Chatterji, I. M. S. Lt. Col. A. D. Longanadan, I. M. S. Lt. Col. N. S. Gill, Major Prakash Chand. Major Aziz Ahmed Major D. S. Raju, I. M. S. Major M. S. Dhillon, Capt. B. S. Pattanayak, I. M. S., Capt. S. M. Hussain, Capt. S. A. Mallik, Capt. A. D. Jehangir, Capt. I. J. Kiani, Capt. Habib-ur.Rahman, Capt. Burhan-ud-Din, Capt. Malik Fateh Khan, Capt. Dhian Singh, Capt. Allah Ditta, Capt. Gurmit Singh, Lt. Amar Singh, Lt. Mumtaz Khan, Lt. Babu Ram, Lt. Kishan Singh, Lt. Puran Singh, Capt. Ram Sarup, 2nd Lt. Rattan Singh, and 2nd Lt. Shiv Singh.

From Thailand.—Messrs. Deb Nath Das, A. A. Rashid, Chuli Shah, L. S. Pandi, M. Sivaram, Sripat Rai, Lalita Misra, Maghar Singh, M.S. Ramsingh, Mr. Sevak, T. Mehtani, Mrs. Laj, S. Mehtani, Pandit Rajunath Shastri, Sardar Amar Singh, Sardar Iswar Singh, Maulvi Akbar Ali and Dr. P. R. Pillay.

From Shanghai.—Messrs. Piara Singh, M. S. Doshi, B. Bobby, and Harnam Singh.

From Manila.—Messrs. Daljit Singh, Mohan Singh, Atma Singh, Inder Singh, and Banta Singh.

From Indo-China.—Mr. T. S. Subramanin.

In an atmosphere of great political awakening and purposefulness the Conference was opened on June 15, 1942, by the Deputy Minister of Foreign Affairs of Thailand, H. E. Vichitr Vichitr-Vadakarn. The day's programme commenced with the singing of the Indian National Anthem, followed by silent prayers for the martyrs of the Indian Independence Movement. Opening the Conference, H. E. Vichitr-Vadakarn addressed the gathering as follows :—

Gentlemen of the Delegation,

I am glad to have the honour of opening this Conference. In performing the pleasant duty, I bring to you a message from His Excellency the Prime Minister, which I shall now read to you :—

In the name of the Thai people, I have much pleasure in welcoming this Conference of Indian Delegates which has been arranged to take place here in Bangkok. My pleasure in welcoming the Conference being held in the capital of Thailand is due to two causes.

Firstly, the aim of this Conference is to rid India of the yoke of tyranny and oppression under which she has been for long suffering, and to restore to India her liberty, so that India may rightly be a country for Indians. Since Thailand has been from time immemorial a land of the free, liberty is deeply-rooted in the heart of the Thai people who cherish their independence more than their very life. The Thais, therefore, sympathise with and support all follow-men, whatever their race, who are striving to attain independence for their motherland. When I learnt that the aim of this Conference was to establish the Independence of India, I gave it my whole hearted support.

Secondly, Thais and Indians are deeply bound together in cultural ties. We, Thais, received the Doctrines of Buddhism and our knowledge of Arts and Sciences from India. Even the words we use in our daily speech and in our writings are many of them derived from India. During the period that India had to contend with foreign aggression and fell under the domination of a race alien in language and in culture, resulting in Indian Culture being deprived of support and maintenance which in time brought on a gradual decay, Thailand undertook the duty of safeguarding

Indian culture. If you visit our National Museum, you will find that we have preserved ancient relics and objects of Art of India in a better state and to a greater amount than those which are to be seen in the Indian Museum at Calcutta. Indiams who have come to reside in Thailand have been received all along in a cordial spirit of friendship by the Thais. Thailand herself has taken up the study of Pali and Sanskrit which are highly prized Indian Culture, in a greater extent than any other country in the world I therefore may safely say that Thais and Indians are bound together in culture in the closest of ties.

For the two reasons stated above, I am happy therefore to have the opportunity of extending my welcome to the Conference for the liberation of India at this capital of Bangkok.

In sending my message for the opening of this Conference, I cannot refrain from expressing my respect for Swami Satyanadapuri, who was one of the prominent figures sharing in the great work of co-ordinating the cultural and spiritual relations between our two nations. I am unable to find words sufficiently appropriate to express my sorrow and sense of loss at his death. I am convinced that his pure soul will come and be present amongst you at this Conference and will help the Conference to achieve success in a satisfactory manner.

Gentlemen, now is an auspicious occasion in which all the Asiatic peoples may collaborate as one in the task of doimg away with all the hardships we have suffered from the oppressive rule of alien races. Japan has taken the lead for the liberation of Asia. It is therefore an opportunity for all the Asiatic people to unite their strength and hearts with Japan for the accomplishment of this important task. As India is the mother country of Religion, Culture, Arts and Sciences, as she has been the world's teacher from olden times, the light of India's soul has therefore never been extinguished, but will henceforth shine gloriously brighter, fanned by the unity, endeavour and perseverance of all of us.

I therefore pray the protecting grace of the Triple Gem and all the sacred powers of the Universe to guard and protect the Indian delegates assembled here, so that you will be endowed with good health, united in spirit and strong in wisdom in order to carry out the work of this Conference to the desired successful conclusion for the freedom and happiness of India and of all the Asiatic peoples.

(Sd.) Field-Marshal P. Pibulasonggram,

Prime Minister.

In addition to this message from His Excellency the Prime Minister which I have just read to you, I wish to add an expression of my own sincere hopes for the smooth progress of this Conference and its final conclusion with the desired success. The auspicious moment has arrived. I have much pleasure, Gentlemen, in declaring the Conference opened".

The message of the Thai Premier was translated into English by a lady announcer of the Thai Broadcasting Station and into Hindustani by Mr. Charanjit Rai Narula of the Bangkok League Committee.

The chairman of the Reception Committee of the Conference—Mr. Debnath Dass then read his address. Welcoming the delegates he said :—

Comrades,

It is a great honour for me to welcome you all to-day. While doing so on behalf of the Indian Independence Conference and your thousand comrades of Thailand, I wish to convey at the outset my heartfelt thanks to the people of Thailand and Japan, who made it possible for all of us to meet and embrace each other especially at this time when we need most. Words are poor carrier of the feelings of inner heart but that being the only means of expression on such occasions, I thank the authorities of Thailand and Japan for all the manifestation of their sincere feelings in helping us to serve the cause, we stand for.

While embracing you, however, my mind goes to him—the one who blessed with all the great heritage of Bharatavarsha, carried the message of her cultural supremacy into this land of the Yellow Robe. The confluence of his head and heart became the meeting place of the giver and the given. Swami Satyanandapuri who has lived with us, the one who is living in us, the one who has not cast the shadow of separation even on departure, the one who has gone farther only to come nearer, is no more with us ! We feel lonely to-day and welcome you in his name—the name that spells truth and love.

We are deprived also of the services of our respected compatriots, Giani Pritam Singh, Capt. Mohd. Akram and Nilkhantha Ayer. To-day when we are assembled, let us give homage to those martyrs, who have left us only to leave behind a great legacy of love for freedom.

Friends ! the land of our birth, Hindustan, is passing through a most crucial period in her history. The history of struggle for freedom that was confined into the prison-walls, has now spread all over and India's struggle for existence has now become the world's struggle. India, who was for century and a half lulled into a dosing whale of humanity by an arrogant imperialism, born of greed and robbery, has now become a mother of a conscious mass. India's fateful hour has now struck as Deshbandhu Subhash Chandra Bose has told and every Indian must now make his decision—decision that no power on earth can undo. The immense sacrifices that our compatriots at home have made for the last seventy years since India's first struggle for freedom in 1857, to lift India from the dark cell of degeneration are now in the hearts of our hearts. We bow our heads down to those, the torch-bearers of freedom, who created for us a field on which all of us stand and see light amidst surrounding darkness. When the rest of the world was still living in awe of the roaring British Lion, the unarmed youths of India were shedding their blood and thus proving that, though India lost everything, she has not lost her soul. This is India's spirit, the spirit that knows no fear, the spirit that steel cannot subdue, neither can fire subjugate. To-day already a gigantic struggle for national emancipation is on in India. India, the fountain-head of all struggles of India's Liberty and Life, is definitely to-day at the parting of ways with Britain and those reactionary non-entities allied with it.

Friends ! the awakening of India has a special significance to the world and a particular hope to humanity, since India is a country with a mission, a nation with a power to contribute to the cause of human welfare. In the conception of her nationalism, when civilisation found its cradle on this quaint land, she has been led by one spirit—the spirit of contributing to the welfare of humanity.

It was this spirit, as Swamiji observed, which moulded her national life and brought perfection to her individual self. It was this spirit that in the days of our death-like slumber kept aglow, even in the darkest days of her life, the light of culture and civilisation, the glimmer of hope that one day she might stand erect before the world and raise with her unshaking hands the torch of truth and love she had lighted with the flame of her life. It is because of this spirit that the hands that were stretched to choke her to death, succeeded only in rousing her to self-consciousness.

All Indian national organisations therefore to be living organism represent such creation, wide and integral, embracing in fact the whole scheme and scope of national life. The central principal of our national struggles, is physical transformation and to evolve collective body or entity —a nation within a nation, with a definite culture, education, religion and society, founded on that inner realisation, through a process of individual and collective purification so as to prepare a field of culture in the truth of unity, yet revealing every variety of India's self-expression and upbuilding a political and economic foundation, whose model is no exact proto-type but the adoption of modern requirements of the ancient great principle native to her life and genius of India. An organisation to be an Indian organisation must be therefore a fountain spring of SADHANA or in other words becomes a spontaneous flow of the Realisation, Resignation, and Service. India is intent to enjoy freedom only within the larger freedom of the world. "Who lives," to quote Pandit Jawaharlal Nehru, "if India dies and who dies if India lives."

To-day we have to create this India. India may be a subcontinent but with all her varieties, basically India is a single country. India may be compared with a garland. A garland is composed of so many flowers but all flowers are tied into one with a single string fastening them together. Take away one flower and it will lose its beauty. Such is India. And such are we, when we embrace each other before we march with faith in Man and God to do our duty towards our motherland. Let our services be complimentary to those that are rendered by our comrades-in-arms at home. Let us die, so that India lives.

Comrades, you have come from different places. Let us take ourselves as little rivulets as if springing up from different places only to break ourselves into a river—the river that will break itself finally into the mighty ocean of India's Liberty and Life. On this most auspicious occasion, let us pray with a craving heart like the Poet: "Where the mind is without fear and the head is held high." Let us cry out with prophetic fire like the Poet: "The injustice, you dread, is far more coward than you. So shatter the shackles of this imaginary fear and rally round the Mother—Mother India." Out of this vision of Viswakavi Rabindranath and in the creation of Mahatma Gandhi, the greatest man of the world, has risen the spirit of Modern India on whose forehead slavery has not put its mark neither has fear cast its shadow.

We, their children, who meet to-day under the able guidance of Sree Rash Behari Bose, the pioneer of our movement for freedom in East Asia, must now make a decision,—a decision that will accelerate

Two views of the Bangkok Conference

Mrs. S. R. Mehtani addressing the Conference

The Visitors are listening with rapt attention

the creation of a Free, Happy and United India—an India which the Poet visualised and the superman is creating. The burden is ours. We have to carry it. The success is assured, once we put faith in India.

We are grateful to those who have been showering on us sympathy and encouragement in helping us carry this burden. The spontaneous sympathy from far and near will ever remain as a treasure. We thank every one of you.

" Bande Matarm. Inqlab Zindabad, Azad Hind Zindabad !"

Mr. Rash Behari Bose was then formally elected President. He delivered the following Presidential Address :—

" Your Excellencies, Friends and Compatriots !

" Allow me to express my sincere thanks for the great honour you have done me by calling upon me to occupy this chair and guide the deliberations of this historic conference. While greatly appreciating this expression of love and affection for me, I am not unaware of the fact that along with this honour you have placed on my shoulders a great responsibility by electing me the President of this Conference. However, if I have obeyed your command and taken this chair in spite of my knowledge of the intricacies of the problems that will come before this conference, I have been prompted to do so by my great faith in your spirit of co-operation and your sincere desire to put your heads together and to come to useful decisions without wasting much of your time on unnecessary discussions and arguments. I am sure I can count upon your unreserved help and co-operation in successfully conducting the business of the conference.

" As I stand here, my thought goes to the unfortunate air accident, last March, that claimed the lives of our four valuable comrades—Swami Satyananda Puri and Gyani Pritam Singhji of Bangkok, and Captain Akram and Mr. Nilakanda Iyer of Malaya, while they were flying to Tokyo to attend our Indian Independence Conference.

" We can well realise the great loss to our cause at such an important period of our struggle and we all feel it very deeply. However, brethren, let us take it as inevitable and pray for the peace of their souls. In our grim final struggle against British Imperialism, we shall have to offer great sacrifices. Many of us will have to lay down our lives before the world can see India free. It can be well said that these four comrades have given us the lead, of which our compatriots in Thailand and Malaya can be well proud of.

" During and since 1857, when we first revolted against British Imperialism in India, hundreds of thousands of our most respected and beloved compatriots have laid down their lives in their efforts to free our motherland. We cannot forget the fact that they have nourished the seeds of Swaraj with their blood and it is the result of their supreme sacrifices that we are to-day so near our goal and can hope with confidence to achieve independence in the near future. World knows only a part of the long list of those Indian victims of British Imperialism. Let us pay respects to the memory of those numberless known and unknown comrades. Placed as we are to-day, we can do very little beyond that. But the time is fast approaching when in every city and town in India, we shall find a worthy monument erected in their memory and we Indians will pay homage to them and look upon them with pride.

"Our homage is also due to those respected leaders and workers as well as the organisations that have in various ways made untiring efforts since 1857 to liberate our country from bondage. Their list is in no way small and in no way their contributions were negligible. Let us pay our respects to that greatest living Indian Mahatma Gandhi, who, with his magic wand, roused the Indian masses from the centuries-long slumber and has created self-confidence in them. We can have no doubt that when the new and true history of India will be written, Mahatma Gandhi's name will have to be mentioned as the Saviour of India.

"I do not want to take your time by going into the details regarding India's struggle for freedom since 1857. Suffice it to say that although the failure of our revolt of 1857 was a great blow to the nation and although a general depression had overwhelmed the country, our efforts to overthrow British rule never ceased. Under the circumstances prevailing in those days, the activities had to be carried on underground and within a limited scope; and whenever there was an opportunity, a revolt was attempted. After minor preparatory stages our first effort on a large scale was made when the war of 1914-1918 started. Our workers were active everywhere. The Indian army was prepared to join the revolt. A part of the Indian army had actually revolted rather prematurely. We thought we were going to succeed. Unfortunately we did not meet with success on that occasion. Thousands of our compatriots had to pay the highest price of patriotism. Thousands were sent to the Andamans and Mandalay and hundreds of them still remain rotting in prisons and concentration camps.

"During that war of 1914-1918 the British had been partially successful in receiving India's co-operation by telling lies and making false promises. Our people were misled by the fine phraseologies of the shrewd British diplomats. They promised us freedom after the war, as they are doing even during the present war. But soon after the conclusion of that war, it was realised that the British not only did not mean to keep their promises but definitely wanted to take away even that shadow of civil liberty that the Indians were having in pre-war days. When they protested against that, the response from the British side was in terms of bombs, bullets and machine-guns. Needless to mention that the tragedy of the Jallianwala Bagh of Amritsar in April, 1919, is still fresh in the memory of every one of us and the wound has not yet healed. It really cannot be healed until and unless we have completely destroyed the power that was responsible for the great humiliation of our people.

"Every tragedy, however, has a lesson and so had the tragedy of Jallianwala Bagh. The blood of more than one thousand of those innocent martyrs, that included even our women and children, could not go without significant results. The great upheaval that swept India from one corner to the other, and the great movement of Non-Co-operation and Civil Disobedience that has been carried on by the Indian National Congress since 1919 and that has wonderfully organised the masses of India for political struggle, were undoubtedly the direct result of the massacre at Jallianwala Bagh.

"We all must bow our heads in reverence and be greatful to those brothers and sisters who by giving their lives at Jallianwala Bagh have created a new life in India. As we know to-day, millions and millions in India are prepared and determined to suffer and sacrifice their all for the cause of their motherland. When in 1939 the war in Europe started, Britain once again began to indulge in jugglery of words in order to secure Indian co-operation and help. But to the great delight of us all, to this very day the nationalist leaders in India have refused to be misled and have continued to resist all British efforts to drag India into war. Our respect goes to Mahatma Gandhi for the most admirable way, he has led the nation clear of all dangers of being entangled in this war.

"With this background in India, the Greater East Asia War was declared on the 8th December, 1941. No matter in which part of the world he or she might be living, whatever might be his or her attitude towards Japan, I refuse to believe that there was a true Indian patriot who was not extremely delighted and gratified in his heart of hearts when the great news of the declaration of War by Japan against the Anglo-American races reached his or her ears. I refuse to believe there is any true Indian patriot, whatever be his or her career or conviction, who might not have rejoiced, as from day to day, the mighty Imperial forces of Japan on land and sea and in the air went on administering crushing blows against their imperialism in Asia, and the British Imperialist bases in these parts began to totter one after the other like houses of cards. For is there a man whose eyes cannot withhold joyous tears when he sees before his eyes the power of the greatest enemy of humanity and peace, the greatest aggressor of centuries being destroyed? Those of us, who were destined to live and work in Japan, had particular reasons to be overjoyed at these most welcome happenings.

"We have been working in Japan for decades so that we can see Japan in a position to stand by the oppressed Asiatics and to liberate Asia. We were anxiouly awaiting the day when Japan would fully realise the great significance of creating a free and united Asia and would feel convinced that it was in the interest of Japan herself, as also for the rest of Asia if not for the world as a whole, that the octopus grip of the Anglo-Saxon Imperialism in the East must be destroyed root and branch. We all were fully convinced that Japan alone was in the position to take the honour. Thus when on the morning of the most auspicious day, the day of the Enlightenment of Lord Buddha, we heard the most auspicious news of Japan's declaration of war against our common enemy, we felt that our mission in

Japan was fulfilled. We felt convinced that India's freedom was assured. Being in Japan for decades, I knew well that Japan was not in the habit of talking and debating unnecessary and meaningless things. I knew well that she was not in the habit of taking any serious step unless she had fully weighed her strength and was convinced of her success. I therefore did not share the views of those who thought that due to her continued military activities in China, she was too exhausted to challenge the mighty Anglo-Saxon, or the so called ABCD combined forces. I was one of those who had not the slightest doubt that the war in China was a prelude to the real war against Powers who were actually responsible for the continued fratricidal conflict between China and Japan. Happenings on the international chess board during the past more than ten years have been suggesting that such a worldwide conflict was inevitable. It was also apparent that the question of Indian freedom could be successfully solved only when Japan rose in arms against British Imperialism.

" Now that Japan and Thailand have taken up arms against our common foe, the joint efforts of our worthy allies ensure the doom of the British Empire and our complete victory is assured.

" These effective efforts on different fronts to destroy our common enemy, bring us a reminder regarding our own duties and responsibilities in this common effort for our common cause. We must ask ourselves what we have done and what we are going to do to contribute to this great cause. Only praising Japan, Germany and Italy will not entitle us to the position for which we are craving. We must contribute our mite and must make the greatest sacrifice we can make. Then alone can we command the respect and consideration of our worthy allies and then alone we can claim a place worthy of a great nation like ours in future international assembly.

Realising this very important fact, and our duty towards our motherland at this most important juncture, we in Tokyo promptly met on the 8th of December, 1941 at the Rainbow Grill and decided upon a programme of action. My compatriots formed a committee and asked me to lead the movement and I gladly agreed to abide by their decision. We at first undertook to consolidate Indian opinion in East Asia in favour of a definite fight from without. Meetings were held in different centres of Japan and resolutions were passed emphasising the solidarity of our compatriots, the great need of declaring Independence of India by destroying British Imperialism, and expressing confidence in our work.

On the 20th December, 1941, for the first time in the history of Indians in Japan, a Conference of nearly fifty representatives of the Indian residents in Kobe, Osaka, Yokohama and Tokyo—all the four cities, where Indians reside—was held at the Railway Hotel at Tokyo to consider the problems. A resolution was passed calling upon the Indians to realise the gravity of the situation and the danger ahead of India. The resolution read as follows :—

"Whereas the continued defeat of the British and their allies in Europe and Africa has sealed the fate of the British Imperialism in Europe.

Whereas the most decisive destruction of British sea and land forces by Japan in the East has given a death-blow to the power and prestige of British Imperialism in Asia.

Whereas the war is fast approaching the shores and borders of India, the British stronghold, Axis powers may be obliged to invade India in order to destroy the main source of British fighting strength.

Whereas such an invasion will bring unimaginable and extremely unusual hardships, miseries and sufferings to millions of innocent and helpless Indians in cities, towns and villages, and

Whereas the only way to avoid this most unhappy situation is to declare complete independence of India from British rule and to cut off all possible connections with British Imperialism in every possible way immediately;

The Indian Nationals residing in Japan assembled in this Conference, most seriously and earnestly appeal to the Indian National Congress and the people of India to immediately declare Independence and to capture all power from the British in India and to take immediate effective steps to stop each and every source of Indian aid to British Imperialist War and to declare on behalf of the people that India has no desire whatsoever to be involved in this conflict and has never been willing to help Britain.

Our representatives were sent to Shanghai and on 26th of January this year, a huge gathering of the Indian residents of Shanghai was held in Young Men's Association hall when similar resolutions as passed in Tokyo were very enthusiastically passed and our movement was given unanimous support.

In the meantime we established contact with the military and civil high commands in Japan and began to impress upon them the necessity of helping India in her struggle for freedom for the very achievement of the great object for which Japan had declared war against British and America. We made it clear to them that so long as British Imperialism in India continued, Japan could not expect a final victory in this war. At last we succeeded in prevailing upon them and General Tojo, the Prime Minister of Japan, openly declared before the Imperial Diet that his Government was prepared to help the Indians in our efforts to free our country from the long bondage. In his declaration before the Imperial Diet on the fall of Singapore he said :—

"It is a golden opportunity for India, having, as it does, several thousand years of history and splendid cultural tradition, to rid herself of the ruthless despotism of Britain and participate in the construction of the Greater East Asia Co-Prosperity Sphere. Japan expects that India will restore its proper status of India for the Indians and it will not stint herself in extending assistance to the Patriotic efforts of the Indians. Should India fail to awaken to her mission forgetting her history and tradition, and continue as before to be beguiled by the British cajolery and manipulation and act at their beck and call, I cannot but fear that an opportunity for the renaissance of the Indian people would be forever lost."

The declaration offered us great encouragement and we felt convinced that India could safely hope to be free before the East Asia War comes to an end. Counting upon the promises of General Tojo, we established our headquarters at Sanno Hotel and started our activities and preparations in right earnest. We decided that a Conference of the representatives of Indian organisations in various parts of East Asia should be held for exchanging views regarding our future move. With the help of the military authorities things were conveniently arranged and the representatives of our compatriots residing in Malaya, Honkong and Shanghai along with us of Tokyo, sat in conference for three days and arrived at certain decisions and framed the preliminary constitution for the working and progress of our movement. Those friends from abroad, who participated in Tokyo Conference, had occasion to come in contact with responsible members of the Japanese Army in Tokyo and to know more and more about the standing of our movement, Discussion at the Tokyo Conference were varied and we did our best to lay down a solid foundation upon which we could base our plan of action in future. We all know that the Conference in Tokyo was held at a time when things were less settled than they are today. Friends from East Indies were not present. We were deprived of the valuable help and advices of our friends in Thailand due to the unfortunate accident. Burma and Andamans were still in the hands of our enemies. We, therefore, were unable to come to a decision that could be claimed to be representative of the views of our compatriots in East Asia as a whole. We, therefore, decided to hold a larger and most representative Conference at a later date when the decisions taken at Tokyo were to be ratified. This Assembly in which we are participating to-day is the result of that decision.

"The responsibility to convene this Conference was placed upon my shoulders and I was asked to hold it in this city. I am sorry that the Conference was delayed by a couple of weeks. We expected to arrive here earlier but due to extraordinary period, through which we are passing, things could not be always done as expected and we have to adjust ourselves according to circumstances.

"I know I have exhausted your patience by chronologizing the events and activities during the last more than six months. But, it was necessary to acquaint you with what has happened and how we have proceeded, before we sit down to business and put our heads together to knock out far reaching decisions.

"Friends, we all realise the gravity of the situation and also the fact that we are passing through the most important period of India's history. I don't want to waste time on long speeches. We had enough of that during the last more than five decades. We really cannot afford to waste our time on meaningless talks and arguments. Those who want to really serve the motherland cannot have much time to talk. If we go on talking without coming to any concrete decision, time will not wait for us and we shall be left only to shed tears at our past folly, and it will be too late to mend things. I know there are knotty problems that will come before you for discussions and will need your most careful consideration. I know you will have to do a lot of thinking and face a lot of doubts from within before you can decide. But, if you have come with grim determination to thrash out a positive, concrete, and actually useful plan, you will be able to come to quick decisions. Let us all fully realise our responsibilities towards our land of birth and let us realise well, that our down-trodden country cannot afford to lose this golden opportunity that comes only once in centuries. Our brothers and sisters have in hundreds of thousands laid down their lives and have suffered and sacrificed for more than a century so that our country may be once again free. Let us rise to the occasion and carry their efforts to success so that the souls of martyrs in Heaven may find peace and be pleased. Let us rise and act so that the great preparations that Mahatma Gandhi has made during the last more than two decades, may bear fruit and our children in future may think of us with pride and respect as the members of a free nation.

"I know many of you have come with doubts and suspicions regarding the ultimate fate of our country as the result of our activities. I assure you that I can well appreciate your feelings of uncertainty and your desire for security and yet I believe they are based on false promises. Having bitterest experiences of Imperialist exploitations for centuries, we have begun to doubt even our good friends and if we insist on this attitude, the world will go on and we shall be left behind to regret our indecision.

"I want to sound a note of warning here. Our enemies have always been suceessful in keeping us divided and creating false impressions in our minds on such occasions. On many occasions in the past, we have missed opportunities to free our country by being victims of lying British propaganda. I can only hope that we shall not repeat our folly. Our doubts and suspicions are to a great extent the results of shrewd and well-thought plans of our enemies to sabotage our efforts. Those of us who have intelligence enough and who are not blind to facts and happenings can see the way clearly.

"We should feel thankful to the Governments of Japan, Germany, Thailand and Italy for their most friendly attitude they have been showing towards our cause. We must be particularly thankful to Japan for the most encouraging and hopeful definite promise of help in our sacred cause Let us not forget the words of Pandit Jawaharlal Nehru when he said :—

> Success often comes to those who dare and act; it seldom goes to cowards.

"I make an earnest appeal to you all friends to see that when you conclude your session, you have a most practical and workable plan of action for India's freedom so that we can start our work right after the Conference and march ahead. We are fortunate enough to have the most valuable help of our Indian Army at our disposal. They deserve our great respect for the great service they have already rendered to our cause by refusing to serve the enemies of India. But their greater service is still awaiting our decision. No one can doubt the bravery of our soldiers in a righteous fight for a righteous cause. Our sympathy goes to the families and friends of those Indian soldiers who have, erroneously believing that they have been fighting for a right cause, lost their lives in Europe and Asia. They have been misled by the same propaganda of lies by Britain that is responsible for the unfounded suspicion in the minds of so many of us. I bow my head to the bravery of our soldiers and we should have no doubt that with their wholehearted support we are going to win our final fight against British Imperialism. Let us stand shoulder to shoulder and let us march hand in hand to success. Let us remember we have one indivisible

Nation—India—one enemy,—England,—one goal—Complete Independence. Bande Matram.

Mr. Koh Ishii then read the following telegraphic congratulatory message from the Japanese Premier General Hideki Tojo. :—

It is with the greatest of pleasure that I send you my heartiest congratulations on the occasion of the convention of the Indian Independence Conference in Thailand, our ally, on the initiative of the leaders of the 2 million Indians living in East Asia to create a new epoch in the movement for Indian independence.

Since the outbreak of the Greater East Asia War more than half a year has elapsed. During this period the British defences in Asia for the placating of India have practically been wiped out by the gallant Imperial forces and a golden opportunity to realize the long cherished aspiration of Indian independence has come.

At this juncture if the leaders of the two million Indians in East Asia in calling this conference respond to Japan's true desire for the Indians to create India for the Indians, Japan is quite prepared to give her unstinted support as it has been announced from time to time, and I might add that the Axis Powers are ready to co-operate in according their full support.

Britain, which is meeting with defeats in Asia, Europe, Africa and in all theatres of war, is facing an extremely miserable state of affairs which she brought on herself by her own misdoings. She is now demanding great sacrifices of India through her usual crafty way of threat and supplication. However, the far-sighted and able patriotic Indian leaders, wisely realizing the heavenly bestowed destiny of India, and fully cognizant of the world affairs, are determinedly resisting Britain, a fact for which I want to express my deepest respect. Though the construction of India for the Indians constitutes my most sincere desire, India still remains British territory, and military establishments, as well as military forces, are being daily strengthened. Japan is firmly determined decisively to destroy Britain and she will be compelled to take action so long as British military strength remains in India.

In order to rescue India from war disaster, it is necessary that Britain should give up her ambitions in India or India herself must sever her relations with Britain on her own initiative. Fortunately, as I believe, the present Conference represents the general public opinion of the Indian people of the East, I pledge that Japan is fully prepared to support the independence movement.

In congratulating most earnestly upon the success of the present Conference I hope sincerely that the Indian people will fully understand Japan's true intentions, and, with the people both inside and outside India working in close co-operation, achieve their cherised hope of independence.

Mr. Koh Ishii also read the following congratulatory message from Mr. Shigenori Togo, Foreign Minister of Japan :—

I have the pleasure to express my sincere respects for the patriotic ardour of the Indian leaders representing the Indians in the

Greater East Asia, on this occasion of the Indian Independence Conference. As is known to the Indian people, the British domination over India, from its beginning, was due to the unimaginable false and crafty policy of alienation and also at the same time to the British military strength in India.

However, the military bases in East Asia have completely been swept away and England's fate is now hanging in the balance. Under such circumstances Britain is now resorting to desperate all-out methods such as propaganda in which she is maliciously alleging that Japan, Germany or Italy has certain ambitions in India and to deceitful proposals concerning the revision of Indian administration in an attempt to win over the Indian people to enlist them in the defence of British Empire. There is no other time than the present when the Indians must be on guard against British machination.

Japan has no desire whatever toward India except to see her realize the restoration of freedom and has the firm determination to destroy Britain and America as has been announced previouly by Japan. The Indian people who are now faced with the golden opportunity should discard trifles and devote themselves to greater moral principle. They should endeavour internally to unify the general public opinion and externally co-operate with Japan, Germany and Italy to destroy British Imperialism to bring about the realization of the aspiration of Indians.

As the result of the conference I firmly believe that the independence movement will be put under a unified control, thus to enhance the early achievement of the independence, for which I want to express my sincere congratulations."

Mr. Anand Mohan Sahay, leader of the delegation from Japan, then made a speech in Hindustani, while Mr. N. Raghavan, President of the Malaya Branch and leader of the delegation from Malaya, spoke in English. In the course of his speech Mr. Raghavan said that India, their mother country, was in danger. She had been enslaved by the British imperialistic expansion of the 19th century and India had been fighting for her independence all the time. Mother India had produced more than 400 millions of her sons and daughters and now she was calling to them. She was calling to her sons and daughters abroad to go to her, to assist her, to escape from the chains and to save her from being trodden down. There was no better opportunity than the present time when they had universal co-operation to release India from the tryanny of British imperialism. The speaker called on all the sons and daughters of India to come to the aid of their enslaved mother, who was now in ragged and soiled clothes.

After Mr. Raghavan, General Mohan Singh G.O.C. of the Indian National Army, spoke in Hindustani for more than one hour. "For nearly a century we had been fighting without arms," he said. "Let us thank the Almighty God that to-day Japan the mighty Eastern Power, is our friend. For humanity's sake and with Mahatma Ghandhi's choicest blessings let us fight for the peace and liberation of our country." The General assured the leaders of the Indian Independence

Movement that services of the I. N. A. would be placed at their disposal, but the I. N. A. would fight under the command of Indian officers only and would exclusively work for the freedom of India.

Colonel N.S. Gill then spoke in English. He stated that it was a shame that the people from three tiny islands in the west of Europe could hold and dominate an ancient and civilized nation like Indians. The domination dated back to the 19th century and ever since India had fought for her liberty and independence inch by inch sacrificing hundreds of thousands of her patriotic sons. In his boyhood he had heard the girls in a village in India sing a song which encouraged the men to fight for India's independence and freedom. That song, he said, was handed down from father to son from the day of domination of India by foreign Power. With the aid of Nippon as well as Germany and Italy India now had the golden opportunity which would never occur for centuries again for the patriotic off-springs of India to drive away the oppressors and robbers of India's wealth and free India for the Indians.

Mrs. Sibaghram, the wife of the proprietor of Karachi Store, Bangkok, made a speech in Hindustani.

The speeches of Mr. T. Tsubokami, the Japanese Ambassador in Thailand, of Dr. E. Wendler, the German Minister, and of Signor Guido Crolla, the Italian Minister in Bangkok, then followed :

"I feel it a great honour to have the opportunity to be present at this historic Indian Independence Conference that has just been opened," said Mr. Tsubokami.

"The independence of India has been the long cherished aspiration of the Indian people; its freedom has long been nourished by the three hundred fifty million Indians. As a member of the Asiatic races we Japanese have also ardently desired the realization of the hope of India for Indians.

"It is a matter of congratulation that the time has become ripe for Indian independence and its signal fire is now about to be lighted in a corner in East Asia. That this conference is being held in the capital city of Thailand, the people of which enjoy the greatest understanding of Japan, cannot be said to be coincidental. The Indian leaders who have assembled here from all parts of Asia are patriots who have endured the harsh sufferings of imprisonments, of having been obliged to seek refuge in foreign lands, of exerting themselves through long years of hardship with unabating hope for the noble cause of seeing their country become free. Their efforts have not been in vain and at this Conference the dawn of their aspiration is now about to be realized. I can see quite well how great must be their joy and satisfaction. We Japanese who, as your comrades in your struggle against the British injustice for the liberation of the peoples of East Asia, obviously cannot be disinterested in this most great and significant enterprise.

"The results achieved by the Imperial Japanese forces on land and sea and in the air for the last six months since the outbreak-of Greater East Asia War have been unprecedented in the world's history of war. Hongkong, Singapore and Rangoon, supplemented by Manila and Netherland Indies, were a sries of fortifications for the preservation of the security of Britain and at the same time the bulwark to defend India.

"As India was Britain's lifeline, it was indispensable that she should have constructed these series of double and treble re-inforced impregnable lines of fortifications in Asia to defend her lifeline. However, these groups of fortifications have helplessly succumbed before the irresistible Japanese forces.

"Moreover, the British fleet in the Indian Ocean has been speedily annihilated and the Japanese navy is now carrying out operations in even the extreme south of Africa. The mastery of the Indian Ocean is no longer in the hands of the British navy, and thus the defence of India which Britain had built at great effort through long years has completely vanished. India has now virtually become a defenceless 'island of seclusion'.

"Concerning the present India we see two significant factors, namely: firstly, Britain cannot any longer enlist the wealth of India for its economic and military needs; and secondly, as the yoke of Britain over India has been broken, the chance for the independence of India has become imminent. In other words, the fall of the British Empire signifies the realization of the independence of India. Under such circumstances this Indian Independence Conference has emerged. Its purpose is identical with one of the objectives of the Greater East Asia War which is to liberate India from Britain.

"In this connection one thing must be made clear and that is that Japan, Germany and Italy in relation to the Indian problem have had the closest understanding and co-operation from the beginning to the end. These three nations, following the conclusion of the tripartite treaty, have been and are standing arm in arm to destroy Britain, their common enemy. That the three nations, since the beginning of the war, have mutually been carrying out their tasks in crushing the Anglo-Saxon forces amply demonstrate how completely the tripartite treaty is being carried out. If we are to assume that the independence of India means the overthrow of Britain, it is clear that the three nations have been and are working in perfect agreement. That the three nations do not have any ambition toward India also demonstrate that there will be no conflict of interests among these three nations.

"Britain and America who are no longer able to defend India are now resorting to propaganda to cause dissension among the Axis Powers, but unless the latter happen to be exceptionally stupid, there is little hope that they will fall victims to such childish propaganda. It is our intention to have made it clear for the Indian brethren that they will even be backed up by the joint strong support of Japan, Germany and Italy.

"India is now being blessed with a heaven-sent opportunity. Hence if she should lose this opportunity she cannot hope for another such chance for independence. The eyes and ears of the whole world, including the three hundred fifty million Indians, are now focussed on the developments of this Conference. As you reflect on this fact you must no doubt realize that every word you say and everything you do carries with it tremendous responsibilities. Generally speaking, in order to accomplish great things it is necessary to discard trifles and unite in the execution of the general objectives. The cause of Japan's epochal achievements rests on just this principle and on the spirit of her national unity.

"Now is not a time for argument but a time for action. India's independence can be achieved through the united action of entire Indian nation. I believe that the success or failure of the Conference rests solely on your spirit of co-operation.

"Sharing in your faith I pray from the bottom of my heart for the success of the Conference."

"It is especially gratifying to me as German Minister in Bangkok," stated Dr. Wendler, "to be able to accept the invitation to attend the opening session of this Conference at which prominent representatives of the Indian people will deliberate as to the means to shape and safeguard the future of India in accordance with the wishes of the Indian people.

"I need hardly emphasize that Germany too takes a lively interest in these questions as was also stressed a short time ago by the fact that the German Chancellor received at his headquaters the well-known champion of the Indian Independence idea, Subhas Chandra Bose. The world war raging to-day will spell the end of the dominion of the British and Americans who have ever subjugated and used for their own purposes the peoples in their power.

"The nations allied to each other by the Tripartite Pact. Germany, Italy and Japan, will see to a just New Order, terminating Anglo-American tutelage over the rest of the world. Thus also the possibility arises for the Indian people, after nearly two centuries of subjugation by the British, a subjugation which has cost India so much misery and suffering, to shape the future destiny of their country according to their will.

"The German people have shown the greatest sympathy towards the people of India. The outstanding cultural achievements of India during the course of her long history dating back thousands of years, have always been the source of special interest in Germany. Germany was also the first country in Europe in which the great values in the spheres of Indian philosophy and poetry were fully appreciated. It is therefore self-evident that the German people, notwithstanding the titanic struggle in which they find themselves involved, even at the present time follow with much sympathy the significant happenings in India and, together with the peoples of Italy and Japan, show the greatest interest in the fight for freedom of the Indian people.

The Great Powers of the Tripartite Pact are all the more in a position to raise their voices as sincere friends of the Indian people since, they have no territorial interests whatsoever in India. They have but one desire:

that India and her people, in free self-determination, should be heading for a better future and develop to a level corresponding with the riches of the Indian soil and the great gifts of its inhabitants.

"It is indeed a source of deep gratification for me," stated Signor Guido Crolla, the Italian Minister in Bangkok, "to attend the opening session of this Conference which, thanks to Thailand's hospitality, gathers here to-day the representatives of the various Indian Movements in the Far East. The bonds between India and Italy date far back in history. They were existing even before the Roman Empire, which was a great attempt of unifying western and eastern cultures. In the Middle Ages the daring exploits of an Italian, Marco Polo, brought the two worlds closer again, while the Republics of Venice and Genoa were intensifying their trade with India through the Mediterranean. In more recent times Indian culture found and still finds in Italy many scholars and admirers and the Italian youth is taught in school how to appreciate the contribution given by India to the history of humanity. The Italian people who have for so long hardly struggled to recover their unity and independence cannot feel but sympathy and understanding towards the suffering and aspirations of the Indian people.

"Italy's interest for the cause of Indian Independence is deeply rooted in the past. Indian exiles have alway found in Italy a most cordial welcome and hospitality. This particular sympathy, which is spontaneous, lively and disinterested, has recently found expression in the institution of a society in Rome called 'The Friends of India,' where the Indian patriots of undaunted faith and sincerity, such as Iqbal Schedai, are working for the cause of Indian liberty followed by the friendly and unanimous encouragement of the Italian public opinion. 'The Friends of India' wish to create as closer connections as possible between cognate associations existing in Germany, Japan and Thailand with a view to attaining the final aim through a better and greater co-ordination of their respective efforts. The enduring passion of the Indian people is approaching is its decisive moment.

"The war which the Tripartite Powers are victoriously waging against India's secular oppressor is destined to create a new order in contrast with the old one ruled by Anglo-Saxon selfishness and abuse. Within the frame of such a New Order the Indian people, after having shaken the British yoke, shall, as a free Nation, find the place which their high civil and cultural traditions entitle them to. Italy, Germany and Japan have no territorial ambitions in India. Their support is therefore all the more disinterested and their friendship all the more sincere.

"The representatives of Free India gathered in Bangkok to-day are confronted with the highly responsible task of shaping the future destiny of their own country in accordance with the wishes and the interests of the Indian people. In unison with Germany and Japan, Italy is wishing this Conference the best success."

Mr. Narulla then read the following message from Mr. Subhas Chandra Bose to Mr. Debnath Das, Chairman of the Reception Committee.

"I am delighted to have your message inviting me to your Conference which is going to meet under the distinguished presidentship of the revolutionary leader, Rash Behari Bose. Since it is not possible to join you in person, I must content myself with sending you this message conveying my most cordial greetings. The branches of the Azad Hind Sangh (Friends of India Society) in Europe also associate with me in sending this message.

"After Stafford Cripps' departure from India, the last phase in our national struggle has begun. In this historic struggle all nationalists whether in India or outside must play their part. The experience I have gained during the last 18 months has convinced me that in our fight against British imperialism, the Tripartite Powers are our best friends and allies outside India and I have no doubt that they will gladly render us such assistance as we may need. But the emancipation of India must be the work primarily of Indians themselves. We who are the vanguard of the national army have the sacred mission of leading the national struggle to a successful conclusion. Tough I have clear and definite views regarding postwar reconstruction in India, it is the Indian people in free India who must determine the future destiny of the country and of the Free Indian State.

"My own objective study and observation in different parts of the world for 18 months has led me to the irresistible conclusion that Britain will lose this war and that the British Empire will be completely dismembered. All the forces that are striving to destroy or weaken the British Empire are helping India's emancipation, while all forces that are endeavouring to save the British Empire are attempting to perpetuate India's slavery.

"It is a matter of profound gratification to all nationalists outside India that all nationalists inside India are united in the aim of India's independence. We, who form the vanguard of the national army, feel however that the time will soon come when it will be necessary to take up arms in the final stage of the struggle. And we also feel that since the British Empire is seeking help all over the world and is trying to flood India with foreign soldiers and foreign war material, it is the right and duty of the Indian nationalists to accept any help that may be offered them. Given the right leadership and the necessary capacity, the Indian people will undoubtedly be able to overcome all obstacles and win their freedom. When the crucial moment arrives nobody will be able to prevent my entering India again with a view to participating in the final struggle.

"I am convinced that during the course of this war India will be free. India's liberation will mean the expulsion of Anglo-American imperialism, the goal of the victorious Japanese Army. The freedom of India will also afford powerful stimulus to freedom movements all over the world.

"I am glad to find that the branches of Azad Hind Sangh in Europe are doing their very best to participate in the national struggle and are preparing for the post-war reconstruction that will follow. It is now time to link up Indian nationalists all over the world in one all-embracing organisation. I wish all success to your

Conference and I ardently hope and trust that it will prove to be a further mile-stone in our march towards victory.

"Inquilab Zindabad! Azad Hind Zindabad!"

In moving a vote of thanks at the conclusion of the open session of the Conference Colonel G. Q. Gilani stated that when he was in Thailand he did not feel strange, because the culture and architecture of the Thai people were similar to those of the Indians. He felt no doubt that Thailand and India had been friends in old days and that fact could be proved by the most hospitable attitude and sympathy shown by Thailand towards the Conference. He thanked Thailand, the Land of the Free, for allowing the Conference to be held in her capital as well as for honouring the Conference with a message from her Premier.

FUTURE OF INDIA.

Momentous decisions on which would depend the future of India were taken at the Bangkok Conference, which concluded its sessions on June 23, 1942. This Conference endorsed the policy laid down by the Tokyo Conference that the complete independence of India free from foreign control, interference or domination shall be the object of the Movement. It decided that the organisation for carrying out the Movement should be known as to the Indian Independence League and framed the constitution of the League with its sphere of operation extending over the whole of East Asia. Its policy vis-a-vis the Indian National Congress was also clearly defined.

The formation, control, status and scope of the Indian National Army were discussed at great length and important decisions bearing on these matters arrived at. The Army was placed under the direct control of the Council of Action of the League. Any military operation contemplated by the Army against the British in India should conform with the wishes of the Indian National Congress, expressed or implied.

This Conference laid down in definite and unmistakable terms what the future relationship of Free India with Japan should be and in a business-like manner wanted the Imperial Government of Japan to endorse this policy by a formal declaration.

By way of crowning their deliberations the delegates brought their efforts to a happy issue by deciding to invite Sjt. Subhas Chandra Bose the Man of the Hour, who was then known to be living in Germany after his mysterious disappearance from his home at Calcutta early in 1941, and to offer him the leadership of the Movement in East Asia.

The resolutions passed at the Conference are as follows :

(1) Whereas it is the objective of the War of Greater East Asia to destroy British Imperialism in the East ;

And whereas it gives an opportunity for India to realise the goal of complete independence ;

And whereas it is the belief of this Conference that a new and re-generated Asia of Free Nations is certain to arise as a result of this said War;

This Conference expresses its sincere gratifications at the war policy of Japan and conveys to the Imperial Government its wishes for the continued successes of the Imperial Japanese Armed Forces.

(2) This Conference conveys to all the Powers fighting against British Imperialism its sincere congratulations and prays that their efforts may meet with complete success.

(3) This Conference places on record its sense of deep gratification for the most determined manner in which the nationalist leaders at home have been trying to refuse to be drawn in this War on the side of the British and their Allies and for the frank and definite demand for the withdrawal of the British from India.

In the opinion of this Conference, unless the British withdraw from India and the Allied Forces cease to make use of India as a base for war operations and war preparations, unimaginable and innumerable sufferings will be the lot of the people of India.

(4) Resolved that a movement for achieving complete and immediate independence of India be sponsored by this Conference.

(5) Object. This Conference endorses the view of the Tokyo Conference held in March, 1942, that the complete independence of India, free from any foreign control, domination or interference of whatever nature, shall be the object of this movement and is emphatically of opinion that the time has arrived to take the necessary steps for the attainment of that object.

(6) Resolved that the Indian Independence Movement sponsored by this Conference shall be guided by the principles indicated below :—

(a) That Unity, Faith and Sacrifice shall be the motto of the Indian Independence Movement.

(b) That India be considered as one and indivisible.

(c) That all activities of this Movement be on a national basis and not on sactional, communal or religious basis.

(d) That in view of the fact that the Indian National Congress is the only political organisation which can claim to represent the real interests of the people of India, and as such be acknowledged the only body representing India, this Conference is of the opinion that the programme and plan of action of this Movement must be so guided, controlled and directed as to bring them in line with the aims and intentions of the Indian National Congress.

(e) That the framing of the future Constitution of India be done only by the representatives of the people of India.

(7) Resolved that an organisation be started for carrying on the Indian Independence Movement and it shall be known as **The Indian Independence League.**

(8) Resolved that the Indian Independence League shall immediately proceed to raise an army called the Indian National Army from among the soldiers (combatants and non-combatants) and such civilians as may hereafter be recruited for Military service in the cause of Indian Independence.

(9) Resolved that for the purpose of financing the Independence Movement, the Council of Action be authorised to raise funds from Indians in East Asia.

(10) Resolved that a request be made to the Nippon Government that it may be pleased to place immediately all Indian soldiers in territories in East Asia under their control, at the disposal of this Movement.

(11) Resolved that the formation, command, control and organisation of the Indian National Army be in the hands of Indians themselves.

(12) Resolved that it is the earnest desire of this Conference that the Indian National Army from its inception be accorded the powers and status of a free National Army of an Independent India on a footing of equality with the armies of Japan and other friendly Powers.

(13) Resolved that the Indian National Army shall be made use of only :—

(a) For operating against the British or other foreign Powers in India.

(b) For the purpose of securing and safeguarding Indian National Independence, and

(c) For such other purposes as may assist the achievement of the object, *viz.*, the Independence of India.

(14) Resolved that all officers and men of the proposed Indian National Army shall be members of the Indian Independence League and shall owe allegiance to the League.

(15) Resolved that the Indian National Army shall be under the direct control of the Council of Action and that the said Army shall be organised and commanded by the General Officer Commanding, Indian National Army, in accordance with the directions of the Council of Action.

(16) Resolved that in the event of military action being taken against British or other foreign Powers in India and for the said purpose the Council of Action may be at liberty to place the military resources available to it, under the unified command of Indian and Japanese Military Officers under the direction of the said Council of Action.

(17) Resolved that before taking any military Action against the British or any other foreign Power in India, the Council of Action will assure itself that such action is in conformity with the expressed or implied wishes of the Indian National Congress.

(18) Resolved that the Council of Action shall make all efforts to create an atmosphere in India which would lead to a revolution in the

Indian Army there and among the Indian people and that before taking military action the Council of Action shall assure itself that such an atmosphere exists in India.

(19) In view of the great urgency and imperative necessity of informing and covincing our countrymen in India and abroad and the friends of India all over the world of the meaning and purpose of this Movement and in view of the fact that propaganda in and outside India is one of the most effective means of waging the war for Indian Independence, this Conference resolves to take immediate steps to carry on active and vigorous propaganda by broadcasts, leaflets, lectures and by such other means as may be found possible and practicable from time to time.

(20) That all foreign assistance of whatever nature shall be only to the extent and of the type asked for by the Council of Action.

(21) This Conference places on record its grateful appreciation of the support and encouragement given to this Movement by the Imperial Government of Japan and resolves that the Council of Action be authorised to approach if and when necessary the said Government with a request to render such monetary help as may be required from time to time for the successful carrying out of the object of his Movement on the distinct understanding that such monetary help is to be treated as a loan repayable to the Imperial Government of Japan by the National Govenment of India.

(22) Resolved that the Imperial Government of Japan be requested to be good enough to provide all facilities for propaganda, travel, transport and communications within the area under the control of the Imperial Government of Japan in the manner and to the extent requested by the Council of Action and also all facilities to come into contact with the national leaders, workers and organisations in India.

(23) Resolved that the Imperial Government of Japan be requested to be good enough to arrange with the local authorities concerned that in matters of administration affecting the Indian community, the Indian Independence League in the respective places, and in places where there are no branches of the League, recognised leaders of the community approved by the League Branch nearest to such places, be consulted.

(24) Resolved that the Government of Thailand be requested to be good enough to consult the Indian Independence League (formerly known as the Indian National Council and the Independence League of India) in matters of administration affecting the Indian community in Thailand.

(25) This Conference, while recording its greatful appreciation of the various pronouncements made by General Tojo, the Premier of Japan, expressing the preparedness of the Nipponese Government to give its unstinted support to the cause of Indian Independence, reiterates the resolution of the Tokyo Conference that in further clarification

of the attitude of Japan towards India, the Imperial Government of Japan be good enough to make a formal declaration to the effect :—

(a) That immediately on the severance of India from the British Empire, Imperial Government of Japan shall respect the territorial integrity and recognise the full sovereignty of India, free of any foreign influence, control or interference of a political, military or economic nature.

(b) That the Imperial Government of Japan will exercise its influence with other Powers and induce them to recognise the national independence and absolute sovereignty of India.

(c) That the framing of the future Constitution of India will be left entirely to the representatives of the people of India without interference from any foreign authority.

(26) Resolved that this Conference is committed to a definite policy of the closest co-operation with Japan and it shall on eliciting an official definition satisfactory to this Movement of the term "Greater East Asia Co-prosperity Sphere" and its implications, endeavour to persuade Independent India :—

(a) To be a member of such Sphere or a member of any other international combine of which Japan is a member, on a footing of equality with Japan ; and

(b) To confer on Japan the most favoured nation treatment on a reciprocal basis.

(27) Whereas it has come to the knowledge of this Conference that Indians in the territories, which are now freed from the domination of the Anglo-Saxons and their allies by the Imperial forces of Japan, own considerable movable and immovable properties in these territories ; and

Whereas owing to the exigencies of the War, a number of Indians had to leave these territories leaving behind their properties without making arrangements for their care and management ; and

Whereas the Imperial Government of Japan has promised its unstinted support to the cause of Indian Independence ; and

Whereas enormous amount of money is required to carry on and complete the object of the said Movement in East Asia; and

Whereas an appreciable steady income is likely to be derived from the said properties in the said territories; and

Whereas in the opinion of this Conference the handing over of such properties to the Indian Independence League by the authorities concerned on the distinct understanding that the said properties are to be returned to their rightful owners when claimed, will be welcome as a sign of goodwill and encouragement towards this Movement.

Now this Conference resolves that the Imperial Government of Japan may be pleased to arrange with the authorities in the territories now freed from the domination of the Anglo-Saxons and their Allies by the Imperial forces of Japan to hand over properties owned by Indians (including those owned by Indian companies, firms or partnerships) and left behind by them owing to the exigencies of the War, to the Council of Action of this Movement, in trust for their rightful owners, to manage and control the said properties and advance the income thereof for the use of this movement to be repaid as and when claimed by the said owners.

(28) This Conference, having learnt with regret that Indians residing in certain countries under the occupation of the Imperial forces of Japan are being treated as enemy aliens and suffer hardships and loss in consequence, resolves that the Imperial Government of Japan may be pleased to make a declaration to the effect (a) that Indians residing in the territories occupied by the Imperial forces of Japan shall not be considered enemy nationals so long as they do not indulge in any action injurious to this Movement or hostile to the interests of Japan and (b) that the properties both movable and immovable of those Indians who are now residing in India or elsewhere (including the properties of Indian companies, firms or partnerships) be not treated by Japan as enemy properties so long as the management or control of such properties is vested in any person or persons residing in Japan or in any of the countries occupied by or under the control or influence of the Imperial Japanese forces and to instruct the authorities concerned in the respective territories to give effect to this policy as early as possible.

(29) That this Movement adopts the present National Flag of India and requests the Imperial Government of Japan and the Royal Government of Thailand and the Governments of all other friendly Powers to recognise the said flag in all territories under their jurisdiction.

(30) This Conference requests Sjt. Subhas Chandra Bose to be kind enough to come to East Asia and appeals to the Imperial Government of Japan to use its good offices to obtain the necessary permission and conveniences from the Government of Germany to enable Sjt. Subhas Chandra Bose to reach East Asia safe.

(31) This Conference places on record its deepest appreciation of and grateful thanks for the co-operation, assistance, and support extended to this Movement and its objective by the Imperial Government of Japan.

(32) That no unauthorised publicity be given to any of the resolutions, adopted at this Conference, but a manifesto be issued by this Conference, setting out the purpose and policy of this Movement and in corporating such decisions and details as may be found proper and beneficial to be made public.

(33) This Conference gratefully acknowledges the sincere and friendly attitude, the Governments and the people of Germany and

Italy have adopted towards our struggle for freedom and places on record its deep appreciation and thanks for the offer of assistance and co-operation extended by them to this Movement.

(34) This Conference places on record its grateful thanks to the Government and people of Thailand for the opportunity given to hold this Conference at Bangkok, for their kind hospitality, and for their sympathy and co-operation in India's struggle for freedom.

The following constitution of the Indian Independence League was adopted at the Conference :

(i) The Indian Independence League shall consist of :

(a) A Council af Action,

(b) A Committee of Representatives,

(c) Territorial Committees, and

(d) Local Branches.

Local Branches.

(ii) a. Local Branches of the Indian Independence League may be formed only at a public meeting of Indians in any locality who shall elect a Committee and a President.

b. Vacancy on such Committee or in the Office of the President may be filled up by the Committee.

c. All Indians above the age of 18 shall be entitled to be members of such Branch on compliance with rules of such Branch.

d. No such Branch shall be recognised as a Branch unless the Territorial Committee as constituted hereinafter accords, and continues to accord, to such Branch due recognition; provided however that all Branches of the Indian Independence League now in existence and recognised in the various Territories mentioned in article (vi) hereof shall, until otherwise decided upon, be recognised by this Movement (Indian Independence Movement).

Territorial Committees.

(iii) Representatives elected by the Committees of Local Branches in each Territory shall form a Territorial Committee and the Territorial Committee shall make such rules as it may consider necessary for the effective working of the Movement within the Territory.

(iv) The Territorial Committee in each Territory shall guide, supervise and control the work of the Movement within its Territory and shall also elect representatives as constituted hereinafter.

(v) Territorial Committees and Committees of Local Branches under them shall have power to make rules not inconsistent with the rules made by the Committee of Representatives or in case of Local Branches by the Territorial Committees.

Committee of Representatives.

(vi) a. A Committee of Representatives shall be constituted by civilian representatives selected by the Territorial Committees in the Territories hereinbelow set out and by representatives selected by the Indian National Army :—

Japan and Manchukuo	...	...	...	4
Philippines	...	...	...	2
Thailand	...	...	...	6
Malaya	...	...	...	14
Burma	...	...	...	21
Borneo and Celebes	...	...	...	1
Hong Kong, Canton and Macao	...		...	2
Other parts of China including Shanghai			...	2
Indo-China	...	...	...	1
Java	...	...	...	2
Sumatra	...	...	...	1
Andamans	...	...	...	1
				57
Indian National Army	...	...	...	33
				90

b. The Council of Action shall be at liberty to include in the above list of Territories any other Territory, and fix the number of representatives from such Territory to the Committee of Representatives, providing in that event for increase in the representatives from the Indian National Army equal to two-thirds of the number fixed for such Territory.

Oath of Secrecy.

(vii) Every member of the Committee of Representatives shall sign the Oath of Secrecy in the prescribed form before he takes the seat on the Committee.

Policy and Programme.

(viii) The Committee of Representatives shall be responsible for the general policy and programme of the Indian Independence Movement and its decision shall in every case be final and binding on each and every member of this Movement.

Alteration of Decisions.

(ix) The Committee of Representatives shall have power to alter, amend or rescind any previous decision made by it, including any decision arrived at in this Conference.

Quorum.

(x) No meeting of the Committee of Representatives shall be valid unless two-thirds in number of the Members of the Committee are present (either in person or by proxy).

Council of Action.

(ix) A Council of Action consisting of a President and four (4) members, of whom at least one half shall be from Indian National Army in East Asia shall be appointed by the Delegates to this Conference.

Mr. N. Raghawan

Member Council of Action and
President I. I.L. Malaya

Col. Niranjan Singh Gill

The Right-hand man of
General Mohan Singh

Col. G. Q. Gilani

Member Council of Action

Mr K. P. K. Menon

Member Council of Action

The first President shall be Sjt. Rash Behari Bose and the four members shall be :—

1. Sri N. Raghavan
2. Capt. Mohan Singh
3. Sri K. P. K. Menon
4. Col. G. Q. Gilani.

Vacancies.

(xii) Any vacancy in the Council of Action caused by death, resignation or otherwise of Members not exceeding two in number at a time may be filled up by the other Members of the Council and in the event of more than two such vacancies the Council of Action shall call a meeting of the Committee of representatives to fill such vacancies.

Duties and Powers.

(xiii) The Council of Action shall be responsible for the carrying out of the policy and programme of work laid down by this Conference and as may hereafter be laid down by the Committee of Representatives and shall deal with all new matters that may arise from time to time and which may not be provided for by the Committee itself.

(xiv) For the proper and efficient carrying out of the work, the Council of Action shall have power to create as many Departments as are neeessary and to appoint and dismiss administrative officers and staff whenever necessary.

(xv) The Council of Action shall have no power to alter or amend the policy laid down by this Conference without the sanction of the Committee of Representatives.

Meeting of Committee of Representatives.

(xvi) The Council of Action may at any time summon a meeting of the Committee of Representatives to be held at such places as the Council may decide provided that necessary facilities for travel to Representatives and at least 14 days' notice of such meeting have been given to the Secretaries of the Territorial Committees and to the Headquarters of the Indian National Army. On a requisition by 20 members (Representatives) hailing from more than one Territory such a meeting shall be called by the Council of Action and the necessary notices and facilities for travel shall be given.

Control.

(xvii) The Council of Action shall have general superintendence and control over all Branches of the Indian Independence League in all territories mentioned in article (vi) and over the Indian National Army.

Register of Organisations.

(xviii) The Council of Action shall cause to be kept a register of all the Territorial and local organisations and may remove therefrom the names of any such organisations and withhold or withdraw recognition of any such organisations.

Collective Responsibility.

(xix) The Council of Action shall have collective responsibility.

Portfolios.

(xx) The allotment of Portfolios shall be amongst the Members of the Council of Action and at the discretion of the President.

Headquarters.

(xxi) The Headquarters of the Movement shall be at Bangkok or such other place as may hereafter be decided upon by the Committee of Representatives or the Council of Action.

Privilege.

(xxii) The deliberations of the Committee of Representatives and the Council of Action shall be privileged and no action of a disciplinary character can be taken against any Member in consequence thereof by any Branch or Territorial Committee or by the Indian National Army.

Alteration of Constitution.

(xxiii) Changes in the Constitution of the Indian Independence League may be made only by a vote to that effect by three-fourths of the Members of the Committee of Representatives.,

---

CHAPTER VIII

LEAGUE PREPARES FOR THE STRUGGLE

The following four or five months saw great activity at the Indian Independence League Headquarters at Bangkok. Provincial Leagues already working in Malaya and Thailand were reorganized. A new branch was opened in Burma. A network of local branches was formed all over these countries under the Provincial Leagues. The following portfolios were entrusted to different members of the Council of Action :—

1. Sri Rash Behari Bose—Home and Finance.
2. General Mohan Singh—General Officer Commanding or C-in-C of I. N. A.
3. Sri K. P. K. Menon—Publicity and Propaganda.
4. Sri N. Raghwan—Organisation and Mass Contact.
5. Col. G. Q. Gilani—Military Training.

Besides Sri B. K. Das who worked as Secretary of the Central League office, Sri S. A. Ayar, Sri D. S. Deshpande, Col. N. S. Gill, Sri A. M. Sahay and Sri A. S. Nayyar were devoting full time to the movement and proved to be very useful.

Broadcasts were begun to be given under the name of "Indian Independence League Headquarters Radio" from Bangkok Radio Station. Sri S. A. Ayar was put in-charge of publicity and broadcasting under Sri Menon. A daily paper 'Azad' was also started. Sri Bose and Sri Deshpande undertook an extensive tour of East Asia to organize League branches. Sri Debnath Das was elected President of the Thailand Provincial League. Sri S. Ali Khan, Sirdar Ishar Singh and S. Bachan Singh were the active supporters in this branch. The Malaya League was the best organized under the Presidentship of Sri N. Raghwan. This League published many pamphlets and tracts. A number of newspapers was also started and broadcasts were given from the Singapore Radio Station under the name of the League. Burma Provincial League was also reorganized. Sri C. B. Parasad was put in-charge of the branch in place of Sri Lathia. As Burma was to be the centre of farther activities of the League, Sri D. S. Deshpande was deputed there as President.

Formal branch of the I. I. L. could not be organized in Indo-China due to the hostile attitude of the French Government, but the propaganda from the "Azad Hind Radio Saigaon" made up fully for this deficiency. It proved to be of great help to the movement. Col. Ehsan Qadir and Col. Hassan were in charge of this work.

While the organisation and propaganda work was in full swing, General Mohan Singh was busily engaged in the most important and arduous task of organizing and equipping the Indian National Army. He knew that the I. N. A. was to play the chief part in the Indian Freedom Movement, and he wished to make it worthy of the great task. The General had also doubts about the intentions of the Japanese, so he wanted to make the Indian National Army a great force—a force as could successfully counteract even the Japanese, when a contingency arose. Originally, he intended to raise an Army of two lacs, but the Japanese stood in the way of expansion. The I. N. A. now consisted of about 17,000 armed and equipped soldiers. Another contingent of 25,000 trained soldiers was kept as surplus volunteers. The Japanese did not equip them with arms. It is estimated that about two lacs more were ready to join the I. N. A., but they were not allowed to be enlisted by the Japanese.

The following Brigades and Sections constituted the Indian National Army :—

(i) Field Force Group—It consisted of 1/14 Punjab Regiment, 3/17 Dogra Regiment, 1—2/18 Garhwal Regiment (all infantry battalions), an artillery regiment, a signalling company and an armoured corps—Commander Lt. Col. Bhonsle.

(ii) Gandhi Brigade—Commander Major S. S. Brar.

(iii) Nehru Brigade—Commander Major M. Z. Kiani.

(iv) Azad Brigade—Commander Major Parkash.

(v) S. S. Group—Commander Major Taj.

(vi) Intelligence Branch—Commander Tajumal Hussain.

(vii) Military Hospital.

(viii) Medical First Aid Corps.
(ix) Engineering Company.
(x) Military Propaganda Unit.
(xi) Reinforcement Group.

A training camp under the command of Captain Shah Niwaz was started at Singapore. The general outlook of the soldiers was completely changed. Instead of being mercenary soldiers, they were now the Army of Liberation of their Motherland. While in British Army, they were kept ignorant of all political, economic and social problems and were mostly illiterate. General Mohan Singh undertook to enlighten the common soldiers of his army. Discourses on topics of national importance, international problems, history of Indian National Movement, Imperialism, Capitalism Socialism, lives of Indian National leaders and such other subjects were given from time to time. General Mohan Singh gave instructions to every unit, that no soldier should remain illiterate. After some time political literature was supplied in the forces. The ordinary soldier began to take interest in politics and his mental outlook was greatly developed. For the special training of officers another camp was opened under the command of Col. Habib-ul-Rahman.

National spirit was infused in the I. N. A. by various ways. They were taught to live and take their meals together in common kitchens. Festivals of all religions were celebrated jointly. Differences of caste, creed and religion did not stand in the way of complete unity. The Army was inspired by the lofty ideals of Unity, Faith and Sacrifice. Every soldier had taken a solemn pledge to sacrifice his all for the honour of his motherland and the national tri-colour. They were taught to equip themselves fully for the coming struggle. This was a unique movement in our history of national struggle and was to play an important part in the future. Needless to say that credit of it all goes to General Mohan Singh.

CHAPTER IX

THE PARTING OF WAYS—I

Burma incidents precipitate matters

We have seen that the Bangkok Conference was followed by great enthusiasm among all classes of Indians in East Asia—military as well as civil. Indian Independence League and Indian National Army were now fully organized and stood on a firm footing. The whole of Burma was now in the hands of Japan. On the other hand situation in India itself had greatly changed. The All-India Congress Committee had passed the "Quit India" resolution on August 7, 1942 at Bombay. This was followed by wholesale arrests of the top-ranking Indian leaders, including Mahatma Gandhi, Pandit Jawahar Lal and Maulana Azad. Then followed the unfortunate disturbances of August 1942 and consequent ruthless vengeance of the British. All these revolutionary events further encouraged the leaders of the Indian Independence Movement and they thought that that was the opportune time to gain their freedoms.

But this enthusiasm was marred somewhat by the uncertain attitude of the Japanese Government. At no time had the Indians placed complete faith in the intentions of Japan. Some of them suspected that Japan had designs on India and they wanted to be on the guard so that they should not fall from frying pan to the fire and their efforts and sacrifices may not end only in the change of masters.

To begin with most of the patriotic Indians were not unaware of the fact, that Indian National Congress at home was wedded to non-violence and more especially, it was opposed to any kind of invasion of India by the Japanese or with the help of Japan. They realized that it was their duty to ensure the safety, dignity and integrity of India, after the British were ousted. And so before taking any further forward step it was necessary to clear matters, to understand their position and pursue a clear-cut policy.

All this required clarification from the Japanese Government on certain points and that clarification was not forthcoming in spite of repeated requests. The patience of the Council of Action was exhausted as time rolled by. Misgivings, suspicion and fear grew, when the Japan Government tried to evade the issues raised in the resolutions of Bangkok Conference—nay, it was working against the spirit of these resolutions. The Conference wanted the Indian Independence League and Indian National Army to be recognized by the Japan Government. It wanted a full, formal and solemn declaration regarding the intentions of Japan to recognize and support the absolute independence and full sovereignty of India, immediately on the removal of British rule in India. And it had waited for it for full six months.

Several incidents occured to aggravate the situation and we shall now narrate these one by one.

At the time of occupation of Burma by the Japanese, a number of Indians, left that country without making arrangements for the care and management of their movable and immovable property. According to international law, Indians were to be treated as enemy nationals and ownerless Indian properties in Japan had to pass into the hands of Japanese Government. As Indians in East Asia had made common cause with Japan, the Indian Independence League rightly thought that Indians were not to be treated as enemy aliens. Consequently it had passed a resolution in the Bangkok Conference, requesting the Japanese Government to hand over the ownerless Indian properties to the Indian Independence League, on the distinct understanding that their income would be utilized to carry on the movement and these will be returned to their rightful owners when claimed. What transpired after this request and how the resolution was treated, will be clear from the following report of Mr. Deshpande and Mr. Prashad of the Indian Independence League Rangoon to the League Headquarters at Malaya. The report needs no comment and fully reveals, what little regard there was for the League on the part of the Japanese authorities. No wonder, that this incident opened the eyes of the Council of Action and made it restless.

It appears that the Japanese were bent upon treating the ownerless Indian property, as the property of enemy nationals and wanted it to be managed by the Indian Independence League according to their instructions. What was more annoying, was the fact that any ordinary Japanese soldier could break open the locks of the Indian property under the control of I.I.L. and take away what he liked. No action was taken against these intruders. The League rightly protested against this high handedness, but their protest fell on deaf-ears.

The report runs as follows:—A scheme for the management of the ownerless Indian property in Burma was handed over to us through Mr. Yutani. After perusal of the same, we found that certain amendments were essential. On the 10th October 1942, we went to Iwaguru Kikan office and had a talk with captain Tsuchimochi. We informed him that we had received a scheme from the Political Department for the management of Indian Ownerless Property in Burma, but the scheme needed certain amendments to keep the prestige of the Indian Independence League—both the Headquarters and the Burma Branch.

Captain Tsuchimochi told us that the scheme had already been signed and sealed by the Commander-in-Chief and hence any amendment was out of question. Still he asked us to submit to Iwaguru Kikan a copy of the amendments suggested, adding that he would see how far he can make the English rendering of the scheme (original being in Japanese) better worded to make it acceptable for us Naturally we parted with great misgivings, in as much as we found that the original scheme will remain as it was, but the English rendering only is to be improved, if possible. We, however, promised to bring our amendments for his perusal.

We took two days to prepare our amendments because in view of what had transpired, we had to make the minimum amendments to the scheme to make it acceptable to us. We are forwarding a copy of the original scheme as well as that of our amendments for your perusal and we are sure, you will agree with us, that the acceptance of the original scheme by us would mean to ignore the spirit of the Bangkok resolutions.

Thinking on these lines, we approached the Iwaguru Kikan office on the 12 th Oct., to acquaint them with the bearing of the acceptance of the scheme by us on the Independence Movement, and to request them to accept the necessary amendments. Of course, we wanted to discuss the matter and come to a mutual understanding. Mr. Yutani of the Political Department of Military administration was also present besides Lt. Col. Kitabe, and Captain Tsuchimochi of the Iwaguru Kikan.

We quote below the conversation that took place between us :

Lt. Col. Kitabe: Since I have other work to attend to, I will not be here and hence I shall tell you whatever I have to say in this matter, before I go. In the first place I wish you to clear your misunderstanding on two points. The first point is that you always seem to refer to the Bangkok resolutions. It was all right for the Bangkok Conference to pass those resolutions, but you will be mistaken to think that those resolutions are binding on the Japanese Government. The Japanese Government have never announced that they have accepted all the resolutions passed at Bangkok by the Indian Independence Conference. What the Japanese Government have up to now said about the resolutions amounts to that they would help the Indian Independence Movement to the best of their capacity. Moreover, the Japanese Government have never accepted the Council of the Indian Independence League as a Government body with whom they could enter into any treaty or pact. Therefore, what I would like to say is, that, although you may look up to the Council of Action for orders or instructions, it is not necessary for us, who represent the Japanese Government, to always respect those orders and instructions which the Council of Action may issue for you.

Incidently, Col. Kitabe also mentioned, while talking about the Council of Action. "The Council of Action being a body without any territory to rule over and without any financial status, it cannot be looked upon as a Government, but it is only an organisation having come into existence to fight for India's Independence and deriving its power from the Japanese Government. Any decision of the Council of Action, in order to be worked upon, must be such as to be found acceptable to the Japanese Government."

He added, "It is ridiculous for the Council of Action to make any decision without trying to ascertain whether it is acceptable to the Japanese Government or not." He urged us not to lose sight of this "important" point while seeking help from them in carrying out our activities.

Mr. Deshpande: Even if we accept the argument advanced by you in principle, it is yet essential for the Japanese side to adopt ways and means which would save the prestige of the Indian Independence League. Already there is an under-ground propaganda to the effect that the League is for them to invade India. In view of this fact, is it not of utmost importance for the Japanese not to take any step which would only strengthen the public misgivings and misapprehensions? Likewise is it also not of great importance for the Indians to act in every way so as to be able to keep their head erect before the Indian public and to behave with self-respect before the Japanese?

Col. Kitabe: Since the Indian Independence League and its activities are solely dependent on the help and assistance given by the Japanese Government, why not the public be told straightway that the Indian Independence League works under the leadership of the Japanese Government. In my opinion it would be better to do so in order to avoid a lot of misunderstandings in future. Whatever resolutions passed at Bangkok have been accepted by the Japanese Government are left to the discretion, so far as their interpretation is concerned, of the Commanders-in-Chief of different occupied territories, and as such we should always bear in mind that the way of application of the resolutions in one territory may not be the same as in another. He emphasized that we should never bring any complaints to him, that a certain Bangkok resolution had been interpreted and given effect to in different way here (Burma).

In continuation of the subject it was pointed out to us that in the Japanese system of working, the Commander-in-Chief of each occupied territory is to act solely on his own responsibility. Each Commander-in-Chief receives only cryptic instructions embodying main lines of policy, and he is left to act upon them using his own discretion as to the details. (This point was also told to us previously on the 10th by Captain Tsuchimochi.

At this point Col. Kitabe went away.

Mr. Yutani wanted to discuss the amendments to the scheme of the management of Indian ownerless property suggested by us.

Mr. Yutani : Indians here are labouring under the wrong impression that the ownerless Indian properties belong to Indians. Absentee Indian property according to the International Law is enemy property and belongs to the Japanese Government, and the Japanese Government have never intended to make a secret of this fact. What properties do you have here ? You are all paupers. It is the generosity of the Japanese, which you must acknowledge and appreciate, that entrusts you with the management of the absentee Indian property. But mind that you can only manage it under the control and discretion of the Commander-in-Chief, who is the sole owner of the properties. In assuming ownership of such properties, you must understand that the Commander-in-Chief has not acted high handedly. He has only followed the injunctions laid down by the International Law. It is you, who, in trying to quote the letter of Bangkok resolutions, presume that the absentee Indian property belongs to the Indians and not the Commander-in-Chief. You must understand that this position adopted by you is weak and untenable and the quicker you give it up, the better for all concerned.

Mr. Parshad : We have nothing to say about the ownership of the absentee Indian property according to the International Law : neither we are ungrateful to the Japanese Government for their generosity in helping our movement and handing over the management of the ownerless properties to us, but we always expect the Japanese Government to help us to keep the prestige of the Indian Independence League in the eyes of the Indian public, because the management of Indian properties is our secondary work, our main activity being Indian Independence.

Mr. Yutani : Prestige—What prestige ? Notion of prestige is a false notion. The prestige of Indians becomes secondary to the execution of the order of the Commander-in-Chief. Any one living in Burma must obey the order of the Commander-in-Chief for the duration of the war. The Indian Independence League also cannot be exempted. The Indian Independence League should not think that it is an independent body—that it has already achieved independence. Do not be swollen-headed.

Mr. Parshad : We only want you to treat the Indian Independence League better than a mere servant executing the orders of and working under the Japanese Government. We agree that the Commander-in-Chief is the sole man in charge of Burma and every one has to obey his orders.

Mr. Yutani : Certainly you are servants. The Commander-in-Chief can command anyone in Burma to do the work, and any insubordination can be treated as treason. Why should you be ashamed to work as a servant ? If the Commander-in-Chief is showing any leniency to you, you should not mistake the same far indulgence. You must realise and appreciate why Japanese Government have offered to help the cause of Indian Independence. Try to be grateful for that, instead of indulging in finding faults about this order and that instruction issued by the Commander-in-Chief.

Mr. Parshad : We think that the Indian Independence League has to carry on the movement for India's independence with the help of the Japanese Government, but it is not to act or behave like a puppet to the orders and instructions that may be given to it in connection with Independence Movement. We think the Japanese Government itself would not like the Indian Independence League to be ralegated to such a position.

Mr. Yutani : We do not want you to be puppets. But if we do, what is the harm in being puppets ? Why is a puppet bad ?

Mr. Deshpande : Why do you think a puppet is good ?

Mr. Yutani : (To Captain Tsuchimochi in Japanese). You cannot argue with these people, because the Indian way of arguing amounts to indulging in useless feats of hair-splitting. Until these people drop this habit, there cannot be perfect understanding between them and us. In my opinion, they must be plainly told that the Commander-in-Chief has every right to direct, guide and control the activities of the Indian Independence League.

Capt. Tsuchimochi : I agree with you on this point in so far as the Indian Association is concerned, but, although the League activities may be watched by the Commander-in-Chief, yet they will not be guided and controlled by him.

Mr. Deshpande : As it is, the management of the Indian ownerless property leaves the League no time for the Independence Movement activities and to undertake to manage it under the scheme presented to us by you makes the task all the more less thankless. We would feel very much relieved to wash our hands off this business and let others be appointed by you to do the work. On our part we would gladly co-operate and assist them as far as we can, but we are convinced that it is not worth while to accept the work in the name of the League under the present scheme.

Captain Tsuchimochi : Why is it not worth while for the League to manage it ?

Mr. Deshpande : As it is, our predecessors, that is, the Rangoon League, has been and is being made the butt of the public blame. The reasons are that they had undertaken a task, for the successful execution of which they had neither the power nor the authority needed. The result was mismanagement for which the public, not knowing where the real fault lay, began to hold the League responsible.

Captain Tsuchimochi : The authority and power were duly delegated to the League and, if there was mismanagement, the League was rightly held responsible for it by the public.

Mr. Parshad : As agreed upon by you, the League had posted its labels on ownerless properties, buildings, godowns, etc. Any ordinary Japanese soldier would come and tear off the label, break open the godowns and carry away whatever he likes, or if the soldier was a little more considerate he would simply tear the League labels and paste his own, the posters reading enemy property, or property held under control by this or that unit or the military supply department, and so on. Cases like these are every day brought to our notice, about which we have been telling you, but the frequency of such acts only shows that from what you speak to us, even you have no authority to put a stop to it. And now it is the talk in the town that in such cases it is no use going to the League since it is impotent. Our predecessors had a hard task coping with such public opinion, and it is precisely the same which we want to avoid. Consequently, we do not want to have anything to do with the management of the Indian ownerless properties unless we have the necessary power and authority.

Capt. Tsuchimochi: If you find the soldiers removing the League lables and pasting their own you can remove their lables and again paste the lables of the League, since the soldiers are ordered not to tamper with Leauge lables which are pasted always with the sanction of the Military Administration Department.

Mr. Parshad : This is easier said than done. Cases are not wanting wherein our people were beaten, in some cases severely, by solidiers for no fault whatsoever, and supposing that a soldier sees one of our men removing their label and it enters into his head to give the man a good hiding, who is there to stop him from doing so ?

Capt. Tsuchimochi : In such cases we admit there is very little to do but the remedy I would suggest is for you to employ watchmen from the cooly class, who have no sense of self-respect and who get beaten to-day and forget about it to-morrow. And in some cases we also may be able to redress the wrong done.

Mr. Yutani : You talk of power and authority, and as I have already told, you, power and authority cannot be delegated to you. As a matter of fact, power and authority cannot be vested in anybody except the Commander-in-Chief.

Mr. Parshad : We realise this, and hence in our amendments we have asked co-operation and assistance of the Japanese Authorities. For instance, we want to borrow a number of soldiers from you, who would see that looting and tampering with the labels are not done.

Mr. Yutani: This we cannot do. We are already short of hands. Perhaps this may be one of the reasons, why we asked you to manage the Indian ownerless property.

Mr. Parshad: You want us to do the work without any power, while your promise of assistance is inadequate, and naturally all the blame for mismanagement will be ours.

Mr. Yutani: You have to take this as it is. Originally everyone in the Military Administration Department was opposed to the idea of asking Indians to manage their ownerless properties, but it was I whose efforts have been responsible for persuading them to agree to let the Indians manage it. Then again, it was thought that only the Rangoon ownerless property should be handed over for management to the Indians. This was thought to be a trial measure. Nobody has any confidence in the ability of the Indians for the efficient carrying out of this work, and so they argued that, if the Indiams showed themselves efficient in the management of the Indian ownerless properties in Rangoon, the question of handing over to them all the Indian ownerless properties throughout Burma for management could be thought of. Here again I stood up like a rock and argued in favour of the efficiency and ability of the Indians for such kind of work, and ultimately I am glad to say that my views prevailed. Moreover, we had no idea of asking the Indian Independence League to do this work. We could have very well asked the Indian Association to do it. But there, through the good offices of the local Iwakuro Kikan, it was agreed upon to ask the League to undertake the work. And now we find, that you are letting us down. There cannot be greater ingratitude than this.

Mr. Parshad: We are grateful to you for being so considerate and agreeing to the request of the Iwakuro Kikan to allow the Indian Independence League to take charge of ownerless properties of Indians in Burma. But under your scheme the Indian Indepen-dece League is relegated to the position of an agent, a servant and an employee of the Japanese Government. We only want the League to be treated in a better manner.

Mr. Yutani: Our scheme was prepared in view of the fact that we had to deal with people like Mr. Lathia, who with his subordinates proved himself very inefficient and incapable. Look, how they have bungled the whole affair. Their mismanagement was another reason why we had to prepare a scheme wherein all rights of control, guidance and supervision had to be reserved for the Japanese Authorities. And now that the scheme has been signed and sealed, we can only assure you that we have confidence in your capacity to manage the work, and we shall assist you in the best possible way. Drop the argumentative attitude, accept the scheme as it is, do not find flaws in the working and start the work. If you are reluctant to take it up, we will have no other way but to ask the Indian Association to do it.

Mr. Deshpande: We would feel very much relieved in that case.

Capt. Tsuchimochi: It is absolutely inadviable to dig up old graves now and ask the ghost of the Indian Association to do it. As everybody knows, both the bodies have been formed into one, which for all practical purposes is the Indian Independence League, and it is unwise to split it into two organisations, which may only cause mischief and trouble in future.

Mr. Yutani: With this attitude of hair-splitting and narrow mentality I feel pessimistic if Indians can ever achieve independence.

Mr. Deshpande: Mr. Yutani, I think it is just the other way.

Capt. Tsuchimochi: You cannot say so, Mr. Yutani. Unless it is people like these who fight for self-respect, who else do you think can fight for independence? I admit that we are partly responsible, if the Indians have begun to think in terms of already being independent. But we (Iwakuro Kikan) had no other way. We had to flatter them, cajole them and assure them that it was their movement; they were to carry it out, and our help would be only to such extent as requested by them; and that we had no other interest in their movement. Only by adopting such attitude we have been able to put their doubts at naught. The concrete manifestation of this fact, you now find in the formation of the Territorial Committee. From now on I feel sure both the Territorial Committee and ourselves will understand each other in the true perspective and also will know where each of us stands with regard to the other.

:CHAPTER X

THE PARTING OF WAYS

Council of Action in a Fix

The attitude of the Japanese Military towards the 60,000 Indian Prisoners-of-war during the early days of the occupation of Malaya was most inhuman and intolerable. In the beginning only lime rice was supplied to them. Most of the prisoners fell ill of dysentery. They were half-starved, bare-footed, ill-clothed, and malaria-stricken. In this connection the services rendered by Sardar Budh Singh of Kuala Lumpur to minister to the wants of the Indian prisoners of war in the camps at Kuala Lumpur, Singapore and Kluang deserve special mention. He with a band of selfless and indefatigable workers collected foodstuffs, medicines, clothings, cooking utensils, blankets, mosquito-nets, beddings and books to alleviate the sufferings of the prisoners.

In the circumstances the call of their enslaved Motherland was irresistible, and 16,000 of them immediately rallied under the banner of liberation raised by Gen. Mohan Singh and formed the Indian National Army. Another 16,000 expressed their willingness to join the freedom struggle and were kept as surplus volunteers. The Japanese Military Authorities promised Gen. Mohan Singh that they would not interfere with his activities to expand the Indian National Army as and when necessary and that they were prepared to equip that Army to the strength of 400,000. But subsequent events proved that the Japanese did not intend to keep their promise. While Gen. Mohan Singh was given to understand that all the Indian prisoners of war had been placed under his control, the news that 600 officers who had not joined the Indian National Army would be assigned special war duties under the Japanese authorities surprised him. There was doubt even about the Japanese, allowing the surplus volunteers to join the I.N.A. It became clear to Gen. Mohan Singh that the Japanese did not want the I.N.A. to be expanded, so that it could play a worthy part in the liberation of India and that they wanted to make use of the Army only for propaganda purposes. Finally the Japanese Authorties demanded that 900 men from the I.N.A. should be sent to Burma, to which demand Gen. Mohan Singh did not accede. He stated that no movement of Indian troops could take place before a clarification of Japan's intentions towards India was made.

That all was not well with the inner working of the Movement after the Bangkok Conference was evident from the very critical discussions that were going on in the Council of Action during the later part of November, 1942, and which found expression in the following memorandum submitted to Col. Iwakuro on November 29, 1942.'

The Counil of Action had a series of meetings recently, when it took stock of the whole situation concerning the Indian Independence Movement in East Asia and the development of the revolutionary struggle in India. The enormous increase in the number of members in the Indian Independence League, the wide network of league organizations throughout East Asia, the tremendous enthusiasm seen everywhere for the cause which we stand for, and the spirit of sacrifice manifested by all classes of Indians in East Asia, have given us immense satisfaction in the progress of the movement made possible by the help and co-operation of the Imperial Government of Japan. The rapid march of revolutionary events in India, resulting in the growing number of strikes, rebellions, sabotages and other mass actions, has further raised our hopes and leaves us in no doubt regarding the intentions and determination of our countrymen to overthrow British rule and to regain our independence at any cost. We have now reached a stage at which we feel that, before we take any further forward move, it is necessary to clear matters, to understand our position perfectly and to pursue our policy precisely, without which it is impossible for us to do any effective work for the attainment of our object. We are unfortunately so placed that we have not so for been able to contact with leaders in India and ascertain their view regarding our policy and our plains. This makes our responsibility all the the more sacred and onerous. The time would not be distant when we shall have to deal with a Provisional National Government in India and, when that comes, we must be in a position to convince that we have taken every possible step to maintain the safety, dignity and integrity of our country when once our goal of Independence has been reached. We have, therefore, after very careful consideration, come to the conclusion that it will be advantageous, and in the interests of our Movement, to request the Imperial Government of Japan to favour us with a reply at the earliest possible opportunity and to clarify the position on the following points :—

(1) A copy of the Bangkok Resolutions has been forwarded to the Imperial Government so long ago as the 22nd July, 1942. Though we have been working on the basis that such resolutions would be accepted by the Imperial Government, we are not yet in a position to know exactly where we stand with regard to these resolutions. We do not conceal the fact that anxious enquiries are still being made by many leading members of our community regarding these resolutions and we find it difficult and even embarrassing to give them a satisfactory reply. It is therefore of urgent importance to us to request the Imperial Government to be good enough to inform us, formally and at the earliest possible opportunity, regarding the acceptance of the Bangkok Resolutions and if there are any resolutions to which the Imperial Government cannot give their support, we shall be glad if they would kindly define their attitude towards the same.

(2) Recognition of the Council of Action as the Supreme Executive of the Indian Independence Movement in East Asia and the acceptance of its status as such is absolutely necessary in order that the Council of Action may function efficiently.

(3) The Imperial Government must no doubt be aware of the propaganda that is being carried on by the British Government in India regarding the intentions of Japan. Although we have had some declarations from H. E. the Premier, Gen. Tojo and other leading statesmen of Japan to the effect that Japan has no political or military ambitions in India, we would respectfully suggest that a full, formal and solemn declaration binding on the present and future Government of Japan regarding the intentions of Japan to recognise and support the absolute independence and full sovereignty of India immediately on the removal of British rule in India is found essential to instil complete confidence and to place the movement on an effective and proper footing.

(4) As a corollary to the acceptance of the Bangkok Resolutions, it is necessary that the formation and existense of the Indian National Army on the principles laid down in the said resolutions should be formally and publicly recognised and all facilities offered for its expansion with a view to making the army a strong and efficient one to carry out the great purpose for which it is intended. We are conscious of and profoundly grateful to the Imperial Government of Japan for the great help they are rendering Indians in connection with this movement. And with further support, which we have no doubt will be forthcoming, we shall be able to attain our goal of Independence in the immediate future.

Council of Action,

Indian Independence League.

On receipt of this Memorandum Col. Iwakuro became worried and wanted the Council of Action to meet him without any delay. The following are the minutes of the joint conference of the Iwakuro Kikan and the Council of Action held at Col. Iwakuro's, bungalow Singapore on Dec. 1, 1942 at 10-0 A. M. on the issues raised in the Memorandum :

There were present Col. Iwakuro, Col. Maki, Lt. Col. Kagawa, Major. Ogawa, Mr. Senda, Mr. Koyama, Mr. Takaoka, Messrs. Rash Behari Bose N. Raghavan, K. P. K. Menon, B. K. Das, General Mohan Singh and Col. Gilani. Lieut. Kunizuka acted as interpreter.

Col. Iwakuro said that he had received a letter from the Council of Action. He was surprised to see that letter, and wanted to know why that letter had been sent. The matter was rather serious. That was why he wanted the Council of Action to meet him. The Council should tell him frankly why that letter had been written.

Mr. Menon : The reason for sending this letter was that we do not know yet where we stand. To begin with, the whole basis of our Movement is Bangkok Conference, made possible by the support and assistance of Nippon Government. Added strength to the Conference was given by the presence of Ministers of Axis Powers. The Council of Action came into existence as a result of Bangkok Conference. During the progress of the Conference and after the Conference, we were given to understand that a reply to the resolutions would be forthcoming. Some of the resolutions cannot be given effect to without knowing what is accepted, what not accepted and what accepted with modification. After the Bangkok Conference, two or three informal conferences were held, at which the Council was told that a reply would be forthcoming. When people made enquiries we told them that our resolutions had been forwarded to Tokyo and that we awaited reply. The Council carried on for two months. Then when the Council met about two months ago, it was informed of Col. Iwakuro's letter dated 10th July, 1942, which is nothing but an acknowledgement of receipt of the resolutions. Then the Council wrote a letter on the 5th Sept. Col. Iwaguro told the Council that the letter would create misunderstanding, if sent to Tokyo. That is why the letter was withdrawn. Many things happened subsequently which considerably weakened the Council's position. We can now hardly justify the position of the Movement in the eyes of the public, I refer to certain statements made by Col. Kitabe in a conference between the Burma League representatives and the Kikan representatives : " The League has mistaken that Bangkok resolutions were accepted by the Japanese Government or the Council of Action recognised......ridiculous for the Council of Action to make decisions without finding out whether acceptable to Japanese Government......League......no prestige......puppet......Tsuchimochi flatter, cajole......no other interest in Movement......Here Mr. Menon referred at length and quoted from the report submitted by the Rangoon Branch. This discussion shows what little regard there is for the Independence Movement. Even in Malaya in some places very little is known to some Japanese officers about the Indian Independence Movement.

The Army is Council's Army. But actually it is neither strong nor efficient, which we want it to be. It is not allowed to announce the existence of the Indian National Army publicly. Propaganda from India is vicious. It is considered necessary that to win over India the Japanese Government should declare their intentions. Premier Tojo's four or five previous declarations do not go far enough. Declaration contemplated should be binding on the present and future Governments of Japan if it is intended to win over the people in India. Naturally the Council does not set out what should be the contents of the declaration, but it should be a full, formal and binding declaration. We know that Imperial Rescripts are issued only in exceptional cases. But the case of India affects 1/5th of the people of the world. But if Imperial Rescript cannot be issued, solemn and clear ponouncement in the best manner by the Imperial Government will do. Without declaration there will be practical difficulties in carrying on the work, e.g., as to the collection of money meant for the training of volunteers. If the people ask why money is being collected, we cannot mention about the I.N.A. Indians' hatred for Britain is far more than Japanese, we being direct victims. We can win freedom with the co-operation of Nippon. But our people want Japanese to tell us frankly where we stand.

Col. Iwakuro says he understands the position. But he wishes to ask a few questions. Regarding Burma discussions, he enquires if the Council is sure that the report of Burma discussions is ture, or if the misunderstanding is due to wrong translation. He points out that in his view such a state of affairs should not exist in Burma. He says that if the Japanese Government did not recognise the Independence Movement, anybody who carries on such a work would be arrested ; the same with the Council of Action. He points out that if there is anything in Bangkok resolutions that is harmful to the Japanese Government, it can prohibit the carrying out of that part of resolutions. The Bangkok Conference resolved to form the I.N.A. This cannot be done without negotiations with different departments. There must be some difficulties during the course of negotiations. As to a reply to Bangkok resolutions, he has submitted the resolutions to Tokyo for reply. He received instructions to reply in the form set out in his letter dated 10th July, 1942. Perhaps the Council desires a reply dealing with each resolution. He refers to the Japanese constitution and usage, and says that when political parties in Japan ask questions of the Government, reply is never given in the name of the Government. The League is a political body, not a Government. It is like a child in mother's womb and you cannot make arrangements with a child in mother's womb. The Imperial Government has stated that (1) Japan has no ambition in India, and (2) Japan will help Independence Movement. The resolutions of Bangkok Conference have already been put into practice. He have studied Bangkok resolutions and finds 80 per cent. or so have been given effect to in practice, but there may be some friction or difficulties.

Mr. Menon mentions that he does not know why the I.N.A. is not recognised and Col. Iwakuro says : The reason for not announcing the existence of the I.N.A. is that if announced there will be great political effects. If the I.N.A. is to be used for military purposes in India it is better to keep it secret. The military effects are more important than political effects—that is why it is being kept secret, not because the Imperial Government does not recognise it. I have discussed with

Mohan Singh this question. who agreed with me. The decision is to announce the existance of the I.N.A. when military operations start. It will then have both political and military effects.

Mr. Menon has said that it is a big political movement—true, and therefore, not a matter of rules and regulations. It is not necessary to make the League strong from legal point of view. Therein lies the difference between Indian and Japanese point of view.

Declaration.—Col. Iwakuro says he appreciates the Council's viewpoint and points out that Premier Tojo has already made declarations on various occasions. The Government's view is that further declaration is unnecessary. These declarations are binding on successive Governments, just as Prince Konoye's declarations regarding China are binding on all successive Governments. If a situation arises when a further declaration is necessary, the Government will make another declaration. He says he has tried his best to give effect to the Bangkok resolutions. If something goes wrong, it may be due to him or to the Council of Action. He invites free discussions from time to time.

Collection of Money :—Col. Iwakuro says that this has close connection with Japanese Administration. Kikan should be informed beforehand so that matters can be explained to the Administration.

Prisoners of War :—Col. Iwakuro says that they are under the Japanese control, intended to be used for work. If Mohan Singh wants to pick up men for the I. N. A. from prisoners without consultation with Japanese authorites, there would be trouble. He says that sometimes he feels Indians do not discharge their responsibilities but blame the Japanese. Both sides should discharge their duties. I am sorry for the above reasons I am not in a position to submit the letters to Tokyo Government.

Mr. Menon says that the Council has not come there to blame Col. Iwakuro. It only asks for assistance to solve difficulties. He wants Col. Iwakuro to approach these questions from the Council's viewpoint.

Col. Iwakuro says the main reason for difficulties is that negotiations have not been carried out well. As to Burma discussions both sides lost temper; the result is as has happened there. This may be also due to wrong interpretation. When he was 15 years old, he entered Japanese War Department, then newly created. The personnel was about 20. There was no work, we spent the whole time in discussions and questioning regulations. But when there was work, these questions did not arise. In his view, when work is done, there is no time to think of legal quibbles.

General Mohan Singh says that the question at issue is Bangkok resolutions. Before the Bangkok Conference started it was said that the reply would be forthcoming by June 26, 1942. Delegates were detained till that date. The leaders from all territories met Col. Iwakuro on the 26th. but they were told that the reply was delayed. The Conference was fixed for the 29th. On the 29th they were again told that the reply was delayed. He asked all the delegates to go back, telling that resolutions in principle were accepted.

Col. Iwakuro says he never said that resolutions were accepted in principle. Gen. Mohan Singh agrees that it was not said in so many words, but such an atmosphere was created. Now wherever one goes the question is asked whether the reply has come. We were never told that Government could not reply.

Col. Iwakuro says that there are two ways of accepting resolutions: (1) a formal open acceptance, and (2) recognition in practice. He points out that it is technically impossible for the Government to enter into a treaty with the Council of Action. Until formation of Nanking Government, Japan never gave formal acceptance. Otherwise, there may be misunderstanding of constitutional position.

Mr. Senda says that only two points have not been dealt with yet. (1) Government's declaration after the Bangkok Conference; and (2) definition of Co-Prosperity Sphare. Regarding the expansion of I. N. A., we have first to consider the question of accomodation ration etc. Expansion will take place when circumstances, permit.

Mr. Raghavan says that Col. Iwakuro will remember that the last letter was withdrawn at his suggestion. But this letter has been written after a great deliberation. He would like him to submit this letter to Tokyo as showing uneasiness in the minds of the Council of Action. He says that one important point is to gain the support of Indians both in India and in East Asia. Therefore, a declaration after the Bangkok Conference having regard to Bangkok resolutions is thought essential. Not merely the Council of Action but outsiders also want to know the attitude of the Japanese Government and their reactions to Bangkok resolutions. Even before the Bangkok Conference the Japanese Government expressed sympathy and support for the Indian Independence Movement. After the Conference a forward step should have been taken.

Col. Iwakuro says that if a declaration was made after the Bangkok Conference, it might appear that it was a Japanese show.

Mr. Raghavan emphasises three important reasons why a declaration after the Bangkok Conference was necessary: (1) The Bangkok Conference was given a lot of publicity. But as no declaration was made thereafter, Indians do not know the Japanese Government's attitude. (2) In some quarters amongst the Japanese there is no understanding about the Independence Movement. (3) Premier Tojo's declarations were not merely with regard to India, but referred to other countries also. If the position *re* India is going to be same as, for example, Burma, then we are not satisfied. He wants a more comprehensive and binding declaration.

Col. Iwakuro says if a declaration was made after the Bangkok Conference, there would have been great political significance. But now five months have elapsed. Therefore unless a declaration coincides with some great event happening in the future, it would have no political significance. He says he will ask Tojo Government to make a declaration on such an important occasion. He tells the Council of Action of something very confidential. Before the Bangkok Conference the Japanese

Government approached Germany and Italy and wanted to issue a joint declaration regarding India. The German Government replied the time was inopportune, as German armies had not advanced much into Egypt. "I admit a more comprehensive declaration should be made on a great occasion."

Mr. Senda says the Government has recognised the Independence Movement. That is why they organised Iwakuro Kikan. They also authorised the raising of an Army. Iwakuro Kikan is representative of the Government. He points out that according to Japanese way of thinking a declaration in Parliament is the most important thing and that in times like these when a treaty is a mere scrap of paper the main thing is not any document but goodwill on both side.

Mr. Raghavan says the Council was never told that a declaration would be made. He inquires if there is a way of communicating to the Council Government's views on Bangkok resolutions through Iwakuro Kikan without recognising the Council of Action as a juristic persona. He says he is not asking for a treaty or pact. If a formula can be arranged by which this difficulty can be got over, it will be very helpful to the Council of Action.

Col. Iwakuro says that if the Japanese Goverment suppressed the Independence Movement, it would go underground and carry on. He points out in the Russian Revolution Lenin had no support from foreign Governments, yet he carried out the Revolution. He urges the Council to remember that this is a revolutionary movement.

Mr. Koyama asks why if the Japanese Government does not trust this Movement, is this big Iwakuro Kikan organised.

Mr. Raghavan : That is what the people are asking us—why is this organisation (League) without recognition from Tokyo ?

Mr. Koyama : The Council of Action is not a real Government and it is only a political body. The Government therefore cannot make any formal promise to the Council. The case of Nanking (Chinese) Government is different. It has territory, people and sovereignty.

Mr. Senda says it is necessary for the Independence Movement to have the moral support of the Imperial Government—this is better than a legal contract.

Col. Iwakuro ; "I have instructions to help this Movement."

Mr. Senda : "Iwakuro Kikan is a new creation to help the Movement."

Col. Iwakuro says he has received orders to help create political organisation and army to carry on this Movement. In each particular case where difficulties arise, he should be informed and he would solve the difficulties one by one.

Mr. Koyama says the Tokyo Government has received information that there are quarrels within the Indian community. There is no unity amongst Indians even in East Asia with a friendly Government helping the Movement.

Mr. Raghavan points out that if the Tokyo Government is really receiving correct information, it should know there is a good deal of anxiety amongst Indians as to the fate of Bangkok resolutions.

Mr. Koyama says that if there is strong unity among the leading persons in the Movement, other Indians would not worry about these matters.

Mr. Menon says there is complete unity amongst Indians regarding this Movement and the people are united in asking for these assurances. The Council of Action is united on this issue. There is no use evading the main issue by talking about unity.

Mr. Koyama : "The Imperial Rescript is a sacred one. Nobody can ask for it. It must come from the Emperor himself."

Mr. Menon says the Council knows of this; that is why no mention of Imperial Rescript is in Council's letters.

Col. Iwakuro enquires whether these questions are asked because some Indians do not support this Movement or because they find that the organisation is not working properly.

Mr, Raghavan replies that questions are asked because people want the Movement to be put on a firm footing. There should be no misunderstanding between the Japanese and the Movement. Leaders' duty is to see to this.

Col. Iwakuro says that this organisation is not a puppet organisation —he does not want it to be treated as a puppet. The Japanese Government will help the Movement spiritually without asking for any returns. He says the Movement should be such as to need no assistance from Japanese side. He points out, if the Japanese Government recognises the League officially before it has done any concrete work, it will be of no good to the Movement. In his opinion the Council should ask for two things. (1) Not to make it a puppet. (2) Japan should ask for nothing in return for assistance rendered to the Movement. He says that if a declaration is asked for, the Council may become a puppet.

Mr. Senda says that the Movement should be run by Indians, that is why Japanese have been very careful and have remained behind the curtain.

Mr. Koyama says that in his opinion there are three categories of Indians : (1) Those ready to sacrifice life and property for the Movement. (2) Those who find Japanese stronger than the British and so join the Movement. (3) Those who are pro-British. He enquires how many Indians are in category No. 1.

Mr. Raghavan replies that even amongst Japanese there are three categories : (1) Those who are solidly behind the Independence Movement. (2) Those who are indifferent to the Movement. (3) Those against Indian Independence, for instance, Mr. Yutani, but he is not the only one.

Mr. Senda says Mr. Yutani is very pro-Indian. In the course of Burma discussions he must have lost his head. There were tempers on both sides.

Mr. Koyama—There may be both Indian and Japanese, whose attitude is indifferent to the Movement, but the duty of the League and the Iwakuro Kikan is to convert them.

Gen. Mohan Singh—Do I understand under present circumstances, that Col. Iwakuro does not think it right to forward this letter ?

Col. Iwakuro—Yes.

Gen. Mohan Singh—Will you do your best to help us, as you are doing now ?

Col. Iwakuro—Yes.

He summed up the position further thus :—

(1) I cannot submit the letters to Tokyo, asking for a reply to Bangkok resolutions, after such a long time ; I have already submitted the Bangkok resolutions to Tokyo. (2) I shall do my best to persuade the Japanes Government to make a declaration at the opportune moment. (3) I shall help the Movement to the best of my ability. Difficulties should be reported to me as and when they arise and not allow them to accumulate and then come in a body for a stiff formal Conference.

CHAPTER XI

·THE CRISIS

General Mohan Singh's tough rssistence.

In the foregoing chapter we have seen that the Council of Action was not satisfied with this state of affairs. The Japanese knew, that it was General Mohan Singh, who was responsible for all the trouble. so they tried to bring him round. On the one hand they wanted him to carry out the movement of a unit of the I.N.A. to Burma, as originally arranged and on the other hand, they wanted to evade the issues raised by the I.I.L. The General was not prepared to compromise the honour, prestige and liberty of India at any cost. No flattery or praise, no jugglery of words, no threats and pressure could make him acquisce. Neither favours nor frowns could deflect him from duty. He presented a bold front to the vascillating tactics of the Japanese.

The following discussions between General Mohan Singh and some of the Japanese high officials are a clear proof of the General's ability, courage and fearlessness, as also of his statesmanship and grasp of international problems :—

1. DISCUSSIONS BETWEEN GEN. MOHAN SINGH AND LIEUT. KUNIZUKA.

Date 1st, 2nd Dec. 1942. Time 10 P.M. (Dec. 1) to 1-0 A.M. **(Dec. 2).**

Kunizuka.—I have been sent by Col. Iwakuro with a special message for you. He is greatly worried and upset about your attitude. He has also been informed that you are the chief instigator in the whole show. He wants to know, why suddenly you have lost confidence.

Gen.—Our today's document was very clear. It explains our feelings and I do not think, it requires any further amplifications. It has been put up by the Council of Action as one body and does not require any individual opinion.

Kunizuka.—Col. wants some points cleared. If we do not trust each other, then the whole show will be very difficult.

Gen.—I think I trust the Japanese side more than anyone else here, otherwise how could I start the tremendous work of raising the Army Not only this ; all the officers and soldiers have placed their implicit trust in me. Therefore I have got all the more reasons to clear the whole position, otherwise I am not worthy of the trust of my men. And you can take it that this morning's document is the voice of the Army.

Kunizuka.—You know the Japanese way. We care, more for our words and sincerity than for a piece of paper. You remember that when you met with Major Fujiwara, for the first ten or twelve days you put everything in writing and wanted everything in writing. Both sides were very suspicious of each other. Then suddenly you changed your mind and told Major Fujiwara "I am going to take a bold step like a blunt soldier I am, without placing complete trust in you from my side, I cannot expect you to trust me. From now onward, I do not want anything in writing. I have placed implicit trust in you and Japanese side. It is upto you to keep this trust or betray it. I take this risk. I will go all-out and also request all soldiers to join me in this matter of trust." Then after that you were so quick in changing the people that some times it took you half an hour to convert the soldiers and send them back, who had just run out from the front. You did not possess any paper to convert people but it was your own 100% trust, that placed their trust in you. They never asked you for papers. It was this action of yours, which was greatly admired by the Japanese side. Major Fujiwara completely fell in for you and he often said that he would give up his life rather than see such a man being betrayed. You know from you experience, how the Japanese side went all out to help you. There was never any misunderstanding. Now why cannot you start with similar trust with Col. Iwakuro. We trust you fully, as you know yourself.

Gen.—As for indivduals where trust is concerned I have got liking for Fujiwara and I am much obliged to Col. Iwakuro. I am prepared to go to any extent for these gentlemen in my individual trust and personal friendship. But we feel it our duty to safeguard and take all necessary steps and precautions to ensure the interest of India.

11. DISCUSSIONS BETWEEN GEN. MOHAN SINGH AND MAJOR OGAWA

Time 6 P.M. to 8-30 P.M. 2nd Dec. 1942.

Ogawa.—The question of move to Burma was decided with you and all preparations were completed and now you have suddenly stopped it.

If this is not carried out as arranged, it will be difficult to carry out these moves in future.

Gen.—I have already informed you the reasons in my letters. (He didn't seem to have read the last letter and was explained).

Ogawa.—You should have consulted the Council of Action first, but now as the arrangements have been made, it is desirable that the move should be made.

Gen.—The Council of Action has decided and the move will not take place.

Ogawa.—You should claim your position in the Council of Action and push this question forward.

Gen.—I am a party to the decision of the Council of Action and don't differ and cannot push this question.

Ogawa.—Advance party was sent without their consultation.

Gen.—That ought not to have been done. In view of yesterday's discussions, situation is very grave and the question of the move is of secondary importance. Unless the major issue is tackled, no move will take place.

Ogawa.—All arrangements with harbour people and naval authorities have been made and programme already worked out and unless this move is carried out, there wouldn't be any sympathy from the Japanese side. No apology on this matter later on will be accepted. It shall be carried out now.

Gen.—Move will not be carried out. It simply can't be done.

Ogawa.—If you cannot see your way through the Council of Action as regards this move, you better resign.

Gen.—The question of resignation does not arise, as I fully agree with the decision of the Council of Action. The question of resignation is my personal affair and I do not need advice on that.

Ogawa.—It is a big question. It is a question of all Japanese and all Indians. If you don't carry out this move, you will lose confidence of the Japanese.

Gen.—I do not wish to gain the confidence of the Japanese at the cost of losing the confidence of the Indians.

Ogawa.—If you miss this opportunity, you will be losing a golden chance for gaining the independence of the whole of India.

Gen.—This is, why we are very serious about it. If it had been a personal matter, I would have done it. We understand this is the question of the freedom of the Indian people. That's why, we have stopped and further moves till the fundamental questions are decided.

Ogawa.—The contents of your letter are very serious. You should have verbally talked instead of writing it.

Gen.—Yes, they were very serious. That's why I put them in black and white. I thought in writing it will be better.

Ogawa.—After you had written the letter, I met you so many times. Why didn't you talk about it ?

Gen.—I had written the letter and it was upto you to discuss, if you felt like doing so. In my letter, I asked Iwakuro Kikan that before contemplating any further move the matter should be referred to the Council of Action, but the reply received was in the form of an order saying that the army i.e., I.N.A. will proceed to Burma in December and January. This, we thought, was an insult of the Council of Action. Therefore we decided that the moves will be postponed pending the decision of the Council of Action.

Ogawa.—It was Kunizuka's English.

Gen.—I think, it was someone else's draft.

Ogawa.—I will ask you again to reconsider this question, for the problem of shipping is very difficult.

Gen.—We are facing much more difficult problems. Till our problems are solved, I am afraid, I can't do it.

Ogawa.—I want to know your problems.

Gen.—I don't propose to carry out any discussion on them. It is a thing for the Council of Action to discuss and decide.

Ogawa—But I have come here to find something.

Gen.—You were present at yesterday's discussions and there is nothing more than that.

Ogawa—But that was settled. Col. Iwakuro cleared the difficulties and explained to you the Japanese constitutional difficulties and I think, you were all satisfied.

Gen.—What makes you think, we were satisfied, We were not only not satisfied but were disappointed.

We have taken a very serious view of the whole situation, and we are deciding our future action in view of yesterday's so-called satisfactory discussions.

Every word of the letter was very carefully studied and we think our letter was the only honourable course left for us.

Ogawa—But we are putting all resolutions in practice and when Mahatma Gandhi is carrying out his gigantic struggle, you are worrying for a scrap of paper.

Gen.—We know, how to carry on this movement. We were carrying on since long and, if necessary, we will carry on in future without your help. No words can please us. We have been betrayed and cheated many a times. We do not wish to take a step forward with you, till India's interests are completely safeguarded. We have learnt these lessons with bitter personal experiences.

Ogawa—We are always true to our words. You can see from Manchuria. We have given her independence.

Gen.—This is exactly, what we do not want. Who says, there is any independence in Manchuria ? India is already much more free than your so-called free and independent Manchuria.

Ogawa.—The question of Manchuria is slightly diffeient. There are five different races.

Gen.—The recial discrimination is your own creation. This is exactly what the ruling nations generally do. Racial problems in Russia are much more serious than in any other country in the world. But Russians are well united and Russia is a powerful nation. You have supported the British policy of several states in Malaya. Before the British came in India. India was one state. Now 2/3rd is under the British, while 1/3rd is divided into 560 Indian Native States. This is how an Imperialist power divides, and sub-divides and weakens the country, but we know India is one and will remain as one.

Ogawa.—Yes, we quite agree. It should be one and we will, like to see it strong and united.

Gen.—It can be your idea or idea of any other, foreign imperialistic power.

Ogawa.—Why have you suddenly become so suspicious ?

Gen.—By your sudden and straight refusal to a genuine demand of Bangkok resolutions and moreover by seeing your ideas of independence of Malaya and Burma.

Ogawa.—You cannot compare India with Malaya and Burma. India will be more independent.

Gen.—What do you mean by ' more.' India will be absolutely independent. No one can stop it. As a result of our constitutional fight with the British, we have achieved quite a good deal of personal freedom. If you will try to relieve the British we will continue to fight with you till we have achieved our final goal. Your object in our country is to fight the British and our object is to achieve complete independence.

Ogawa.—It is your county and we are just assisting you. You take all the assistance and should not ask for any assurance.

Gen.—Yes, it is our country and our countrymen have been so far fighting alone and they never requested for any assurances. Even now, if we were going to fight the British alone we would never have asked for assurances, or promises. But as the things stand, we are going to take a very big foreign army in our country, placing our own services at the disposal of that Army, it is only logical that we must have a clear-cut policy laid down to protect our interests and national prestige. We can never tolerate that India should change hands. In that case we shall have to start a new fight, with twice the fury and determination.

Ogawa.—By the time war starts the declaration will come.

Gen.—We want to be sure of everything now. By that time it might be too late.

Ogawa.—Col. Iwakuro's idea is, that the Council of Action cannot work independently. It is a very passive body and Independence League has no ability to guide this big movement. This is why KIKAN is here to help you, Independence League will never be able to do anything. It is only the army which has done and is capable of doing something great.

Gen.—I disagree. We Indians are capable of conducting this movement. It is lack of assurances from your side, which have weakened the League and made her cautious and reluctant to take any plunge in the dark. The way, you are crushing the Malayans here and completely Japanising them, has created suspicion in the mind of Indians.

Ogawa.—Our intentions about India are absolutely clean and in the next session this question will get further clarification.

Gen.—If your intentions are so noble, why don't you officially announce them? Anyhow it is difficult for the Council of Action to wait for the next session. I don't know what they will decide, but I can assure you it will be a very delibrate and cautious decision.

III. DISCUSSION BETWEEN GEN. MOHAN SINGH AND COL. IWAKURO

Time.—8-50 P.M. to 10. 30 P.M. 2nd Dec, 1942.

Col.—Iwakuro was not in his usual happy and cheerful mood. He looked worried and depressed. He said "I am very sorry, that mutual dissatisfaction and suspicion has started and we have started thinking in these terms. I am sorry that your side has taken this attitude. I never said, this was a Japanese puppet movement; on the contrary I have the firm conviction that this is entirely an Indian show and we are trying our utmost to help and support this glorious attempt. But I cannot understand, why you have taken this drastic step. After very thoughtful deliberations, we have come to this conclusion that it is of no use to continue this movement in the present prevailing atmosphere. It is much better to stop it. I entirely leave it to you to do anything you think right and those of you, who don't think it advisable to continue any further can go back to their previous status, *i.e.* the prisoners-of-war. Do as you please; we don't impede in any way. It is very tragic that my genuine efforts have gone in vain. I am feeling very lonely and depressed. I feel, I have been betrayed by my own beloved son. Visualising the whole thing, I clearly see the fundamental differences of two different characters.

Gen.—I am very sorry that this sort of stage has arisen. This movement was a child of my dreams. All my energies were devoted day and night to bring about the successful realisation of those dreams. I never started it to be ended in such an abrupt manner. It will be a tragedy from my viewpoint if this mighty fabric fail before fulfilling the cause, for which it was raised. The Council of Action, after careful deliberation and thoughtful consideration, drafted the letter requesting a reply to the Bangkok resolutions. We also considered all possible reactions from your side and were prepared for all eventualities. The letter was discussed in detail yesterday in concurrence with you and it is extremely regrettable that we went back dissatisfied by the unaccommodating welcome given by you. The Japanese side should also be blamed for this. On our return from Tokyo, Major Fujiwara told us that Tokyo resolutions were accepted in principle but subsequently you told us the contrary and later on regarding the Bangkok resolutions, you gave us some vague promises, which never materialised. Naturally we had to become suspicious. Now we thought that the time had come, when we should exactly know where we stand.

Col.—After Bangkok resolutions I tried my best to get the formal reply for you but unfortunately there were so many constitutional difficulties that it was impossible to get the required reply, but at the same time our Government decided to give practical shape to the various resolutions. At such a critical moment, when Mahatma Gandhi is engaged in life and death struggle for the emancipation of Indians from the British yoke, it is regrettable that this suspicious atmosphere has started. You are ignoring the practical application and just worrying for a mere scrap of paper.

Gen.—We Indians are very accommodating. We always trust people and this has been our national character and in fact our present plight is the direct outcome of our placing too much trust in the British at one time or another. We have been repeatedly betrayed and cheated and that's why we have developed a suspicious nature. As individuals, we are prepared to trust you and several other Japanese friends but our national trust is a very sacred trust and much above mere individual trusts and I am afraid we are not satisfied with what we have heard or seen so far in this respect from the Japanese side.

Col.—I am still trying my best to assist you in every possible way and I am sending these M.Ps. to Japan with a personal message. I am also forwarding some special instructions in this matter. I have been preparing these papers for the last two months. It may be our last interview but I would like to show you my views forwarded to my government for kind consideration.

Salient Points of the Letter Forwarded.

1. Japanese should fully help in satisfying the burning desire of patriotic Indians for complete independence.

2. Japan should bring about friendly relations between Indians and herself *i.e.* the spirit of goodwill and good neighbourhood.

3. Japan should not force the Indians to join any sphere politically, economically, militarily and culturally.

4. Japan must respect the territorial integrity and full sovereignty of India.

5. All treatment should be on equal basis and on mutual understanding.

6. Japan should not aspire for new interests in India beyond already existing before the War.

7. All Indian property to be handed over to the Indian Government soon after the occupation.

8. On the request of the Indian people, Japan should give all technical advice and assistance.

9. Japan should not interfere in any of Indian internal affairs and all occupied territories should be immediately handed over to the Congress or Indian Independence League.

10. In case of external invasion, on India's request, Japan should give all possible help. Defence of India should entirely be left in the hands of the I. N. A.

While the British are still there, the Japanese will fight the British and utilize the aerodrome, landing grounds and other stratagical points.

I have been working day and night writing so many training pamphlets for the I. N. A. and it is a great tragedy to stop this show at this stage. I feel that you have let me down and betrayed.

Gen.—It is none of my business to advise the Japanese Government but I must say Japan will make a great blunder, if she invaded India before absolutely clarifying her status and position. India has been fighting the British for the last 150 years with all possible means and methods at her disposal and she will continue to fight Japan, till she has attained her one and one objective i. e., complete Independence. India has seen many invaders and history proves that all of them met their final end on the same side. Today India is politically awakened and she can never be subjugated. A Free, Strong, and Friendly India will not only be a great asset to Japan but will also contribute for the peace, prosperity and deliverance of mankind.

Col.—I love my country as you love yours and quite agree with you. It is equally bad for my country to invade India with any selfish intentions. In Manchuria we have been quite true to our declaration because we declare all five races should equally benefit by the new order. Prince Konoye's promises are still being carried out to the last word in China.

Gen.—Before we started this movement, we knew of your policy in Manchuria and China. We have seen your ways in Malaya and heard about Burma and this is the reason that we are very careful about our commitments. Our only hope was that Japan will be wise enough to adopt a different policy in different territories. We cannot tolerate these types of governments in our country, so before taking any further step, we want definite assurances.

Col.—I quite agree with you. India's question is a seperate question and I am trying my best to request the Premier to issue a clear and formal declaration. Please understand the Japanese viewpoint; we are absolutely ready to co-operate whole-heartedly.

Gen.—I will talk the whole matter with my colleagues in the light of what you have told me just now. Till then I am not in a position to say anything on this major issue.

Col.—This Burma incident has caused great misunderstanding, which was all enacted in hot temper. Mr. Yutani is a strong supporter of Indian cause and he fully understands Indian problems and Indian character.

Gen.—I beg to differ. Col. Kitabe is a soldier and head of Iwakuro Kikan Burma and he should not have been influenced by Mr. Yutani. In fact Mr. Yutani repeated and supported what Col. Kitabe himself said and moreover I don't agree that Mr. Yutani has the foggiest idea of Indian character and Indian problems. He might have come across some labour or cooly classes of Indians or he might have associated with some rich ignorant Indians. It is only today that I have received a letter from Mr. Parshad written by Mr. Yutani ordering him to dismiss two gentlemen working in his office and employ someone else. I do not think you will appreciate, if this thing is done to you by someone and yet you say that he is very pro-Indian and is helping the Indian cause. I would like to point out that Mr. Deshpande, who has been brought up, educated and married in Japan and who was a staunch supporter and admirer of Japanese people, is not at all satisfied with the whole show after working for the last few months. He is trying his utmost to get away from this Movement as soon as circumstances permit him to leave this farce.

IV. DISCUSSIONS BETWEEN MAJOR FUJIWARA AND GEN. MOHAN SINGH.

Dated December 3, 1942 Time 12 noon to 3 p. m.

INTERPRETER Lieut. KUNIZUKA.

Fujiwara.—I was surprised this morning to listen to so many things about you and I was much worried about this situation, which has so suddenly arisen. The question of move to Burma is an extremely serious question and I am very badly involved in it. In these days the transportation problem is supposed to be a major issue. I did my best to fix a ship for the I. N. A. This was done at the cost of Japanese troops scheduled to go there. The programme of the movement of the troops was charted out after consultation with you and your final approval and this sudden turn now has created a great amount of anxiety. I am personally responsible for this particular move and if this is not carried out according to plan, it will be a dark spot in my career and will bring down my prestige every where. I might have to commit Hari-Kiri. If this move is stopped, the Japanese side will be completely shocked and it will create grave ill feeling. You know both of us have worked very hard for the creation of the I. N. A. This is my firm conviction that all minor differences can be solved by mutual consultation and co-operation. But such serious step taken at this stage will shake the foundation of this glorious movement, which you and I have laid for a noble cause. You should always try to take a broader view and your attitude towards these minor things should not be an attitude of a common individual but of a great leader. There are several people who are trying to separate us by vicious propaganda. It is unfortunate that there is language barrier separating us and some times creating minor misunderstanding.

Gen.—I feel extremely sorry that such a state of affairs has arisen. You very well know how dear this movement is to me and I have solely devoted my best energies to bring about the successful realization of this only and only mission of my life. The present situation has taken a serious turn and the only honourable course left for us, is to stop and see, where we actually stand. The movement of troops is a minor affair in comparison with the basic issue and that is why, we have unitedly decided that no moves will take place until and unless the fundemental problems are decided once and for all.

Fujiwara—It is not a minor affair. The movement of the troops may be a minor thing but the reaction of stopping it, will create great suspicion and will alienate the sympathies and best wishes of the Japanese. Although I am not in direct touch with you but still I am responsible for Indian affairs in the Japanese Military Headquarters. I won't like the slightest misunderstanding at this critical juncture and will personlly try to explain the whole situation to the members of the Council of Action.

Gen.—The Council of Action has very carefully thought over it from all angles, and I am sure that the decision stands final and irrevocable.

Fujiwara—In times of war, transport arrangement is very important and on minor incidents movements are never cancelled.

Gen.—It is strange that you think it to be a minor incident but for us it is the pivot of the whole organisation and the whole show might be suddenly stopped, if it is not tackled satisfactorily, and immediately.

Fujiwara—It is the first time in history that Indians and Japanese have come in closer contact for a common cause. It is a pity that still we do not understand each other's mentality. Whatever our present trouble be, it should be kept as a family secret, which cannot be done if the move will be cancelled.

Gen.—I quite agree that it should be kept secret but the Council of Action has decided on some principles and they are ready to sacrifice anything for the preservation of those noble principles.

Fujiwara—Iwakuro Kikan is all out to help you but they are facing certain constitutional difficulties in tackling this affair. The G. O. C. who is directly under the Imperial Government has got full powers and instructions to help this movement whole-heartedly. General Tojo's declaration was also sanctioned by His Imperial Majesty the Emperor. It is the first time in the world history that an army has been raised like this.

Simultaneously with these discussions the Council of Action were holding day to day discussions amongst themselves. Minutes of two meetings of the Council of Action (4th and 5th Dec.) are given here to place before the reader the view-points of different members of the Council.

Minutes of the meeting of the Council of Action held at Room No. 75. Sea View Hotel, on 4th December at 1 p. m.

Sri Rash Behari Bose, President, Sri N, Raghavan. Sri K. P. K. Menon, Gen. Mohan Singh, Col. Gilani, Sri B. K. Das. Secretary, were present.

President enquired of members of their attitude on the questions arising out of yesterday's discussion. Menon says they have considered the situation—he, Mohan Singh and Gilani have decided to resign—says it is better, the whole Council should resign in a body. Tables draft of letter of resignation.

President says he has decided that no troop movement should take place now. He takes the responsibility for this decision. Says with regard to Couecil's request to Col. Iwakuro to forward the letter dated 29th, November, 1942, he will take up the matter. Asks for time to deal with those questions. He hopes all outstrnding questions would be solved satsfactorily by the end of next month. Requests Council Members that all work shoul l be carried on and assures that there will be no movement of troops outside Malaya until questions solved. Requests Council to leave these questions to him for solution.

Raghavan says that the Council should take the stand that Bangkok resolutions should be implemented.

On President's assurance that no movement of troops outside Malaya will take place and other questions will be taken up by him, draft letter of resignation is withdrawn.

Raghavan says President should write to G. O. C. that he has decided that there should be no movement of troops (I. N. A.) without Council's sanction or approval. G. O. C. should refer to Iwakuro Kikan or Japanese authorities to deal with the Council of Action on question of movement of troops.

Council agrees with this suggestion.

As to civilian volunteers already recruited in Malaya, Council reaffirms its previous decision that they should be taken into I.NA. forthwith.

The Council decides that all questions of administration, finance, etc., regarding I. N. A. must go first to the President and be dealt with by the Council of Action and that letter to that effect be sent by the President to Colonel Iwakuro.

The Council adjourns till tomorrow 10 a. m.

Minutes of the meeting of the Council of Action held at Room No: 75. Sea View Hotel Singapore at 10.30 A.M. on December 5, 1942. All the members and secretary were present. Col. N.S. Gill attended the meeting with permission.

The President reports that he saw Col. Iwakuro the previous day, explained to him the position and informed him of his decision that the movement of 900 troops would not be carried out. Col. Iwakuro said that he would try his best to get satisfactory reply from Tokyo on the points raised by him. The President says his impression is that Col. Iwakuro was genuine when he expressed his views on the matter. Mr. Menon and Gen. Mohan Singn enquired if Col. Iwakuro promised to send the letter dated Nov. 29, 1942, to Tokyo and whether he was prepared to state this in writing. If not, they would have no alternative but to resign. The President answers "No" to the questions and informs that, if necessary, he will deal with these questions with the higher authorities as he had already told. He discusssed the question with Col. Iwakuro on general lines. Col. Iwakuro did not say he would forward the letter to Tokyo but said that he would explore all avenues to satisfy the Council of Action.

Mr. Raghavan says that if they have no faith in the Movement, it is better to scrap the Movement rather than use pin-pricks against the Japanese authorities. The President had asked for time till the end of next month and yesterday the Council had agreed. Nothing has transpired since then for members to insist upon immediate reply. The President met him (Mr. Raghavan) after his discussion with Col. Iwakuro and told him (Mr. Raghavan) that Col. Iwakuro admitted there are two outstanding questions: (1) A declaration by Japanese Government as to their intentions about India; and (2) Answers to the Bangkok resolution. The President is willing to take up these questions with the Tokyo Government, if necessary.

Gen. Mohan Singh, Col. Gilani and Mr. Menon state that the position is just as unsatisfactory and after some discussions state that, unless the following points are considered immediately, they will resign :

1. An assurance that Col. Iwakuro will forward the letter to Tokyo.

2. An assurance that a reply will be given on or before 1st January, 1943. The Council to meet in the last week of December, 1942, to consider the situation.

3. No major action would be taken regarding the I.N.A. Routine work of the Movement to be carried on in the mean time.

4. Practical action regarding the I.N.A. to be taken on the following points forthwith :—

(a) All surplus volunteers and prisoners of war are to be placed under the control of the General Officer Commanding I.N.A.

(b) No major movement of personnel, of surplus volunteers and of prisoners of war, either inside or outside of Malaya should take place in the meantime.

(c) All guards and detachments now working under the Japanese authorities must be under the control of the G.O.C.

(d) Advance party in Burma should be informed that no further action should be taken until further orders from the G.O.C.

The President informs the Council that he will place these matters before Col. Iwakuro and obtain his views thereon.

These discussions clearly show that the Japanese were putting continuous pressure on General Mohan Singh to act according to their wishes, they even threatened him with grave consequences but General refused to be a puppet in their hands. Sri Rash Behari Bose was trying to effect a compromise between the Japanese and other members of the Council of Action, but to no purpose.

While these discussions were going on, the Japanese precipitated the matter by the arrest of Col. N.S. Gill. Col. Gill was in charge of the I.N.A. in Burma, and had recently come back. The Japanese suspected him to be a British agent. The Japanese Military Authorities came to the residence of General Mohan Singh in the early hours of, Dec. 8, 1942 and, in spite of Gen. Mohan Singh's protest took Col. Gill under arrest. The arrest of a trusted colleague added fuel to the fire. Gen. Mohan Singh was beside himself with rage. He called on Major Fujiwara at Mr. Senda's bungalow at 9.30 A.M. the same day and demanded an explanation, regarding the arrest of Col. Gill. Lt. Ratan Singh (General Mohan Singh's private Secretary) was also present. M. Senda also took part in the discussion, which lasted for 2½ hours.

Major Fujiwara started with apologies that such an incident had happened at that time and he hoped that the General had not taken it seriously. He asked the General whether he could suspect Col. Gill. The General replied, "Nothing doing,—not at all." Major Fujiwara went on to explain the charges against Col. Gill. "Gill had been watched right from the beginning and they were sure he had a complete network of (British) spies in and out of the I. N. A. During March he selected six trusted officers to convey to the British Government in India, what was happening in the Far East. Out of the six, two had succeeded in crossing the border and the remainder were arrested and had given the Japanese the information about Col. Gill's activities. In Tokyo I was warned not to trust Col. Gill by some of the Indians there to whom Col. Gill had told what he thought of the Japanese. In Saigon Col. Gill telephoned to someone that this Movement was nothing and that he was definitely pro-British. However, Col. Gill played so well with me, (Maior Fujiwara) that I had no suspicion whatsoever that Gill was a British espionage agent. Col. Gill requested him to make me the C. in C. and said that Mohan Singh (G.O.C.) was nothing. I told him that I had already given my word to Mohan Singh and I would never divert but I promised him that he would be a useful partner.

"After his return from Tokyo Col. Gill started his activities and we thought that he would be harmful to the I.N.A. We despatched him to Bangkok. Before he left Syonan he told his trusted colleagues that he (Col. Gill) might be shot at Bangkok and told them to carry on their mission and not to believe whatever he said in public. At Penang Col. Gill confessed to an Indian merchant that he was anti-Japanese. At Bangkok Gill tried to do as much harm as possible to the Japanese and the I.N.A. The Japanese M.P. warned me regarding the activities of Gill, but I took no serious notice about that In Burma suspicions were aroused by Col. Gill's movements and the M.P. again reported but no serious view was taken. As soon as Gill returned to Syonan the Japanese M.P. warned me to watch Col. Gill's activities. On the 18th Nov., 1942, six British spies landed by parachutes on Pegu and they were arrested. From investigations and after deciphering the British code, Japanese authorities came to the conclusion that Col. Gill was a British agent. Those six parachutists confessed that they had three objects :—

(1) To contact Col. Gill and Major Dhillon ; (2) To spread confusion and distrust between the Japanese and the I.N.A.; and (3) To find the movements of the Japanese forces.

Under these charges Col. Gill was taken for investigation.

During this time Mr. Senda interrupted now and then on other matters like :—

(1) Do not doubt Japanese sincerity.

(2) There were technical difficulties regarding the clarification.

(3) The announcement was not made because of strategic reasons.

(5) The Japanese C-in-C has already sent circular to the Japanese to treat Indians as comrades-in-arms, etc. You had a sincere and open heart and now must not crush this movement.

To these, G.O.C. replied suitably in this manner :—

1. From the very beginning I came and started these activities with complete sincerity.

2. After the Bangkok Conference the formation of the I.N.A. was done in full trust.

3. Now I am honour-bound to safeguard the interests of the men under, me, so that they may not be exploited and for this and several other reasons I have taken this step.

4. Individuals do not matter and I am prepared to take all the blame.

To these Mr. Senda nodded and agreed that whatever he (G.O.C.) had done, he had done in full sincerity and he wished that as soon as the matter was clarified, the movement would flourish.

After this General Mohan Singh said : " Whatever has happened was not unexpected on our side. We were ready for this show. Regarding Col. Gill. I cannot believe, and I will not believe that he is working for the British. From my close association with him and from the work he has done for me, I have not the slightest doubt. This incident can be looked at by a disinterested person as follows : (*a*) That I have called Col. Gill from Burma and have handed him over to the Japanese for my own personal reasons ; (*b*) That you believe that the present deadlock has been created by Col. Gill and to get rid of him you have taken him away ; and (*c*) To separate him from me during this juncture. Under all these circumstances my position becomes awkward. As I have told you that not one Gill or one Mohan or one Bose but hundreds may have to be sacrified to achieve our goal. I do not matter. It will be the greatest blot on me not to take the responsibility. I have done all these and I stand by all my actions. May I ask a few questions regarding Gill again :—

Q. Can I meet the six parachutists that landed in Pegu ?

A. Impossible. They are under the charge of the M.P.

Q. Can I meet the officers despatched by Col. Gill ?

A. I think it is not possible.

Q. Can you name these officers ?

A. Yes, I shall give you detailed news of them, after I get them from the M.P.

Q. Can I see Col. Gill now and then ?

A. As the M.P. have full powers, it is not possible but after the investigation, I think, it will be possible.

Q. Can you tell me the approximate dates of the arrest of the officers and when they crossed the border ?

A. During August, but I am not certain.

The General then said. " In my view, this step taken by the Japanese is entirely wrong and it does no good to the Japanese. It is a wrong move. Yet it was expected by me. The proper thing would have been that you should have informed me about this earlier. That would not have been so bad. All the same I am of the opinion that you have taken him away, for no reasons except as stated before. I only regret that you are entirely wrongly informed and your move is wrong. It was I who brought about this deadlock, sincerely, too and I should have been arrested.

" I have to fight hard against my conscience and imagination to believe your story about Gill, because in 1939 after the outbreak of the

European War, certain officers (Sikhs) planned to capture the Punjab. I was in it. We decided to put up the claim of Maharaja of Patiala and one senior Officer amongst us took the scheme to Col. Gill at Army Headquarters at Simla. Col. Gill kept that secret to this date. He advised us to wait as it was not the proper time. There can be no other better proof of his sincerity towards India."

At this stage Mr. Senda remarked that as Col. Gill's way of living was completely Anglicised, his personal opinion was that he might like the British, because he had achieved the highest possible post for an Indian in the Army. He was of the opinion that quite unknowingly Gill was pro-British.

To this General Mohan Singh said, " I don't agree with you, because most of the army officers live like the British ; yet we could never change hearts. Whatever it is, Gill never is or was pro-British. Some of us might have liked their ways but not their rule."

Major Fujiwara then requested the G.O.C. to call on Col. Iwakuro and inform him about this meeting.

The G.O.C. replied that he could not do that till he could make up his mind.

Immediately after his return from Mr. Senda's bungalow, a meeting of the Council of Action took place. It was clear that after the arrest of Col. Gill there was no room left for any compromise. Three members of the Council of Action resigned from the Council. Of course a wide gulf now separated these members from the President (Mr. R. B. Bose), who accepted their resignations the next day (9th Dec.) The same day Gen. Mohan Singh called a meeting of the officers of the I.N.A. in the evening and placed before them all the happenings of the last two weeks. It would interest the reader to know the situation and General Mohan Singh's point of view in his own words. Addressing the meeting he said :—

"This lecture was fixed by me yesterday, as I deemed it necessary to clarify the present situation. Just a little before I left my Bungalow I received a letter which has cleared certain doubts and has made our course much easier. You have, I believe, been informed through your senior officers, what has been taking place during the past two weeks. I shall take you a little further back. You all remember that on or about the 15th of November I delivered a lecture to all of you, in which I stated that we had come to a critical stage and that we were on the cross roads. I also advised you that whatever happens, our success lay in unity and sacrifice. I do not think, whether any of you understood the real meanings of those words, but I knew exactly, what serious step I was going to take. On the very same day, I invited all Field Officers at my bungalow and told them that we had reached such a stage that to go further without clarification of the many doubts we had, was not in keeping with our policy. We all were of one opinion that we must get all our doubts cleared now. A few days later, the Council of Action met. In these meetings we discussed all ways and means and finally we drafted a memorandum to the Government fo Japan to be forwarded through Iwkuro Kikan; Just then Col. Gill arrived from Burma. At the request of Col. Iwakuro, we met him and there were many other Japanese gentlemen and there Col. Iwakuro told us that he was not prepared to forward our letter to Tokyo. We all were very much disappointed and dejected. We accordingly informed Col. Iwakuro, how we really felt about the situation.

However, the President, Mr. Bose, assured us that he would do his best to negotiate and we accordingly agreed, knowing fully well what he possibly could do. At this critical stage, Col. Gill's arrest took place. You all know that the I. N. A. is one party and we will sacrifice everything for any member and we will prove that. You all know how much respect and admiration we all have for Col. Gill and his loss to us is very tremendous. At this critical stage, the feelings on both sides were very strained and the slightest mistake on any side would have been disastrous. Our position was that of a weighing measure, when the scales weighed equally and the slightest addition of weight on any scale would have lost the balance.

At such a stage, to separate Col. Gill was not at all desirable. All the same, they did it. Yesterday morning, when it was still dark, the Chief of the M. P. with 17 other officials came and woke me at my bungalow. They were very polite and they produced a written authority. The Chief asked my permission to arrest an officer of the I. N. A. I replied that I should know the name of the Officer and the reason for his arrest. Mind you, I was not taken by surprise, as I expected this show, it was only one day late. He reluctantly told me that he wanted to arrest Col. Gill but would not disclose the reasons. He only informed that this action has nothing to do with the I. N. A. and requested that this should not create any misunderstanding on the I. N. A. side. He told me that Col. Gill was being taken for some very important investigation regarding Thailand and Burma. I replied that unless I know the charges, I must accompany Col. Gill. He was not willing to take me but I went. We went to Oxley Road and there the Chief of the M. P. took me to a seperate place and told me the charges.

I gave him my opinion and told him that it was impossible and I do not for a minute believe the charges. As I had gone there without informing Col. Bhagat or Col. Gilani, who were staying with me, I thought it nececessary to return at once to avoid further misunderstandings. Later, I was engaged with Major Fujiwara and Mr. Senda in discussion regarding Col. Gill for about 2½ hours. After that we went to attend the meeting of Council of Action. Here I informed that the time had come, when we had to come in action. Two other honourable members namely Mr. Menon and Col. Gilani were with me and we three jointly tendered our resignations, which I shall now read out to you. I had not got the reply to this but just before leaving, I got the reply, which accepted our resignations. I shall now read out both to you.

RESIGNATION

Syonan, 8th December, 1942.

The President,

Council of Action,

Indian Independence League.

Sir,

We have been, as you know, during the last few weeks engaged in carefully examining every aspect of the Indian Independence Movement in

East Asia and after long deliberation we came to the conclusion that without clarification of the position on many points it would not be possible nor desirable to go on with our work.

It was with this object that we prepared a memorandum for consideration by the Imperial Government of Japan and sent same to Col. Iwakuro on 29th November, 1942, with a request to forward it to Tokyo and get a reply at the earliest possible opportunity. On his invitation we met him and some other Japanese gentlemen at a conference on 1st December, 1942 when we further placed our difficulties and our point of view before them.

After a discussion lasting for over 2½ hours, in the course of which Col. Iwakuro clearly told us that he was not prepared to forward our memorandum to Tokyo, we returned greatly disappointed, and dejected and we informed him of it accordingly.

On the 5th instant you assured us that you would try to induce Col. Iwakuro to reconsider his decision and wanted us to wait till you were in a position to report us the result of your attempts. Today you were good enough to inform us that your efforts have been unsuccessful so far.

We put our whole soul in the endeavour to preserve this Movement for the purpose for which it was started but we cannot deceive ourselves and the public by pretending that things are going on well and smoothly when in fact, we are thoroughly dissatisfied with the situation in which we find ourselves.

Therefore, we are of the opinion that no useful purpose will be served by our continuing as Members of the Council of Action. We hope that, in spite of the present difficulties, it will be possible for us in the near future to resume our activities under more favourable conditions. But our duty at the present is clear. We are not confident that we shall be able to serve the cause of Indian Freedom in the manner and to the extent that we wanted to serve it if we go on like this.

This situation took a more serious turn this morning by the arrest of Col. N. S. Gill, who is highly admired and respected by the members of the Indian National Army. It is well-known that Col. Gill played a great and noble part not only in the creation and formation of the Indian National Army, but also in popularising the Independence Movement generally. At a time when his presence and assistance would have been of great use to us, he has been abruptly taken away from us, and we cannot conceal the fact that this unfortunate incident has made a deep impression on our minds, as it has no doubt made on yours also.

It is very painful to us to cease our connection with a Movement which we patiently laboured to create and develop, but we shall be proving ourselves false to the great trust imposed on us by our people if we continue our association with this movement under the circumstances in which we find ourselves today.

We, therefore, tender our resignation as Members of the Council of Action and we request you to accept the same.

While we sever our connection with this Movement as members of the Council of Action, it is needless to say that we shall, in our individual capacity, always be prepared to give our wholehearted support and co-operation to the Military Administration of Malaya.

May we take this opportunity to thank you personally for the great courtesy and consideration that you have shown to us during the period that we have been working together.

We have etc.
(Sd.) MOHAN SINGH
(Sd.) Col. GILANI
(Sd.) K. P. KASHAVA MENON

REPLY

Indian Independepence League Headquarters.
Camp, Sea View Hotel,
Syonan, 9th Dec., 1942.

Dear Mohan Singh,

I am in receipt of your letter of resignation of yesterday's date. It was not altogether enexpected. During the last few days, I noted that a crisis was being carefully developed in which the only difference of opinion between yourself and myself was on the point as to whether this Movement should be allowed to be wrecked immediately without our exploring all the avenues to preserve it honourably and in the interest of India. I believed, and still believe, that it could be so preserved. As I had already informed you a number of times, on all outstanding points ot issue, I have been doing my best to negotiate and I only pleaded for some time to continue these negotiations to a definite conclusion consistent with our country's needs and self-respect. I have been making some progress and I reported same to you. I even undertook to go to Tokyo, if need be, and try to get the position clarified to our satisfaction. But, in spite of these assurances on my part and in spite of my plea, I regretted to note, during the discussions that we have had, an atmosphere which was not conducive to joint work and which was fatal to the Movement. In the circumstances, I accept your resignation with great regret and carry on the Movement by myself as President in the best way I can, pending a reference to the Committee of Representatives. I hope and pray God that I shall, in my endeavours to serve our country, receive the full support of my countrymen in East Asia.

I thank you for the last paragraph of your letter, The courtesy and consideration have been mutual.

Yours in Service,
(Sd.) RASH BEHARI BOSE
President,
Indian Independence League,
East Asia.

This is the reply of the resignations. I do not think it proper to lecture about the proceedings of the Council of Action but I do think it my duty to tell you all briefly what has taken place. I am not prepared to give you any opinion about the President. He imagines,

I suppose, that that he can influence the Japanese Govenment but from my experience, I think it is impossible. We three, Menon, Gilani and I are one but Mr. Raghavan is of different mentality and outlook. He wants to act like a theatre-man "hero" and is nothing more or less. He is not at all worried about the cause but himself. He has no other grouse. You might charge me of hasty action but I assure you that it is not so. You know that I took the risk of a soldier and joined the Japanese voluntarily at Jitra. Singapore fell; Tokyo Conference, then Bangkok Conference with great pomp and finally the formation and organisation of I.N.A. itself. The discipline, spirit and the marvellous work done by all of you is self-speaking. No one can say that we failed in our duty. I contemplated the present step only after the formation of 4 more regiments. After training 8 regiments in all, we would have more strength, but circumstances were such that this stand had to be taken now. There were certain factors like the movement to Burma etc. I took this step knowing fully well that all of you are behind me like one man.

Rumours in the town are now being spread that the Army had failed to do its duty, that it had only mercenary outlook and so many other things. At the same time, the right-thinking people know the truth too. We have done our duty and all this outside world understands our position. World is such a treacherous place and people are so clever and cunning that they are even capable of exploiting the partiotism of others for their own selfish ends. It will be the work of future historians, to record, who was right. All that I have done, is with the best intentions. As a Chief Actor of this show, I fully understand the seriousness of this measure. Our President, did not, even weeks after the fall of Singapore, know that there existed Mohan Singh or Indian soldiers. I have laboured and have put all my soul to create this Movement. I can be compared with a man who wants to build a beautiful house and collects with great difficulties all the paraphernalia like bricks, etc. and builds the house. When the house is near completion, can you imagine the builder will destroy that building ?

I have patiently laboured and worked with all my energy to create this Movement and with your help I have succeeded in building this Movement after my very heart. Can you ever imagine that I could come and say to you to wreck it ?

Of the two million Indian residents in the Far East, I say that the majority of them have no interest whatsoever in India. They are only concerned with their own daily bread, and of their leaders, with the exception of very few, none is worth the name. These so-called leaders, just to save their skins, are prepared to sell the 400 millions in India. They love to go about in big cars, attending tea parties and such like things. Can you expect anything noble or honourable from them ?

My conscience says that no one can exploit us and no one will succeed to wreck this movement. These people cannot for a second visualise the extent of the political awakening of the people of India. These tea-party lovers can never wreck us. We will decide with our conscience. Conscience never fails any one. We canot fight imagination and conscience. We have acted as brave men. I recall when Pt. Nehruji said "Success often comes to those, who dare and act, it seldom comes to the timid."

I wish to thank you all for the sincerity and unity shown by you. I shall be failing in my duty, if I do not point out that a wavering element has been discovered. It was firmness, strength of character, love of cause and country, which was required. You were clearly told that this movement was started not for pleasure but hardships. Our path was full of thorns and this is the first one. You know that once Aurangzeb's 50,000 men had to encounter Dara-Shikoh's two Million men together with Raja Jaswant Singh's forces. In the night, when Aurangzeb's forces came to know about the strength of the enemy forces, they began to desert. Aurangzeb came to know of this and in the night, collected all the senior Officers and said that there was no cause to worry, because those who were running away now would have run away tomorrow and those who remain with us will be our partners of death and life. History bears witness, who finally won. Aurangzeb won that battle.

The crisis comes to purify movements like this. True friends are those who remain in misfortune. In major issue, petty things do not matter. We started this movement not for the sake of Japanese, but for a definite and sacred reason and I say, no one can expliot the patriotism of the I.N.A.

Your courage and bold action at this stage, have opened the eyes of a mighty Empire. The Japanese have come to realise, that India is unlike other countries. It is my strong conviction that if India with her own strength, is capable of achieving freedom from a very powerful organization no one from outside can wreck her. Your strong and united action at this stage has had its desired effect. Not one Mohan, but you are capable of producing 1,000 Mohans and India can produce millions. We are not cowards and if our issue is cleared once for all genuinely, we are prepared to act. To fear at this moment, is the meanest thing.

I will get my opportunities to clear my position. As yet, I have only resigned from that impotent body, "The Council of Action" and not from the I.N.A. I shall remain with you till my death. With me are two more honourable members. Remain united whatever happens. If anyone of you in future wants to take risk, do so, but clear all the doubts. Do not for anything be individualists, but follow one man. Have one voice and one party. When I see the brave soldiers singing national songs and doing their work with the best of spirits, my heart goes out to them. I fear for them. My only wish is that the lives of these brave patriots should not be allowed to be exploited by any one. Please do not exploit these poor soliders. I know none of you will ever do it.

You have worked very hard indeed to raise the spirit of the soldiers and now do not allow it to fall. On the country, go on with the noble work. Do not be dejected. Be brave and remain with your men. Encourage them and let the national spirit of the men increase. Remain calm and courageous and no harm can come your way. After all, misfortune comes to a man and we must face our ordeal manfully and calmly."

At this stage Sri Rash Behari Bose issued the following appeal to his countrymen in East Asia to carry on the movement :—

My colleagues of the Council of Action have resigned. The constitution to that extent has broken down and, on behalf of the Indians in East Asia, I, as president, have decided to carry on, pending the election of other members which can be done, according to our Constitution, only by the members of the Committee of Representatives from the various territories of East Asia. In exercising all the powers and duties of the Conncil of Action which, consequent on the resignations of my colleagues, have vested in me I believe I am interpreting the Constitution of our Movement in the most politically sound way and thus respecting the mandate of the Indians of East Asia given to me at the Conference held at Bangkok in June this year. I have from the 9th of December onwards, taken control of the Movement and I once again pledge to serve the cause of Indian Independence without fear and without favour, loyally and conscientiously and to the utmost of my ability. I shall endeavour my very best to interpret the conscience of our people and give effect to their wishes and dictates. I shall not, as far as humanly possible, allow anything, however powerful it may be, to come between us and our objective, namely the absolute independence of India, free from any foreign control, domination. interference or even influence of any nature. In taking over control. I know, and fully believe, that what I have done—to save the Movement for Indian Independence from collapse—will meet with the approval of my countrymen wherever they may be.

As with many of my countrymen, the cause of Indian independence has always been nearest to my heart. For that I laboured ; courted death; courted exile. For full two decades I had been striving my utmost to pave the way for the liberation of our Motherland. It was not only liberation from the British yoke that I wanted, but liberation from any yoke whatsoever. There was a time when even the people of Nippon, among whom I lived, viewed the question of Indian independence with indifference. But I strove on ; and to-day I believe that we have succeeded in securing their sympathy and support—an international asset of no mean importance for any nation to have at the present juncture and for the future. We have secured the sympathy of other nations as well. It would have broken my heart if at this moment I had let this Movement die because some of my colleagues took it into their heads that, unless on every point they had their way, they could not go on. On the other hand, I believe that if there are difficulties in the Movement they can and shall be rectified. If there are doubts and fears, they can and will be cleared. If there be even actual obstructions in our path, it is my firm conviction that those should be removed and the way made clear for achieving our object, the much-longed-for and long-awaited independence of Hindustan. The co-operation or otherwise of any nation, however valuable it may be, is not a rock on which the ship of Indian independence should founder. We shall fight our battles with such help if possible, but without it, if necessary.

The Indian Independence Movement was, as is well known, being carried on even prior to the war. But the declaration of war and the

Japanese attitude towards Indian independence outlined in the statement of His Excellency Premier General Tojo made it possible to work this Movement in various countries in East Asia openly and without hindrance. The Movement was started even prior to the Bangkok Conference. We have been carrying it on now for nearly a year. At Bangkok we were given by the delegates assembled there a definite mandate to carry it on, and as a result of that mandate more organisations, both civil and military were established. We were making progress. Very recently my colleagues felt that some further clarification of our position was necessary for us to work the Movement. With that view I was in complete accord. Where some of us differed was in the contention that without such clarification—and that forthwith—the Movement could not and ought not to proceed. Thus arose a deadlock. In my negotitations for clarification which started immediately on our deciding in the third week of last month to secure such clarification, I found that some time was necessary to obtain results. I therefore, advised the Council that we should give a little time; that, having carried on the Movement all these months, it would not cause much harm, danger or hardship by carrying it on for a few weeks more in the same manner as we had been doing; and that, if at the end of our negotiations we could not get satisfactory arrangements made, we were entitled to consider and change our policy, if necessary. It required a little patience and a good deal of perseverance. I felt happy when after discussions amongst ourselves on the 4th of December, it was agreed that matters should be left for further negotiations and for report by the end of next month. On the 5th of December, however, for no apparent reason, I was informed that some of my colleagues again changed their minds and decision arrived at on the previous day was not to be acted upon. It was then that I realised there was more in the move than what appeared on the surface. Immediately on such realisation I began my fight against the move, against the creation of a deadlock, against the break-up of our Movement and disruption of our work. I pleaded with my colleagues not to resign and precipitate a crisis and a deadlock which would result in hardship, misunderstanding and unhappiness and may ultimately damage our cause. I assured them that I was as jealous of our rights as they were. My stay in a foreign country has not made me any the less a patriot than other sons of India, but has only intensified my attachment and affection to my Motherland.

My colleagues resigned on the 8th of December. I have given deep consideration to their letters of resignation. I am of the view that they should not have resigned without consulting the representatives from the various countries in East Asia. I am of opinion also that it was not necessary for them to have resigned at all, as some of them appeared to have done, for the solution of the matters raised by them. But they are their own best judges and so I have accepted their resignation with regret. Since I am confident that the Movement can only be carried on for India's and India's benefit only, and all outstanding questions solved to our satisfaction, I have taken upon myself to continue the Movement with the support and co-operation of the Indians in East Asia. While, on the one hand, I shall be carrying on with our work, I shall, on the other hand, also spare no pains to negotiate and secure for the Movement every facility and support for which my colleagues and I have all the while been asking. At the earliest opportunity I shall be reporting to my countrymen the progress that I shall be making. In the mean time the work will go on, and none on the civil side need entertain the slightest fear. There shall be as little upsets as possible. The Movement shall be carried on as heretofore. I shall endeavour to put into it, as we go along, even deeper enthusiasm and more vigorous activity. I must assure every Branch of the League and also the Indian National Army that my taking over on myself the rights, duties and responsibilities of the Council of Action need not in any manner mean changes in the constitution, organisation or development of the civil and military institutions that we have endeavoured to create, nurse and nurture during the last few months. I guarantee to them that I shall not be a party to any act that will jeopardise their interests or the interests of our Motherland. Their interests have always formed my sole objective in the work that I have undertaken on myself.

I know I have the trust and confidence of my brothers and sisters in the arduous work ahead. If my opponents call me a puppet, let them do so. But let me assure them that they are sinning against a man whose only end and aim in life is to see his country free, absolutely free and independent, who is as proud of his birth-right as any Indian alive, and who has staked his all and who will stake the last drop of his blood in upholding the honour and integrity of Hindustan. I seek nothing from life except the success of our mission. If once it is accomplished, I shall retire into seculsion in some nook or corner of our beautiful Homeland. The full and complete independence of Hindustan is our objective and let no differences, personal or otherwise, cloud or obstruct the issue. I appeal to my countrymen to continue to render to me and to this Movement their generous support and co-operation in abundant measure, without which nothing can be accomplished, but with which, I have complete confidence, we shall carry on our fight to its successful termination—the attainment of India's independence. Long Live Hindustan! Vande Mataram!

(Sd) RASH BEHARI BOSE
President,
Council of Action I.I.L.

Syonan,
10th Dec, 1942.

Two days later, on December 12, Sri Rash Behari Bose in his new role of a dictator addressed a letter to Gen. Mohan Singh, informing him that the I. N. A. would in future be under his control. This matter had already been the cause of much heated discussion in the Council of Action. Mr. Bose and Sri Raghavan contended that the Council of Action had a right to control and direct the I.N.A. This General Mohan Singh was not going to concede, so he atonce sent the following "Hands off the I. N.A.!" reply, announcing the severance of the Army from the Indian Independence League.

No. 2/M. S.
H. Q., I. N. A., 13th Dec., 1942.

Mr. Rash Behari Bose,
Sea View Hotel, Syonan.

I am in receipt of your letter of the 12th instant. I maintain that with the resignation of the four members of the Council of Action you have no authority to assume any of the powers your claim in your letter.

In the preliminary conference held at Tokyo and again at Bangkok, we were most anxious that no one individual should have dictatorial powers. We frustrated all attempts in this direction. The outcome of these conferences was the creation of a Council of Action and the limiting of the powers of the President to only giving effect to its decisions. You are now striving to invoke the Constitution to do the very mischief that we took so many precautions to avoid.

We are all faced with a grave situation. All the members of the Council of Action save you have resigned. Rule 12 of the Constitution provides how the vacancies on the Council of Action should be filled up, and, until such vacancies are filled up in the manner stated therein, you cannot arbitrarily assume all the powers and functions of the Council of Action. You may be the sole surviving member, but you cannot act for the whole Council especially in view of Rule 19 of the Constitution, which lays down "the Council of Action shall have collective responsibility." If you do, you do it at your own risk.

It is apparent from your correspondence that you are not only totally ignorant of anything pertaining to an army but have some foolish and misguided notions about it. Let me put down a few facts concerning the Indian National Army which may help to clear your mind.

(a) The members of the Indian National Army are pledged to me and me alone by name, and I am pledged to safeguard the honour and dignity of the I.N.A. We form one indivisible whole, we raised and trained the I. N. A. for an honourable cause, that of securing the unfettered independence of India and not to satisfy the passing whims and fancies of any particular individual.

(b) This army will only be part of any movement, if it is convinced that that movement is conducted in the interests of India. It has been found necessary, under the circumstances in which the army was raised and trained, to depart from normal practice and keep the officers informed of the trend of political events. They are fully aware of the position you have held, the part you have played and the manner in which you have played it. There is nothing but disgust and contempt for you. In case you have any false ideas about your popularity in the army after the one or two occasions on which you have had the privilege to visit it, I am more than willing to afford you an opportunity to see their true feelings now.

(c) As already mentioned, the I.N.A. has only one clear object to secure—the independence of India. This cause is sacred to it, and it is prepared to make any sacrifices, to fight any person or persons for the attainment of its goal.

The events of the last few weeks however, have convinced us that, under existing circumstances, we cannot usefully serve our Motherland through the Indian Independence League in East Asia, and we have accordingly thought it fit to sever our connection with it.

I have had the opportunity to come across the false and malicious reports, including your statement issued on the 10th instant "To the Indian Patriots of East Asia," concerning our resignations. They constitute a deliberate attempt to misinform and mislead the public as to the true facts. The versions given are all of your own manufacture and one-sided. I am most anxious that the public should be acquainted with the true facts in order to ensure that their patriotism should not be exploited by unscrupulous people wishing to serve their own selfish ends.

I therefore challenge you to face the public at a meeting at which I shall take the opportunity to present the facts and let them decide as to the correct standpoint for themselves. If you do not call such a meeting forthwith, I will be compelled to issue a statement placing all the facts before the public.

The above letter has not been written to contest or disprove the position you hold for yourself in your imagination. You to me have only been the sole surviving member of a defunct Council of Action, since the resignation of the others. It is merely written as a courtesy and to avoid future unnecessary instructions by you to the army. Needless to say that, if you still persist in writing anything, it will not be answerd.

(Sd.) MOHAN SINGH,
G.O.C., I.N.A.

As the days passed by the rift between the I. N. A. and the League widened, and the distrust created in the mind of Gen. Mohan Singh that the Movement would founder under the leadership of Rash Behari Bose forced the General to issue the following Special Order of the Day for the dissolution of the Indian National Army:

21st Dec., 1942.

Warning Order—Discontinuation of the I.N.A.

The Indian National Army will be dissolved shortly. It is with deep regret and great reluctance that this decision has been arrived at. Circumstances have arisen under which it is impossible for the I.N.A. to forge ahead to achieve its goal, *i.e.* the complete independence of India without any foreign control, influence or interference.

I thank all ranks of the I.N.A. for their loyal and enthusiastic support in this great undertaking. Though we have not been able to achieve our final object, the movement has not been in vain. It has inculcated in us the true national spirit ; it has brought a degree of unity amongst us unknown in the past; and it has shown to us and the world at large what we are capable of, if only we are left to our own selves.

All the members of the I. N. A. are welded together into a patriotic group. We were and are prepared for supreme sacrifice. It is up to everyone to ensure that that sacrifice is directed in one and only direction—the achieving of our goal of independence. Let us never forget that great and beautiful land of ours with its 400 millions—our brothers and sisters. To her freedom we are wedded. I therefore appeal to you all to continue demonstrating that solidarity and unity that you have so admirably manifested before. I know that you will now and always continue to do so. Remember our strength is our unity and our life is for our country.

A confirmatory order will be sent out as soon as arrangements with the Nipponese are complete. In the event of my being separated from you before such an order is issued, the dissolution will take place automatically and immediately. Also at the same time the resignation of all the members of the I.N.A. and their release from all obligations and undertakings to me and the I.N.A. will be taken for granted.

India first and India last. Long live India !

(Sd.) MOHAN SINGH,
G.O.C., I.N.A.

On the morning of the 29th December, 1942, Gen. Mohan Singh was called to the office of the Iwakuro Kikan, Mount Pleasant, on the telephone. The General went there accompanied by his Secretary Lt. Iqbal. Besides some Japanese officers, Sri Rash Behari Bose and his Secretary Sri B.K. Das were already there. As soon as General Mohan Singh arrived. Col. Iwakuro produced before him a letter containing certain conditions under which the General would have to work with the I.N.A. When the General refused to abide by those conditions, he was shown another letter signed by Rash Behari Bose dismissing him from the post of G.O.C., I.N.A. Gen. Mohan Singh was then taken to a sea-side bungalow and kept there under detention for two months. He was afterwards removed to a near-by island and kept there till the end of December, 1943. Later he was taken to Sumatra and detained in that island till the surrender of the Japanese. He surrendered to the British and was brought to Pearl Hell Jail Singapore, where treatment meted out to him in the beginning was most barbaric. He was brought to Delhi on Nov. 28, 1945. He was first kept in the Red Fort. Later on he was removed to Kabul Line Delhi Cantt., from where he was released uncoditionally on May, 4, 1946.

After the arrest of General Mohan Singh begins a most pathetic and heart-rending chapter in the history of the Indian National Army. The I.N.A. had been dissolved and the Japanese wanted to form it again. A vast majority of them stood by their brave General. There was a trial of strengths between the Japanese and these faithful, patriotic soldiers. It was this test that proved to the Japanese, that Indians could not be exploited and when it was a question of their country's honour, they could give proof of being alive. The Japanese were a ruthless barbarous people. It required a lot of guts to say 'No' to them. And in those darkest hours nearly ten thousand of them—the cream of the I.N.A.—had the courage to give a heroic stand and say 'No' to the Japanese, knowing full well that they were courting certain death. Those dauntless heroes had to pay dearly for the stand they had taken to keep the honour and prestige of their motherland. They were sent by the Japanese to New Guinea, Java, Sumatra and other South-East Asiatic Islands. They had to work there as slaves, were poorly fed and had to undergo untold sufferrings. More than five thousand of these young men lost their lives for the sacred cause unheard and unwept. It was their sacrifice that made the Japanese respect Indians and give a free hand afterwards to Netaji Subhas. All glory to these martyrs—the brave sons of India! Their sacrifices would be written in letters of gold in the future history of India.

Before closing this chapter, we may well stop to ponder over the unfortunate happenings of this period—happenings which were responsible for so much suffering and torture. The reader has studied the conflict of the two parties—rather two schools of thought. It will be better not to apportion blame; perhaps it could not be avoided. But we cannot help paying a tribute to General Mohan Singh. His is the most glorious part in the Freedom Movement of India. We have already refered to his statesmanship, his courage, fearlessness and his ready wit. His sense of partiotism, bravery, sacrifice and his love for his men deserve our best admiration. India may well feel proud of her sons like him.

CHAPTER XII

SRI RASH BEHARI BOSE AS DICTATOR

1—The Chaos

After the arrest of General Mohan Singh and some other Army officers a state of chaos and confusion prevailed. The Indian National Army had been dissolved by the General and attempts to revive it by Sri R.B. Bose only met with partial success. The civilian element of the League had also many complaints about its working. The vacancies on the Council of Action had not been filled up. The Japanese Govt. had not made any formal declaration, clarifying in full the policy of Japan towards India. On the other hand, they were frequently interfering in the affairs of the League. The Iwakuru Kikan had established direct contact with minor workers and members of the League, thus undermining its discipline, prestige and strength. It had also organized an Indian Youth Movement. It was thought that third-rate persons, who were puppets of the Japanese and were in their pay had come to the forefront. The real Independence Movement had receded in the background.

In the critical discussions of early Dec. 1942, Sri N. Raghwan, President of the I.I.L. Malaya Branch, had called an emergency meeting of the state Branch Presidents. This meeting was held at Penang on the 8th and 9th Dec. and after hearing Sri Raghwan in detail decided unanimously that the movement should be carried on and complete support be given to Sri R.B. Bose, President Council of Action, but he be requested to secure a clarification of all matters by Tokyo Govt. at the earliest possible date and any further forward move should be decided only after such clarification. In spite of this decision, signs of internal disintegration, as a result of doubts and difficulties were not wanting. The following letter submitted to the President Council of Action by the President and members of the Territorial Committee Malaya, would throw some light on the situation prevailing at this period and the concern and uneasiness of the sponsors of the Movement over its impending failure :

Syonan, 21st February, 1943.

The President,
Council of Action,
INDIAN INDEPENDENCE LEAGUE,
Syonan.

SIR,

We, the President and members of the Territorial Committee of Malaya, have the honour to send you the accompanying Memorandum decided upon by us at our sittings in Penang from 18th to 21st February 1943.

The matters raised in this Memorandum have been those troubling us for some time past and considered by us very carefully and in detail at our said sittings. In presenting this Memorandum to you we would like, lest we should be misunderstood, to make our position clear. Most of us are persons who have been engaged in originating and organising the Indian Independence League Movement in this part of East Asia ever since December, 1941. It is indeed a matter of pain to us that even after more than a year of working, we are still in the stage of evolving understandings on principles, instead of working on details. It is a matter of personal faith and conviction to us that the Indian Independence Movement should be worked to a complete success. With this object in view we have been striving hard in spite of difficulties, but we have at present come to a stage when we find that our objective will not be achieved, if some of the present tendencies are not checked in time, and the Movement galvanised into fresh activity by creating internal unity and confidence and also by securing a full, whole-hearted and correct assistance and co-operation from the Iwakuro Kikan and other Japanese authorities. It is with this end in view that we are forwarding to you this Memorandum.

We hope that we shall not be considered as mere critics, light-hearted or intentionally attempting to sabotage a Movement which we believe in, in the service of which we have sacrificed our time and energy, and for the furtherance of which we stand committed. In fact, to one and all of us this Movement is one of life and death. We therefore request you most respectfully to give this, our Memorandum, your closest attention and consideration and to secure for us a satisfactory solution of the various doubts and difficulties raised therein. We regret that in spite of repeated attempts by us we could not have the privilege of your presence and advice at our sittings.

We hope we have put in only important matters on which we cannot make compromises without compromising our principles and our conscience. It is our belief that in solution of our difficulties and the establishment of complete confidence in mutual relations, lies the resucitation and future expansion of this great Movement, and it is in that connection we have definitely come to the conclusion that we shall have to stand down and let the Branch be run by others if there cannot be any change for the better, any change resulting in the solution of our difficulties and the prevention of future problems of similar nature.

We hope that you will make every effort to help us, and pray that your efforts will be crowned with success. If unsuccessful, we regret we shall have no other option except to tender our own resignations.

Yours in service,

N. Raghavan, President, Malaya Branch; S. C. Goho, Member, Ex. Council; M.K. Lukshumeyah, Member Ex. Council; John A. Thivy, President, Perak Branch, J.N. Bhaduri; Palayil Gopi; D.K. Majumdar; K. P. K. Menon; G. Maganlal ; O. A. R. Arunachalm Chettiar; M. K. Ramachandran; N.K. Menon; S.N.K. Nagappa.

Summary of Memorandum

1. A formal and solemn declaration from the Japanese Government clarifying its policy towards India at the earliest.

2. There should be full co-operation and co-ordination between the civilian and the military sides of the Movement. They should be educated to feel as one.

3. In the matter of recognition of the I. N. A, the civilian members of the I. I. L. should be consulted and their help should be accepted in the matter of expansion of the I. N. A. from amongst surplus volunteers and prisoners of war.

4. The department of information and publicity work should be left entirely in the hands of the Malaya branch of I. I. L., with such advice as may be found necessary of the Iwakuru Kikan.

5. No parties, other than the accredited leaders of the League should receive the confidence of the Japanese and made use of for work in connection with India and Indians.

6. Vacancies in the Council of Action be filled up at the earliest opportunity.

7. Generous assistance should be given to the Malaya Branch of the I. I. L. by the Japanese in the solution of its local difficulties and problems such as education, wages, toddy, labour employment and ecnomic existence and development.

8. It was the agreed policy of the Kikan to take no direct action in matters connected with the Indian community except when asked for by the League. Therefore the attempt to organize an Indian Youth Movement by the Kikan should be stopped.

9. In order to secure unity among Indians. stringent action should be taken against those Indians, who are guilty or reasonably suspected of activities that are bound to injure Indian unity, Indo-Japanese friendship and other vital objects of this Movement and effective assistance should be given by all Japanese authorities in the pursuit of this policy.

10. Similar assistance should be given by the Japanese to the League regarding the collection of donations from the Indian community. Those who are hostile to the Movement or are showing only lip-sympathy should be made to pay.

11. In order to secure more efficient and more united working and success in the common objectives we have in view (a) there should be more of mutual confidence between the Japanese side and the Indian side ; (b) that the Indian Independence Movement should not even appear to have been influenced, run or directed by any one other than Indians ; (c) that there should be a perfect understanding by the Indian Independence League of Japan's exact policy towards India and the methods and means of working out that policy and that for such understanding the Japanese side do give us effective co-operation ; (d) that the principal men of action should be taken into confidence with reference to Japan's plans in advising and assisting the Movement for securing its objective ; (e) with regard to any Japanese action concerning Indians, this Movement

should be taken into confidence ; (f) that before taking any military action against the British in India there should be mutual consultations and discussions between the Indian leaders vitally interested in the Movement and the Japanese advisers and experts as partners in common enterprise.

12. No further forward move is to be made, until the conditions specified above are fulfilled.

13. If satisfactory solution of these difficulties and problems is not possible, all the members of the Territorial Committee and Presidents of various branches would resign.

This ultimatum did not have the desired effect. Sri Rash Behari Bose got it into his head that some persons wanted to break up the Movement and he must frustrate their move. He thought that he would be able to remedy all the difficulties by contacting the Japanese High Command at Tokyo. So he began to clear off the obstacles. Sri Raghavan was forced to resign. Dr. M. K. Lukshumeyah succeeded him as President of the Malaya branch. Other members did not resign, as they thought that their resignations would give facilities to the Japanese to put people of their own choice on the committee and make anti-nationalistic propaganda through such a body. Headquarters of the I. I.·L., were transferred from Bangkok to Singapore, which was to be the base for future operations.

2. The Flame is Kept Burning.

Sri Rash Behari Bose re-organized the Indian National Army under Lt. Col. J. K. Bhonsle, who was appointed Director of Military Bureau. Lt. Col. M. Z. Kiani was made the Commandar of the Army. Training Centres were opened at Singapore, Kuala Lumpur and Rangoon and Col. Ehsan Qadir was put in charge of these. Intensive propaganda was carried on in the civil population as well as the Indian Army (Prisoners of War) by lectures, pamphlets, newspapers and broadcasts.

Sri Rash Behari Bose had virtually become a dictator. No wonder that could not achieve much. Circumstances were such that he was helpless. The Japanese were at that time at the height of their power. It was not possible to get justice from them. Mr. Bose was looking for the opportune time. His country men in the Far East, not realizing his helplessness, were throwing stones at him, but it goes to his credit that he did not let the movement die, in spite of obstacles and setbacks and was able to hand over to Netaji Subhas Chandra Bose a foundation, on which he built a grand edifice.

The following scheme issued by Sri R. B. Bose on April 3, 1943, for immediate adoption would show, what he was doing during this period and what were his future plans :

Owing to a series of "crises" and resignations, the general public has begun to entertain doubts regarding the progress of the Indian Independence Movement. But the fact is that the Movement was never slow in its forward march irrespective of obstacles, impediments and "crises." The time has, however, come when we must examine the background and the surrounding circumstances under which the Movement came into being and I find these factors need radical changes.

Whereas in June, 1942, India was pressing for independence from the British, to-day she is fighting for it against Britain, both spiritually and physically. It was to increase the physical pressure against the British war effort that Mahatama Gandhi recently risked his very life. The collapse of the British war-effort would have meant the retreat of the Anglo-American forces now in contact with the Japanese forces on the Indian border. The extent to which the British forces retire is the extent to which the Japanese forces advance ; and that contact cannot be broken till one side is defeated. What is obvious to us, is obvious to the Indian National Congress. The Congress has considered the consequences and the choice.

The safeguards and assurances made for which we asked in June 1942, are therefore now not necessary. Our job is only to convert the potential strength of the Congress into an actuality and help the Congress in establishing a National Government. The League is not a State, but only the begetter of a State. The future constitution of India as well as the relation of the Indian National Government with Japan will be decided by the Congress itself.

In the past we have followed a system of collective responsibility and elections similar to that adopted by the Congress in peace-time to wrest political control by a process of evolution. But now our object is revolution. In the past the resignation of a member or members had resulted in the dislocation to certain extent of vital departments, Civil or Military. This may be tolerated in peace-time, but never in time of war. My immediate concern is to maintain the League as a fighting organisation. The following interim plan has, therefore, been drawn up to put the League on a war footing.

1. **Introduction**: Freedom cannot be won only by having a longing for it. The success of each Branch of the Indian Independence League will be judged from the number of young men it can educate and train as potential fighting men for the independence of India. The League Branches, therefore, have three main functions : (1) The political awakening of the masses with a view to producing a body of patriots with a revolutionary spirit. (2) To obtain the financial and moral support of all those who cannot take active part in the Movement. (3) To undertake due share of social uplift and relief work without getting involved in local administrative problems. To give concrete shape to item No. 1, a Youth Section will be started immediately. A Women's Section with its own President is to be started wherever practicable. A movement for boys and girls under 17 should also be started. In all Indian Schools Hindustani should be taught as primary language. National Anthem (Bande Mataram) and other patriotic songs shall be sung and significance of daily saluting of the National Flag taught. The body of spirited young people so produced will help in the other activities of the League.

2. **Naujawan Section (Youh Section), 18 to 30 years:** The object is to train Indian youths in East Asia to (1) become revolutionary soliders in the fight for India's independence and (2) to behave as free citizens who with their example will foster the spirit of independence among the inhabitants of occupied territories. It is suggested that where the Vice-Presidents of the local Branches are willing to serve

the National cause actively, they themselves may take over the Youth Section, otherwise suitable young men shall be appointed by the Presidents concerned.

3. **Syllabus:** The following is issued as guide. Time table and periods of training will, of course, vary according to the facilities in each centre.

(i) Weapon Training,—Rifle, Pistol, Grenade, Tommy ·Gun ; A.R.P.; Hygiene Meetings ; Singing of Indian National Anthem : Hoisting of Indian National Flag ; Bicycle trips to places 30 or 40 miles away; Cooking own food; Entertainment—National and Social Dramas.

(ii) Physical Training—Labour, building of wooden bridges, swimming, digging slit trenches, rowing, games.

(iii) Education—Teaching of Hindustani, significance of the War of Greater East Asia, Geography Topography, maps with special reference to India, weak points in British War organisation, and civil administration in India. History of British aggression in India, study of lives of Congress leaders.

(iv) National Discipline—Obey before you command, Spirit of sacrifice, Building of Character, Self-reliance, Right living, Right thinking, Spiritual training, Love for country and elders, Ordinary Military Discipline, Punctuality.

(v) National Culture—Common manners and customs, Army salute, Common food.

(vi) Uniform—Khaki shirt and shorts, Khaki Gandhi Cap with double fold, Tricolour rectangle 3″ × 2″ on the left arm.

4. **Organisation:** Unit of 10 = a Section ; 4 Section = a Platoon; 4 Platoons = a Company; 5 Companies = a Battalion; 3 Battalions = a Regiment; 3 Regiments = a Formation. For the present each Branch should aim at a maximum of one Company at the discretion of the Territorial President. The training will be the entire responsibility of the League Branch and should be carried out on the most economical lines, *e.g.*, those who can afford should be encouraged to meet their own expenses. The Naujawan Section is a popular movement run on the lines of the Boy Scout Movement. Owing to a shortage of Khaki cloth, uniforms may be difficult to obtain, but work should nevertheless begin at once. A tour of inspection will be arranged by this Headquarters during the month of April. Local Presidents will be informed of the programme of the tour, so that they can put their requirements, if any, to the touring party.

5. **Training Centres for · Youth Workers:** (a) Azad School, Syonan: An experimental school for training 50 youth workers will be started at Syonan with effect from the 15th April, 1943. The first course will last two months, at the end of which these trained workers will be available for posting to the Naujawan Section of the various

Branches. (b) Swaraj Youths Training Institute, Rangoon: The Burma Branch is running its own centre at Rangoon on the lines of the Azad School, Syonan. (c) Bharat Youth Training Centre, Kuala Lumpur: Provides spiritual and military training to selected young men of the Youth Sections from all Branches in East Asia. At present 961 youths are under training and will be ready for disposal by the end of June, 1943.

The present scheme for actual military training is for 10,000 volunteers to be trained by the end of this year. In view of the limited training staff that can be spared by the Indian National Army and the expenditure involved, not more than 5,000 youths can be trained at one time. If accommodation is available, the Kuala Lumpur Centre will be expanded to accomodate these 5,000. Otherwise, more centres will be opened to accommodate that number.

The following approximate quota should be kept ready by the middle of June:—Thailand 1,000, Burma 1,000, Malaya 1,000, Hongkong and Shanghai 1,000, Borneo and Sumatra 1,000, and Java, Philippines, Celebes 1,000—total 6,000. All will not be absorbed in the I.N.A. Some will go to schools such as the Officers Training School or the Civil Administration School, while others will go back as fully trained instructors for training the youths in each territory in East Asia. The names of trained personnel will be put on the list of reserve volunteers to be called up when required. Territorial Branches will please inform this Headquarters of the number of youths likely to be forthcoming during 1943. Pocket money at the rate of 8 dollars per head will be given to all those undergoing training at the above centres.

4—SINGAPORE CONFERENCE.

To get a constitutional sanctity for his actions, Sri Rash Behari Bose convened another Conference of Indians in East Asia. It was held at Singapore from the 27th to 30th April 1943. Some extracts from his Presidential address would show how zealous he was to put the League on war footing and how averse he was to "lengthy arguments and unnecessary discussions:"

"It is with mingled feelings of joy and regret that we are meeting to-day to discuss ways and means for the liberation of our Motherland. This is the third time within a short period of one year that we are meeting for one and the same purpose.

I used the words "feelings of joy and regret"—joy because our enemy is being consistently defeated by the Imperial Nippon forces and thus the British chain of Imperialism which is strangling India is being weakened daily and our hopes of independence are brightening; regret, because the actions of some of my colleagues have marred temporarily the speedy progress of our Movement. But with the help of Almighty God all the difficulties have been overcome, the whole Movement has been rejuvenated and placed on a more solid ground than hitherto and I can assure you that if I continue to receive your full support and co-operation, our success is at hand.

Before going any further I shall repeat my words of warning which I gave in the very opening chapter of my speech at the Bangkok Conference. I wish to reiterate the same words, as I hope that it will **not be** necessary for us to meet again before the liberation of India. I said thus: However, if I have obeyed your command and taken this chair in spite of my knowledge of the intricacies of the problems that may confront me. I have been prompted to do so by my great faith in your sincere desire to put your heads togeher and to come to useful decisions without wasting much of your time on unnecessary discussions and arguments. I was prompted by the experience of the Tokyo Conference to give these words of warning but, despite all that, the result of the deliberations of the Bangkok Conference is well known to you. To remedy the shortcomings of the last Conference, it has been necessary for me to call you the representatives of different territories in East Asia, and also the representatives of the Indian National Army. Let us put our heads together once again and work out a plan which should be very short and effective in our organisation and the progress of the Movement. It is a time for action and not words, so you must avoid all lengthy arguments and jugglery of words. Before working out a plan you must remember two points, (a) that Japan is at war and we can expect only what can conveniently be given to us because their needs are above ours and (b) we are preparing to get into action very soon, so the constitution should be as brief and simple as possible.

I appeal to you my friends who have come to participate in this Conference, to divorce all party feelings, suspicions and prejudices and make every effort, so that when you conclude your session, you have a most effective and workable plan of action for Indian freedom, so that we can start our work immediately after this Conference and march ahead.

I hope you have realised the shortcomings of the last two Conferences and will keep aside all old and complicated ideas which are nothing more than mere obstacles in the progress of this revolutionary movement and will work out a simple and straightforward plan which will leave no room for future disturbance.

This is a revolution and there is an international conflagration all round us and I know you will all agree there is no time for discussion and argument. So I advise you once again to sit down and create something which will revolutionize the whole Movement. The masses are itching for action but our existing constitution is so cumbersome and impracticable that we cannot move an inch. All plans should be made on the basis of self-sufficiency because this is our Movement and the major part of it should be workable by us.

In the name of four-hundred million starving Indians for whom you have pledged to lay down your life, I appeal to you once again to create the atmosphere of brotherhood, trust each other and have mutual understanding for this common end of ours. Your plan of action should be such that, as far as possible, only full time workers could be permitted function—people who will be ready to make decisions day and night and from day to day, people who should be ready to serve anywhere and in any capacity, people who will be ready to bear all personal inconveniences of sleeping on the ground, going without food, and, travelling on foot or travelling by whatever conveyance may be available.

Every League Branch should be so constructed and organized that every worker from the Chairman downwards should as far as possible, be a full time self-sacrificing person who should be prepared to bear all hardships and should be prepared to work in the firing line when called upon to do so. Every League official should try to undergo a complete course of military training. May God help you in your efforts!"

Major General Iwakuro also attended the Conference and explained the Japanese side of the matter. But his speech, far from inspiring any confidence, was more of a threat. He wanted the I. I. L. and I. N. A. to be managed by only such people, who believed in the sincerity of Japan. He considered all others as elements of hostile nature and wanted to treat them accordingly.

The most important resolutions passed at the Conference were :

(1) That the Indian National Army is the Army of the Indian Independence League and all officers and men of the I.N.A. as well as all members of I.I.L. shall owe allegiance to the League.

(2) That the entire Indian Independence Movement be placed on a war footing immediately and that the constitution of the I. I. L. be so altered as to enable it to discharge its vital war duties with the utmost speed and efficiency.

Accordingly the written constitution passed at the Bangkok Conference was amended. The most outstanding feature of the new constitution was that the President was invested with almost dictatorial powers, including the right to nominate his own successor, the power to alter, amend or rescind any previous decisions made by him, including any decision arrived at in this Conference and general control over all the branches of the I. I. L. and I. N. A. He was empowered to deal with all the matters, not provided for by this Conference.

But the President did not get much time to work out these decisions, as he left for Tokyo early in June to have discussions with the high Japanese officials and get the clarification of some matters. He had also learnt that Sri Subhas Chandra Bose was coming to the Far East and he went to Tokyo to bring him back to Malaya. He returned early in July, with Sri Subhas Chandra Bose and entrusted all the work to him.

4. Fifth Columnist and Sabotage activities.

From the very start of the Movement. there was some talk of infiltration into India and doing secret propaganda. In the first Singapore Conference March 9, 1942, it was decided to leave this work to experts. After this we do not hear anything about it in the proceedings of the India Independence League.

It seems that most of this work had been taken over by the Japanese themselves. Sri Raghwan started the Swarajya institute in Penang in the spacious building of Free School Greenland. It imparted Military and Fifth Columnist training to the civilians. About 100 young men joined the institute, which was under the charge of Col. Alaggapan. Five Officers of the I. N. A. were appointed for the Military Training, one of them being Col. Sangha.

During the crisis of Dec. 1942, the Japanese decided to send these youngmen to India, for sabotage work. Sri Raghavan came to know of this beforehand and warned them not to move, without the knowledge of the Council of Action. Nevertheless some of them were sent and remain untraced up to this time. Sri Raghawan closed the Swarajya Institute as a protest against the high-handed action of the Japanese. This was also a factor in accentrating the gulf between the I. N. A. and the Japanese.

There were some other revolutionaries, who were working directly under the guidance of the Japanese for the above purpose. From the outset they had not associated themselves with the Indian Independence League and were connected with the Japanese Kikan. Most prominent of these was Baba Usman Khan, who had as his assistants Baba Bannerji at Rangoon and Master Chopra at Penang. Later, after leaving the Swarajya Institute, Col. Sangha also formed a similar party at Batu Farangi. Panjabi Youths, mostly Sikhs joined this Movement. They were given training in receiving and sending wireless messages and doing underground work.

After the arrival of Netaji Subhas Chandra Bose, he took over all these sections under his control. Some of these men were sent to India as spies through submarines or parachutes to contact Indian revolutionaries at home and to foster anti-British feelings in the Country. Most of them came into the hands of the British, were tried and sentenced to death or long imprisonments. Sri S. L. Mozamdar Chittagon; Sri T. P. Kumarn Nayyar Malabar, Sri Ramu Never Ramnad (Madras). There were three or four batches of such spies. Comrade Zahur Ahmad, Sheikhupura, Mr. Mohd. Atta, S. Ajaib Singh, Amritsar; S. Mohinder Singh and perhaps a dozen more were executed in 1943. Ten of these undergoing sentences of 40 years each were recently (Nov. 5, 1946) released from the Punjab Jails They are :—

(1) Col. S.N. Chopra, Hafizabad. (2) Lt. Kanwal Singh Hissar. (3) Lt. Kartar Singh Charsada. (4) Lt. Ram Dulare. (5) Lt. Bhagwat Gautam Gorakhpur. (6) Lt. Sohan Singh Lahore. (7) Lt. Sadhu Singh Amritsar. (8) Lt. Ganga Singh of Nangal Gam, Amritsar. (9) Lt. Sham Lal Pandey Meerut. (10) Lt. Ardheshwar Roy Gorakhpur.

After the arrest of General Mohan Singh, Col. Gilani also came to Penang, with a handful of his men and joined these activities. He took over the command of a school for training I. N. A. propagandists for infiltration into India. About a dozen of his men were sent to India by a submarine. Immediately on landing India, they handed themselves over to British authorities and gave very useful information to them.

Before concluding this chapter, we may do well to sum up the relations of the Japanese to the Independence Movement. The fact is that the Japanese were never sincere in their intentions towards Indians. They wanted to exploit the Indian Independence Movement and the Indian National Army for their own purpose. They did not allow the I. N. A. to grow and did equip it with sufficient arms or ammunition. They issued guns to the I. N. A. without any optical or mechanical instruments, without which it was not possible to fire these guns with any degree of accuracy. Tanks and armoured cars, supplied to the I. N.A., were fit only for ceremonial parades and propaganda photographs. It seems that they were afraid of making the I. N. A too powerful.

The real intentions of the Japanese were to use the Indian soldiers for propaganda work and as spies. They were also used to make up the deficiency of the Japanese soldiers and to defend various islands for the Japanese. And even in performing these duties, then Indian soldiers were given a minor role. The Japanese divided them into groups of eight or ten and placed them directly under the command of the Japanese officer. The treatment meted out to these men, in some cases was harsh and brutal.

General Mohan Singh wanted that the Indian prisoners-of-war who had not joined the I. N A. should be treated well, and should be kept under his command. The Japanese refused to agree to these demands and employed some of the prisoners-of-war as labourers in various islands. Their treatment was most inhuman and barbaric in most cases.

Even after the arrest of General Mohan Singh, the Japanese did not nive up their game of exploitation. They set up a counter organization dalled the Indian Youth Movement and started training centres for the civilians under the supervision of Japanese officers. These camps were put directly under the Indian Independence League and not under the I. N. A. Thus the Japanese tried to create ill-feelings between civilian and the military sections of the Movement.

It is clear that the Japanese had never any interest or anxiety for the freedom of India. They had their own axe to grind. They wanted to drive the British out of India for their own safety, for as long as the British held India and could use it as a base for operation, the Japanese Empire was never safe. To achieve their purpose, they wanted to use the I. N. A. and the Indians of East Asia in their own way. The Indians wanted to help and take the help of the Japanese for their own interest—that of securing the independence of their motherland. The Japanese by helping Indians were doing no favour to India. On the other hand, as long as the Japanese were at the height of their glory and success and the I. N. A. was helpless they went on exploiting it. Even after the arrival of Sri Subhas Chandra Bose they took comparatively poor interest in the welfare of I. N. A. in the matter of supply of rations, arms, medicine and other equipment and in affording other facilities to it, but the towering and impressive personality of Netaji made it impossible for him to use the assistance of the Japanese to his own advantage without undermining the prestige of India.

Netaji Subhash Chandra Bose

Supreme Commandar of Indian National Army

I. N. A.'s Marching Song

Kadam kadam barhaye ja, Khushi ke geet gaye ja.
Yeh zindgi hai Qaom ki, Tu Qaom pe lutaye ja.
Tu Sher-i Hind age barh, Marne se tu kabhi na dar.
Falak talak utha ke sar, Joshe Vatan barhaye ja.
Himmat teri barhti rahe, Khuda teri sunta rahe.
Jo samne tere chareh, Tu khak men milaye ja.
Chalo Dilli pukar ke, Qaomi nishan sambhal ke,
Lal Qile par garh ke, Lahraye ja, Lehraye ja.

Yeh Zindgi hai Qaom ki,
Tu Qaom pe lutaye ja.

Indian
Independence Movement
in East Asia

PART II

Marching to Delhi

By YONE NOGUCHI

Translated by himself from the Japanese

I

"Delhi, Delhi, to Delhi !"
The war-cry replies to a storm of cannon-balls,
And praises the might of powder and smoke.
Leap over the terror that trenches command,
And entrust your bones to a hill of the mother-land !
In a blazing sand your palm grasps,
You will find all the rewards that Death bestows,
And the hunger you suffered from the hundreds of years
Can't be filled till an Independence-feast is spread.

II

"Delhi, Delhi, to Delhi."
The fighting array beats its wings ;
The bugles begin to cry.
The war-wagons groan wild ;
The cannons send up their sacrifice-fire,—
Oh, the heroes the crusaders to win liberty, they go to the front!
They know a night-feast of victory is waiting behind,
And their hunger will be filled at last ;
They know their own history have now to begin.

III

"Delhi, Delhi, to Delhi "
Krishna bids them to burn in lore of the mother-land,
Putting a holy fire on their own souls.
The glory of many thousand years comes to life again,
And will create over the Ganges a rainbow-bridge.
Lo, the snowy citadels of Himalayan peaks
Drive back law-breakers, forbids them not to invade again.
The depthless water of the Bengal gulf
Gets graves ready and waits for their coming.

IV

"Delhi, Delhi, to Delhi !"
The war-cry rings through India's whole land ;
People's blood boils and seethes,
Making an arched squall of anger,
That will never fail to ruin the enemy's camp.
Lo, the anti-British war-men go in majestic line,—
The crusaders to take liberty by force are they !
Ah, what enemy can defy Heaven's will ?

CHAPTER I

THE MAN OF THE HOUR

The Indian Independence Movement was marching slowly on, but all realized that the progress was not satisfactory or encouraging in any way. The lack of a leader, who could inspire confidence and infuse fresh life and vigour in the movement, was being keenly felt. Neither the Japanese nor the Indians could put up with these half-hearted measures; something active had to be done to achieve India's Independence. The plunge had to be taken and a man had to be found, who could shoulder the responsi bility of taking the plunge and bringing it to a successful close. That man was Sriyut Subhash Chandra Bose—the great Indian patriot and revolutionary leader, who had once been the President of the Indian National Congress and was the accredited leader of its left wing—the Forward Block.

Sjt. Subhash Chandra Bose had left his home at Calcutta early in January 1941, disguised as a Pathan and reached Berlin via Peshawar, Kabul and Russia. As early as March 1942 he was mentioned as a likely person to lead the struggle. In the Conference held at Singapore on March 9, 1942, Swami Satyananda Puri had proposed that Sjt. Bose be requested to lead the Independence Movement. But at that time the delegates were mainly concerned with the Tokyo Conference.

The Reception Committee of the Indian Independence Conference Bangkok had invited Sjt. Bose to participate in the conference and he had sent a congratulatory message expressing his inability to come. Majority of the delegates to the conference wanted that he should be declared formal leader of the Movement and should guide its activities from Berlin. But for obvious reasons of lack of communication, and the difficulties in Sjt. Bose's coming to East Asia, the matter was not pressed and the conference merely passed a resolution requesting him to come to East Asia and appealing to the Imperial Government of Japan to obtain facilities for this purpose.

For obvious reasons, the Japanese Government was not very keen in obliging the Indians in this matter. They would better not take any risks and carry on with Sri Rash Behari Bose.

But the arrest of General Mohan Singh on 29th December 1942 and the subsequent dissolution of Indian National Army was followed by great pessimism. The strength and solidarity of the Movement had been broken. Dissentions prevailed in the Indian Independence League and the Army, The Japanese felt that there was lack of willing co-operation from the general Indian public, whose faith on them had been shattered. The Japan Government was also feeling difficulties in the matter of administration.

Under the circumstances, there was no other way of keeping up the Movement except by bringing Sjt. Bose to East Asia and the Japan Government set to it in right earnest. Of course difficulties of safe conveyance were there, and it took a long time before he could reach East Asia. The submarine carrying him from Germany touched the shores at Penang on the first week of June 1943. There were rumours in Malaya of his being seen in Penang and responsible Japanese officers there, confirmed the news that Sjt. Bose was nearing Japan. Two weeks later, it was officially revealed by the Japan Government (on the 18th June 1943) that Sri Subhash Chandara Bose had arrived in Tokyo from Berlin. It was reported that he had called on General Tojo—the Premier of Japan—on June 14, and received his assurance of Japan's friendship and support for the freedom struggle, which he was called upon to lead.

Sri Subhash Bose's arrival in Japan was an epoch-making event. This thrilling news electrified the entire Greater East Asia and infused a new hope and greater enthusiasm in the sponsors of the Indian Independence Movement and the entire Indian community in East Asia. The Man of the Hour had appeared on the scene !

CHAPTER II

SUBHASH BOSE IN JAPAN

Sjt. Subhash Chandara Bose started his activities just after his arrival in Japan. He saw General Tojo on June 14, interviewed the press and addressed a series of appeals to India. He broadcast the following address to his countrymen in East Asia on the 18th June 1943 :—

While I am in Tokyo, I desire to address a few words to you, and I have no doubt that you will give them due consideration. In the first place I desire to thank you most heartily for the warm and enthusiastic welcome that you have given me on the occasion of my public appearance in East Asia, and for the assurance you have given me of your wholehearted support to our efforts to liberate our dear Motherland. I feel overwhelmed at this manifestation of your burning patriotism and spirit of sacrifice. I have received numerous telegraphic, telephonic and postal messages from you direct, while other messages I have read in the press and all these messages have given me great joy and satisfaction.

You know that I have always been an optimist. Nevertheless, I must say that the response that I have received has exceeded my fondest expectations. I can only say in reply that I am proud of you. Since the outbreak of the war in Europe and East Asia I have been saying repeatedly that we Indian people, could not have wished or even dreamt of a better combination of circumstances for helping us achieve our liberty. When world forces are helping us in this way, our task automatically becomes very much easier than what it would have been otherwise. This fact should futher strengthen our self-confidence and optimism and hearten us considerably in the fight that lies ahead of us. I am overjoyed to see that you have already realised, the responsibility of winning freedom. The main work lies at home. It is but natural that they should bear the brunt of the burden and they have been doing so already. But, at the same time, every Indian—no matter where he is living at the present time—has a duty towards his country and he must contribute his due share towards the final victory.

I am convinced that India cannot hope to be free until Indians living abroad perform their duty in this momentous world-crisis. Owing to the fact that the Tripartite Powers have been giving their fullest support to Indian independence, it is comparatively easy for Indians living in an Axis country or in countries controlled by the Axis powers to play their part in the national struggle. Consequently, among Indians who are now abroad, I expect, Indians living in Axis countries or in countries controlled by the Axis powers, will render maximum service to the motherland. Here in East Asia you have seen yourself how deep is the interest in, and sympathy for, Indian independence. The readiness of the Imperial Nippon Government and nation to render any assistance in our national struggle, we may need, has lightened our task to a considerable degree. Consequently, there can be no possible excuse why any Indian in East Asia should not put his whole might in the present struggle.

But though the Axis powers in general, and Nippon in particular, are prepared to help us at any time and have been actually doing so already, the task of liberating India is ours, and ours alone. That responsibility we shall not cast on anybody else because that would be against our national honour. Moreover, we have no right to ask for or expect help from any quarter until we ourselves have first of all done our very utmost. Our sisters and brothers at home have been doing their very best in the circumstances in which they have been placed. But the enemy is ruthless and desperate and he is armed to the teeth. Against such a brutal foe, no amount of civil disobedience, or sabotage, or revolutionary terrorism can be of any avail. If, therefore, we want to expel British power from India, we have to fight the enemy with his own weapons. The enemy has already drawn the sword—he must therefore be fought with the sword.

But it is not possible for our countrymen at home to organize an armed revolution and to fight the British army of occupation with modern arms. This task must therefore devolve on Indians living abroad—and particularly on Indians living in East Asia. Friends! If you compare the history of our national struggle with the histories and struggles in other parts of the world, you will realize we in India have up till now lacked one thing and one thing alone. We lack an organization whereby we can meet force with force. It is our task to supply this one want and thereby eliminate once and for all the only drawback in our national struggle. I therefore desire that all able-bodied Indians living in East Asia should volunteer to fight with me for the liberation of our Motherland.

This is our supreme task and duty, before which no other type of service counts for much. All those countrymen of mine who are prepared to fight for the liberation of India will please get in touch with me at once, directly or through their local organizations. I am confident that with the help of my countrymen in East Asia, I shall be able to organize such a gigantic force as will be able to sweep away British power from India, in conjunction with those who have been already fighting at home. The hour has struck, and every patriotic Indian must advance towards the field of battle. When the blood of freedom-loving Indians begins to flow, India will attain her freedom."

Srijut Bose met at a Press Conference on June 19 and gave the following statement :—

Gentlemen! At the outset I may say that it is for me a great pleasure to offer you my cordial greetings, since I have been for a long time connected with journalism in my own country.

You may be wondering what has brought me to this part of the world and at such a time.

For many long years, British jails in India and Burma had been my residence. But the fact that today I am standing before you in the heart of Nippon instead of sitting idly in a prison house in India is symbolic of the new movement that is now sweeping over my country.

It was in accordance with the will of my countrymen that I left home and homeland more than two years ago and whatever I had done since then was also in accordance with their will.

During the last World War our leaders had been bluffed and deceived by the wily British politicians. That was why we took the vow more than 20 years ago never again to be deceived by them.

For more than 20 years my generation had striven for freedom and eagerly awaited the hour that has now struck—the hour that is for the Indian people, the dawn of freedom.

We know very well, such opportunity will not come again for another hundred years and we are therefore determined to make the fullest use of it.

Gentlemen ! We have so often heard of war that is being waged for the freedom of democracy. But you can very well imagine what my countrymen think of those Powers that talk of freedom and democracy and deny the same to one-fifth of the human race—the Powers that reply to the demand for liberty by terror and brutality and by the massacre of unarmed men, women and children. British Imperialism meant for India moral degradation, cultural ruin, economic impoverishment and political enslavement.

Is it any wonder, therefore, that the Indian people have at last solemnly resolved to end the British yoke ? The present world conflict means for the Indian people the struggle between the forces that want to maintain the *status quo* and those that are determined to overthrow it.

Can any one blame us if in such conflict our sympathy lies with those, Powers that stand for the change—for the New Order ? And when these Powers support our demand for freedom it is but natural that sympathy for them should deepen into enthusiastic support.

The Tripartite Powers have rendered the greatest help to Indian's struggle by waging war against our eternal foe. And they have earned our lasting gratitude by offering us not only sympathy but active support and assistance.

Nevertheless, it is our duty to pay for our liberty with our own blood. The freedom that we shall win, through our sacrifice and exertions, we shall be able to preserve with our own strength.

We, therefore, feel strongly that we should actively participate in the war against our common foe.

The enemy that has drawn the sword, must be fought with the sword. Civil disobedience must develop into armed struggle. And only when the

Indian people receive the baptism of fire on a large scale, will they qualify for their freedom.

Broadcast Address of Sri Bose from Tokyo on June 21, 1943.

Countrymen and Friends ! Since I spoke to you last, no important change has taken place in the general war situation. In the Western theatre, the Anglo-American forces have scored a success, and the fighting in North Africa has come to an end. Anglo-Americans have followed this up by occupying certain islands in the Mediterranean.

But to us, Indians, what is of primary importance is not what is happening at Tunis, Timbuctoo, or in Lampedusa or Alaska, but what is happening inside India and across our frontier.

What is of primary importance to us is that the much advertised reconquest of Burma has ended in a shameful retreat ; the Nippon army is standing on our eastern frontier ; and the Government of Nippon through its worthy Prime Minister, General Tojo, has repeatedly declared its fullest support to the Indian Independence, and its firm resolve to see that the Anglo-American forces and influence are expelled from India ; and lastly, the Nipponese Prime Minister has offered active assistance towards the Indian revolutionaries in their struggle for complete national independence.

What is also of obvious importance to India is the uprooting of British Imperialism in our country.

You know, as well as I do, that when this war broke out, some of our friends thought that the British Government would soon find itself in serious difficulties and that it would naturally be constrained to sue for peace with the Party that controlled the Cabinets in the majority of Provinces in British India.

According to these friends, all that the Congress had to do was to hold on till the British Government was compelled to make the first advance.

A year passed by, but there was no evidence of any change of heart on the part of the British tyrants. Then these friends decided to exert mild pressure on the British Government in an effort to bring about a compromise. In this, steps were taken, but no tangible results followed.

Even the fall of Singapore, the greatest disaster in British military history, according to Mr. Winston Churchill and Mr. Roosevelt, and the loss of Burma, could not bring about any appreciable change. British Imperialism remains inexorable. Men may come and men may go, empires may come and empires may go, but British Imperialism goes on for ever—that is what our rulers continue to think.

You may call it lack of statesmanship or political bankruptcy, or midsummer madness. But this midsummer madness has its own explanation.

The British Empire has grown out of India, The British people know, no matter to which political party they belong, that they need to reap all the resources of India. To them the Empire today means India. They are now fighting madder to preserve that Empire. The cost of recognising India's independence might amount to winning the war, but losing the Empire.

Consequently, no matter what fate besets Britain during the course of this war, the Englishman will endeavour to the very last to keep his Empire, that is, to hold on to India.

Therefore, if I may speak frankly, I would say that it is not a midsummer madness that the British politicians refuse to recognise India's independence though they are in a terrible plight ; it is midsummer madness that we should expect the Englishman to give up his Empire voluntarily !

There is another factor that is against the British Imperialists.

As the Foreign Minister of Germany said the other day, the British Empire had been losing one part of territory to its enemies and another part to its friends during the course of the present war. Moreover, in his frantic endeavour to maintain the Empire, John Bull is now bleeding himself white, making up the colossal loss by exploiting India more ruthlessly with the war effort.

Therefore, according to imperialistic logic, whatever may be the outcome of this war, it would be their endeavour to retain that hard grip over India.

Consequently, no Indian should ever cherish the illusion that one day England will be induced to recognise India's independence.

But that is not to say that British politicians will never again compromise with India.

Another attempt at compromise may be made at any time whether under pressure of a failing military situation, or in order to placate the liberal elements in England and America. But what I want to point out is that by compromise the British politicians will never recognise India's independence, but will only try to bluff the Indian people.

Protracted negotiations are only planned to side-track the campaign for independence and thereby undermine the national will, as they did between December 1941 and April 1942.

Negotiations which were carried on by Sir Stafford Cripps in India last year have done no harm to the British Government in any way. It only interrupted our struggle for freedom.

Therefore, we should, once and for all, give up hope against any compromise with British Imperialism. Our independence admits of no compromise. Freedom is won only when the British and their allies quit India for good. And those who really want liberty must fight for it and pay for it with their own blood.

Let us therefore carry on the fight for liberty, inside India and outside India, with all our strength and vigour.

Let us continue the battle with unshakable faith till the day that, under the combined attack of our friends and allies and of ourselves, the Anglo-American Imperialism—the British Empire—will be broken up and out of its ashes India will once again emerge as an independent nation.

In this struggle there is no going back, and there can be no faltering. We must march onward till victory is achieved and freedom won.

INQUILAB ZINDABAD !

Broadcast Address of S. C. Bose from Tokyo, on June 24, 1943.

Countrymen and Friends ! I want to deal in the first place with the meaning of this war, and the historical facts lying behind it. Well, this war is a clash between the forces that want to maintain *status quo* in the world and the new forces that are determined to destroy it in order to usher in a new order. The former includes the Anglo-American imperialistic powers that have been masquerading under the cloak of freedom and democracy. Victory to these imperialistic powers would mean the perpetuation of our servitude as well as the continued enslavement of many other unfortunate nations.

Some of my countrymen have been expecting that under the pressure of an international crisis, the imperialistic powers like Britain might be induced to recognise the independece of enslaved countries like India, but all such expectations have been completely falsified. Likewise, all attempts previously made by some people to avoid war, and somehow to arrive at a compromise between the two parties, have proved to be fruitless. The result is the present war, which is being fought to a finish, and there is every chance of its being a more prolonged struggle than the last World War.

In this titanic conflict our national interest clearly lies in allying ourselves with those young and virile nations, who are determined to overthrow the *status quo* and thereby give us a chance of winning our liberty.

It should be fully evident that the Tripartite Powers by fighting our age-long enemy and inflicting terrible defeats on him, have been indirectly helping our national struggle to a remarkable degree. If our enemy had not been mortally wounded by these Powers, our task of achiev'ng liberty would have been a hundred times more difficult than what it is to-d‿y. We are grateful for this, but we are even more grateful that the Tripartite Powers are not only content with giving us Indirect help, but have been offering active support and assistance in our fight for freedom.

I know that there are some countrymen of mine who, having been brought up in English institutions and having been influenced by English propaganda, doubt the merits of the Tripartite Powers. *I would ask those countrymen to put their trust in me. For the powerful British Government that has persecuted me all my life and has imprisoned me eleven times, has not been able to demoralise me. No power on earth can hope to do so. And if the wily, cunning and resourceful British Politicians have failed to cajole and corrupt me, nobody else can do so.*

In all the Axis countries I have visited, I have not only studied very closely the public opinion in regard to India, but I have also acquainted myself at first hand with the attitude and policy of the three Governments.

Friends ! The latest declaration of Premier Tojo made at the Imperial Diet on 16th June, 1943, which I had the privilege of hearing personally, following my interview with him on 14th June, was absolutely clear and unequivocal. In the course of that statement which will live in history for all time as an epoch-making declaration, His Excellency said : " Japan is firmly resolved to extend all means in order to help to expel and eliminate from India the Anglo-Saxon influences which are the enemy of the Indian people, and enable India to achieve full independence in the true sense of the term."

Friends ! I know that some anti-Axis people have been making efforts to mislead the Indian people by suggesting that it is unbelievable that the Axis Powers should become so generous as to support India's demand for independence. But to me the attitude of every Axis Power is traditionally both natural and easily understandable. To-day, the Axis Powers and India have a common enemy, and therefore a common interest and objective.

The Axis powers must, in their own interest and in order to ensure their own freedom and prosperity in the future, defeat and overthrow the British Empire. In order to achieve that aim they must expel Anglo-American Powers and influence from India, and they must do this even if the Indian people preferred to remain under the British yoke. Knowing, however, that the Indian people have been struggling for their freedom, the sympathy of the Axis Powers naturally goes out to them.

Moreover, if India could achieve her national emancipation from the British Empire, it will be of advantage to the whole world including the Axis Powers. Reason and commonsense should therefore easily comprehend why the Axis Powers have adopted so friendly an attitude towards the Indian Independence Movement.

Having been completely foiled in their anti-Axis and anti-Japanese propaganda, the Anglo-American Imperialists and their hirelings have fallen back on their last subterfuge.

Referring to Premier Tojo's repeated declarations, they have been saying that these declarations are the embodiment of policies intended to bluff the gullible and credulous people. There is an old saying in Sanskrit which you all know—*Atmawath Manyate Jagath*—which means that a man would judge the world according to his own nature. Being hypocrites themselves, these people think that everybody else is a hypocrite.

However, Premier Tojo has given the most effective and crushing reply to such vile propaganda by declaring to the whole world that before the end of the present year both Burma and the Philippines will have independence in reality. I wonder what new arguments our enemies can possibly invent for their anti-Axis propaganda when this year is out.

Countrymen ! You are aware that towards the end of 1940, since I saw that Mahatma Gandhi had at long last launched civil disobedience campaign, I felt that the honour and prestige of the Indian people had been vindicated, and it was necessary to plan the Indian revolution on a larger scale and in an effective manner in order to bring it to bear fruit.

But for that it was necessary to have information on the international situation and to establish contact with the Axis Powers and to secure the active assistance of our countrymen abroad.

To-day I am in a position to announce to you that all these objectives have been fully achieved.

Firstly, we know the international situation at first hand and we are therefore convinced of our ultimate victory.

Secondly, we know at first hand that the Axis Powers in general, and Japan in particular, are the best friends and allies that the Indian people now have for their struggle for freedom.

Thirdly, all Indians outside India who are not living in countries directly under the control of our enemies, have now been brought together into one well-built organisation. They are following closely developments inside India and on the other hand they are keeping unimpeded contact with international events.

They are making all possible preparations to bring at the right time the maximum assistance to you who have been carrying on this struggle at home in spite of internment, persecution and brutality.

Friends ! You may remember that I have in the past assured you more than once that when the hour strikes, I, and many others like myself, will be by your side to share the glory of fighting and suffering side by side and to share with you the joy of victory as well.

The British Broadcasting Corporation, through its speaker Mr. Brenwood, said that I did not have the slightest intention of fulfilling my pledge. I would like to tell them that my pledge, which had been given not to the B. B. C. but to my countrymen, would be redeemed to the fullness of time.

Now I have taken the third step and I am not far from the Indian frontier. No power on earth was able to hamper my movements since January 1941 ; and no power on earth will be able to prevent my crossing the frontier once again in order to participate in the last phase of our national struggle.

Countrymen and Friends ! In conclusion let me convey through you to our comrades in prison and in internment, my brotherly greetings. Tell them to be of good cheer. They have up held the honour and prestige of our country. Through their sufferings, they have declared to the whole world that enslaved India is at war with Britain.

I and all those who have been working outside India are proud of them. Not a day passes without our paying humble homage to their noble martyrdom. I assure them once again that their sufferings will not be in vain.

India shall be free—and before long. And a free India will throw open the prison gates so that her worthy sons may step out of the darkness of the prison cells into the light of freedom, joy and self-fulfilment.

INQUILAB ZINDABAD !
AZAD HIND ZINDABAD !

In all his statements and broadcasts from Tokyo, Subhash Chandra Bose stressed four main points :—

Firstly, that India's freedom must be won fighting, that the civil disobedience movement must develop into an armed struggle, that the Anglo-Americans have drawn the sword, which must be met with the sword.

Secondly, that the Britain would never, never grant the freedom of India : and India must not fall in the traps that may be set by the crafty British to sidetrack the independence movement.

Thirdly, that the victory of Nippon and the Axis Powers in Europe is assured, that Anglo-American propaganda is meant solely to bolster up their domestic morale and to deceive India ; and that the defeat of the Anglo-Americans is a certainty.

Fourthly, that Nippon and the Axis Powers in Europe are India's friends and allies ; that India must respond to the sincere offer of all-out aid pledged by Nippon for India's battle for independence ; that Nippon will fulfil her pledge of "full independence of India in the true sense of the term."

CHAPTER III

BOSE ASSUMES LEADERSHIP OF THE MOVEMENT

Just after the arrival of Sjt. S. C. Bose in Japan, it had been announced from Tokyo, that he was shortly coming to Malaya to lead the Indian. Independence Movement. The Indians were anxiously waiting for himn The air was surcharged with emotion, when Sjt. Subhash Chandra Bose, oe July 2, 1943, stepped off the plane from Tokyo at the Singapore Aerodrom and for the first time saw with his own eyes India's Army of Liberation (Azad Hind Fauj) drawn up on the Courtyard to provide him with a gaurd of honour. Leaders of the Indian Independence Movement (I. I. League) and representatives of the Indian National Army had also assembled at the courtyard to accord him a right royal reception. They were all conscious that they were witnessing a historic event in India's struggle for independence. Sri Subhash Bose himself was overcome with emotion when he addressed a few words to the Azad Hind Fauj (I. N. A.) and confessed to them that that day was a historic day in his life. He said to them, "The only thing, that we have been lacking so far in our fight for independence, is armed force to fight against the British. You, patriotic warriors have provided that armed force. Let us all march forward together, ready to lay down our lives and thus win the freedom of our Motherland." The men of the I. N. A. in reply gave their solemn pledge and assurance to Sjt. S. C. Bose by giving him three resounding cheers.

This was the first meeting between the Man of the Hour and the Army, which had been waiting for him.

Two days later, on the 4th July 1943, Syt. Subhash Bose formally assumed the leadership of the Freedom Movement and became President of the Indian Independence League in East Asia.

Remarkable scenes of patriotic fervour and enthusiasm were witnessed at the meeting of the Committee of Representatives of the Indian Independence League in East Asia held in Syonan on July 4, when Sri Subhash Chandra Bose assumed office as President of the League in East Asia. From early morning large crowds, not minding the steady drizzle, thronged all approaches to the Cathay Cinema, to catch a glimpse of their leader. Subhash Bose, on arrival at the Cinema accompanied by Rash Behari Bose, was greeted with thunderous ovation from the crowds. The Hinomaru (Rising Sun flag) and the Indian National tri-colour flag adorned the dais. On Subhash Bose's entry into the meeting hall, the whole assembly rose up and greeted him with cheers. From all parts of the hall, cries of "Subhash Bose Ki Jai," "Rash Behari Bose Ki Jai," "Mahatma Gandhi Ki Jai," "Maulana Abul Kalam Azad Ki Jai," and "Pandit Jawaharlal Nehru Ki Jai" rent the air.

The proceedings commenced with the garlanding of the two leaders by girl students of the Ramakrishna Mission. Miss S. N. Saraswathi delighted the gathering with the singing of Indian national songs. The following message of congratulations from Premier Tojo was read :—

"On the occasion of welcoming the great leader Sjt. Subhash Chandra Bose, the Indian Independence League in East Asia holds a meeting of the Committee of Representatives of Indians in East Asia at Syonan, which has been liberated from British bondage. With this welcome to Subhash Bose, you are taking a long stride towards decisive action with renewed and grim determination to achieve India's independence.

"On this occasion, I extend my most sincere congratulations because it is a happy augury not only for India but for all East Asia also. Since the outbreak of the Greater East Asia War, the Imperial Japanese forces have annihilated the enemy wherever he was found and, within a very short time, battered all the Anglo-American strategical points in this part of Asia At the same time, the bonds of unity among Japan, Manchukuo, China and Thailand have been strengthened, and they are irresistibly advancing towards the goal of the establishment of the sphere of co-prosperity in East Asia. With unshakable faith in ultimate victory and the triumph of justice, for which Japan is fighting, the accumulated wrongs and misdeeds of the British are going to be wiped out. Thus the brilliant dawn of Greater East Asia has arrived. This is the golden opportunity for India to liberate herself and such a rare opportunity will never occur again.

" With the outbreak of the Greater East Asia War, Indian nationalists in India rose against their British rulers, and India has thus already attained spiritual independence. The British Empire, which is gasping for a last breath, will, in desperation, choose any means to put off the day of their impending doom, and America is also stretching its devilish hands towards India. In a situation like this, it is by no means an easy task for Indians to achieve India's complete independence : but four hundred million Indians should unite into one solid body and win their own freedom and independenee with their own blood and toil.

" The sincere wish of Japan for the fulfilment of India's long cherished ambition of " India for Indians " has been proved beyond doubt by the repeated declarations of the Government of Nippon. Nippon is inflexibly determined to exhaust all her means to help India in achieving her independence which is the earnest desire of Indians. It is Japan's sincere wish that the active movement for the achievement of India's independence must be intensified both inside and outside India, and the Anglo-American forces must be driven out of every corner of India as early as possible. The world situation is becoming more complicated, and taking advantage of this, the Anglo-American enemies will no doubt intensify their intrigues. Traditionally Nippon is a country which invariably keeps faith where friends trust each other, and so is India.

" I sincerely wish that Indians will not be deceived by Anglo-American intrigues and miss the God-sent opportunity to win their freedom. I trust that Indians, with firm faith in the victory of Japan, Germany and Italy, will fight for justice and righteousness shoulder to shoulder with us. I firmly believe that this is the only way that Indians can hasten the glorious day of their freedom, and I sincerely wish them every success in their brave fight."

Amidst wild cheers of enthusiasm Shri Rash Behari Bose, the Father of the Indian Independence Movement in East Asia, rose to deliver his Presidential Address. He said :—

It is indeed a great pleasure for myself and to you all, that we meet today, so soon after our last conferenee in Syonan (Singapore). But, events are marching fast these days and our Movement for the sacred cause of Mother India has made enormous strides in the two months since our conference at the end of April, 1948. To-day, we are on the eve of the most vital, the most decisive, phase of our fight for the freedom of our Motherland. And I am confident that we are on the threshold of victory.

It is now one and a half years since the Indian Independence Movement was organised in East Asia. For all practical purposes, that historic day, December 8, 1941, when Japan unsheathed the sword of righteousness to destroy the Anglo-American imperialism and to liberate the Asiatic nations from bondage, that historic day marked the inception of the Indian Independence Movement in its present form. You do not expect me, on this occasion, to review the progress of our Movement, to enumerate our efforts, our successes and our failures. You know, we started from scratch, with nothing but our indomitable spirit of service to our Motherland. But soon we found sincere friends and powerful allies and our Movement gathered strength, thanks to your efforts and co-operation, thanks to the patriotic fervour of Indians throughout East Asia. And our most sincere gratitude is due to our Japanese friends, the Government of Japan, the local Military Authorities in every part of East Asia and to the Japanese nation in general.

As you all know very well, we have had our share of trials and tribulations, some trivial, others serious. But thanks to your grim resolve in the battle for India's freedom and to your patience and devotion to duty, our Movement survived all obstacles in its way and emerged with increased strength and solidarity. To-day, the Indian Independence League is an All East Asia Organization which is almost on a war footing. The League's Branches throughout East Asia are functioning smoothly and every Branch is contributing its share to the success of the great event now ahead of us. Friends ! I want to thank you from the very bottom of my heart for all the support, assistance, and co-operation extended to me by you and your colleagues, as well as by my compatriots throughout East Asia, in the fulfilment of the duties and responsibilities you have entrusted to me.

Friends ! I told you that we are now on the eve of a new phase of our fight for India's independence. For decades, India has been struggling against British domination and exploitation. Thousands of Indian patriots have laid down their lives in the cause of India's freedom ; and even at this very moment, all India is at war with Britain. As Mahatma Gandhi, our revered leader, has stressed, "This is a fight to the finish." And, with the help of Almighty God, the fight will be finished with the glorious victory of India and the ignominious defeat of India's enemies, the Anglo-Americans.

Friends ! A casual glance at world events to-day will show you what I mean. Within India, the Anti-British revolution has been going on for nearly eleven months. The British boasted that they would crush the revolution in no time ; but they have failed and failed miserably in spite of all the ruthless terror and repression they unleashed on India's freedom fighters. Beyond the frontiers of India, we Indians in East Asia are girding for battle to supplement the efforts of Indian Nationalists at home. And in support of us, for the assistance of India, we have powerful allies, the Japanese. It was only the other day, while I was at Tokyo that Prime Minister General Hideki Tojo re-affirmed Japan's pledge of all-out aid to India in the fight against the Anglo-American forces. And you will remember that Premier Tojo also made the categorical declaration that it is Japan's policy to assist India to attain full independence in the true sense of the term.

Friends and Comrades in-Arms ! Now you see why I am confident that India's victory is a certainty. As I have told you very often, the odds are in our favour—I mean in India's favour—and against our enemies, the Anglo-American enemies of India. This is our God-sent opportunity—an opportunity that we must take advantage of. For decades India fought Britain single-handed, but to day, India has powerful allies. Japan and her Axis partners in Europe are India's friends and allies. India is with them in this war. The victory of the Axis Powers means the freedom of India ; the victory of the Anglo-Americans means the slavery of India for hundreds of years to come. Therefore, as Indians, our duty is clear. For the sake of India's freedom, for the sake of justice and decency in this world, for the sake of a better order of human life and intercourse, we Indians must work and fight for the victory of Japan and the Axis powers. For, as I have just said, the victory of Japan and the Axis Powers means the victory of India, the freedom of four hundred million Indians, the glory of Asia and a new order in this world.

Friends ! When I left Syonan for Tokyo towards the end of May, I told you I would be back in about six weeks. And I am here now. I want to thank the Administrative Committee of the Headquarters for the most efficient manner in which they carried on the work during my absence and I want to thank you all for the warm reception you accorded me on my return.

To-day we meet here just two days after my return from Tokyo and naturally you would expect me to say something of what I saw and heard in Japan. Well, I was impressed by many things that I saw and heard during my brief sojourn in Japan. I was greatly impressed by the great sympathy for India's cause, on the part of the entire Japanese nation, from His Excellency the Premier down to the man in the street. The freedom of India is stressed on all sides and the entire Japanese nation is prepared to go all-out in helping India expel the Anglo-American enemies and to win the national independence. And you know for yourselves that Japan is fully confident of her ability to help us crush the Anglo-Americans in India. And as for the sincerity of Japan's policy, we have before us the historic example of Burma which will be independent very soon, and that of the Philippines which will emerge as a free country within the course of this year, 1943.

Friends ! This is India's golden opportunity—an opportunity the like of which may never again occur. If we take this opportunity, we save our Motherland, we save the four hundred millions of our compatriots from an alien tyranny that has been crushing them body and soul for over two hundred years. On the other hand, if we miss this opportunity ; we betray our Motherland ; we condemn our four hundred million brethren and the future generations of India, to slavery for ever. Now or never is our opportunity ; now or never is India's chance for freedom.

Friends and Comrades-in-Arms ! You might probably expect me to say something more of what I saw in Japan. Well, I saw in Japan a great and powerful nation in its grim resolve for victory. And remember what I told you just a little while ago ; Japan's victory means India's freedom, India's victory and glory.

In Nippon I saw mighty forces at work, forging weapons of war, and assuring the victory of the Asiatic cause. The unity and determination of the people of Japan are marvellous ; their war efforts, at their zenith. Factories work day and night, turning out warplanes, tanks, arms and ammunition. The huge factories and workshops which once carried on peace-time manufacture, are armament factories now, which means the entire industry of Japan is a war industry. The entire labour of the Japanese nation is now war labour. New docks and shipyards in various parts of Japan turn out warships and merchant vessels to further strengthen Japan's invincible navy and intrepid merchant marine. Training of soldiers, officers and air-men goes on throughout the country and millions of young men are joining the armed forces. And as for the food situation in Japan, I got exactly the same food that I got last year. There is plenty of rice, fish, meat and vegetables ; one and a half years of war has not in the least affected Japan's food situation, thanks to the excellent planning and control by the Government. In one word, I found Japan united as one man, with no thought but of war and victory—the victory of the holy war of liberation, the victory that would mean freedom and prosperity for India and all Asia.

Friends and Comrades-in-Arms ! You might now ask me what I did in Tokyo for our cause, what present I have brought for you. Well, I have brought for you this present (turning to Subhash). Srijut Subhash Chandra Bose needs no introduction to you, to India or to the world. He symbolises all that is best, noblest, the most daring and the most dynamic in the youth of India. As an all-India Leader in the fight against British Imperialism, he stands in a class by himself. He is a brilliant leader and an uncompromising fighter. He has dedicated his life to the cause of Mother India and he richly deserves the name of "Deshsevak Subhas". Eleven times he has been in British political prisons but all that suffering and sacrifice have only strengthened his dynamic will to wage the battle for freedom until victory is achieved.

Friends ! This is one of the happiest moments in my life. I have brought to you one of the most outstanding personalities of our sacred Motherland to participate in our campaign for the freedom of India. The spontaneous and enthusiastic welcome which the two million Indians in East Isia have extended to Subhash is an unqualified assurance to him—and to me and to India—that Indians in East Asia have whole-heartedly placed themselves, and all they have, at his command.

Friends and Comrades-in-Arms ! In your presence to-day I resign my office and appoint Deshsevak Subhash Chandra Bose as President of the Indian Independence League in East Asia. From now on, Subhash Chandra Bose is your President, your leader in the fight for India's independence. And I am confident that, under his leadership, you will march on to battle and to victory. And, of course, I will be always by your side sharing the glory and suffering of the battle, and sharing the joy of victory as well.

Netaji inspecting the serried ranks of Azad Hind Fauj

Major General M. Z. Kiani

Divisional Commandar

Major General J. K. Bhonsle

Chief of Staff

You know I have dedicated my life, in my own humble way, to the cause of our sacred Motherland. That is my life-mission. And as long as there is breath in my body, I shall be the soldier that I have always been—the soldier in the battle for Mother India's freedom. And, of course, I shall not spare myself in giving him all that I can give him—whole-hearted co-operation, assistance and advice in the battle that is now ahead of us.

Friends and Comrades-in-arms! The greatest moment in our lives has come. We are on the eve of the most decisive phase of our campaign; happy and auspicious way in which events are taking shape. So, my friends! have faith in God, have faith in yourselves, have faith in our friends and allies, have faith in their victory which is India's victory as well, and be ready to plunge yourself into the battle—the battle that will lead our sacred Motherland to freedom, victory and glory.

Inquilab Zindabad! Azad Hindustan Zindabad!

Deafening cheers filled the air as Rash Behari Bose announced the appointment of "Deshsevak" Subhash Chandra Bose as President of the Indian Independence League in East Asia. Sri Rash Behari Bose's address was translated into Tamil by Lt.-Col. S. A. Alagappan.

In a stirring address welcoming Srijut Subhash Chandra Bose, Sri J. A. Thivy, Chairman of the Malaya Branch of the Indian Independence League, reaffirmed the pledge of all Indians in Malaya to serve India and the Indian Independence Movement to their fullest capacity, even at the risk of their lives. He said: "We will, by our action, show our implicit faith and trust in you as our Leader".

Lt. Col. J. K. Bhonsle, Director, Military Bureau, made a speech in Hindustani welcoming the new President, on behalf of the army. He said: "We welcome you on behalf of the Army and assure you of unswerving allegiance and steadfast loyality to the cause of India's freedom."

"To us you are a new hope. Your arrival has instilled a new spirit among our soldiers. So far, we had an ideal and a cause to fight for, now we have a leader who will inspire and guide us successfully to the achievement of our goal.

"We are ready and pledged to our Motherland. We only await your orders. You are our leader; we have placed our destinies and the destiny of India in your hands. When you think the opportune time to strike has come, on your orders we shall march forward.

"Ours shall be a grim but a glorious fight. I am sure—nay certain—our soldiers will give a good account of themselves. We will meet the enemy in the field and destroy him there and rid the sacred Bharat Mata from the evil influences of Anglo-American Imperialism for ever."

Before he commenced his address, Sjt. Subhash Chandra Bose paid a well-deserved tribute to the retiring President in Hindustani which was translated into Tamil. It was indeed a touching scene. Subhash Bose said:—

"During and before the last Great War, people in India knew him (the retiring President) very well, but the present generation may have forgotten him. His marvellous services at the risk of his life during the last war for the liberation of India are not only fresh in our memories but are also in the records of the British Imperialists."

Subhash Bose asked the retiring President to continue his activities in the League as the President's Supreme Adviser and to guide him in leading this Movement.

Subhas Bose then delivered the following address :—

Mr. Rash Behari Bose and representatives of the Indian Independence Movement in East Asia !

I thank you from the bottom of my heart for the honour you have done me, by appointing me to the leadership of the Indian Independence Movement in East Asia I accept this responsibility, but I do so with a feeling of extreme humility and I pray that God may grant me strength to fulfil my duty, to the entire satisfaction of my countrymen at home and abroad.

If you were to hear my experience—at home and abroad—since the outbreak of the present war, you would feel, as I do, that the hand of Providence has been protecting us from harm and has been guiding our efforts along the path leading to victory and freedom. This has increased my optimism and self-confidence a hundredfold.

Friends, the time has now come for freedom-loving Indians to act. Action in a war-crisis demands, above all, military discipline, as well as unflinching loyalty to the cause. I, therefore, call upon you, all my countrymen in East Asia, to line up in one solid phalanx under one leadership and prepare for the grim fight that is ahead of us. I am confident that you will do so.

I am glad to tell you that the momentous step taken to-day serves to unite in a common bond, not only the patriotic Indians in East Asia, but patriotic Indians all over the world as well. I have to-day the confidence and support of all freedom-loving Indians abroad, who are actively working for the emancipation of our Motherland. Even Indians now living in enemy countries, where they are unable to work actively for India's freedom, are morally with us in the work that we are doing. Within my knowledge, this is the first time in recent history that Indians living abroad have been united in one organisation, for the attainment of one common goal.

What is perhaps even more remarkable is that patriotic Indians abroad are working in complete harmony with their countrymen at home. I have publicly declared several times that, when I left home and Homeland in 1941, on an important mission, it was in accordance with the will of the vast majority of my countrymen. Since then, despite all the restrictions imposed by the C.I D.—that is, the Secret Service—I have remained in constant touch with my countrymen at home. To-day, I can go so far as to inform you that during the last twelve months, a large number of our representatives have been sent to India from outside, from all directions. Some of them have been captured and shot—for which we shall, in due time, exact full revenge. But many more have been able to evade arrest and, according to latest reports, they are working satisfactorily. Thus, patriotic Indians abroad have been working as genuine trustees of the freedom-fighters at home. I can assure everybody once again that whatever we have done up till now, or may do in future, has been, and will be, for the freedom of India and we shall never do anything that is either against the interest of India or will not be in accordance with the will of our people.

I shall now deal with the question as to how we can win our liberty. Some of my friends at home had hoped, at one time, that at the pressure of an international crisis, the British Government would, in its own interest, accede to India's demand for independence. These friends must have been disillusioned by now, because it is transparently clear that both during and after the War the British Government intends to exploit India more ruthlessly than ever before. That is why Field Marshal Lord Wavell is being sent as Viceroy and Governor-General. I have noticed that certain circles at home are extremely dissatisfied over this appointment and they would have probably preferred a man like Lord Halifax as Viceroy, but I do not share their view. For me, the appointment of Field Marshal Lord Wavell as Viceroy is a prophetic event—a writing on the wall. This ever-retreating Commander-in-Chief is destined to be the last Viceroy of India. Moreover, the military, political and economic exploitation of India which he is bound to intensify, will further embitter the Indian masses and thereby strengthen the gathering forces of revolution.

But though India is in for a period of military dictatorship under the new Viceroy, I anticipate, nevertheless, that in future another attempt at a compromise with India will be made. This attempt will be nothing more than a bluff or a hoax—and our countrymen at home should be prepared in advance to see through it—as they did, when Sir Stafford Cripps offerd empty promises to India in April, 1942. Mr. Winston Churchill, the supreme representative of the British people, recently gave an indication of his mentality when he told the Lord Mayor of London that he did not like even the expression "British Commonwealth", preferring the expression "British Empire" instead. The last Imperialist Prime Minister of England will, no doubt, do his very best to preserve that Empire and any offer that he will make to the Indian people will be only for the purpose of deceiving them. But there is no sense in even thinking of a compromise with an Empire that will soon disappear from the face of the earth.

Those of you who have studied the history of freedom-movements in other lands—as I have done—must have observed that for the achievement of independence, two conditions are essential—firstly, a favourable international situation and, secondly, necessary sacrifice and effort. The first condition has been already fulfilled. If India had to fight single-handed with the British Empire, our task would have been exceedingly difficult. The Tripartite Powers are determined to carry on the war, until Anglo-American Imperialism is overthrown.

Friends! For more than two years I have been constantly travelling with a view to studying the war-situation at first-hand. From this study, I am convinced that, however long this war may last, there can be but one outcome—namely, the complete victory of the Tripartite Powers and their allies. I am not blind to the many difficulties that have to be overcome before Anglo-American Imperialism could be defeated. I am also aware that in a long war, temporary ups and downs are unavoidable and that, at the present moment, the Anglo-American Powers are enjoying a temporary advantage in certain unimportant theatres of war. But the general war-situation—and the strategic position in particular—remains greatly advantageous to the Tripartite Powers, and you will see that, as the days roll by, the Anglo-American Powers will have to suffer one defeat after another.

The British Empire, in spite of all its power and might, has been seeking and obtaining help from every possible quarter. It is therefore but natural that we, too, should look out for sympathy and assistance wherever it is available. Moreover, every freedom movement in history has had to seek some help or other from abroad, before it could achieve success. The logic of events, in the present case, has made the Tripartite Powers our natural allies and there is nothing wrong if we accept their sympathy, or even their help, should we need it.

I know that some of my countrymen, who are under the influence of British propaganda, doubt the sincerity of the Tripartite Powers in their attitude towards India. But common-sense should tell them that it is the most natural thing for the enemies of British Imperialism to support India's demand for liberty. Moreover, with the exception of England a free India will be an advantage to the whole world, including the Tripartite Powers.

Japan's attitude towards Burma and the Philippines will be the most convincing proof of her sincerity and good faith. But apart from this, as a normal human being, I see no reason why I should have any doubt or mistrust with regard of Japan's intentions. Japan was the first Asiatic Power to successfully resist foreign aggression—and Japan knows, more than any other Asiatic power, that, so long as the enslaved Asiatic nations are not emancipated; no Asiatic nation can feel completely safe from the menace of aggression, Moreover, there is in Japan, to-day, what one might call an Asiatic consciousness, which manifests itself in a desire to help other Asiatic nations to achieve their liberation. This is a unique development which affords a golden opportunity to all enslaved nations in Asia to emancipate themselves and set up a new order based on freedom, justice and morality.

If anybody has still any doubt in his mind on this point, I should ask him to place his trust in me. My loyalty is to India and to India alone and not even our enemies will have the audacity to urge that I am capable of betraying my country. And as I said in Tokyo the other day, if the British Government could not demoralise me after persecuting me all my life, nobody else can do so. And if cunning British politicians could neither cajole nor deceive me, no one else can hope to do so.

Every Indian should realise that the victory of the Anglo-American Powers will mean for India continued enslavement and more ruthless exploitation. Our only hope of freedom is therefore in a Tripartite victory. But we should so conduct our own struggle that an Axis victory may simultaneously bring us our liberty.

Friends! We have now the most favourable international situation and the most happy combination of circumstances. Consequently, all that is needed for winning freedom is sufficient effort and sacrifice. Our record in this connection is by no means unsatisfactory. You may remember that in May last year after the departure of Sir Stafford Cripps from India and exactly 85 years after the outbreak of our first war of independence, I declared that our national struggle was entering upon a most significant phase. Since then, we have passed many a milestone on our onward march—the most important of these being the intensification of the Civil Disobedience Movement and the commencement of sabotage activities after the arrest of Mahatma Gandhi in August last. In the history of India's struggle, August 1942 will, therefore, remain an unforgettable landmark, indicating the psychological transition from passive to active resistance. Not content with a civil disobedience campaign, the Indian people are now morally prepared to employ other means for achieving their liberation.

The time has, therefore, come to pass on to the next stage of our campaign. All organisations, whether inside or outside, must now transform themselves into a disciplined fighting organisation under one leadership. The aim and purpose of this organisation should be to take up arms against British Imperialism, when the time is ripe and the signal is given. In order to mobilise all our forces effectively, I intend organising a Provisional Government of Free India. It will be the task of this Provisional Government to lead the Indian Revolution to a successful conclusion. To this end, the Provisional Government will have to prepare the Indian people—inside and outside India—for an armed struggle which will be the culmination of all our national efforts since 1883. When the revolution succeeds and Anglo-American Imperialism is expelled from India, the task of the Provisional Government will be over. It will then make room for a permanent Government to be set up inside India, in accordance with the will of the Indian people.

When all our preparations for the last struggle are complete, it will be possible to bring the Indian struggle into line with the common struggle of the Tripartite Powers against the common foe. By participating in this common fight, we shall be qualifying for our freedom. By shedding our blood in a sacred cause, we shall be paying the price of liberty and, at the same time, we shall be laying the only enduring foundation for our national unity. And last but not least, by winning freedom through our own efforts and sacrifice we shall be acquiring the strength whereby we shall preserve our liberty for all time.

Friends ! In conclusion, I thank you once again from the bottom of my heart for the confidence you have reposed in me and for the assurance of unflinching support that you have given me. I warn you that, though we are absolutely sure of our final victory we can never afford to under-estimate the enemy and we should even be prepared for temporary setbacks. We have a grim fight ahead of us—for the enemy is at once powerful, unscrupulous and ruthless In this final march to freedom you will have to face hunger, thirst, privation, forced marches and death. Only when you pass this test, will freedom be yours. I am confident that you will do so and thereby bring freedom and prosperity to your enslaved and impoverished land.

Inquilab Zindabad ! Azad Hind Zindabad !

As the President of the Indian Independence League in East Asia Srijut Subhash Chandra Bose took the salute at a parade of the Indian National Army on the ground opposite the Singapore Municipal Offices on July 5. Representative detachments of the Indian National Army took up their positions on the ground an hour before the parade was due. Looking smart and agile in his khaki military uniform, Srijut Subhash Chandra Bose, accompanied by I. N. A. bodyguard, arrived at the Parade punctually at 10-30 a.m., where upon the troops presented arms and the bugle sounded. The President then ascended the steps of the rostrum and from there surveyed the serried ranks of the warriors who had sworn to sacrifice their lives in the fight for India's freedom.

Led by the Chiefs of the Indian National Army and accompanied by Srijut Rash Behari Bose, his Supreme Adviser, Srijut Subash Chandra Bose inspected the Army, after which he returned to the rostrum and delivered a stirring message to the officers and men of the Army; Thunderous shouts of "Inqilab Zindabad" "Azad-Hind Zindabad" "Mahatma Gandhi ki Jai" and

"Subhash Chandra Bose ki Jai" punctuated his address. The President said :

Soldiers of India's Army of Liberation and my Comrades,

To-day is the proudest day of my life. To-day it has pleased Providence to give me the unique privilege and honour of announcing to the whole world that India's Army of Liberation has come into being. This Army has now been drawn up in military formation on the battlefield of Singapore, which was once the bulwark of the Brtish Empire This is not only the Army that will emancipate India from the British yoke, it is also the Army that will, hereafter, create the future national army of Free India. Every Indian must feel proud that this Army—his own Army—has been organised entirely under Indian leadership and that when the historic moment arrives, under Indian leadership it will go to battle.

There are people who thought at one time that the Empire, on which the su did not set, was an everlasting Empire. No such thought ever troubled me. History has taught me that every empire has its inevitable decline and collapse. Moreover, I had seen with my own eyes, cities and fortresses that were once the bulwark, but which became the graveyards of by-gone Empires. But standing to-day on the graveyard of the British Empire, even a child is convinced that the almighty British Empire is already a thing of the past.

When France declared war on Germany in 1939 and the campaign began, there was but one cry which rose from the lips of German soldiers "To Paris, to Paris." When the brave soldiers of Nippon set out on their march in December, 1941. there was but one cry which rose from their lips "To Singapore, to Singapore." Comrades ! My soldiers ! Let your battle cry be "To Delhi, to Delhi." How many of us will individually survive this war of Freedom, I do not know. But I do know this that we shall ultimately win and our task will not end until our surviving heroes hold the victory-parade on another graveyard of the British Empire—the Lal Kila or Red Fortress of ancient Delhi.

Throughout my pnblic career, I have always felt that, though India is otherwise ripe for independence in every way, she has lacked one thing ; namely, an army of liberation. George Washington of America could fight and win freedom, because he had his army. Garibaldi could liberate Italy, beeause he had his armed volunteers behind him. It is your privilege and honour to be the first to come forward and organise India's National Army. By doing so, you have removed the last obstacle in our path to freedom. Be happy and proud that you are the pioneers—the vanguard—in such a noble cause.

Let me remind you that you have a two-fold task to perform. With the force of arms and at the cost of your blood you will have to win liberty. Then, when India is free, you will have to organise the permanent army of Free India whose task it will be to preserve our liberty for all time. We must build up our national defence on such an unshakable foundation that never again in our history shall we lose our freedom.

As soldiers, you will always have to cherish and live up to the three ideals of faithfulness, duty and sacrifice. Soldiers, who always remain faithful to their nation, who perform their duty under all circumstances, and who are always prepared to sacrifice their lives, are invincible. If you, too, want to be invincible engrave these three ideals in the innermost core of your hearts. A true soldier needs both military and spiritual training. You must—all of you—so train yourselves and your Comrades that every soldier will have unbounded confidence in himself, will be conscious of being immensely superior to the enemy, will be fearless of death and will have sufficient initiative to act on his own in any critical situation, should the need arise. During the course of the present war, you have seen with your own eyes what wonders. scientific training, coupled with courage, fearlessness and dynamism, can achieve. Learn all that you can from this example and build up for Mother India an absolutely first class modern army.

To those of you who are officers, I should like to say that your responsibility is a heavy one. Though the responsibility of an officer in every army in this world is indeed great, it is far greater in your case. Because of our political enslavement, we have no tradition like that of Mukden, Port Arthur or Sedan to inspire us. We have to unlearn some of the things that the British taught us and we have to learn much that they did not teach. Nevertheless, I am confident that you will rise to the occasion and fulfil the task that your countrymen have thrown on your brave shoulders. Remember always that officers can make or unmake any army. Remember, too, that the British have suffered defeats on so many fronts, largely because of worthless officers. And remember also that out of your ranks will be born the future General Staff of the Army of Free India.

To all of you I should like to say that in the course of this war, you will have to acquire the experience and achieve the success which alone can build up a national tradition for our army in future. An army that has no tradition of courage, fearlessness and invincibility cannot hold its own in a struggle with a powerful enemy.

Comrades ! You have voluntarily accepted a mission that is the noblest that the human mind can conceive of. For the fulfilment of such a mission, no sacrifice is too great—not even the sacrifice of one's life. You are to-day the custodians of India's national honour and the embodiment of India's hopes and aspirations. So conduct yourselves that your countrymen may bless you and posterity may be proud of you.

I have said that to-day is the proudest day of my life. For an enslaved people, there can be no greater pride, no higher honour, than to be the first soldier in the army of liberation. But this honour carries with it a corresponding responsibility and I am deeply conscious of it. I assure you that I shall be with you in darkness and in sunshine, in sorrow and in joy, in suffering and in victory. For the present. I can offer you nothing except hunger, thirst, privation, forced marches and death. But if you follow me in life and in death—as I am confident you will—I shall lead you to victory and freedom. It does not matter who among us will live to see India free. It is enough that India shall be free and that we shall give our all to make her free. May God now bless our Army and grant us victory in the coming fight !

Inquilab Zindabad ! Azad Hind Zindabad !

After the address, the President took the salute at the march past that followed. The procession of India's soldiers of freedom was led by a long line of mechanised units, proudly flying the Indian National Tricolour, followed by the infantrymen in smart turn-out, proud and erect with confidence, firm in faith ready to lay down their lives in the cause of their Motherland.

The following day, Tuesday, July 6, 1943, in bright sunshine, and on the former battlefield of Singapore, the Premier of Nippon witnessed a parade of India's Army of Liberation, in the presence of Srijut Subhash Chandra Bose.

Premier General Tojo stood at the top of steps of the Singapore Municipal Offices, and surveyed the solid phalanx of the soldiers of India's Army of Liberation.

To the serried ranks of the Indian National Army drawn up on the esplanade, the sight of the Premier of Nippon, General Tojo, and Srijut Subhash Chandra Bose; the uncrowned King of Free India, standing side by side, and taking salute at the Parade was a rare experience and a wonderful tonic to the already high morale.

The following address of welcome was presented to Premier Tojo by Srijut Subhash Chandra Bose on behalf of the Indian National Army :—

Your Excellency, on behalf of the Indian National Army, I have great pleasure in offering Your Excellency a most hearty welcome this morning. I desire to express our profound appreciation of the great honour Your Excellency has done us by spending so much of your valuable time in order to review our Army. This day will ever remain a red-letter day in the history of the newly organised Army of Free India. Your Excellency's presence among our soldiers to-day, immediately after sending an inspiring message to the Indian Independence League Conference yesterday, has given a powerful impetus to our revoluntionary struggle.

The Army that stands before Your Excellency to-day knows that it will have to fight for India's liberty. It is also conscious of the many difficulties that still beset the path to victory and freedom. But this Army is determined to achieve India's liberty at the cost of any sacrifice. In this task the Army has the active support of all Indians in East Asia, whose enthusiasm knows no bounds.

In conclusion, I beg to assure Your Excellency of our unshakable determination to fight with you shoulder to shoulder, through joy and sorrow, through sunshine and darkness, till complete victory is achieved and till India regains her lost liberty.

Indian National Army re-organized

The first work of Syt. Subhash Chandra Bose after assuming the President ship of Indian Independence League, was to reorganize the I. N. A.

The following Communique was issued from the I. I. L. H.Q. Singapore on July 8, 1943 :—

The Indian Independence League in East Asia has organised an Army. This Army will be known as the Azad Hind Fauj or the Indian National Army

The Azad Hind Fauj or the Indian National Army has sworn allegiance to the cause of India's complete independence.

Azad Hind Fauj Warriors

Marching in a procession in Singapore

A procession of civilians in Bangkok led by S. Ishar Singh (first from the left) Minister of State

The officers and men of the Azad Hind Fauj or the Indian National Army have dedicated their lives to the sacred task of expelling the British from India and establisheding an India for Indians.

The Spokesman of the League made the following statement after reading out the communique issued by the Indian Independence League Headquarters :—

You have just listened to the official announcement of the Indian Independence League Headquarters, that the League has organised an Army which will be known as the Azad Hind Fauj or the Indian National Army. You have also heard that this Azad Hind Fauj or the Indian National Army has sworn allegiance to the cause of India's complete Independence, and the officers and men of the Army have dedicated their lives to the sacred task of expelling the British from India, and creating an India for Indians·

Freedom Or Death

I wish to make it clear to the world that the Indian National Army has been organised solely by Indians, and consists of picked soldiers from Indian volunteers who have taken a solemn oath to achieve the complete independenee of India by fighting the British and wiping out of India all trace of the two centuries of British rule. They are anti-British in every fibre of their being, and they are inspired by the Spirit of Independence. They have dedicated their lives to the cause of India's freedom ; they have no thought of personal comforts, luxury or profit ; their one motto is "Freedom or Death" to quote Mahatma Gandhi's dictum ; and they are ready to lay down their lives in the fight for India's complete Independence.

This is the first time in India's history since the advent of the British, that a truly Indian and truly National Army has been raised.

The sole object of the I. N. A. (Indian National Army) is to destroy the British power and influence in India and to make an India for Indians.

As I said earlier, the I. N. A. is a picked fighting force of Indians, selected on the basis of volunteer system. The men of this force are burning with the anti-British spirit and spirit of Independence.

Uniform And Training

The anti-British spirit permeates the entire I. N. A., it is organised on a system best adapted to the Indian genius and is in tune with the revolutionary war which the I. N. A. is expected to wage when the time for action comes.

The training of the I. N. A is also adapted to Indian spiritual and cultural heritage and Indian military tradi ions. A strong anti-British spirit and the spirit of Independence are the basis of the moral and spiritual training undergone by every single soldier of the I. N.A. from the Commander down to the soldier. Their training goes on from morning till night. As soldiery, the entire I. N. A. is bent upon beating the British tactics and it is well trained and equipped so to do.

The uniform of the officers and men of the I. N. A. also conform to the Indian spirit, Indian genius and Indian environments.

The British have been ruling over India by sedulously following their policy of "Divide and Rule." They carried this policy into the Indian Army also thus keeping alive the difference of race and religion in the Indian Army, and thus preventing the growth of national consciousnes in the Army. Fully realising the diabolical nature of this "Divide and Rule" policy of the British, the organisers of the Indian National Army have laid the axe at the very root of this tradition. All distinctions of class, caste, creed and religion have been abolished in the Indian National Army which has been organised on truly national lines. There are no water-tight compartments based on the religious faiths of members of the I. N. A. Every man of the I. N. A. feels that he is an Indian first and Indian last. His goal is the liberation of India from British rule; and his motto is Unity, Faith and Sacrifice.

I. N. A. And Nippon Army

The officers and men of the I. N.A. are undergoing an intensive training course of enlightenment and culture to fit them spiritually for the sacred task before them.

Spartan living is one of the marked features of the I. N. A. and Indian manners and customs have been given an honoured place in the general conduct of the I. N. A.

To wipe out every trace of denationalisation, deliberately fostered by the compulsory use of English language, and to establish strong bonds of affinity between the officers and men, the Indian language has been adopted as the medium of communication between officers and men at the barracks and on the field.

I would most emphatically stress once again that the I. N. A. is entirely of the Indians and for the Indians. And the only task to which the I N. A. has solemnly dedicated itself is the winning of India's Complete Independence.

In a speech delivered at the Mass Meeting held in Singapore on July 9, 1943, Sjt. Bose explained why he left home and Motherland.

Sisters and brothers! Let me, first of all thank you for the exceedingly warm and enthusiastic welcome that you have given me to-day. I am particularly thankful to my sisters who have boldly come forward in such large numbers to give expression to their patriotic feelings. From what I see to-day, I am confident that in the coming fight, my countrymen in Syonan and in Malai will play a leading part. What was once a bulwark of British Imperialism has now become a bulwark of Indian Nationalism.

Next, I would like to tell you quite frankly what made me leave home and homeland on a journey that was fraught with danger of every kind.

You know that I have been actively working in the independence movement ever since I left the portals of the University in 1921. I have been through all the civil disobedience campaigns during the last two decades. In addition to this, I have been repeatedly put in prison without trial, on the suspicion of having been connected with secret revolutionary movement—whether non-violent—with which I have been familiar. I may also assert without the slightest exaggeration that there is no nationalist leader in India who can claim to possess the many-sided experience that I have been able to acquire. In the light of this experience, I came to the conclusion that all the efforts that we could put forward inside India, would not suffice to expel the British from our country. If the struggle at home had sufficed to achieve liberty for our people, I would not have been so foolish as to undertake this unnecessary risk and hazard.

To put it briefly, therefore, my object in leaving India was to supplement from outside the struggle going on at home. Without this supplementary help from outside it is impossible for anybody to liberate India. On the other hand, the supplementary help from outside which the national struggle at home so urgently needs is in reality very small. This is because the defeats inflicted on the British by the Axis Powers, have shattered British power and prestige to such an extent, that our task has been rendered comparatively easy.

The help that our countrymen at home needed and still need is a two-fold one—moral and material. Firstly, they have to be morally convinced that their victory is assured in the long run. Secondly, they have to be given military help from outside. In order to do the first, one had to study objectively the international war-situation and thereby find out what the result of the war was going to be. To do the second, one had to find out what Indians outside India could do to help their countrymen at home and also if it was possible to obtain help from the enemies of British Imperialism, should that need arise. Friends! I am now in a position to tell you that both these objectives have been fulfilled. By travelling abroad, I could see things for myself and could study the respective positions of the belligerent powers. Thereafter, when I came to the conclusion that the defeat of Anglo-American Imperialism was assured, I conveyed the information to my countrymen at home. Then, I was delighted to find that my countrymen all over the world were wide awake and were anxious to undertake their share of the national struggle. I was also gratified to find that the Axis Powers—and Japan in particular—were really eager to see India free and they were prepared to render any help that was within their power, should the Indian people desire it.

As to the attitude of Indians abroad, I do not think that there is any man or woman who does not want India to be free and who is not prepared to help the national struggle. As to the attitude of the Axis Powers and of Japan—if anybody has the slightest doubt or suspicion I can easily convince him with overwhelming proofs that outside the ranks of our countrymen, they are the best friends we have in the world today. Moreover, I can ask you to trust me. Not even my enemies will have the audacity to say that I am capable of doing anything against the interests of my country. And if the British Government could not demoralise me or deceive me or allure me no other power on earth can do so. Therefore, believe me when I say that if you want any external help in your struggle against British Imperialism, the Axis Powers will come to your aid. But whether you do need any help or not, is for you to decide—and it goes without saying, that if you could do without any help, it would be the best course for India. At the same time I should add that if the almighty British Government can go round the whole world with the begging-bowl asking for help everywhere—even from the enslaved and impoverished people of India—there is nothing wrong in our taking help from outside, if we are forced to do so.

The time has come when I can openly tell the whole world, including our enemies, as to how it is proposed to bring about our national liberation. Indians outside India—particularly, Indians in East Asia—are going to organise a fighting force which will be powerful enough to attack the British Army in India. When we do so, a revolution will break out, not only among the civil population at home, but also among the Indian Army which is now standing under the British flag. When the British Government is thus attacked from both sides—from inside India and from outside—it will collapse and the Indian people will then regain their liberty.

According to my plan, therefore, it is not even necessary to bother about the attitude of the Axis Powers towards India. If Indians outside and inside India will only do their duty, it is possible for the Indian people to throw the British out of India and liberate 388 millions of their countrymen.

There may be croakers who will say that if 388 millions of Indians cannot expel British power from India, how can three millions living abroad hope to do so? But friends, look to the history of Ireland. If three million Irishmen living under the British domination—under a form of martial-law—could, with the help of five thousand armed Sinn Fein volunteers, bring the British Government to its knees in 1921, why cannot three million Indians backed by a powerful movement at home, hope to throw the British out of India, when the aid of powerful Japan is readily available?

I must, however, say that Indians living abroad and particularly in East Asia, must put forward thir maximum effort. In order to do so effectively, it is my intention to set up a Provisional Government of Free India The task of this Government will be to mobilise all the resources of the Indian people and lead the fight against the British Army in India. When the campaign succeeds and India is free, the Provisional Government will make room for the permanent Government of Free India, which will be set up in accordance with the will of the Indian people.

Friends ! You will now realise that the time has come for three million Indians living in East Asia to mobilise all their available resources—including money and man-power. Half-hearted measures will not do I want Total Mobilisation and nothing less—for we have been told repeatedly, even by our enemies, that this is a total war.

You see before you today a part of India's Army of Liberation—the Azad Hind Fauj or the Indian National Army.

They held their ceremonial parade the other day in front of the Town Hall. Thereafter, they have resolved that they will not rest till they hold their victory-parade before the red fortress of ancient Delhi, They have adopted the slogan—" Onward to Delhi—Onward to Delhi !" Friends ! Let the slogan of the three million Indians in East Asia be—"Total Mobilisation for a Total War."

Out of this total mobilisation, I expect at least three hundred thousand soldiers and three crores—that is thirty millions—of dollars. I want also a unit of brave Indian women to form a "Death-defying Regiment" who will wield the sword which the brave Rani of Jhansi wielded in India's First War of Independence in 1857.

Friends ! We have for a long time, been hearing so much of the Second

Front in Europe. But our countrymen at home are now hard-pressed and they are demanding a Second Front. Give me Total Mobilisation in East Asia and I promise you a second front—a real second front for the Indian struggle.

Summary of Speech delivered at a meeting of Indian Women held under the auspices of the Women's Section of the I. I. L., Singapore Branch, on 12th July, 1943.

Sisters ! First of all I want to thank you from the bottom of my heart for the grand welcome that you have given me this afternoon. I am purposely calling it a grand welcome because I cannot conceive of a more magnificent welcome than what you have given me this afternoon. At the same time I want to thank you also for the great enthusiasm which you exhibited the other day, when we had our Rally at the Padang in front of the Municipal Offices. Not only myself but also the other friends and guests who were with me on the platform were exceedingly impressed by the brave manner in which you stood the rain and inclement weather and stuck to your posts till the very last. I know that some of you had brought your babies also along with you. Your brave attitude and your profound enthusiasm on that occasion have deeply impressed all of us. I have no doubt that after this good beginning your work will progress rapidly from day to day.

You all know, as well as I do, of the part our women at home have taken in the Freedom Movement, especially during the last twenty two years. From the very beginning of the new awakening in India our women have taken a prominent part, in all spheres of public life. But this has been particularly evident since the year 1921 when the Congress was reborn under the leadership of Mahatma Gandhi. It is not only in connection with the Congress Movement or the Movement of Civil Disobedience but also in connection with the secret revolutionary movement that our sisters have played a noble part.

In fact, it will be no exaggeration for me to say that there is no sphere of public activity, there is no department of national endeavour, in which Indian women have not played a prominent part. What is more, there is no suffering which Indian women have not gladly and bravely shared along with our men in the course of several decades of our national struggle. Whether it is a work of touring from village to village without food and drink, whether it is a task of lecturing at one meeting after another, whether it is task of carrying the Freedom message from door to door, whether it is a task of leading processions along public streets in defiance of the official orders and in spite of lathi charges by the inhuman British Police, or whether it is a task of running election campaigns or whether again it is a task of facing bravely imprisonment and persecution, and insult and humiliation of every kind, nowhere have our women been found wanting. And last but not least, our sisters, our brave sisters, have also played a prominent part in the secret revolutionary movement. And they have shown that when the need arises they could, like their brothers, shoot very well.

If today I express my fullest confidence in you, in your capacity to suffer and to fight for the freedom of your country, it is not an empty compliment which I indulge in, simply for the purpose of rousing your enthusiasm. If I do so, it is as a result of my personal experience. I know what our women are capable of, and therefore I say without the slightest exaggeration that there is no work, there is no sacrifice, there is no suffering, which our sisters are not capable of.

The time has now come for us to make the last and final effort in order to achieve the liberation of our Motherland. Such an opportunity is indeed rare in the life-time of a nation. Certainly in our life-time this opportunity will not come again, and perhaps not even for another one hundred years. I must say that it is the Grace of Providence .that this opportunity has suddenly presented itself to us. And if we grapple this opportunity and make every effort to undergo every sacrifice, we shall be able to achieve once and for all our national emancipation.

I know that among us there are men who have at one time thought that the British Empire was an everlasting Empire, there are men who thought at one time that it is unbelievable that the British Empire can ever cease to exist, but history tells a different tale. History teaches us that every Empire has its fall just as it has its rise. And the time has come for the British Empire to disappear from the face of this world. If you remember, sisters, I told you the other evening at the Padang that at least we who stand on the battlefield of Singapore, at least we should be convinced, and we are convinced, that the British Empire is a thing of the past. We have seen with our own eyes how that Empire has disappeared from this part of the world and we will see how it disappears from another part of the world also—from India as well.

I remember having read years ago a book written by an Englishman called Meridith Conrade. Referring to India he remarked in that book that once the Indian people are united, it would be impossible for the British to continue their domination over India. And in the course of his remarks, he said that an Empire which rose in a day will vanish in a night.

I said in one of my radio talks not long ago that it took twenty long years to build Singapore and it took only seven days to evacuate Singapore. Well, I cannot expect that we shall be able to drive out the British from India within a week, but if we calculate mathematically we can find in how many weeks we shall be able to drive the British out of India as well when the final campaign is launched.

Sisters, I hope that each and every one of you has the fullest confidence that the time has come for us to make the final effort for our emancipation. I hope that each and every one of you has the fullest confidence that the ultimate outcome of this war can only be the defeat and overthrow of the Anglo-American Imperialism, and it is only out of the defeat of Anglo-American Imperialism that India can hope to win her freedom. That is why I have always been asserting that India's freedom is bound up with the final victory of the Axis Powers. To-day both the parties, India and the Axis Powers, have a common enemy, and therefore, we have a common goal. We have to fight against the common enemy no matter what the sacrifice involved may be, and through our common suffering and sacrifice to win our liberty.

Even if it is possible to get our liberty without suffering, sacrifice and struggle, I am sure that it is not worth having, because freedom that is obtained without sacrifice and struggle would be difficult to be retained even if we are free. Therefore, if you want to liberate yourselves from the British yoke and thereafter to preserve your independence, once and for all, if you desire that never again in history should we lose our freedom, then it is necessary that in the course of our national struggle we should acquire that strength whereby we may win, and thereafter be able to preserve our liberty for all time. Therefore we have to pay the price of freedom, and the price of freedom is suffering, sacrifice and struggle. I have no doubt in my mind that we shall be able to put forward the necessary sacrifice and struggle, we shall be able to undergo cheerfully the necessary suffering, and thereby we shall not only be able to free ourselves from the British domination but thereafter we shall be able to retain our freedom for ever.

Sisters, the time has come for us to begin our final preparations for the final struggle, in right earnest. We have no time to lose. No one can predict when the call may come, when the march would begin. We must, therefore, be so prepared that whenever the call comes we should be immediately prepared to begin our march. As I said the other day there is but one thought in our minds, there is but one cry which rises from our lips—"*Onward to Delhi, Onward to Delhi*!" The campaign which will be begun here in Syonan, which has become the grave-yard of the British Empire, that campaign will end only when we drive out the British from India and occupy our Metropolis. And then we shall parade finally in celebration of our victory before the famous Red Fort of Delhi.

Sisters, we had at one time conservative men amongst us who thought that women had nothing to do with the national struggle, and that it was entirely a man's affair. I hope that there are no such men in our midst today. On the contrary, I am convinced that until and unless Indian women play their due part in the national struggle, India can never hope to be free. And if I am so optimistic to-day of our speedy emancipation, it is, because I am equally optimistic of the part that Indian women will play in the coming struggle.

When I talk of your playing your part in the coming struggle, I do not forget the part that our sisters at home are already playing in the struggle at home. I do not forget that there are hundreds, perhaps thousands of our sisters rotting in British jails in India to-day, and it is their sacrifice, which is inspiring the entire youth of our country. I have no doubt that our friends at home, men and women, oys and girls, will go on doing their part, but we know that that alone will not be enough to win our liberty. All the efforts that they may possibly put forward will not suffice to expel the Britishers from India; therefore we have a duty to perform and that duty is to bring assistance to India from without.

Here in East Asia we have got a population close upon three million Indians and I have no doubt that if we can bring about Total Mobilisation of our resources, in manpower, in money and in other resources, we shall be able to bring that help to India which will enable our countrymen at home to finally overthrow the British yoke.

CHAPTER IV

REORGANISATION OF THE LEAGUE

Sooon after his assumption of the office of the President, Sri Subhash Chandra Bose issued the following circular for reorganising the League :—

Indian Independence League Headquarters

7, Chancery Lane,
Syonan, 13th July, 1943.

In view of the new responsiblities that the Indian Independence Movement has to face in the near future and in view of the wave of enthusiasm, that is visible among Indians in East Asia, it has become necessary to reorganise the Indian Independence League. The first step in this direction is to reorganise the Headquarters of the Indian Independence League. For this reorganisation, some of the existing Departments have to be expanded, while other new Departments have also to be set up. I am giving below the scheme of reorganisation. I shall watch carefully the result of this organisation and in the light of experience, I may make further changes—if and when necessary.

Departments :—1. Military Bureau, 2. Recruitment, 3. Training, 4. Supplies, 5. Finance, 6. Publicity, Press and Propaganda. 7, Health and Social Welfare, 8. Overseas, 9, Women, 10. Reconstruction, 11. Education and Culture and 12. General Secretary.

Department of Recruitment. This Department will organise Recruitment for the Azad Hind Fauj (Indian National Army) all over East Asia in a systematic way. This is a new Department.

Department of Training. The existing Youth Department will be absorbed in this new Department. The work of this Department will be to provide some kind of training for all recruits throughout East Asia until the Army is in a position to take over these recruits and put them into military barracks.

The existing Training Institutes will be managed by this Department and if necessary, more may be started. The present staff of the Youth Department will come under this Department and fresh appointments will be made, if and when necessary according to the amount of work that has to be handled by the Department. The Head of the Youth Department will become the head of the Department of Training.

Department of Supplies. The function of this new Department will be to collect supplies from all over East Asia for the Indian Independence Movement in general and for the Azad Hind Fauj (Indian National Army) in particular for present and future use.

The existing Stores at the Headquarters of the Indian Independence League will henceforth be managed by the Department of supplies.

Department of Health and Social Welfare. The existing Welfare Department will be absorbed in this Department. The new Department of Health and Social Welfare will have two sub-departments namely: (a) Medical, and (b) Social Welfare.

The existing Welfare Department with its staff will be absorbed in the sub-department of Social Welfare. The head of the Welfare Department will become the Head of the Sub department of Social Welfare. The medical Sub-department will be under a junior Medical Officer. The whole department of Health and Social Welfare will be under a Senior Medical Officer.

Overseas Department. The work of this new Department will be ;

(a) To direct and stimulate the work of the Branches

(b) To establish new Branches where necessary

(c) To maintain regular contact between the Headquarters and the different Branches.

Women's Department. This will be a new Department. The work of this Department will be to organise Indian women throughout East Asia and direct and stimulate their activities in connection with the Indian Independence movement.

This Department will also recruit women for the Army and will organise a Red Cross Department from among Indian women and girls.

Reconstruction Department. The work of this new Department will be :

(a) To prepare plans for the future—particularly in connection with future administration in India.

(b) To train men for future administration, etc.

Education and Culture. This will be a new Deparment. The function of this Department will be to direct the educational and cultural activities of Indians in East Asia and to provide for additional facilities in this connection, in so far as it is possible for the League to do so.

General Secretary's Department. The functions of this Department will be :—

(a) To maintain liaison with the *Hikari Kikan

(b) To co-ordinate the work of the different Departments

(c) To perform any special duties that may be assigned by me from time to time.

This Department will have a sub-department, to be called the House Sub-department. This sub-department will deal with problems arising out

*After Major General Iwakuro had departed from Malaya to take up another appointment leaving the Kikan in charge of his successor Col. Yamamoto, the Kikan came to be known as "Hikari Kikan," "Hikari" meaning light and glory.

of the daily work of the Indian Independence League Headquarters, *e. g*, (a) Transport and Petrol, (b) Buildings and their equipment, (c) Light, Telephone, etc., at the Headquarters, (d) Medical Staff, and (e) Arrangement for the stay of guests coming from outside.

When the work of the House Sub-Department increases it may be necessary and advisable to convert it into a full-fledged Department.

Establishment. Questions dealing with establishment (*e. g.*, appointments, allowances, transfer, etc.,) will be dealt with by me. The Departments concerned will, however, make recommendations from time to time.

Existing Staff ;—The existing Staff will all continue to work for the League in future. Transfers from one Department to another may, however, be made, if found to be necessary, in order to give effect to the re-organisation scheme outlined above.

Detailed Instructions—Detailed instructions with regard to the working of each Department will follow.

(Sd.) SUBHASH CHANDRA BOSE
President,
The Indian Independence League,
East Asia.

The following circulars were issued by the Departments of Recruitment and Training to provide detailed instructions for the working of each department :

Indian Independence League Headquarters

(Department of Recruitment)

7, Chancery Lane,
Syonan
23rd July, 1943.

Subject : Recruitment

You may be aware by now that the Headquarters of the Indian Independence League have been re-organised and that in order to effect the *Total Mobilisation* of our man-power and resources, several new departments have been started. In accordance with this plan, this Department has come into existence and it is the earnest desire of our President that at least 300,000 men (including women volunteers) be recruited for the coming fight for India's freedom.

Regarding the training of these recruits, the newly formed Training Department will address you separately. I shall only tell you this that we do not want to call up these recruits at once. In fact, the training will be done in three stages. In the first stage, recruits should not leave either homes or their professional work—and they should do only morning or evening drills. In the second stage, they will be brought into camps for whole-time training—when these camps are started in different parts of East Asia. In the third stage, they will be brought into Military Barracks when they will become full-fledged members of the Azad Hind Fauj (Indian National Army).

It will be considered a breach of discipline if any recruit suddenly gives up his professional work, or leaves his home, before he is called up for whole-time training.

To carry on the recruitment of volunteers for the Indian National Army in a systematic way, the following machinery is being set up :—

1. Under each Territorial Committee, the Chairman of every I.I.L. Branch will be the Recruiting Officer for his own area.

2. Under each Branch, the Chairman of every I.I.L. Sub-branch will be Assistant Recruiting Officer and will be responsible for recruitment within his area.

3. The Recruiting Officer (Branch Chairman) will supervise and co-ordinate the work of the Assistant Recruiting Officers. In case any Assistant Recruiting Officer fails to do his work properly, the Recruiting Officer will have authority to remove him and appoint a new Assistant Recruiting Officer in his place—after obtaining the approval of the Chairman of the Territorial Committee.

4. The Chairman of each Territorial Committee will be the Chief Recruiting Officer for his area. He will supervise and co-ordinate the work of the Recruiting Officers within his area. In case any Recruiting Officer fails to do his work properly, the Chief Recruiting Officer can remove him and appoint a new Recruting Officer in his place—after obtaining the approval of the Secretary of the Department of Recruitment of the I. I. L. Headquarters.

Duties Regarding Recruitment

1. Each recruit should fill in an enrolment form and hand it over to the Assistant Recruiting Officer.

2. These forms should be collected and sent to Headquarters through the Recruiting Officer and the Chief Recruiting Officer.

3. Owing to extreme emergency, old forms are being made use of, until revised forms are printed by this Department.

4. In case of shortage of printed forms, typed enlistment forms may be used by any Recruiting Officer or Assistant Recruiting Officer.

5. Each Officer, either R. O. or A. R. O., who is directly responsible for recruitment should keep a register of all the recruits who have applied for enlistment within his area—together with all particulars regarding each recruit.

6. Every C.R.O., R.O. and A.R.O., will please note that there will be no age restriction for recruits applying for enlistment. Printed forms of enlistment which contain age restriction should be amended accordingly.

7. Each Assistant Recruiting Officer should arrange for the Medical Examination of each recruit within his area. If necessary, he will take the help of the R.O. in this connection and the R. O. will, if necessary, take the help of the C.R.O. in this connection.

8. The forms of enlistment duly filled in should be forwarded to Headquarters, together with the Medical Officer's report.

9. No recruit should be rejected by the Medical Officer simply because he does not come up to the Army Standard—provided he is otherwise physically fit.

10. Each Branch or Sub-Branch as the case may be, should meet the expenses in connection with recruitment.

11. Enlistment forms together with the Medical Officer's report should be sent to Headquarters regularly once a fortnight. The first instalment of enlistment forms should be sent up as soon as possible.

12. In order to facilitate and expedite the work of recruitment the Headquarters will send to each Territorial Committee one or more Military Recruitment Advisers. The C.R.O., R.O. and A.R.O. are requested to make the fullest use of these Advisers.

Secretary,
Department of Recruitment.

Indian Independence League Headquarters

(Department of Training)

Subject—Training

In view of the total mobilisation in which Netaji requires not only the youth, but all able-bodied men to serve irrespective of age, the existing Youth Department has been absorbed in the Training Department.

2. The training being imparted to the Youth Sections by the I. S. I. and the Azad School Graduates at the local centres in Malaya will be continued under the direction of the "Member in Charge Training" of each branch or sub-branch.

More Instructors for local training will be sent to Malayan Branches on demand by the Malayan Chairman.

The demand from other territories should state the approximate number of recruits likely during the next 3 months.

3. The system of training will mobilise the manpower of East Asia in successive stages :—

1st. Stage. *Local training* in the nature of part time instruction for 2 hours in the morning or evening, every day as far as possible.

This is the responsibility of the territorial Branch and its Sub-branches. Recruits should neither leave their profession, nor their homes.

It will be considered a breach of discipline if any recruit suddenly gives up his professional work, or leave his home, before he is called up for whole-time training.

Instructors for this purpose will be provided from I. N. A. and from men trained in Central Camps.

Officers of the Azad Hind Fauj (I. N. A.) who are on recruiting or other duty will be utilized wherever possible to supervise such training and to help the Local Chairman in matters of Military Training and Organisation.

2nd Stage. Central Training in Central Camps under the Direct Control of this Headquarters.

(i) **Ordinary Camps ;** (ii) **Special Camps.**

(i) Territories will be informed of their quota for ordinary camps as and when Camps are ready. Although no high educational qualifications are needed, the best men from local training Centres must be selected to make up this quota.

The first ordinary Central Camp will open in Malaya on or about August 15. The total quota of 5,000 is alloted to Malaya. Detailed instructions later.

(ii) *Special Camp.* The highest possible educational qualifications are needed for candidates for special Camps.

Three such Camps, the Azad School, Syonan, the B. Y. T. C., Kuala Lumpur, and the Swaraj Youth Training Institute, Rangoon, are already in existence.

Another Camp, the Azad School, Penang, for 100 volunteers will open during the first week of August 2603. As other territories will not be able to send candidates in time, the quota of 100 will also be required from Malaya.

Other territories should proceed with the task of sifting good material and must send in applications as soon as possible.

3rd Stage. Training in Azad Hind Fauj.

This will begin as soon as the Army is in a position to absorb the men permanently.

When the system is in full swing, volunteers from the 1st and 2nd stages of training will provide a large reservoir for the I. N. A.

4. *Conditions and Allowances.* In addition to free clothing, board and lodging, men in all central camps will receive a normal pocket allowance.

5. *Training Syllabus and Organisation for the 1st Stage* will remain the same as given in "Interim Plan" dated 13-4-2603 except that more emphasis will be laid on Physical Fitness, Route Marches, and Military Training.

A simple specimen programme for the month of August is given below :—

Once a Week : Route March Distance to be increased from 5 to 15 miles.

Daily : P. T. 45 mins., Spiritual Training : 20 mins., Drill : 45 mins., Instructions for next day and rest 10 mins,

Total :—2 hours.

Sundays and Holidays : Special lectures for spiritual and political training.

6. *Finance*. The expenses in connection with training will continue to remain a territorial responsibility as far as the 1st Stage of training is concerned.

Secretary,
Training Department.

CHAPTER V

SUBHASH BECOMES SUPREME COMMANDER

The Indian Independence Movement was now gaining rapid momentum. To concentrate all the activities, it was thought proper to invest the whole power in one outstanding personality. Consequently Sjt. Subhash Chandra Bose took over the Supreme Command of the Indian National Army on July 25, 1943. The following Special Order of the Day was issued :—

In the interest of the Indian Independence Movement and of the Azad Hind Fauj I have taken over the direct command of our army from this day.

This is for me a matter of joy and pride—because for an Indian, there can be no greater honour than to be the Commander of India's Army of Liberation. But I am conscious of the magnitude of the task that I have undertaken and I feel weighed down with a sense of responsibility. I pray that God may give me the necessary strength to fulfil my duty to India under all circumstances, however difficnlt or trying they may be.

I regard myself as the servant of 38 crores of my countrymen, who profess different religious faiths. I am determined to discharge my duties in such a manner that the interests of these 38 crores may be safe in my hands and that every single Indian will have reason to put complete trust in me. It is only on the basis of undiluted nationalism and of perfect justice and impartiality that India's Army of Liberation can be built up.

In the coming struggle for the emancipation of our Motherland, for the establishment of a Government of Free India, based on the goodwill of 38 crores of Indians and for the creation of a permanent army which will guarantee Indian independence for all time, the Azad Hind Fauj has a vital role to play. To fulfil this role, we must weld ourselves into an army that will have only one goal—namely, the Freedom of India—and only one will—namely, to do or die in the cause of India's freedom. When we stand, the Azad Hind Fauj has to be like a wall of granite ; when we march, the Azad Hind Fauj has to be like a steam-roller.

Our task is not an easy one : the war will be long and hard but I have complete faith in the justice and in the invincibility of our cause. 38 crores of human beings, who form about one-fifth of the human race, have a right to be free and they are now prepared to pay tbe price of freedom. There is consequently no power on earth that can deprive us of our birthright of liberty any longer.

Comrades! Officers and men! With your unstinted support and unflinching loyality, the Azad Hind Fauj will become the instrument of India's liberation. Ultimate victory will certainly be ours, I assure you.

Our work has already begun. With the slogan, "Onward to Delhi!" on our lips, let us continue to labour and to fight till our National Flag flies over the Viceroy's House in New Delhi, and the Azad Hind Fauj holds its victory parade inside the ancient Red fortress of India's metropolis.

SUBHASH CHBNDRA BOSE,
Sipah-Salar.
(Supreme Commander)

Headquarters, Sipah-Salar,
Azad Hind Fauj, (I.N.A.)
25th July, 1943.

As the Supreme Commander Srijut Subhash Chandra Bose on a later occasion addressed the I.N.A. Officers on their duties and responsibilities. He said :

Brother Officers! It is my wish that we should be familiar among ourselves, and all of us should know what is our object ; what are our duties and responsibilities and how to discharge these duties and responsibilities satisfactorily.

First of all, I will myself tell you something about me. Because, I wish to let you know what is my individuality and what is my individual life, as, in future, we shall have to work together and tread the same path.

After the university career, I entered the political world. The most important question at that time was this : What Indians did during the last war ? What was the result and what were the experiences and lessons we got for the future ? In India and in England it was our experience that the policy of our leaders was wrong. Of course, we were depending upon our leaders for action. But we young men and students were thoroughly disappointed. In our minds there was only one idea, that the mistake committed by our leaders in the last war should not be committed again. We thought, if we get an opportunity in future, we will not make such mistakes.

There was another big question. In Europe, after the war, in the year 1918 and 1919, there were many changes ; new governments were coming into existence, which had not existed before the war. The Czechs ceased to be a part of the Austro-Hungarian Empire. Another race, the Poles, formed their own government. When I went to Europe, I had the opportunity of meeting two or three Indian leaders there. They all advised me that if we want to do anything for our Motherland we should study the history of the war and the experiences of such history should be utilized for our fight against Britain. We began to learn and understand things. We came to know how some leaders of Czechs went out of their country for doing propaganda and for getting help from the enemies of Austria and Hungary. They joined hands with Britain and France against Austria, Hungary and Germany.

The Poles, too, formed an army of 30,000 and took part in the war. It was their fortune that Germany and her allies were defeated, and after the war, they were able to form their own government.

There is no reason why we should not also go by the same path, and taking advantage of the international situation, we should fight shoulder to shoulder with the enemies of Britain, to get complete freedom.

The people of Ireland also took advantage of the war. They openly revolted under the Sinn Fein Party against the British. In the City of Dublin, the Sinn Fein Party had an army of 3,000 only. They had also an army of 10,000 strong in the country. Something went wrong with their plans and the rebellion that started in Dublin did not spread to the countryside. Anyhow they kept the City of Dublin under their control for eight days. The revolution occurred during Easter, and so the revolution is called the Easter Revolution. Though the revolt did not materialise in 1916, it again broke out in the year 1919, just after the war. They had only 5,000 volunteers. This time it was different. War was over. From England troops could be brought to suppress the rebellion. Even then this army of volunteers numbering 5,000 carried on their fight and in the end the British were brought to their knees.

In 1921, we began working in India with all the experiences that we had from the study of the history of the last war. At that time as you know, Mahatma Gandhi had launched the Non-Co-operation Movement enthusiastically with the specific idea in mind that when an opportunity offers itself, we should take up arms against the British. We knew also that Germany would try to take revenge and then would come our opportunity as well.

We joined the Congress in 1921 under Mahatma Gandhi, because there was no other way to carry on our fight to keep up the honour of the nation in the face of terrible British oppression. Hindus and Muslims were united. But we knew definitely that by Civil Disobedience Campaign India would not be completely free. Of course the movement did create the political consciousness among the people, and it prepared the people for armed struggle. From 1921 onward we were waiting for an opportunity to take up arms, and that opportunity was a war in Europe.

This is not my individual view but it is the view of many young men who came under Mahatma Gandhi in 1921. Certainly there were a few young men who believed in non-violence, but many of them were strong supporters of violence and they were awaiting the proper time to strike.

I went to Europe in 1933 and remained up to 1936. My idea in going to Europe was to study the situation and to know what was going to happen next. During my stay in Europe I visited Berlin and made acquaintance with certain Government officials and met Fuehrer Hitler. I plainly asked them when they were going to strike at Britain so that we might also take up arms simultaneously against the British. They replied that they were not at all going to fight Britain and they hoped that all their demands would be fulfilled by Britain. They were for a compromise with Britain. However, they expressed their sympathy for Indian freedom. I argued with them about the British hypocrisy and their cunning policy as Indians know best about that by personal experience, and warned them that, when Britain thought that the German power was getting stronger, she would openly come into conflict with Germany. In the end I told them : "Britain is our traditional enemy. We will fight her, whether you support us or not". But I had no doubt that war would start in Europe soon, Anybody could understand this, by having a look at the preparations that were going on in Germany. When I went to Europe this time, I reminded them of what I said in the year 1936.

My idea in saying this is that I came back from Europe with a strong conviction of what was going to happen. The new party that came in power in Germany was always for a fight. I clearly understood that the German demands would not be accepted by the British and if the British found the Germans growing a bit strong, they would fight the Nazis. In 1938 when I went to Europe I noticed some changes. Germany was beginning to understand that the British would never fully accept their proposals. In September 1938, when the Germans put forward the case of Sudetan Germans, Mr. Chamberlain rushed to Munich to come to an agreement with Herr Hitler. There was a time when all parleys of international value generally used to take place in London. But when I saw the British Prime Minister, Mr. Chamberlain, going to Germany, leaving his own country and when he accepted the German demands, I realized the secret. It was the first time in the history of the British that a Prime Minister of England relegating the usual custom, proceeded to a foreign country to accept the demands of another nation.

Then I started propaganda in India that a war in Europe was inevitable and it was the duty of Indians to be alert and to try to force Britain to accept our demands, and if they did not, to prepare ourselves for a fight. I was noticing the reaction of the public to my propaganda, and I was convinced that the full support of the general public was with me. But our leaders were thinking in a different way, particularly Mahatma Gandhi whose policy was to wait and see. But we young men were not deterred by this policy. We redoubled our propaganda. We were asking the people of India to take advantage of the golden opportunity that would be presented to them in the near future.

In the annual session of the Indian National Congress at Tripuri in March 1939, I tabled one resolution demanding freedom for India within six months and such an ultimatum to be sent to the Government. In case this demand was not conceded in that period, we should prepare the people for a fight against Britain with whatever might we possess. It was, of course, in the nature of an ultimatum and the resolution was introduced, keeping in view the tense international situation and knowing full well that a conflagration would begin in Europe within six months.

When the war actually started in September 1939, the public began to realize that what I said in March was correct. It was our duty at that time to unite all the Nationalist forces and bring pressure on the British Government to concede to our demand, and if unsuccessfnl, to fight for it. But our leaders were thinking and acting in a different way. They were under the impression that Britain would become weak in the course of the war and to get the Indian help, they would come to an honourable agreement with the Congress. I tried to point out the absurdity of such a notion and told them whatever might be the weakness of Britain during the war they would never allow to rid themselves of the power in India. The weaker they grew the more powerful would become their grip on India. Without India they would not be able to prosecute the war successfully. They would begin looting and plundering the country's resources as they got weaker and weaker.

In March 1940 when the Congress Session was in progress, we expected a forward step. But Gandhiji had his own way. He was to wait and see. We began to lose our minds, come what may, to start our own movement. An anti-war movement was started throughout the country. It became somewhat serious ; many people courted imprisonment. Meanwhile I got information that Gandhiji himself would launch a civil disobedience movement in November as the Government did nothing. I heaved a sigh of relief that if Gandhiji starts a movement, it will have world-wide reperenssions. The whole world will come to know that Indians are fighting for freedom. All the nations will think that Indians deserve freedom. We will surely get the sympathy of the world to have saved our honour.

But I thought that by the weapon of Civil Disobedience alone we will not achieve freedom. The movement would surely bring pressure on the Government and hamper its war effort, but the government would never consider our demand. That was my idea. We were thinking what to do. What new method should be adopted. Young men were doing their bit with bombs and revolvers. We got into touch with these young revolutionaries. I knew their strength. They were real revolutionaries with high spirits. But their strength and sacrifice were not enough to achieve complete independence for our Motherland.

It was then we began scanning the pages of history and found many an example and learned many a lesson. The American example was before us. I began to realise, and even came to the conclusion, that without outside help the Indian revolution would not be successful. The United States got a lot of help from France. Even Generals were despatched from France. In the history of the world, it is not a new thing to get assistance from other nations for winning freedom for one's country.

The news we got in India were twisted and more of a propaganda nature. It was natural that Britain should do so. But to understand the real situation of the world by remaining inside India was not possible. What would be the result of the war and how the war would end and who would win in the end ? What were the ideas of Indians abroad, how they were thinking about India's fight for freedom, how to get help from them for India's independence and whether it was possible to get material help from the enemies of Britain ? These were the questions which made us think that somebody should be sent outside India I thought of sending some persons to foreign countries. Certainly it was a most difficult task, strictly restricted as our movements were. I thought also that such a person should leave India as the British really "understand" and as the Indian people seriously take. At last I decided myself to get out of India.

I was in jail at that time. To get out of the jail was a difficult problem. To slip away from jail would make it difficult for me to leave the country in view of the British C. I. D. At last I decided to go on hunger-strike. This decision was taken after steeling my heart, that I would either die or get out of the jail. When my decision was made known to the Government it created a stir in the official circles as they never wanted to see me die in the jail. The Superintendent of the jail came and entreated me not to undertake hunger-strike. He argued that if all the prisoners went on hunger-strike the King's Government would come to a stand-still, and warned me that if I died in the jail it would be my own responsibility. My hunger-strike went on for six days. They tried to forcibly feed me but I was determined to die the way of Jatindra Nath Das. After seven days, a secret conference took place at Governmeut House. They wanted to do something as the medical report about my condition was serious. They set me free with the idea of rearresting me after a month. I got information of this in good time. Meanwhile some arrangements could be made for my escape from India and I left my country.

Experiences I had a lot, after leaving my homeland. I was listening in to both the radios. I had the privilege from the German authorities to hear the enemy radio and propaganda. I had the opportunity of visiting all the fortifications and other defences all over Europe. After these personal experiences, I have no doubt what will be the result of the war. As I said in your prade the other day, the war will be a prolonged one but there will surely be one result, that is, the collapse of Britain, and her empire.

Now the question is this. What is the position of India under these circumstances ? The destruction of the British Empire is certain, and the whole map of the world will be changed. What will be the position of India in the new map ? The British will be driven out of India, and what should be our position then ? We should think about this. There are three alternatives ;

One is to keep away from the war and to have a neutral attitude.
Second is to go and beg for freedom from the new invader and
the third is to take part in the war with the enemies of Britain and qualify ourselves for freedom.

I know what alternative you prefer. For us there is but one alternative that is, to fight hand in hand with the enemies of Britain and contribute our share in the destruction of British Empire.

The internal situation in India is very grave. It is our duty to encourage and support the forces that are in India doing, their bit against Britain. What is the internal situation in India to-day ? The whole population is against the British Government.

People are carrying on the fight without arms. To suppose millions of unarmed people, a small army of thousands equipped with all modern arms is enough. When I had the privilege of meeting Herr Hitler, I took the liberty of asking this question of India and sought his advice as to what path we should tread. The Chancellor of Germany, who is himself an experienced revolutionary, giving his opinion, said that a well-equipped army of a few thousands would be able to control millions of unarmed revolutionaries. He added that so long as an external power did not knock at the frontier no change could be expected in the internal situation. We should form part of this external power. We hear so much nowadays of a second front. It is we, who should create a second front in India. It would have been possible for them to face us in both the fronts, had not the Axis Powers crippled and maimed them. The Axis Powers had made our work easier. We are thankful to them for doing this, but at the same time, it is incumbent upon us to do our duty towards our motherland. To do this work an army of 50,000 is enough, but we should be prepared to raise an army of 300,000.

The question now is this : What are the duties of this army ? There are two duties which this army will have to perform. The first and important duty is, of course, to fight the enemy and free our motherland ; the second one is also no less important. After the enemy is defeated, we will have to do tremendous work in India. By freeing India our duty will not be over. Our army is revolutionary one, and as revolutionaries we have two duties to perform. *The first one, as I said before, is to drive the enemy out of India, and* the second duty is to form such a powerful army in India that will face any nations put together, and to defend India forever against foreign invasion.

Friends! We all should think that we will never remain slaves. We have already had a very good taste of this slavery. To protect our motherland from any foreign aggressors, it is the duty of all of you to form the strongest possible army in the world. As far as ability and efficiency are concerned, I may tell you that you are second to none. We were not getting proper training and opportunity but whenever these two things were offered to Indians, they have shown their mettle. Not only in military, but in politics, economics, science, sports, etc, we Indians are not in any way backward. Indians are efficient and able. The Almighty has created them like that. Of course, we have to learn much from the world and we are prepared to do so. And with this learning and the natural efficiency and ability of ours and with full confidence, we are forming this army.

For the success of an army, military training only will not suffice. Take the case of France. Up to 1939 the French Army was considered the best in the world. It was really so. They had a lot of materials, aeroplanes, heavy guns, etc. In addition there was the 'impregnable' Maginot Line to protect them. Why then France fell within so short a time? There was only one reason and that was, there was no *josh* in them. After the last war, such a feeling was created in France that they should take rest as the enemy had been defeated once for all. That was not so in Germany. In Germany the cry was 'revenge.' One nation was thinking in terms of revenge and sacrifice. That is why the French people had their disastrous defeat. The French people had lost their spirit and the Germans were seething with the spirit.

After the Azad Hind Fauj parade, I had a talk with Premier Tojo who congratulated me for the grand parade. He also said that the success of an army mainly depends on the moral training they get. I assured him that that will be given special attention.

The Nipponese attach much importance to this 'spirit'. For instance, see the spirit of the defenders of Attu Island. They knew they could not win against such a numerically superior army. They could have easily surrendered. But they did not do so It was against the honour and glory of their motherland. The whole garrison of 2,000 sacrificed their lives fighting the enemy.

I may also mention about the brave defenders of Stalingrad. They were at one time surrounded by the enemy, and they were even given an ultimatum by the Germans to surrender. They did not surrender and carried on their fight, even though the enemy were 200,000 strong that surrounded them. Such was the spirit of the brave defenders of Stalingrad.

We should create such a spirit in our men. The responsibility of the Officers is great. A Sepoy can afford to leave the battlefield but an officer cannot do so. He is a responsible man and only an army led by such responsible officers will be successful in the end. So, your work is tremendous. There is no other work greater and nobler than the work you have undertaken.

Our sisters and brothers in India are facing even bigger ordeals with cheer and enthusiasm. For the Indian Independence and for India's welfare, there is no greater work than this.

While in Europe, I tried and I was successful in forming a small National Army. I have brought photos of the army. In Berlin and Rome Indians are thinking and doing things as you are thinking and doing here. Everywhere in the world, wherever there are Indians, a new spirit, a new awakening has come among Indians.

CHAPTER VI

PREPARATIONS FOR MILITARY CAMPAIGN

Netaji's Eventful Tour

Events were now moving fast. By the rare qualities of his head and heart, Syt. Subhash Chandra Bose had gained the full confidence of his countrymen ; dissentions had disappeared, all the forces had been mobilised and all had gathered round his banner. His past services and sacrifices in the cause of freedom movement in India counted a great deal. The Indians in East Asia realized that he was the Man of Destiny and conferred on him the title of " Netaji "—the Great Leader.

With great enthusiasm and vigour, working day and night and knowing no rest or sleep, Netaji was fast preparing for the last struggle. His capacity of work knew no equal. We are wonderstruck to see, what he achieved within 20 days, after his arrival in Singapore. He had addressed several public meetings, had reformed and consolidated the Indian Independence League and had reorganised the Indian National Army. He called several meetings of the sponsers of the Movement and officers of the Indian National Army and saw the Japansese authorities at Singapore, in order to impress upon them his viewpoint. He was naturally now anxious to personally contact Indians, living in other parts of East Asia and to foster close relations with Governments of other countries, whose co-operation was necessary for his cause, viz., that of Burma, Thailand. Indo-China etc.

Consequently he took an extensive tour of these countries. Leaving Singapore by Air on July 25, 1943, he returned to headquarters on August 11. The most memorable event of his tour was his presence in Rangoon at the historic occasion of the Declaration of Burma's Independence on August 1. He personally exchanged felicitations with the Head of the New Independent State of Burma, Dr. Ba Maw, and thus cemented the ties of traditional friendship and sympathy between India and Burma.

Srijut Subhash Bose conveyed to Dr. Ba Maw India's heartfelt congratulations to Burma on the latter's attainment of her Independence. Himself engaged at the moment in preparing for the final battle for India's Independence, Srijut Bose felt a peculiar thrill and great inspiration in witnessing the rebirth of Independent Burma, next-door to his own dear Motherland.

Five days earlier during his sojourn in Bangkok, as the State guest of the Government of Thailand, Syt Bose had an intimate personal talk with Field-Marshal Pibul Songgram, the Thai Premier, which lasted for one and a half hour. This meeting undoubtedly resulted in deepening Thailand's sympathy with the Indian Independence Movement, and ensured even greater support of the Thai Nation and the Government for the total mobilization of the Indian Community in Thailand.

Thus Syt. Bose's whirlwind tour of this part of East Asia was another milestone in the consolidation of the Asiatic nations, which were already independent, which had just attained independence and which were on the threshhold of independence. The leaders of these nations fraternized with each other and established personal contacts that were so essential for understanding, sympathy and co-ordination of the efforts to create an Asia for Asiatics.

Another and a vitally important achievement of the tour, was the tremendous enthusiasm aroused among the Indian communities in Thailand, Burma and French Indo-China, Ever since the arrival of Srijut Subhash Bose at Syonan in the middle of June, Indians in Bangkok, Rangoon and Saigon had been on the tiptoes of expectation of his visit to these cities. And when he did arrive in their midst, the enthusiasm of Indians in these places rose to feverpitch, and they gave a resounding demonstration of their readiness to march under his banner to sacrifice their all and their very lives, in the coming bloody struggle for India's independence. When hearing his impassioned words, their faces shone bright with hope and confidence that victory was at sight.

Leaving Singapore by air on July 25, Srijut Subhash Bose arrived in Bangkok the same day ; after a three-day stay there crowded with engagements, he arrived in Rangoon by air on the 29th, returned to Bangkok by plane on August 4th, left for Saigon on the 9th and arrived there the same day, left for Singapore on the 11th, reaching Headquarters the same evening by plane.

On arrival at the Bangkok aerodrome on July 25th, Srijut Subhash Bose was given a rousing welcome by the Indian community who had gathered in large numbers to receive him. On the way from airport, Srijut Subhash Bose alighted at the Victory Monument of the Thais and laid a wreath ; later in the day he paid courtesy calls on high Nippon authorities in Bangkok.

Next day, July 26th, Srijut Bose called on the German Minister, and the Italian Minister, met leading Indians in Bangkok, and was entertained by the local Indian community, the Nippon Ambassador and Nippon military authorities. On July 27th, he addressed a mass rally of Indians at the Chulankorn University hall, was entertained by the German Minister, met the Thai Premier for one-and-half hours, received the Thai and Axis press representatives, and was entertained to dinner by the Thai Foreign Minister.

The following day, July 28th, he left for Rangoon where he arrived on July 29th and was welcomed at the airport by high Nippon officials and leading Indians of Rangoon. In the course of the day he paid courtesy calls on the Nippon Commander in-Chief and highranking Nippon officers, visited the Burma Government offices and Indian Independence League organization and was the guest of honour at a dinner given by the Nippon Commander-in-Chief.

The next day, July 30th, he took the salute at the Parade of the Swaraj Young Men's Training Institute, visited the Broadcasting Station, was guest of Dr. Ba Maw at lunch, addressed a mass meeting of Indians, and was later entertained at dinner at the Oriental Club.

The following day July 31st, Srijut Subhash Bose received the press representatives and addressed the executives of the Indian Independeace League.

The first of August, a historic day for Burma and all Asia, and a day of hope for India—declaraion of Burma's Independence—Subhash Chandra Bose was personally present at the epoch-making ceremony of the proclamation of Burma's Independence.

He sent a message of congratulations to the Head of the New Independent State of Burma, Dr. Ba Maw on the achievement of Burma's aspirations. The same evening he attended the State Banquet to celebrate the Independence proclamation.

The following day, August 2nd, Srijut Subhash Bose granted interviews to leading citizens of Rangoon and later called on the first Nippon Ambassador to Burma.

August 3rd was spent in interviewing leaders of the Indian community in Burma.

Arriving in Bangkok the next day, August 4th, he again called on the Thai Premier.

The Italian Minister entertained the Indian leader on August 5th ; later in the day, Srijut Subhas Bose addressed a public meeting and gave interviews to leading Indians in Bangkok.

On August 6th, Srijut Subhash Bose was host at a Garden Party to Nippon and Thai officers and officials and Indians, and was guest at a dinner given by the Nippon Ambassador.

After spending two more busy days in Bangkok, the leader arrived in Saigon on August 9th. During his brief stay of two days at Saigon, he called on the Commander-in-chief Nippon Forces in Indo-China, the Admiral in Indo-China, and Nippon Ambassador in Saigon. He attended a public reception in his honour organised by the Indian community who demonstrated their determination to do their bit in India's last War of Independence.

Leaving Saigon on August 11th by air, he arrived in Singapore the same evening.

The following detailed proceedings, recording the speeches and Press interviews of Netaji, will show the exact position of the movement at the time and its future :—

1. Press Statement on the achievement of Burma's Independence

From 1925 to 1927 I used to gaze from the verandah of my cell in Mandalay Prison on the palace of the last independent King of Burma and I used to wonder when Burma would be free once again. Today Burma is an independent State and I am breathing the atmosphere of that liberated country.

Right in the midst of a World War, an indepnedent State is born in Asia, out of the ashes of British Imperialism and out of the smouldering ruins left behind by the fleeing British. In November, 1941, the then Prime Minister of Burma was in England, pleading with his British rulers for a small measure of self-rule, but all his entreaties were treated with contempt and scorn. The people of Burma, thereupon, took up arms against the British, co-operated with the armed forces of Nippon and hounded the British out of Burma. They now have their reward for all their suffering and sacrifice.

During the nineteenth century, India through her own enslavement, offered a jumping-off ground to Briiain's armed forces for attacking and subjugating Burma. Burma has now repaid us by turning the British out and offering her independent territory as a springboard for India's National Army, in its attack on Britain's Army in India.

The pledge given by Japan's worthy Prime Minister, General Tojo, now stands redeemed. While Sir Stafford Cripps gives promises of Dominion Status and of Pakistan after the war—and while Sir Dorman Smith claims to rule Burma from Delhi with the help of his typewriter—Burma with the help of her ally, Nippon, has succeeded in overthrowing the British and winning her liberty. This has very great significance for India, for Asia, and for the whole world.

The news that India's next door neighbour Burma, is now free has thrown our rulers in New Delhi into epileptic fits. They are panic-stricken that the example of Burma will now inspire the Indian people to rise in arms against their alien oppressors and they are busy devising more ruthless methods for suppressing the nationalist movement. But nothing on earth can keep India enslaved any longer and just as the peacock emblem now flies over the Government House in Rangoon—so will the tricolour soon fly over the Red Fortress of Delhi.

2. The following speech was delivered on Rangoon Radio on August 1, 1943

Countrymen and Friends ! Today is the first of August, 1943. Today an event of great historical importance has taken place. Right in the midst of a World War, an Independent State has come into being. Burma—our neighbour has achieved her Independence and she has now her own national Independent Government. Long Live Free Burma !

You all know that when the war in East Asia broke out in December, 1941, the people of Burma deeided to utilise the opportunity for recovering their lost liberty. Instead of co-operating with the British Government, the vast majority of Burmans did their best to help in expelling the British from the country, and the result is that today, not only has Burma been liberated from the British altogether, but she has actually realised her long cherished goal of Independence.

The Independence of Burma in this momentous crisis in world history, has a two-fold significance for us. It shows, in the first place, what a nation can achieve, if it knows how to seize an opportunity which histoty has offered.

Secondly, just as the conquest of India supplied the British with a jumping-off g ound for their attack on Burma in the nineteenth century—similarly, the emancipation of Burma has supplied the Indian Independence Movement in East Asia with a spring-board, for its attack on Britain's Army of occupation in India, during the twentieth century.

Burma was deprived of her liberty long after India was. Nevertheless Burma has stolen a march over us and has attained her liberty, while we are still passing through the throes of revolution. On behalf of the Indian people and of myself, I offer my warmest congratulations to the people of Burma on their achievement—and I heartily wish them increasing progress and prosperity in the days to come. I offer also my hearty felicitation to His Excellency Dr. Ba Maw, the head of the New and Independent State of Burma and I wish him all success in the discharge of the manifold responsibilities which have now devolved on him. It is a source of great pleasure and gratification for me that so soon after meeting Dr Ba Maw in Syonan, during the first week of July, I can offer him my greetings and congratulations as the head of the new and Independent State of Burma.

Friends, you are aware of the many promises which the British Government has given to the Indian people during the course of their rule in India—promises which have always proved to be mere scraps of paper. You are aware also that these promises have been repeated since the outbreak of the present war and all sorts of silly excuses have been put forward to show that in the midst of a war, transference of power from British to Indian hands cannot take place. As against this example, we now see that right in the midst of the war, the promise of liberty made by the Prime Minister of Japan, His Excellency General Tojo, on behalf of his Government and nation, has been fully redeemed. Where there is a will there is a way and this statesmanship and generosity on the part of Japan, will bring into bold relief the hypocrisy of British politicians—while they will demonstrate the real character of Japan's state policy.

The Independence of Burma will, I am sure, be soon followed by the Independence of the Philippines. Asia is now on the threshold of a new era in her history. This is a unique opportunity for all the suppressed nations of Asia to rise and effect their emancipation. It is above all the sacred duty of the Indian people to seize the present golden opportunity and fulfil their age-long aspirations.

The liberation of Asia cannot be complete until India is free. The Indian people must, therefore, rise and liberate themselves and thereby help the emancipation of other Asiatic nations. Above all, India must seize the hand of friendship which Japan has offered to India and to other suppressed nations of Asia. Confronted by a common foe, the people of India must march shoulder to shoulder with the brave Nipponese nation, till the enemy is overthrown and India recovers her lost liberty.

INQUILAB ZINDABAD!
AZAD HIND ZINDABAD!

3. Addressing a mammoth rally, attended by more than 10,000 local Indians, Srijut Subhash Chandra Bose, President of the Indian Independence League in East Asia in a stirring speech on July 30, exhorted Indians in East Asia to rise as one man to oust the British from India, declaring :

"We can win our independence only if we are ready to sacrifice our lives and property." He emphasized : "By shedding our blood we will be creating a real united India."

"The time for total mobilization has come," Mr. Bose declared, stressing that Indians in East Asia must realize that the opportunity to serve India has come to them.

He added : " Death is certain. Everyone has to die sooner or later. But you must realize that there cannot be a more glorious death than death to free one's own country."

He pointed out that Indians, although moved by the desire for independence, have hitherto been unable to achieve freedom because " we had no arms."

"By means of civil disobedience and Satyagraha, we could surely harass the enemy, but these weapons were insufficient to drive out the enemy from India," Mr. Bose said.

"Today, however," he declared, "the situation has changed and Indians have been able to organise a powerful army outside India. The Indian National Army has been declared to the world. It is no more kept a secret."

Utilizing this powerful army and internal situation in India, Mr. Bose expressed his confidence that Indians both within and without India will be able to expel the British from India.

Pointing out that the organization of the Provisional Government of free India is essential for the successful penetration into India, Mr. Bose told his listeners : "I am going to make the announcement of such a Government at the right time "

He added, when such a Government is formed, its only work will be to prepare for the fight, mobilize and fight. And then we enter India and after the final victory, the work of the Provisional Government would be over, and it will be left to the 38 million Indians to establish a new and permanent Government in India."

He concluded by exhorting all Indians, young and old, men and women, rich and poor, to exert their supreme effort for the glorious realization of Indian independence.

4. Srijut Subhash Chandra Bose, President of the Indian Independence League, in a recent interview, granted to a Domei correspondent, at Rangoon predicted that the attainment of independence by Burma will greatly accelerate the Indian Independence Movement.

Slowly and in well-studied phrases, the great Indian leader first noted that the significance of the historic event in Burma lay in the fact that everything happening in Burma, would have far-reaching repercussion in India

Bose traced back the mutual history of the two countries, especially emphasizing the fact that Burma was at one time a territory of India when both suffered under the British rule.

The majority of Indian nationals are well aware of this mutual history, not to mention the geographic proximity of the two countries, Bose said.

Thus the fact that Burma has now released herself from the tyranny of Britain and has declared her independence is something very close to Indians. This event is sure to inspire the Indian people whose faith in their own independence is firm beyond description.

Subhash Chandra Bose added that the Indian people at home are sure to expect great aid from the Burmese in gaining their own independence. The Indian National Army is already placing high hopes on independent Burma, Bose revealed, because the army will now be able to advance to the Indian frontiers without having to worry about its rear which will be guarded by the Burmese.

He unstintingly praised Prime Minister Dr. Ba Maw, saying Burma couldn't have obtained a better leader to start the country on its brilliant way of progress. He added Dr. Ba Maw is supported by a very capable cabinet, emphasizing especially that the appointment of Major-General Thakin Aung San, who is highly popular with the youths to the post of Defence Minister has greatly bolstered the Government.

Confidence, that Mahatma Gandhi and a large number of his followers would extend their wholehearted moral, if not complete physical support, once the Indian National Army successfully penetrates into India along with the projected Provisional Government of Free India, was expressed on July 31, by Subhash Chandra Bose, President of the Indian Independence League in East Asia at a press conference following his arrival in Rangoon.

The fiery Indian national leader declared that although Gandhi may not support fighting with arms because of his steadfast adherenee to his long advocated principle of non-violence, it is certain "he will not oppose us."

Howeverer, once the proposed Provisional Government has successfully penetrated into India there is every possibility Gandhi will lend his full support, Bose stressed.

"Among his followers most of them will support us though we do not expect older men," Bose declared, pointing out that more and more younger men of the Gandhi group are coming over to the side of the advocates of violence.

Bose's statement was made in response to the question as to whether rumours were true that an agreement exists between him and Gandhi regarding the conduct of the Indian independence movement.

Explaining the reason for his conviction, Bose recalled Gandhi's attitude at their last meeting in Wardha in June 1940. "In my last meeting I tried to persuade Gandhi to abandon his non-violence stand but he did not agree", Bose said, "When I finally told him that if he would not come over to our side we would do it ourselves, he laughed and said "I shall be the first to congratulate you, if you succeed." Bose recalled.

Questioned regarding the existence of anti-Nippon feeling in India, Bose declared that anti-Nippon sentiment in India had undergone a vast change since the outbreak of the war.

There has been a big landslide in favour of Nippon with Premier Tojo's repeated declarations that Nippon desires nothing but the well-being and freedom of India.

Although there are still a few people who doubt Nippon's intentions, the number is smaller now." Bose stressed adding, "These very doubts regarding Nippon's intentions can, and are being dispelled".

In this connection the visiting Indian leader said, "the formation of the Indian National Army is proof that it is not the Nippon army alone which is fighting but "We are fighting for Asia."

He added that the formation of the proposed Provisional Government will be further proof that Nippon has no designs on India.

Anti-Nippon sentiment, he said, constitutes the reaction of some groups who are either pro-Chungking or pro-Soviet. The argument in their groups is that the Nippon army is simply going to attack India, but this reasoning is weak as it is actually not the Nippon army but the Indian Army which is taking the lead.

As to the effect of Burma's independence on India, Bose said "Burma's is like a test case ; the independence of Burma will help us greatly in our fight. The moment we show Burma is free, we show that the argument against Nippon is false."

Burma's independenee, he said, will have a much greater effect on India than the Philippines because Burma is geographically closer to India.

Bose pointed out that Burma's independence is significant for three essential reasons : (1) It refutes the argument that Nippon is solely concerned with creating a Greater East Asia for herself ; (2) Burma formerly was a part of India ; and (3) Burma's indepedence opens a direct route of aid to India.

Discussing the effect of India's independence on Britain, Bose said, as India has come to assume an integral part of the British Empire, India's freedom will be a terrific blow politically, morally, and spiritually to the British. The expulsion of the British from India, militarily means that Britain will be deprived of all hopes of retaking Burma not to say of recovering lost territories in Asia. Moreover, when the British are permanently driven out from Asia, the British will be unable to maintain their military strength in Iran and the Middle East which depend on India for supplies."

Under such circumstances, Bose expressed the view that the Axis should first tackle Britain which is weaker than the United States.

There are two ways of defeating Britain. The first is the occupation of the British Isles which however does not seem possible at present. The other is to undermine the base of British resistance by driving ont the British from India.

Although the Americans have sent reinforcements to India they are not strong enough yet to take over control of India from the British, he said, Therefore, Indians should expel the British from India before the Americans realised their aims.

Questioned as to what he thought about the anti-Axis war aims, Bose declared that politically there seems to be no agreement between Britain and the United States. Pointing out the clashes between American and

British interests in Africa and Australia and the friction between the two countries and the Soviet Union regarding the administration of Polish occupied territory, Bose remarked : "If you compare this with the Axis you can find no such clashes among the Axis. Militarily the Axis powers are more strategically located both in Europe and Asia. Thus the Axis are in a better position to defend themselves when the occasion arises," he said.

Contrary to conditions during World War No. 1, the Anglo-American powers steadily are destined to grow weaker from a protracted struggle while the Axis will become stronger. Hence Bose said, there is no doubt of the Axis' growing strength.

Commenting on his impression of Burma and its leaders, Bose said he thought "Dr. Ba Maw is the best choice that could have been made. In Burma you have not got a better man."

He added, he believed, Dr. Ba Maw could succeed although the latter has a difficult wartime task ahead. "All the ministers have self-confidence which is very important and his work will be made easier by the co-operation of old officials."

"On the other hand the vouger generation and former revolutionary elements such as Major-General Aung San are giving their full support to the new Government, thereby assuring Burma's success," Bose concluded.

5. Immediately after Netaji's return from tour, a mass meeting was held at the Farrer Park, Singapore on 15th August 1943. In a stirring speech Netaji described the impressions of his tour and his future plan of action, He said :—

" Sisters and brothers ! Indians all over East Asia are meeting today in unprecedented numbers for a two-fold purpose. They are, first of all, celebrating the Independence of Burma. They are also reiterating their demand that the British quit India at once and they are reaffirming their unshakable determination to continue the struggle till the complete independence of India is achieved.

" You may be aware that I had the good fortune to be in Burma when the declaration of independence was made on the 1st of August and the new independent State of Burma was brought into existence, along with the first Cabinet of Free Burma.

"The whole ceremony was a most solemn and impressive one and I am thankful to Providence that I could witness with my own eyes the birth of a new and independent State just across the Indian frontier. By the nemesis of history Burma's independent State was established in the same place which was the seat of British power and authority in Burma.

" As I was witnessing that historic ceremony on the morning of the 1st of August—I could see vividly with my mind's eye—the ceremony of hoisting our national flag over the Viceroy's House in New Delhi as well as the Victory Parade which the Azad Hind Fauj (Indian National Army) will hold inside the ancient Red Fortress of Delhi—when the British are finally expelled from India.

".Friends ! You know perhaps that Burma was not new to me and that I had spent 2½ years in prisons in Burma, when the British were in occupation of that country. But it was a new Burma and a free Burma that I visited this time.

" In that free Burma, the Nipponese Military Administration has been completely abolished ; Dr. Ba Maw is head of the new State, as well as Premier and Commander-in Chief, and he has formed a cabinet ; he will be advised by a Privy Council. Independent Burma has declared war on Britain and America who are still dreaming of reconquering and re-enslaving Burma ; Independent Burma has entered into a Treaty of Alliance with Nippon ; the Nippon Ambassador is already in Burma ; Ambassadors of other countries will soon be in Rangoon ; Burmese Ambassadors have been accredited to other countries ; Nippon has decided to transfer all the Anglo-American enemy properties in Burma to the new Burmese State.

" These properties include factories, harbours, railways, telegraphs, and telephones. Thus, the Burmans will govern their country according to the wishes of the Burmese people ; and they have an army manned and officered exclusively by themselves. Last but not least, today the Peacock Emblem—the national flag of Burma and not the Union Jack – is flying over the office and residence of the head of the State—Adipadi Dr. Ba Maw.

" Today my heart is full of my recent experiences in Burma and it will take me hours and hours, if I were to narrate all I have seen and heard there. I shall therefore end this topic by relating only a few things. First of all, about Rangoon jail.

As I had lived in Rangoon Jail for several months in 1927, I wanted very much to re-visit that place. But I was not allowed to do so, because that Jail is no longer used for Indian prisoners.

It is now used exclusively for British war-prisoners.

Friends ! Think of the day when we shall avenge ourselves for the incarceration of hundreds of thousands of Indian patriots by converting all the prisons in India into Camps for British War-prisoners. Prepare from now for that glorious day !

" I had the privilege of having long discussions with Adipadi Dr. Ba Maw and his Ministers and I am glad to tell you that a complete aggreement was reached on problems of common interest.

" The Adipadi has promised all-out aid to India in the coming stuggle for Indian Independence. Burma and India will now march shoulder to shoulder against the common enemy—and when the enemy is vanquished and peace is established, we shall live in complete amity and accord like good neighbours.

" It would interest you greatly to hear that the Adipadi Dr. Ba Maw is alive today to lead his people, through the grace of Providence.

" He was a prisoner in North Burma when the war in Burma began and the British wanted to take him by force to India—or in the alternative to kill him in prison. But God willed otherwise. He managed to escape from prison with the help of some Government Officials and later on, he received the assistance and support of the victorious Nippon Army.

" Friends ! On behalf of the Indian Independence Movement I desire to offer my warmest congratulations to Adipadi Dr. Ba Maw, to the Ministers of the new cabinet and to the people of Free Burma on the independence that they have won and I desire also to convey our sincerest good wishes for the everlasting freedom and prosperity of Burma in future.

" We are fortunate to have in our midst today the members of the Burmese deputation who recently visited Tokyo. They are led by His Excellency U. Ba Lwin wha has been appointed as the first Burmese Ambassador to Thailand. I beg to offer—on your behalf and on mine—the warmest welcome to His Excellency U Ba Lwin and his colleagues and I request them to convey personally our message to the people of Burma when they arrive in Rangoon.

" Friends ! The independence of Burma has thrown fresh responsibilities on our shoulers. After the expulsion of the British from Burma, the road to India has been opened and we have to march along that road.

" Until the British are driven out of India the Freedom of Burma cannot be safe. The freedom of India is, therefore, necessary—not only for Indian people but for Burma as well.

" A year has rolled by since Mahatma Gandhi was put in prison for the crime of demanding the withdrawal of the British from India. Since then, the civil disobedience movement, as well as sabotage activities, have gone on with unabated vigour. But we have not won freedom. And we shall not win freedom, till we put up a second front on the Indo-Burma Frontier and call upon the Indian people and the British Indian Army to take up arms against the British and their allies in India.

" Providence has ordained that it is the task of the Indians in East Asia to put up the second front which the Indian people have been demanding. For this, we need a total mobilisation of our manpower and resources in East Asia.

" I want 300,000 men and women for the Azad Hind Fauj (Indian National Army)—including the Rani of Jhansi Regiment. I am thankful to the Youth of Syonan and Malai for offering themselves for enlistment in such large numbers But the money that has been forthcoming from Syonan has not been enough. I want from Syonan at least 15 million dollars for our national struggle and I know that this is not too much for you.

"I am hoping that the day is not far off when we shall be able to set up a Provisional Government of Free India. When this is done, we shall march into India under the leadership of our own Government.

" I want to inform my comrades in the Army and among the civil population that the Indian National Army is now on the move. It is a long way from Syonan to Delhi—therefore we have to begin our march as early as possible.

" All those who are fit and ready for action—must now begin to pack up. During the next two months, a large portion of the Army will be on the road to India—and when the Army moves, the Independence League Headquarters will also move nearer to India. I am longing for the day when our Headquarters will be shifted to the Indo-Burma Frontiers.

"Today, with a feeling of great humility, I venture to make a prediction —namely, that before the end of this year, we shall stand on Indian Soil.

Of course, the Indian National Army will also be with us. But I want to know how many of you (in addition to our army) would like to accompany us in our march to India ?

In Rangoon I had heard that when the British fled from the country, last year, above five lakhs of Indians joined them in the flight. Out of these five lakhs, one lakh died on the way—out of hunger, thirst and disease.

This sacrifice was of no use to India. If, on the contrary, one lakh of Indians had fought for freedom and died for it, India would have been free to-day. If five lakhs of Indians had gone to India with stones and brickbats, they could have killed about one lakh of Britishers.

Therefore, I invite you to join us and our army, and march with us to India. If you lack any arms now, you will get them from our countrymen in the British Indian Army when you reach the Indian frontier.

The British Army will actively join us in the coming struggle and fight the common eneny. I assure you that today Marshal Wavell is one of our best friends—because the army that he is now raising in India will be of great help to us in the coming struggle against the Britishers.

From the civil population in East Asia, I desire to invite 700,000 men to march with us and with our army to India. I want one man for each of the 700,000 villages in India.

Unlike the 500,000 Indians who fled panic-stricken to India from Burma, these 700,000 men will travel to India to deliver our message to every village in India.

That message will be a very simple one—namely, that the British have been completely wiped out of East Asia—that Burma is now independent and that it is now India's turn to strike for her liberty. When this message is delivered to every village in India, I am sure that revolution will break out from one end of the country to other.

Do not worry at all about the situation in Europe. I have been in Europe long and know all about the strong and weak points of the Axis powers. Do not be misled by enemy propaganda.

Whenever the enemy has a slight advantage anywhere, he indulges in such noisy propaganda that one would think that the enemy has already won the war. Knowing the European situation, I want to tell you that whatever may happen in Europe, the situation in India will remain quite unaffected—namely, it will be always easy for us to win liberty and oust the Britisher, if only we put forward the necessary effort.

The sooner we make the effort, the better for India. I know that there are a few Indians here in Syonan, as elsewhere, who still think that the British will return once again to these parts. This is only a proof of their utter degradation as a result of slavery over a long period.

These people are so degraded that even if they see India liberated, they will probably not believe their own eyes, but will think it is a dream. Fortunately, the number of these men is microscopic.

Friends ! Let the whole world know, and let our enemies know, that all Indians in East Asia are united, regardless of religion or caste and that they are determined to fight for the freedom of their common Motherland.

Let them know that the Indian National Army has come into existence and that it is daily growing in numbers. Let them also know that a Women's Regiment—the Rani of Jhansi Regiment—has also been orgauised and that it will march alongside of the Azad Hind Fauj.

And finally let them know that our Army is on the move. The day is not far off when India's national flag will fly over Delhi just as Burma's Peacock Emblem is now flying over the former Government House of Rangoon. And when the independence of India is achieved, all the 38 crores of Indians will be free Indians—proud and happy human beings, pledged to maintain their liberty for all time.

It is to-day a very great pleasure for me to see so many of my Muslim country men in this gatherings of ours and thank them heartily for the welcome they have given me and for the handsome purse they have offered for the Indian Independence Movement. And let the whole world know, and let our enemies know, that all Indians in East Asia are united regardless of religion or caste and they are determined to fight for the freedom of their common motherland.

6. The Next day—August 16, 1943—Netaji had his first Press interview, in which he emphatically declared that that was the opportune time for military action, to strike the blow for India's freedom. He enumerated the reasons for his coviction as follows :—

(1) Indian Independence League and Indian National Army had been re-organized.

(2) Indians were becoming more anti-British due to their stiff attitude.

(3) The establishment of Independent Government in Burma morally helped the Independence Movement.

(4) Economic situation in India had deteriorated.

(5) Burma aad Thailand had assured him of their fullest support as well as grant of certain facilities, when the battle began.

Netaji revealed that, while he was in Rangoon, he started the work of reorganizing the Indian Independence Movement and preparations were under way in Burma for the accommodation of the Indian National Army.

Netaji told the Press that Burma would be the future centre of activities, so he expected to return to Burma in the near future to resume the work of making adequate preparations.

Netaji outlined his plans for a Provisional Indian Government and declared that its early establishment was necessary because it would give Indians within India the assurance that there was no need for anxiety as to the future, if a Provisional Government was already created.

Speech delivered at Kuala Lumpur on the 5th September 1943.

Friends ! I want to thank you most heartily for the purse you have presented to me this evening. It is a handsome purse, but I shall call it handsome, only if you regard it as a first instalment. Considering, what other towns are paying and within a very short time ; considering also what Ipoh has paid as a first instalment, I am sure that Indians in Kuala Lumpur will be anxious to see that this contribution is multiplied atleast five times and if you cannot do that, I am afraid, you will be doing a great disservice to your country. You are very proud of your city and rightly too. It is the second city in this part of the world and if you enjoy the prestige, you must fulfil the responsibilities that follow from that distinction and prestige.

I will now tell you that what we want in cash is only a part of our total requirements. The time has come when we have to give our all in the service of our mother-land The days of minimum sacrifice are over. The time has come, when each and everyone of us has to think of the maximum sacrifice, which he or she is able to offer, and that sacrifice has to be in human life, in money, in other resources, which are necessary in order to equip a modern army for its marches. I am glad to know that you citizens of Kaula Lumpur and Selangor state are anxious to do your duty in every respect and my only remark andrequest to you is to expedite your collections as soon as possible so that our army may be equipped sooner than many expect and be ready to march to the field of action.

From my experience, I am convinced that so long as the Indian people remain unarmed, so long as the British Government has a modern army under its control and so long as we do not take up arms for our struggle for freedom, we shall not be able to achieve independence for India. I do not know of one instance—of one single instance—in the whole history of mankind where a nation has been able to achieve full independence without resorting to arms, but apart from history, our natural experience in the course of several decades has convinced us that we have to take up arms in the final stage of our struggle if we want full independence and not a diluted form of it. So long as peace reigned all over the world it was practically impossible for the Indian people to get arms and fight with arms. It was impossible for the people inside India. It was also impossible for people outside India, but thanks to this war, what was impossible four or five years ago has today become possible. If you want arms you can get them not inside but outside India. If you want to build up a modern army and equip it with the modern weapons, you can do so today. Five years ago you could not do it even if you wanted to. That is why I say this war has been a God-sent opportunity to us. It has given us a unique opportunity for achieving not Dominion Status or Colonial self-government, but full and complete independence.

The only question I would like to put to you as Indians is whether you really want full and complete independence. If you do so you must pay the price. You must organise a complete modern army and march with that army to India.

To-day the British have one front—the Indian national front, you might call it—inside India. The British with their army are able to cope with this Indian national front. If you can put up a second front—not a bogus second front, but a real second front then it will be imposible for the British to maintain their position in the country. I am convinced when the Indian National Army appears on the frontier of India its very appearance will be a clarion call to the people in general and also to the Indian army to rally round the banner of Indian revolution. This is not a wishful dream on my part. I know the people at home are fully aware of our activities in East Asia and the British too are aware, but we do not care. The time has come when we could openly proclaim to the whole world what we have been doing, what we are doing and what we are going to do in the future. Our brethern in the Indian Army who to day are standing under the Union Jack are anxiously waiting for the Indian National Army on the continent of India. That is the position at home without any exaggeration. It is therefore our duty to hurry with our work and see that the National Army goes to the aid of India as soon as possible.

Ever since the existence of the Indian National Army was announced to the world and its intention of marching to Delhi, you will be surprised to learn that there has been a complete change in the tactics of British propaganda. Up to recently British propagandists have been saying that to day Nippon has become the enemy of India and that its army intends to march into India, but ever since they realised that the Indian National Army had been formed and is getting ready to march into India, there has been a complete change in the attitude and also in the tactics of British propagandists and now they are anxiously trying to work up the Indian people to take a stand against the Indian National Army. The British Government knows, as much as as we do, what the attitude of the Indian people and the Indian Army will be when our army appears on the frontier of India, and that is why they are anxious to do their best to win over the Indian people to their side so that they may take a stand against the Indian National Army.

But the most unexpected surprise came to me when I was told that British propagandists on the occasion of a Hindu Festival had appealed to the Hindus of India to get ready to fight their brothers who are going to march in from outside. These British propagandists even went so far as to say that the good old days have come back again !

Friends ! The Anglo-Americans have found out now a new Napoleon. According to the Anglo-Americans, Lord Louis Mountbatten is amphibious. He is a master in land and sea operations. Well, what is the career of this amphibious monster ? He is the hero of Dieppe. Dieppe was an attempt by the British army to land in France and to expel the Germans from that part. Within 24 hours they were completely wiped out and there ended all the heroic exploits of Lord Louis Mountbatten. Because of his achievement at Dieppe he has been made commander-in-chief of the South East Asia command. I challenge you to show me one country in the world today where promotions are made not for success, not for victories, but for defeats. It is a unique achievement of the British army and its government in this war. I can assure Lord Louis Mountbatten that a much bigger and greater Dieppe is waiting for him in East Asia.

Perhaps, there are some people living in East Asia, and even in Malai, who are still hoping and dreaming that the British will come back. We have heard of them. There are a few such men in Syonan also. I can only pity them. You know what Syonan was and is to day. The British—I do not say it, I only repeat it—took twenty years to build Singapore and how many days to get out ? Seven days. This is an achievement and still there are people who believe they will come back ! The biggest bulwark of the British Empire is now the biggest graveyard of that Empire and it shall be a graveyard. The days of the British Empire are over. If you have any doubt turn over the pages of history. Every Empire has had its glory and also its decline. The British Empire had its glory during the last war and since then its decline has become very rapid and we have witnessed with our own eyes the last phase of the decline.

I have always said that the last war brought about the disappearance of the two Empires—the Ottoman Empire of the Turks and the Austro-Hungarian Empire. This war will see the end of the British Empire and out of the ashes of that Empire will rise a free India. The two things are identical—the defeat and dismemberment of the British Empire and the creation of an independent India. If you want India to be free you have to work and fight for the overthrow and dismemberment of the British Empire.

British propaganda of late has adopted new tactics and that is to utilise to the best advantage the small success they have achieved in Africa and Sicily. If you were to listen to the propaganda that British agents have been carrying on all over the world you would think that with the occupation of Sicily they have already won the war. I know something of Europe, not only of peace-time Europe but war-time Europe, and I know all these places where fighting has taken place. I know also the strength and weakness of the Axis powers in Europe and from experience I want to assure you that whatever may happen in Europe has no bearing on the situation either in India or East Asia. Whatever may happen in Europe, Indians will be ready if only we put forward the required effort. Therefore, do not hesitate for one moment by any propaganda the enemy may carry on to-day or tomorrow and be firm in your belief and faith that it has become possible for Indian people to achieve independence.

First of all is it a very big effort that we have to bring an army of 200,000 to 300,000 to India? Look at the millions and millions of people fighting on all fronts in different parts of the world. For the salvation of 38 crores an army of 300,000, or even 400,000 is nothing at all and it is possible for the people of East Asia to contribute enough men for this army. It is possible also for the people in East Asia to contribute money and every material for the equipment of this army. Therefore, let us concentrate all our energy on the one task of organizing an army and bringing it to perfection as soon as possible.

Friends, our task to-day is to bring perfection as soon as possible to the army that exists to-day, along with it we have to expand our army because the war is going to be a long and hard one. We want more and more young men to come in and get training. I congratulate you that you have in the heart of Kuala Lumpur one of our camps where Indian young men are trained for the coming fight for freedom. Well, it is not only in Syonan and Kuala Lumpur that they are being trained to-day. Malai is dotted with camps and many of these camps were formerly camps of the British army. They have been turned over to us for our use. That reminds me that when we go to India we shall also find ready-made barracks for our national army. We won't have to build new barracks. From Calcutta to Bombay and from Rawalpindi to Madras, there are splendid barracks not for the Indian army but for the British Tommy, but these splendid barracks are going to be taken for our Indian National Army and I promise to give the British in return all the prisons for their use.

Friends! to defeat Britain we shall need help from outside. The enemy is asking for help all over the world. The almighty British Empire, over which the sun never sets, that mighty British Empire is going round the world with the begging bowl. It is not merely at Washington that they are asking for help but all over the world, even the poor Indian people, the slaved Indian people, are not spared. Even Indian people have to do their share in men, money, munitions and war materials. They are begging even Indian people to help them in their hour of need. We have to fight today not merely the might of Britain but the combined might of Britain and her allies,—a most powerful combination. If we are to fight and win we shall need help and take help when the time comes, but there will be no humiliation in accepting or asking for help when we have first done our duty.

At this juncture, the duty of the people of East Asia is to put forward the maximum effort Remember you have an opportunity of doing something which your countrymen in other parts of the world cannot do. What can Indians in Europe, Africa, America or even in England do? They are helpless. I know many of them are dying to serve and fight for their country's freedom but it is impossible for them to do so. They are unable to organise an army or join the National Army but all that is within your reach, if you only make it your mission you can join the National Army and work for its success. Therefore, when the call of sacrifice reaches your ears do not flinch. Thank Providence that He has given you of all Indians in the world a unique opportunity to serve your country and fight for your country's independence.

Netaji in Bnrma again

The Indian National Army was to be on the move at an early date and for this purpose elaborate arrangements in Burma had to be made. Netaji, therefore, again came to Burma for a week and supervised and inspected the arrangements personally.

During his short stay at Rangoon, Netaji visited the Mausoleum of Bahadur Shah, the last Emperor of Free India. A mass meeting was held at the tomb on Sunday, September 26, 1943. Amongst those, who attended the function were His Excellency Dr. Ba Maw and his colleagues.

Netaji laid a wreath on the tomb and paid profound homage to the mortal remains of Bahadur Shah, who fought for the overthrow of the British rule in India. The following is a summary of his speech at the time :—

Your Excellency and Friends ! Today we have assembled here near the tomb of Bahadur Shah, the last Emperor of free India. It is perhaps strange, may be a lucky coincidence of history, that while the remains of the India's last Emperor rest on the soil of Burma, the remains of the last King of free Burma now rest on the soil of India.

We in India and in Burma have all along felt bound together historically by the most profound ties. And this coincidence of history is one of the most convincing proofs of these ties between Your Excellency's nation and ours.

We are, both of our nations, passing through a common fight against our common foe and we therefore consider it to be in the fitness of things to have a small celebration before the mortal remains of our last Emperor, so that on the one side we might rouse the fire that burns within us and at the same time, strengthen further the ties that have bound Burma and India so long and that will bind us together for all time.

We are profoundly grateful to Your Excellency and to the honourable members of the Government for the honour that has been done us by your gracious presence in this function,—a function which is pregnant with important and historical events in the days to come.

As I have done so before, once again I should like to express our unshakable determination to fight with our Burmese friends, shoulder to shoulder, assured of the magnanimous help and support of Nippon, so that we may bring about the final overthrow of British Imperialism which will on the one side bring India her lost liberty and at the same time remove once for all the menace to Burma's safety and independence.

This time, we express our unshakable determination before a sacred memorial, before the mortal remains of the last fighter for India's freedom, the man who was an Emperor among men and at the same time, a man among Emperors. We cherish the memory of Bahadur Shah. . We Indians, regardless of religious faiths, cherish the memory of Bahadur Shah not because he we was the man who gave the clarion-call to his countrymen to fight the enemy from without, but because he was the man under whose flag fought Indians form all provinces, Indians professing different religious faiths, the man under whose sacred flag Muslims and Hindus and Sikhs or at least freedom-loving Muslims, Hindus and Sikhs, fought side by side in the war that has been dubbed by the English Historians as the Sepoy Mutiny, but which we Indians call as the First War of Independence. And now when we are engaged in the last war for India's independence, it is all the more necessary for us to renew our unshakable determination, to fight this last war for independence to a finish, regardless of all sufferings and sacrifices, regardless of all difficulties on our path, regardless of the length of this war, so that at long last the enemy, the common enemy of Burma and India will be finally overthrown and we will be free not only within our homes, but free as comrades marching shoulder to shoulder to fulfil the common destiny of mankind.

Your Excellency, with us it is the practice to offer donations and contributions at shrines like this. As a token of our inner feelings and faith I can think of no better donation or *Nazar* than to offer in the name of the last hero of India's First War of Independenee, Emperor Bahadur Shah, a small contribution of Rs. 250,000 to be handed over to Your Excellency as a very small token of our love and admiration for Burma and all that Burma stands for, a small donation which Your Excellency may utilise in a manner considered best by yourself.

And now I shall close these few remarks by quoting the English meaning of a couplet which was composed by Bahadur Shah himself, "As long as the last particle of faith exists in the souls of India's freedom fighters, the sword of India shall continue to penetrate the heart of London."

His Excellency Dr. Ba Maw delivered the following speech :—

Mr. Bose and Friends ! I can assure you that it gives us very great pleasure to be with you on an occasion like this.

As your great Leader has spoken just now I recall his battle call to you 'To Delhi'. Yes, if that is your battle call, if you are marching to Delhi, it is befitting that you shall gather together at the tomb of the last great Indian emperor, the last man who represented the Delhi Dynasty. It is befitting that you should come to a sacred place like this to seek inspiration

Netaji with Dr. Ba-Maw

At the Tomb of Bahadur Shah at Rangoon

Netaji being garlanded by Pandit Raghu. Nath Shastri Secy. Territorial Committee Thailand

Ladies also acclaiming the declaratior war by the Provisional Govt. of Ind
23-10-43

and strengthen your great enterprise. We, Indians and Burmans, have under tragic circumstances lost touch with our past history. It is our duty to maintain this contact with past morally. It is therefore right that whenever occasion offers we should go back to the past, go back to our national memories, for there lies our true heritage.

We Burmans also attach a great deal of importance to certain sacred spots, to certain victory-bringing earth as in Shwebo. I hope for you Indians this earth will bring victory, as we Burmans believe that the sacred earth in Shwebo,—if we march across it,—will surely bring success to any enterprise.

While your Leader on behalf of the Indian community has been good enough to donate two and a half lakhs to any Burmese cause worthy of such charity, I accept it in the spirit in which he has offered it to us. In these days when you have a great task ahead of you I could realise the importance of finance. I know that two and a half lakhs, although your Leader may have described it as a small and trivial sum, is not small and trivial It is an important sum from the point view of view of your very great and difficult and expensive task.

I know that when you are nursing a movement like yours, when you are getting ready for a colossal march to India, to Delhi, a sum like this represents in a real sense a certain sacrifice on your part and if I accept it from you, it is as a token of your deep appreciation of Burma, of your sympathy for the Burmans who have suffered in this war.

It is a deep appreciation of your generosity and therefore I say, your love for this country, and it is therefore in that spirit that I return you my deep thanks for the gift

I wish to join you and I am certain, members of my Government also wish to join you, in paying reverence to this last great Hero of past India. We Burmans will march with you in that spirit, we Burmans will be with you and follow the spirit of Bahadur Shah which I am sure will go marching on, and led by that spirit of the last great Delhi Emperor you will surely return to India.

It is my firm conviction that the past and the present can together capture the future. The present without the past is not helpful as much as the past without the present is dead. Therefore as I have said I appreciate it and I am glad that you have come to a sacred piece of land that reminds you of a great past. If you follow your past leader, as I am sure, you will follow your present great leader, victory will be yours and India will be independent as surely as Burma today is independent

CHAPTER VII

PROVISIONAL GOVERNMENT OF FREE INDIA

After his return from Burma, the stage was set for the formation of the Provisional Government of Free India. On October 21, 1943, a Conference of the Indian Independence League, attended by delegates from all parts of East Asia and thousands of Indians from all over Malaya was held at Singapore. The proceedings began with a welcome address by Mr. M. K. Ramachandram, which was followed by a detailed report on the working of the League by the General Secretary Lt.-Col. A. C. Chatterji. Netaji Subhash Chandra Bose then ascended the rostrum and delivered the following stirring address :—

Friends! First of all, allow me to offer you a most cordial welcome to this Conference, which has been convened at very short notice. The purpose of this Conference is to take stock of our progress and achievement since we met here in July last and then to take the necessary steps for the early attainment of our national goal.

The first task to which I addressed myself after taking over the Presidentship of the Indian Independence League in East Asia was the reorganisation of the League Headquarters with a view to putting it on a war footing. This work was undertaken early in July and several new Departments were opened in the Headquarters. The reorganisation of the Headquarters was effected according to the programme of "Total Mobilisation" of all the resources of Indians in East Asia—resources in men, money and materials. Following the organisation of the Headquarters, branches of the League throughout East Asia were also reorganised on the same basis and effect was given everywhere to the new programme of "total mobilisation."

The next task to which I addressed myself was the reorganisation of the Azad Hind Fauj (or the Indian National Army). To this end, I took over the direct command of our army. Since then, some changes have already been made in our army reorganisation and in future some more changes will be needed. Simultaneously with changes in army organisation, the morale of the Army as a whole has been considerably strengthened and improved. One indication of the present morale of our army is the joy and enthusiasm which light up every face, when a Unit is transferred northwards from Singapore. I am glad to tell that to-day the slogan that is on the lips of every member of the Azad Hind Fauj is the slogan—"ONWARD TO DELHI." In fact, it would be no exaggeration to say that the Army as a whole is earnestly longing for the day when it will be transported to the frontier of India.

While speeding up the spiritual and technical training of the existing Army with a view to making it ready for action, the work of expanding the Army has also been taken in hand. I am happy and proud to inform you that the morale of the new recruits has come up to our highest expectations. As to the number of new recruits, I may tell you that though the whole of

Netaji Subhash Chandra Bose

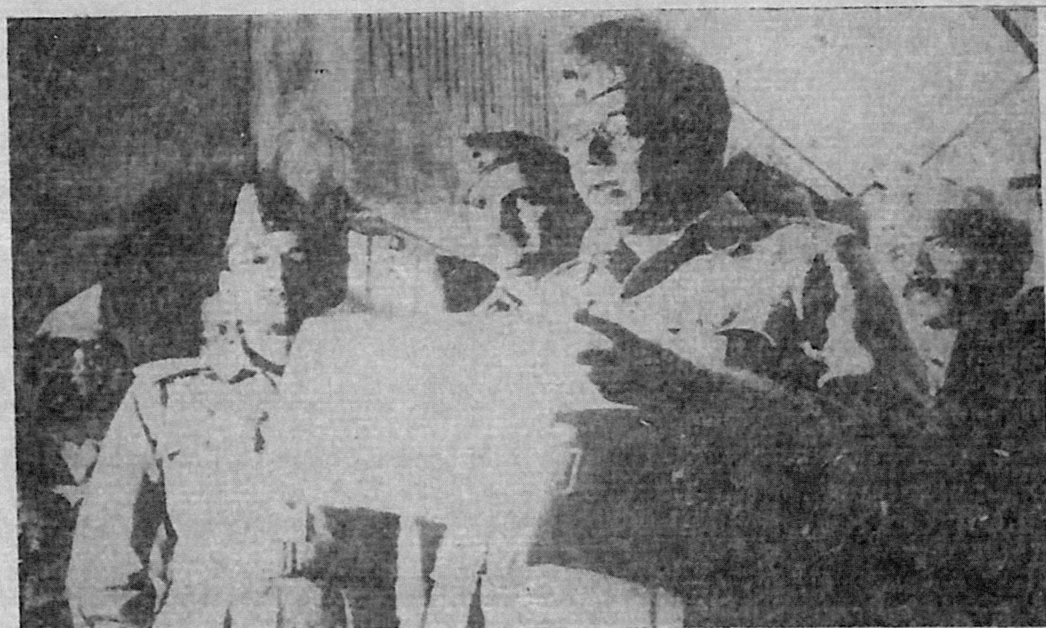

Reading the Proclamation of the Provisional Govt. of Azad Hind with him from the right are Mr. Dev Nath Dass (Advisor), Lt. Col. A. C. Chatterji (Minister for Finance), Lt. Col. M.Z. Kiani and Mr. Karim Ghani (Advisor)

The Famous Cathay Building Singapore

Where the Provisional Govt. of Azad Hind was formed and Azad Hind Broadcasting Station was situated

Malaya is now dotted with our Camps, we have still a very large number of recruits in hand, for whose training we have not yet been able to make the necessary arrangements. Nevertheless, we hope that in future we shall be able to make such arrangements that every recruit who volunteers may be taken care of at once. To this end, training Camps are being opened in other parts of East Asia as well—*e.g.* in Thailand, Burma, etc.

It is not our young men alone, who have been volunteering everywhere in large numbers. Our young women also are coming forward enthusiastically to volunteer for national service of every kind. We have therefore, found it necessary to organise a Rani of Jhansi Regiment, in which our sisters will be given military as well as Red Cross Training. The Central Training Camp for the Rani of Jhansi Regiment will be opened in Syonan on the 22nd October.

In accordance with the scheme of "total mobilisation," strenuous efforts are being made everywhere to collect funds for the Independence Movement and also to purchase and collect supplies necessary for our Army. The response has on the whole, been very encouraging. Among the middle and poorer classes, the spirit of sacrifice hitherto exhibited has been remarkable and affords satisfaction and pride to every freedom-loving Indian. As for the richer classes, they are slowly coming forward and I hope that in future they, too, will not lag behind the rest of the Community in the matter of national service and sacrifice.

Since July last besides carrying on an extensive propaganda among the Indian Community as a whole, we have been also concentrating on those sections of the Community who have been lukewarm or indifferent in the past. I am glad to be able to report that in this respect as well, we have made considerable progress. There is to-day a general desire among all sections and strata of the Indian community in East Asia to do everything possible to further the cause of Indian Independence and they are anxiously waiting for further steps to be taken in that direction.

During the last few months, the situation inside India has been developing in a manner favourable to our cause, though it has meant more and more suffering for the people. The political attitude of the British authorities remains as reactionary as ever, though occasionally high-placed officials talk glibly of compromise. All the known and recognised leaders of Indian nationalism are behind the prison-bars, along with a very large number of our political workers and fighters. There is no possibility that this situation will change, though it is not unlikely that a futile attempt may be made once again to dupe the Indian people into a dishonourable compromise with Britain.

The political unrest in India has been greatly accentuated by the famine conditions prevailing in several parts of India—and particularly in Bengal. There can be no doubt that these famine conditions have been largely due to the policy of ruthless exploitation of India's food and other resources for Britain's war purposes, over a period of nearly four years. You are aware that on behalf of our League, I made a free and unconditional offer of one hundred thousand tons of riee for our starvng countrymen at home as a first instalment. Not only was this offer not accepted by the British authorities in India—but we were given only abuse in return. On the other hand, frantic appeals made by public institutions in India—like the Calcutta Municipality for instance, to President Roosevelt and Prime Minisetr Churchill, for food supplies for the starving millions in India evoked no response at all. The only satisfaction that we can derive out of this heart-rending situation is the thought that hunger always breeds revolution.

I am happy to be able to tell you that the general world situation remains as favourable for the success of our cause as it was before the anti-Axis powers obtained some success in North Africa and in Italy. Our countrymen at home realise this, Consequently, the only effect of the recent happenings in North Africa and in Italy has been to further strengthen the anti-British feeling in India and the determination of the people to throw off the British yoke. So far as the Indian Independence League in East Asia and the Indian National Army are concerned, the determination to fight for and win liberty has been rapidly increasing with the passage of time, regardless of any developments in other parts of the world.

You are probably aware that since July last, I have toured more than once in the mainland of Malaya, in Thailand, in Burma and in Indo-China. The enthusiasm among our countrymen that I have met with everywhere has not only been encouraging but has added greatly to my feeling of confidence and optimism.

For Indians fighting for their liberty, whether at home or abroad, achievement of indedendence by Burma in August last and by the Philippines this month (*i.e.* October) has come as a very great inspiration. Indians throughout East Asia have celebrated both these occasions by holding meetings and demonstrations and have conveyed their heartfelt congratulations to the independent Governments of Burma and the Philippines. Simultaneously, they have realised more keenly than ever before the added responsibility which has now fallen on the Indian people to bring about the final emancipation of Asia by expelling the British and their allies from Indian soil.

In my visits to Thailand and to Burma, I was fortunate enough to make personal contact with His Excellency the Prime Minister and other Ministers of Thailand as well as with His Excellency Adipadi Dr. Ba Maw and the other Ministers of the Burmese Government. From both Goverments I obtained not only sympathy and goodwill for our struggle, but also assurance of help in every possible way.

I would like to inform you also that we have been planning and preparing, not only for the coming struggle, but also for post-war reconstruction. We can visualise the conditions that we shall find at home when the Anglo-Americans and their allies are expelled from our country. We have therefore set up a Reconstruction Department in our Headquarters, where the problems of post-war reconstruction are being studied. People are also being trained for work of rapid reconstruction within India simultaneously with the progress of military operations. In short, we are not leaving anything undone in our preparation for the coming fight for freedom and for the task that we shall have to undertake thereafter.

From every point of view the stage is now set for the next stage of our campaign. We have now to adopt measures both of a political as well as of a military nature.

With regard to measures of a military nature, Indians in East Asia and, in particular, members of the Azad Hind Fauj (Indian National Army) are eagerly looking forward to the day when we shall be able to cross the frontier of India and launch the last fight for our freedom. But before we can do that some political measures have to be adopted. We have for instance to form the Provisional Government of Azad Hind (Free India) and commence our struggle under the leadership of that Government. The formation of such a Government at this juncture will have a profound effect on Indians throughout the world and it will afford a powerful impetus to them in the struggle that lies ahead. In fact, our countrymen in East Asia have been eagerly desiring and expecting the inauguration of the Provisional Government of Azad Hind.

The Indian Independence League, being the only representative organisation of Indians in East Asia and enjoying the full confidence of the entire Indian community, is competent to form such a Government. By virtue of the powers vested in me under the Constitution of the Indian Independence League it will be my task to form the Provisional Government of Azad Hind.

It would naturally, have been the best thing if such a Government had been constituted inside India and if that Government had launched the last struggle for liberty. But things being what they are in India and all the known and recognised leaders being in prison, it is hopeless to expect the formation of a Provisional Government within the frontiers of India. It is equally hopeless to expect the last fight for freedom to be organised or initiated within the country. It is consequently for the Indians in East Asia to undertake this solemn task.

I may, however, remark at this stage that there are several historical precedents for a Provisional Government being formed outside the frontiers of a country, There are also historical precedents for award of freedom being launched from outside the country.

But though the initiative in the political as well as in the military fields has to be taken outside the frontiers of India, it is no secret to-day that the Independence Movement abroad has been working in the closest harmony with the Movement at home. Whatever we have been doing outside has the fullest support, not only of the civil population of India, but also of a large section of Britain's Indian Army. It is also no secret to-day that there is a regular and unbroken contact between patriots working at home and those working abroad. The British authorities have, from time to time arrested, tortured and killed some of our liaison agents—but that has not disturbed our communications in any way. In view of all these facts, there is not but the slightest doubt in our minds that when we cross the Indian frontier with our Army and hoist our National Flag on Indian soil, the real revolution will break out within the country—the revolution that will ultimately bring about the end of British rule in India.

Friends ! what we are doing here at present is but a preparation for the final struggle. That struggle will begin only when we cross the Indian Frontier Then will commence the historic march to Delhi—the march that will end only when the last Englishman is either expelled from India or is thrown into prison—when India's National Flag flies over the Viceroy's House and when the Azad Hind Fauj holds its victory parade inside the ancient red-fortress of India's Metropolis.

Friends ! I cannot end this address without expressing our heart-felt thanks to the Government and people of Nippon and to the Imperial Nipponese Army and Navy for the sympathy, help and co-operation that we have received in so generous a measure. The day will certainly come—and that too soon—when we shall give tangible proof of our gratitude for the assistance that we have received in the past and that we are going to receive in future, during one of the darkest hours in our history. In the meantime, all that we can do is to offer a humble token of our appreciation of and gratitude for the magnanimous sympathy and help that we have been receiving. As a small token of our gratitude, I have offered, on behalf of the Indian Independence League, a sum of money adequate for the purpose of manufacturing and equipping five aeroplanes for the Imperial Nipponese Army and five aeroplanes for the Imperial Nipponese Navy. Apart from this, I want to assure the Government and people that however long and hard the struggle may be, we Indians are determined to fight shoulder to shoulder with them till our common enemy is overthrown. We are absolutely convinced of the ultimate victory of Nippon and her Allies, just as we are of our own national liberation.

And now, friends, I have to declare that I shall announce the composition of the Provisional Government of Azad Hind in the afternoon session to-day.

The Conference reassembled at 4 p m. The hall was packed to overflowing, as in the morning session. Netaji Subhash Chandra Bose arrived punctually at 4 p.m. accompanied by Col. Yamamoto, chief of the Hikari Kikan. Before proclaiming the inauguration of the Provisional Government of Free India, Netaji moved a message of thanks to the Imperial Government of Japan for their kind help in the Indian Independence Movement and two messages of congratulation to Burma and the Philippines on their attainment of independence. The messages were readopted by the Conference with acclamation.

Netaji then made a statement in Hindustani explaining the significance of the formation of the Provisional Government. The statement, which was translated into Tamil by Mr. M. K Chidambaram was as follows :—

As a student of history, and, in particular, of revolutions in different parts of the world, during 22 years of my public life, I always felt that what India was lacking in her fight for freedom were two things—a National Army and a National Government to lead that Army to battle. In the course of the present war, thanks to the brilliant victories achieved by the armed forces of Nippon, it became possible for Indians in East Asia to organise the Independence League and the Indian National Army.

The creation of a National Army lent reality and seriousness to the whole Independence Movement in East Asia. If this Army had not been organised, the Independence League in East Asia would have been a mere propaganda organ. With the creation of the National Army, it became possible, as well as necessary, to set up a Provisional Government of Azad Hind (Free India). The Government is born out of the Independence League for the purpose of launching and directing the final struggle for India's freedom.

In setting up this Provisionial Government we are, on the one hand, meeting the exigencies of the Indian situation and are, on the other, following in the footsteps of history. In recent times, the Irish people set up their Provisional Government in 1916. The Czechs did the same during the last

World War. And, after the last World War, the Turks, under the leadership of Mustapha Kemal, set up their Provisional Government in Anatolia.

In our case, the Provisional Government of Azad Hind will not be like a normal peace-time Government. Its functions and its composition will be of a unique kind. It will be a fighting organisation, the main object of which will be to launch and to conduct the last war against the British and their allies in India. Consequently, only such departments will be run by the Government as will be necessary for the launching and the prosecution of the struggle for liberty.

The Cabinet will consist of a certain number who will represent the civil department of the Government —while there will be others representing the Armed Forces of the Government. Since the purpose of the Government is to fight for Independence, the armed forces have been given a large representation on the Cabinet.

Besides the ordinary Ministers of the Cabinet provision has been made for a number of Advisers to the Cabinet. In this manner, the Provisional Government will maintain close and organic connection with the entire Indian community in East Asia and mobilise all their resources for the coming struggle.

When the Provisional Government is transferred to Indian soil, it will assume the functions of a normal government operating in its own territory. Many new departments will then be started.

With the formation of a Provisional Government of Azad Hind the Indian Independence Movement has obtained all the pre-conditions of success. It remains now to start the final struggle for Freedom. This will begin when the Indian National Army crosses the frontier of India and commences its historic march to Delhi. This march will end only when the Anglo-Americans are expelled from India and the Indian National Flag is hoisted over the Viceroy's House in New Delhi.

The Conference hall resounded with loud and prolonged cheers as Netaji announced the composition of the Provisional Government as follows :—

Subhash Chandra Bose (Head of the State; Prime Minister and Minister for War and Foreign Affairs).

Capt. Mrs. Lakshmi (Women's Organisation .

S. A. Ayer (Publicity and Propaganda).

Lt.-Col. A. C. Chatterji (Finance).

Representatives of Armed Forces :

Lt.-Col. Aziz Ahmed,

Lt.-Col. N. S. Bhagat,

Lt.-Col. J. K. Bhonsle,

Lt.-Col. Gulzara Singh,

Lt.-Col. M. Z. Kiani,

Lt.-Col A. D. Loganadan,

Lt.-Col Ehsan Qadir.

Lt.-Col. Shah Nawaz.

A. M. Sahay, Secretary (with ministerial rank).

Rash Behari Bose (Supreme Adviser).

Advisers :

Karim Gani, Debnath Das, D. M. Khan, A. Yellappa, J. Thivy and Sardar Ishar Singh, A. N. Sarkar (Legal Adviser).

The Ministers and Advisers thereupon ascended the dais and took their seats behind Netaji.

The most touching scene was when Netaji took the Oath of Allegiance to India in the name of God. Netaji was visibly moved when he began reading the Oath in Hindustani. He seemed to feel the tremendous reponsibility he was taking on his shoulders. After he had read a few words he was so overcome that he put his kerchief to his face to wipe a few drops of tears. A wave of emotion swept the whole audience, when the Head of State and Prime Minister read the following Oath :

"In the name of God, I take this sacred oath that to liberate India and the thirty eight crores of my countrymen I, Subhash Chandra Bose, will continue this sacred war of freedom till the last breath of my life.

I shall remain always a servant of India and to look after the welfare of thirty eight crores of my Indian brothers and sisters shall be for me my highest duty.

Even after winning freedom, I will always be prepared to shed even the last drop of my blood for the preservation of India's Freedom."

Netaji was followed by the members of the Government pledging in the name of God their loyalty to Netaji Subhash Chandra Bose, the Head of the State and Premier, and consecrating themselves entirely to the service of Mother India. Each individual Member stood at attention before Netaji and took the following Oath :

In the name of God, I take this holy oath that to liberate India and the thirty eight crores of my countrymen I,......................will be absoutely faithful to my Leader Subhash Chandra Bose and shall be always prepared to sacrifice my life and all I have for fulfilling this pledge.

Netaji cordially shook hands with each of the members to the accompaniment of hearty cheers from the audience.

The following Proclamation of the Provisional Government of Free India was read in Hindustani by Mr. A. N. Sahay, in Tamil by Mr. Chidambaram and in English by Netaji himself :

After their first defeat at the hands of the British in 1757 in Bengal, the Indian people fought an uninterrupted series of hard and bitter battles over a stretch of one-hundred years. The history of this period teems with examples of unparalleled heroism and self-sacrific. And, in the pages of that history, the names of Siraj-ud-doula and Mohanlal of Bengal, Haider

Ministers of the provisional Govt. of Azad Hind (21-10-43)

(First row) 1. Lt Col. A. C. Chatterji, 2. Lt. Col. J. K. Bhonsle, 3. Netaji Subhas Chandra Bose, 4. Captain Mrs. Lakhshmi, 5. A M. Sahay, 6. S.A. Ayyar
(Second row) 7. Lt. Col. A.D. Loganadan, 8. Lt. Col. Ehsan Qadir, 9. Lt. Col. N. S. Bhagat, 10. Lt. Col. M.Z. Kiani, 11. Lt. Col. Aziz Ahmad, 12. Lt. Col. Shah Niwaz, 13. Lt. Col. Gulzara Singh

Netaji Subhas Chandra Bose with S. Ishar Singh Minister of State and Chairman I. I.L. Thailand and Col. D. S.Raju Personal medical advisor to Netaji

Mr. Johan A. Thivy
Minister of State and Secretary to the Provisional Govt. of Free India

Netaji Amidst Friendly Powers

The Assembly of Greater East Asiatic Nations in a group photograph taken in front of the Imperial Diet Building in Tokyo, in which the historic meetings were held (Nov. 5-6, 1943) In the front row, from left to right: Prime Minister Ba-Maw of Burma; Prime Minister Chang Ching-hui of Manchoukuo; President Wang Ching-wei of the National Govt. of China; Prime Minister General Hideki Tojo of Japan; H.R.H. Prince Wan Waithayakon of Thailand; President Jose P. Laurel of the Philippines; and Subhas Chandra Bose, Head of the Provisional Government of Free India, who attended the assembly in the capacity of an observer. Behind them are standing their respective staff and Ministers of Govt.

Netaji and Wang Ching-Wei
Premier of China

Netaji and Abhai Wonges
Premier of Thailand

Netaji and Ba-Maw
Premier of Burma

Ali Tippu Sultan and Velu Tampi of South India, Appa Sahib Bhonsle and Peshwa Baji Rao of Maharashtra, the Begums of Oudh, Sardar Shyam Singh Atariwala of Punjab and last, but not least, Rani Laxmibai of Jhansi, Tantia Topi, Maharaj Kunwar Singh of Dumraon and Nana Sahib—among others—the names of all these warriors are for ever engraved in letters of gold. Unfortunately for us, our forefathers did not at first realise that the British constituted a grave threat to the whole of India and they did not therefore put a united front against the enemy. Ultimately, when the Indian people were roused to the reality of the situation, they made a concerted move—and under the flag of Bahadur Shah, in 1857, they fought their last war as free men. In spite of a series of brilliant victories in the early stages of this war, ill-luck and faulty leadership gradually brought about their final collapse and subjugation. Nevertheless, such heroes as the Rani of Jhansi, Tantia Topi, Kunwar Singh and Nana Sahib live like eternal stars in the nation's memory to inspire us to greater deeds of sacrifice and valour.

Forcibly disarmed by the British after 1857 and subjected to terror and brutality, the Indian people lay prostrate for a while—but with the birth of the Indian National Congress in 1885, there came a new awakening. From 1885 till the end of the last World War, the Indian people, in their endeavour to recover their lost liberty, tried all possible methods—namely, agitation and propaganda, boycott of British goods, terrorism and sabotage—and finally, armed revolution. But all these efforts failed for a time. Ultimately, in 1920, when the Indian people, haunted by a sense of failure, were groping for a new method, Mahatma Gandhi came forward with the new weapon of non-co-operation and civil-disobedience.

For two decades thereafter, the Indian people went through a phase of intense patriotic activity. The message of freedom was carried to every Indian home. Through personal example, people were taught to suffer, to sacrifice and to die in the cause of freedom. From the centre to the remotest villages, the people were knit together into one political organisation. Thus, the Indian people not only recovered their political consciousness, but became a political entity once again. They could now speak with one voice and strive with one will for one common goal. From 1937 to 1939, through the work of the Congress Ministries in eight provinces, they gave proof of their readiness and their capacity to administer their own affairs.

Thus, on the eve of the present World War, the stage was set for the final struggle for India's liberation. During the course of this War, Germany, with the help of her Allies, has dealt shattering blows to our enemy in Europe—while Nippon with the help of her Allies has inflicted a knockout blow to our enemy in East Asia. Favoured by a most happy combination of circumstances, the Indian people to-day have a wonderful opportunity for achieving their national emancipation.

For the first time in recent history, Indians abroad have also been politically roused and united in one organisation. They are not only thinking and feeling in tune with their countrymen at home, but are also marching in step with them, along the path to Freedom. In East Asia, in particular, over two million Indians are now organised as one solid phalanx, inspired by the slogan of "Total Mobilisation." And in front of them stand the serried ranks of India's Army of Liberation, with the slogan, "Onward to Delhi" on their lips.

Having goaded Indians to desperation by its hypocrisy and having driven them to starvation and death by plunder and loot, British rule in India has forfeited the goodwill of the Indian people altogether and is now living a precarious existence It needs but a flame to destroy the last vestige of that unhappy rule. To light that flame is the task of India's Army of Liberation. Assured of the enthusiastic support of the civil population at home and also of a large section of Britian's Indian Army and backed by gallant and invincible allies abroad, but relying in the first instance on its own strength, India's Army of Liberation is confident of fulfilling its historic role.

Now that the dawn of freedom is at hand, it is the duty of the Indian people to set up a Provisional Government of their own, and launch the last struggle under the banner of that Government. But with all the Indian leaders in prison and the people at home totally disarmed, it is not possible to set up a Provisional Government within India or to launch an armed struggle under the aegis of that Government It is, therefore, the duty of the Indian Independence League in East Asia, supported by all patriotic Indians at home and abroad, to undertake this task—the task of setting up a Provisional Government of Azad Hind (Free India) and of conducting the last fight for Freedom, with the help of the Army of Liberation (that is, the Azad Hind Fauj or the Indian National Army) organised by the League.

Having been constituted as the Provisional Government of Azad Hind by the Indian Independence League in East Asia, we enter upon our duties with a full sense of the responsibility that has devoled on us. We pray that Providence may bless our work and our struggle for the emancipation of our Motherland. And we hereby pledge our lives and the lives of our comrades in arms to the cause of her Freedom, of her welfare, and her exaltation among the nations of the world.

It will be the task of the Provisional Government to launch and to conduct the struggle that will bring about the expulsion of the British and of their allies from the soil of India. It will then be the task of the Provisional Government to bring about the establishment of a Permanent National Government of Azad Hind constituted in accordance with the will of the Indian people and enjoying their confidence. After the British and their allies are overthrown and until a Permanent National Government of Azad Hind is set up on Indian soil, the Provisional Government will administer the affairs of the country in trust for the Indian people.

The Provisional Government is entitled to, and hereby claims, the allegiance of every Indian. It guarantees religious liberty, as well as equal rights and equal opportunities to all its citizens. It declares its firm resolve to pursue the happiness and prosperity of the whole nation and of all its parts, cherishing all the children of the nation equally and transcending all the differences cunningly fostered by an alien government in the past.

In the name of God, in the name of bygone generations who have welded the Indian people into one nation and in the name of the dead heroes, who have bequeathed to us a tradition of heroism and self-sacrifice—we call upon the Indian people to rally round our banner and to strike for India's Freedom. We call upon them to launch the final struggle against the British and all their allies in India and to prosecute that struggle with valour and perseverance and with full faith in final victory—until the enemy is expelled from Indian soil and the Indian people are once again a Free Nation.

Signed on behalf of the Provisional Government of Azad Hind.

SUBHASH CHANDRA BOSE (Head of the State, Prime Minister and Minister for War and Foreign Affairs) ;

Capt. Mrs. Lakshmi (Women's Organisation) ;

S. A. Ayer (Publicity and Propaganda) ;

Lt.-Col. A. C. Chatterji (Finance) ;

Lt.-Col. Aziz Ahmed, Lt.-Col. N. S. Bhagat, Lt.-Col. J. K. Bhonsle, Lt.-Col. Gulzara Singh, Lt.-Col. M. Z. Kiani, Lt. Col. A. D. Loganadan, Lt.-Col. Ehasan Qadir, Lt.-Col. Shah Nawaz (Representatives of the Armed Forces) ;

A. M. Sahay, Secretary (with ministerial rank) ;

Rash Behari Bose (Supreme Adviser) ;

Karim Gani, Debnath Das, D. M. Khan, A. Yellappa, J. Thivy, Sardar Ishar Singh (Advisers) :

A. N. Sarkar (Legal Adviser).

Syonan, Oct. 21, 1943.

CHAPTER VIII

PROVISIONAL AZAD HIND GOVERNMENT DECLARES WAR

The first meeting of the Council of Ministers of the Provisional Government of Azad Hind (Free India) was held at the official residence of Netaji Subhash Chandra Bose at 9 p.m. Friday Oct. 22, 1943. Netaji presided.

The first item on the agenda of this first meeting of the Council of Ministers was a resolution, paying homage to all those, who are carrying on a heroic struggle against the British inside India, and are undergoing tremendous sufferings and sacrifices, and those who have laid down their lives in the cause of India's freedom.

The Council of Ministers also discussed the general political and economic situation in India.

The Japanese Board of Information announced at 11 a.m. on 23rd October that the Japanese Government had recognised the Provisional Government of Free India. The text of the announcement reads as follows :—

The Provisional Government of Free India, having been established with Mr. Subhash Chandra Bose as the Head, the Nipponese Government, in its firm belief that it is a great forward step towards the realisation of an independent India, for which the Indian people have long aspired, has recognised it as the Provisional Government of Free India, and hereby declares its intention to extend every possible co-operation and support in the Provisional Government's effort to attain its objective."

The second meeting of the Council of Ministers of the Provisional Government of Azad Hind met at midnight at the official residence of Netaji Subhash Chandra Bose on the 23rd/24th October, 1943

Advisers also attended the meeting.

The political, economic and military situation in India was again discussed and the following decisions were arrived at unanimously :

The Provisional Government of Azad Hind declares war on Britain and the United States of America.

The Provisional Government of Azad Hind places on record its deep appreciation of the message conveying the news of the recognition by the Imperial Government of Nippon of the Provisional Government of Azad Hind The Provisional Government of Azad Hind expresses its grateful thanks to the Imperial Government of Nippon for the generous offer of wholehearted co-operation and assistance contained in the above message.

"The Provisional Government of Azad Hind declared war on Britain and America at 5 minutes past midnight last night" roared Netaji Subhash Chandra Bose addressing an audience of 50,000 Indians on the maiden, opposite the stately Municipal Buildings of Singapore at 4 p.m. on Oct. 24.

The air was rent with lusty shouts of "Inqilab Zindabad." "Azad Hind Zindabad" and "Netaji Ki Jai."

"We have declared war because our strength has increased a hundred-fold," proclaimed Netaji Subhash Chandra Bose. Frenzied cheering greeted this Challenge to the enemies of India's freedom. Then Netaji uttered a note of grim warning to the mammoth gathering.

He declared : "I want you to demonstrate to the world that you are resolved as one man to follow up this declaration with action that will show to the world that you mean bloody war when you declare war. The British know very well that I say what I mean and that I mean what I say. So, when I say 'War' I mean WAR—War to the finish—a war that can only end in the Freedom of India.

"But I warn every one of you, to think very carefully before you raise your hand to pass this resolution of the Provisional Government of Azad Hind declaring war on Britain and America. If you too mean it, if you too are ready from this moment onward to sacrifice everything, all you have in this world and your lives, to translate this declaration into action, if you mean to lay down your lives, in the coming fight for India's freedom, then stand up and raise your hands," said Netaji Subhash Bose.

This was the signal for an outburst of frenzied demonstration. The audience of 50,000 rose to its feet, wild cheering broke out, fifty thousand

Brave sons of Hind !

The only thing you lacked, was arms !

throats shouted revolutionary slogans for full fifteen minutes without a break. Where fifty thousand heads were seen a few moments earlier, was now seen only a forest of bayonets, which stood about twelve feet from the ground, the men of the Azad Hind Fauj and Volunteers having spontaneously raised their rifles and rested the butt-ends on their shoulders. They stood there like that and shouted revolutionary slogans. The civilians standing behind them, men, women and children raised both their hands and went on cheering their solemn assurance to Netaji ; and on the 15-foot-high platform Netaji stood like a lion grim and determined, witnessing this feverish enthusiasm.

Then the crowds broke the cordon ; in wave after wave they advanced towards the platform where Netaji was standing and cheered him until their throats went hoarse.

The following is Netaji's speech at the Mass Rally :

When I addressed you last on October 17th, on the occasion of our meeting to congratulate the Philippines on its achievement of Independence, I told you that Burma and the Philippines had become independent and that the next would be India's turn. To-day I feel joy in informing you that the turn of India has now come and the Provisional Government of Azad Hind has been established by us and recognised by the world.

When we look back at the succession of events which had slowly but steadily led to this important landmark in the history of our Independence Movement, we could clearly see that everything has been happening under the guidance and help of Providence. The will of God has been with us and if to-day the Provisional Government of Azad Hind has been established, it is a Government which has been declared to the world in the fulness of time and fitness of things.

With the beginning of the present War in Europe, our life-long enemies, the Britishers received their first blows in the West and became weakened thereby. If they had continued to receive blows in the West only, the cause of Indian Independence could not have benefitted thereby. But when the Greater East Asia War started in the East, our enemies received greater blows and became more weakened by one defeat after another. More important and significant than their losses in the East was the fact that a new door—a door undreamt of by them—was opened in the East for the emancipation of India.

The British strategists had always expected a menace to India from the North Western Frontier ; litttle did they envisage the possibility of an Army of Liberation marching into India from the Northern Frontier. They never dreamt of this possibility ; nor were they prepared to defend an attack from this direction.

There is another interesting aspect of this question. Even supposing that the Britishers, suffering defeat after defeat in the West, had retreated up to the North Western Frontiers of India, even that would not have helped the cause of Indian Independence. Because there in Western Asia, we do not have any colony of Indians. On the other hand, Destiny had kept three millions of Indians in East Asia. And when the enemy was driven out of East Asia and the help of Asiatics was forthcoming, the material was there in these three millions of Indians for a real bid for Independence.

With the Britishers driven to North East Frontiers of India—to the Indo-Burma borders—a golden opportunity thus arose for liberating India, and if the Indians in East Asia had not risen to the occasion, even that opportunity would have been lost. But the Indians in East Asia, I am glad to say, did not fail India at this great hour ; they heard the call of the times and organised themselves into the Indian Independence League and started the formation of the Indian National Army. A retrospective survey of the events of the past few years clearly shows that Destiny had prepared the stage in an undreamt of way for the final war of Indian Independence. Things have happened steadily in the fulness of time and the fitness of things and who can deny when I say that by the grace of God, India's Hour has come, that India's turn to be free has come.

When I came to East Asia and took up the lead of this movement, my first objective was to re-organise and strengthen the Indian Independence League, and to reform and stabilise the Indian National Army.

In my address to you on the 15th August, I told you that I am determined to set my foot on the holy soil of India before the end of this year. I always mean what I say. Mine was not an empty declaration or a mere boast. Since then, our preparations have been continuing slowly but steadily. You will remember the Military Review which took place here on this maidan on July 9, and this morning you would have noticed that the Indian National Army which took part in the Review was far smaller than that of July last. I revealed in my address at the Military Review this morning that a considerable part of the Indian National Army had left Syonan already and that they were on the road to India. All our preparations have been proceeding in a satisfactory manner and recently it became necessary to take another and more important step, a decisive stop in our march towards Independence.

The question would naturally arise as to what would be the leadership under which the Indian National Army would fight. And it was right time for us to clear our position. The world in general and Indians in particular had to be told under whose leadership the Indian National Army was going to fight and who would take over the territorial rights in India when the enemy is driven out. And so, at the right time, we established the Provisional Government of Azad Hind at the Conference of Indians in East Asia held on the 21st October.

If we had formed such a Government three years ago, the world would have called it a farce ; and the enemy might have called it a propaganda stunt But the Provisional Government having now risen as a natural sequence to the organisation of three millions of Indians in East Asia and the establishment of the powerful Indian National Army, even our enemies would have to think twice before calling it a propaganda stunt. The present Provisional Government of Azad Hind is not a plaything ; it is a solid and powerful body having as its sanction the will of the three millions of Indians united as a granite wall by the Indian Independence League and having as its support the Indian National Army.

In forming this Government, we have made no innovations because it has always been part of the technique of revolution to declare a Provisional Government just on the eve of a final War of Independence. Many examples are available in history for the adoption of this method. We have, for instance, the case of the Czechs and the Irish as well as the case of Mustapha Kemal who formed a Provisional Government of Anatolia before the Turkish War of Independence, By taking this step on the 21st October, we have not only acted at the right time but we have also adopted the right method.

It is true that it would have been better if such a Provisional Government could have been established within the frontiers of India. But under the present circumstances it is not practical politics to have such an organisation like the Indian Independence League or such an armed force like the Indian National Army within the frontiers of India. And any Provisional Government declared within India without the proper organisation and armed strength would be a farce ; it would be some thing which our enemies could suppress in no time. This being the truth, and taking all the factors into consideration, patriotic Indians cannot but come to one and only conclusion that the only practical path for the achievement of our Independence is the path which we have now chosen.

In the proclamation of the establishment of the Provisional Government of Azad Hind on the 21st October, I have clearly defined the objectives and limits of this Government. We are not a Government like the ordinary administrations established in normal times ; and hence, we have not followed the normal method nor have we opened departments which are essential only for the administration of a country in normal times. The first and foremost function of this Government is to wage the war of Independence and hence our Cabinet is primarily a War Cabinet.

Secondly, this Government would undertake to administer the liberated territories during the transitionary period only. We shall continue to function till the last Englishman is driven out of India, till India becomes independent and law, order and peace are restored in Free India and till a Permanent Government of Free India is set up according to the will of the thirty-eight crores of Indians in India. I appeal to you and to every Indian in East Asia to read the Proclamation issued by us on the 21st October and to understand fully the true significance of our Provisional Government.

I would also take this opportunity to emphasie that if a few have been elected as members of the Government it does not mean that the vast majority are absolved of their duties or responsibilities. For the sake of administrative convenience and necessity, a few have been made members of the Government, but the responsibility of the Government lies equally on all the Indians in East Asia.

Those who have assumed functions in the new Government machinery have not assumed any grand positions ; they have assumed in fact greater burdens and responsibilities. The path of this Government is not a path of roses and very soon this Goveenment will have its trial on the battlefield. You must not think even for a moment that there has been any elevation of individual position.

If there has been any elevation of position, it has been that of India and the Indians Who can say that by the formation of this Government and its recognition by the world, the status and position of the Indians have not increased in the eyes of the world ? You must realise that this is your Movement and that this Government is your Government, and that your duties as members of the Indian Independence League have now increased ten-fold.

We have two great tasks before us, The first task is to make full and final efforts with a view to crossing the frontiers and setting foot on the holy soil of India before the end of this year. The second task is to continue our work and carry on our preparations for a long war. The retreat of Britishers from India would mean the final destruction of the British Empire and so it is only natural that the British will try to cling to India with all their might.

It is not going to be an easy affair to drive the Britishers from India, but I am confident that once we are on the Indian soil we shall get necessary help and strength from the Indians in India. The Indians in East Asia, however, should realise that their efforts must continue as ever till our final objectives are achieved.

I would once again reiterate that our programme of Total Mobilisation muts be carried out with greater vigour as a sequel to the formation of our Provisional Government. I would once again repeat my appeal for Men, Money and Materials. It is the duty of the Indians in East Asia to see that there is a continuous stream of men, money aad materials forthcoming till we achieve final victory.

I may say in this connection that my call for men to rally ronnd the Colours has been receiving satisfactory response. The way young Indians in East Asia have come forward as volunteers and the way in which our sisters have responded to my call to form the Rani of Jhansi Regiment have been inspiring indeed.

And about the offer of money and materials, I may say here that the response from the poorer and middle classes has been encouraging. I have come across instances of the spirit of sacrifice among our poor brethern which would bring tears to the eyes of even a stone-hearted man. A washerman came to me and gave his "all" and further said that he hailed from Jhansi and he would like to march along with our sisters of the Rani of Jhansi Regiment as their washerman. A poor ill-clad Indian who was a barber came forward with 200 dollars which represented his savings for years and gladly offered it for the cause.

Especially moving are the sacrifices of our Gowala brethren. These brothers came, gave all the cash they had, all the cattle they possessed and offered themselves as Volunteers for the Indian National Army. The poor classes have been showing by their actions and example the meaning of Total Mobilisation. It is only the rich who want to know whether Total Mobilisation means five or ten per cent of their savings. The poor, have been spontaneously coming forward with their all and their own selves.

It is high time that the rich revolutionised their outlook. They should realise that when a Volunteer joins the ranks and goes to the front he does not ask whether he should spill five per cent or ten per cent of his blood. He goes to the the front to spill every drop of his blood. The life of one such volunteer is to me more precious than millions of dollars. What I would ask the rich to understand is that if they do not want to come forward to give their lives, they should at least come forward to give their possessions.

I have heard that some of the rich people have been saying that we are a nuisance and that the nuisance would be over when we leave Syonan on our march to India, I want them to know that though we may march, the

March Past of the Azad Hind Fauj

Netaji taking the salute

Netaji inspecting the Azad Hind Fauj (23-10-43)

Indian Independence League would still be here carrying on our "Home Front" programme while we are engaged on the fighting front. We cannot spare the rich ; we cannot spare any Indian because ours is a life and death struggle and we are determined to carry on our fight to victory by all means and at any cost.

I have also said that some of our rich friends are thinking of changing their nationality to dodge the Indian Independence League's demand for funds. To these misguided friends, I have to say that there are only two alternatives before them ; either they must become true Indians and do their duty at this hour of need or they must say that they are friends of Britain and be treated as such. In East Asia, there is no room for Britishers or their friends except in jails and the time is not far off when in India also their position will be the same. I hope there will soon be a re-orientation of outlook among the few rich Indians who have not satisfactorily responded to our call.

I shall now inform you of two very important decisions of the Cabinet of the Provisional Government of Azad Hind and place them before you for your ratification.

There was a time when the Britishers in their propaganda tried to ignore or belittle our Movement in East Asia Now they have taken it seriously and for want of any other tactics they have resorted to abusing me from their radio stations. The tactic of abuse is the last refuge of the weak, of those who are at their wit's end.

But it is significant that the enemy has realised our strength and he understands that ours is not a mere propaganda stunt. The reactions and repercussions of the establishment of our Provisional Government has been world-wide and it will be no exaggeration if I say that it has created panic both in London and Washington.

The enemy radio stations were rather quick this time in flashing out the news of the formation of our Government through their broadcasts. Meanwhile, we have received the recognition of the Imperial Government of Nippon, and this, I must say, is a historic event of tremendous importance. If this recognition was a solitary act without any precedent there could have been opportunity for people to question the *bona fides* of this gesture. Buf, fortunately, this has not come as an innovation This has come as one of the corollaries of Nippon's Asiatic policy based on justice and equality. The world has heard of this policy ; it has already heard of the independence of Burma and then of the Philippines and so the recognition of the Provisional Government of Azad Hind has come as the natural result of this policy.

The Anglo-Americans have been proclaiming from their house-tops that they were the champions of Liberty and Democracy but their actions have repeatedly given the lie to their claims. Apart from their determination to maintain their hold on India, they have enslaved independent countries like Iraq and Iran. They have been and are trying to enslave free Burma.

In contrast to this, we have the action of Nippon in recognising Independent Burma, Independent Philippines and now the Provisional Government of Independent India. Our Nippon friends have always been showing us every sympathy and now, by this recognition, they have rendered us the greatest moral assistance for which we are greatly thankful. And so, the

Council of Ministers of Azad Hind have unanimously passed a resolution deeply appreciating this gesture of Nippon. I place their resolution before you for your ratification.

"The Provisional Government of Azad Hind (Free India) places on record its deep appreciation of the message conveying the news of the recognition by the Imperial Government of Nippon of the Provisional Government of Azad Hind. The Provisional Government of Azad Hind expresses its grateful thanks to the Imperial Government of Nippon for the generous offer of wholehearted co-operation and assistance contained in the above message."

Our thanks are due to Premier General Tojo for his great interest in Indian Independence. We have to thank also Colonel Yamamoto, the Chief of the Hikari Kikan, for his co-operation, especially in the establishment of the Provisional Government of Azad Hind.

The next Resolution which was unanimously adopted by my Council is a more important one. The Council after discussing the political, economic and military situations in India came to the unanimous conclusion that the hour has struck for the declaration of war against Britain and America by the Provisional Government of Free India.

Last night at 12'55 a.m., we declared war through the radio and it is interesting to note that at 2 a.m., the enemy radio stations also gave out the news of our Declaration of War. This shows how alert they are in watching what steps we are taking. The Britishers know me well enough during my fight against them in India and they know well enough also that I will not make a declaration without having the strength to enforce what I say. Our declaration is not again a propaganda stunt. The coming events would show that we meant what we said.

Before I place our resolution declaring war on Britain and America before you for your ratification, I would ask you to realise its implications and to give your decision after full consideration.

Our Declaration, I repeat, is not an empty threat. We are resolved to carry it out with the last drop of our blood. And when I ask you to ratify it; I do not want to have the resolution carried in a formal ceremonial way. Your ratification would mean that you are as much resolved as we are to shed your last drop of blood in enforcing the Declaration, I know that I need not put this question to the Indian National Army because I know their mind and their deep anxiety to be on the Road to Delhi. I am now asking the Civilians as to whether they are one with us in making this Declaration, because if they are one with us they should come forthwith to give the fullest effect to our Programme of Total Mobilisation.

Friends! I want you to realise that we are now taking part in a meeting which is not a propaganda show; this is not a ceremonial affair. We are here at a historic meeting to decide on a life and death issue. If we succeed in the project, thirty eight crores of Indians will be free. If, on the other hand, as God forbid, we fail, for at least another century our Nation will be doomed to slavery and untold misery. I have told you at the outset how the hand of God has created this golden opportunity for us, I have shown you how we have moved from stage to stage and we have reached the right opportunity to strike at our enemy, I have told you how we now have the organisation, the army and the Provisional Government of Azad Hind recognised by the world and how we have secured every help and support. Are we going to fail India at this great hour in her history ?

Realise all these things, consider deeply all the implications of a Declaration of War and if you decide to take the war path, if you feel in your heart of hearts ready to face anything and everything in the historic fight against the British, if you feel that you are ready to give body, soul and all to fight our enemy until victory is won, then rise and give your ratification to our War Declaration by your acclamation.

Friends ! My joy and pride knows no bounds at having witnessed the outburst of enthusiasm and spirit of revolution in you, and your thirst for Independence. With this spirit permeating the hearts of the Indians in East Asia there could only be one sequel to our Declaration of War. And that is a fight which cannot fail to end in victory and with this demonstration of the united will and unified spirit of the Indian Nation, it may be an easy victory over our enemies. The meeting is now over and I would appeal to you to calm yourselves and to return to your homes, resolved forthwith to make every effort to bring our war to a victorious conclusion.

I would, lastly, call upon you to give three cheers for Revolution, for Free India and for the Government of Nippon.

At the 83rd session of the Imperial Diet which met on October 26, in Tokyo, Premier Gen. Hideki Tojo made the following reference to India in his speech :

" Turning to India, we find her 400,000,000 people still under Britain's ruthless heel and, with the ambition of the United States recently added to that pressure, they are continuing to experience indescribeble miseries The cruel rule of Britain and the outrageous conduct of the Anglo-American forces have further intensified the friction and antagonism betweem them and the Indian people, thus creating a profound social confusion accompanying an unprecedentedly great famine. The grave situation which is becoming aggravated day by day and month by month, is admitted even by Britain and the United States themselves.

" With many Indian patriots thrown into prison by the British and millions of innocent people thrown into agonies of starvation, the conditions in India at present are indeed tragic and the object of common grievance of all humanity. Such a situation we can by no means leave to take its own course. At this very juncture, Indians who hold their motherland close to their hearts have risen in unity under the leadership of the great patriot Mr. Subhash Chandra Bose and on the twenty-first of this month, the Provisional Government of Free India was established. Thereupon Nippon proceeded to recognize that government on the 23rd.

" It is truly a great pleasure for us to declare to the world through this chamber that Nippon is determined to support that government consistently in the future and to put forth her utmost efforts for the independence and emancipation of India.

" The complete independence and freedom of India and the lasting prosperity of the 400,000,000 Indian people are what Nippon sincerely desires. I have not the slightest doubt that in this purpose Nippon may count not only upon the wholehearted co-operation of all Greater East Asia peoples but also meet the earnest desire of all high-minded peoples throughout the world.

" It is my strong conviction that this rising tide of the movement for India's emancipation with the active co-operation of the peoples of Greater East Asia will inevitably bring, in the not distant future, the glorious day of independence and prosperity to India."

In a statement on the sppech by Premier General Hideki Tojo, Netaji Bose declared :

"The historic ulterance of His Excellency the Premier of Nippon General Tojo, at the extraordinary meeting of the Diet held on Oct. 25th will bring joy and inspiration to the hearts of Indians all over the world. This uttrance has special importance since it is the first public declaration of the Premier of Nippon after the recognition of the Provisional Government of Free India by his Government.

"The first speech of His Excellency represents a fitting climax to a series of soul-inspiring pronouncements on the Indian question since the fall of Singapore last year The Indian people owe a special debt of gratitnde to him for the personal interest in and sympathy for Indian Independence that he has consistently cherished and demonstrated.

"I am confident that Indian people will give practical proof of this gratitude on field of the battle "

Within a week of its formation the Provisional Government of Free India was recognised by nine free Governments of the world *viz.* Japan, Germany, Italy, Burma, Thailand, Mauchoukus, Phillipines, Croatia and National Government of China. It also received a message of sympathy from Ireland.

CHAPTER IX.

RANI OF JHANSI REGIMENT

Ever since the formation of Indian Independence League, it was felt that Indian women in East Asia could also do a lot to further the cause of India's Independence. It was such a great task that every man and every woman was required to come forward to sacrifice his or her utmost for this cause. Indian women could not help their brothers in various ways *e.g* preparation and collection of bandages, first-field dressings and other requirements, collections of funds and articles required by the troops, inspiring young men and women to do their duty in this critical hour etc.

It was with this view that Indian women began to take part in relief and Red Cross work. In March 1943 a Women's Section of I. I. L. was formally inaugurated. All the branches of the I. I L, throughout Malaya, Thailand and Burma started women's section. But it was with the arrival of Syt. Subhash Chandra Bose that the movement underwent a revolutionary change and gathered a fresh momentum. As early as 9th July 1943 (only a week after his arrival at Singapore) Netaji asked for men as well as women volunteers. The women of Singapure readily responded to the call

Bannet Charge

G rls of Regiment of Rani Jhansi being trained

A Soldier of Azad Hind

Firmly determined to recover his motherland

At the women's meeting held three days later, forty young women presented a guard of honour to Netaji. This marked the beginning of Rani of Jhansi Regiment.

Mrs. M. K. Chidambaram was elected chairman and Miss Saraswathy secretary of the Women's Section I. I. L. Singapore branch. Dr. S. Lakshmi was appointed secretary of the Headquarters. These energetic ladies undertook an extensive tour of Malaya and Thailand in the following two months to start branches of the Women's Section and enlisted volunteers for the Rani of Jhansi Regiment. The response was very encouraging. The first central camp for the training of volunteers was opened at Singapore on Oct. 22, 1943, after the formation of Provisional Government of Free India. The day coincided with the birthday of Rani of Juansi and was celebrated with great pomp and show. Netaji himself performed the opening ceremony.

The entire audience composed mostly of women, young and old, rose to its feet and broke out into delirious cheering when Netaji called upon the Indian women to march shoulder to shoulder with their brothers of the Azad Hind Fauj and be ready to lay down their lives on the battle-field for the sake of India's freedom.

Nataji Subhash Chandra Bose arrived punctually at 5 p.m. and was received by Mrs. M. K. Chidambaram, the president of the Women's Section. Netaji then inspected the guard-of-honour presented by an armed unit of the Rani of Jhansi Regiment, in the company of Capt. Mrs. Lakshmi. The tricolour national flag was hoisted by Netaji to the accompaniment of a national song.

The meeting then began with an address of welcome by Mrs. Chidambaram who declared that it was indeed a glorious coincidence that the Free Government of Azad Hind should be inaugurated and announced to the world on the birth day of the Woman Warrior of Hindustan.

Capt. Mrs. Lakshmi, in her capacity as Secretary of the Women's Section, I.I.L Hqrs., East Asia, presented the following report on the progress of the movement :—

We have gathered here this evening to celebrate the birthday of that most illustrious daughter of India—Rani Lakshmi Bai of Jhansi—and I am sure you will all agree that the only way in which we can pay true homage to her memory and avenge her death at the hands of our British enemy is by sacrificing our all in this our final struggle for independence. Today we Indian women in East Asia are starting on the most glorious journey in our history—a journey which we begin here in Syonan but will end only in Delhi when our beloved Netaji hoists the flag of Free India on our ancient Red Fortress. I shall give a brief account of the events which have gone to make this historic day.

Even since the formation of the Indian Independence League in East Asia, Indian women have been taking part in the activities of the League, especially in relief work and Red Cros work. In March 1943 our then President Srijut Rash Behari Bose formally inaugurated a Women's Section in Syonan and all League branches throughout East Asia were instructed to immediately start Women's Sections. With the arrival of our Netaji in Syonah in July our whole movement has undergone a revolutionary change and has gathered fresh momentum. He has given us a programme—Total

Mobilization of our Man Power and Resources against the enemy and a War Cry "Chalo Delhi" ! Knowing fully the past traditions and the present conditions prevailing in our Motherland Netaji has not been content to mobilize our men alone—he has given our women the most wonderful opportunity of our lifetime—the chance of proving ourselves to be the brave and true daughters of Mother India—thus following the noble examples of the Rani of Jhansi, Chand Bibi and the thousands of our sisters at home who even today are undergoing hardships and sufferings in their gallant fight against our enemies.

On the 9th of July at a mammoth rally of Indians held in Syonan Netaji called for volunteers. Along with our men our women also readily responded to his call. At the Women's meeting held here on the 12th of July a guard of honour consisting of 40 young women was provided to present arms when our Netaji arrived. It was an eye-opener not only to those present on that historic occasion but to the whole world as it clearly showed that our women were as determined as their brothers to drive the enemy out of their Motherland.

That day marked the beginning of the Rani of Jhansi Regiment. Two days later a Women's Department was formed at the Indian Independence League Headquarters and immediately steps were taken to organize the Indian Women of East Asia into one body with a view to recruiting volunteers for the Rani of Jhansi Regiment. All Territorial branches and Committees were immediately informed of this momentous step and asked to reorganize the axisting Women's Sections along these lines. The most striking feature was the fact that even before the various Women's Sections were formed, applications poured in from women all over Malai asking to be enlisted immediately as volunteers in the Rani of Jhansi Regiment. This fact is all the more noteworthy when it is remembered that most of these applicants had neither seen nor heard Netaji. His message had however reached them and having implicit faith in his leadership they were willing to follow him.

At the end of July the Member-in-Charge of the Women's Section in Syonan, Mrs. M. K. Chidambaram and the Secretary, Miss Saraswathy, with Lt.-Col. Alagappan of the Azad Hind Fauj made an All-Malaian tour. They addressed public gatherings of Indians at all the important towns and in many places helped in the starting of Women's Sections. Everywhere they found the spirit and enthusiasm very high and many women clamouring to be sent to Syonan immediately for training. In this connection I must point out that the response has come from women of all classes and strata of our society. Women who are all actuated by one and the same motive—namely, service and self-sacrifice in the cause of our National Freedom.

From the very beginning efforts were made to open a Central Training Camp (either in Syonan or on the mainland) but as there was considerable delay in obtaining a suitable place, part time training was started in many centres. The start was made in Syonan where part-time training was begun on the 19th of July ; it consisted of Military Training by instructors from the Azad Hind Fauj and lectures in First Aid. Similar training centres were started later at the Seletar Naval Base with the consent and help of the Imperial Nipponese Naval Authorities and about a month later in Johore Bahru and Penang. Centres which could provide no facilities for Military training started First Aid training and Hindustani Classes.

We were fully rewarded for our initial enthusiasm as Netaji during his tours and on every occasion made special mention of the Rani of Jhansi Regiment and the part we women were expected to play in the coming struggle. Everywhere spirited women, young and old, came forward and offered their services for a cause they all hold sacred. Training Camps have already been started both in Thailand and Burma. We expect our sisters from Thailand to join us here soon while our sisters in Burma are expecting us all to join them on the completion of our training ready for the final stage of our journey.

Our Camp is ready today but before it is formally opened by our Netaji, it is my most pleasant duty to thank all those who have worked so hard to make this an accomplished fact. First of all I must thank His Excellency the Mayor of Syonan and other authorities of the Syonan Tokubetusi for giving us permission to use the site of the existing barracks. Our heart-felt thanks are due to the Manager of the Chettiars' Bank for bearing all the expenses for the repair and reconstruction of the camp. My thanks are also due to my colleagues of the I. I. L. Headquarters, members of the Azad Hind Fauj and the authorities of the Hikari Kikan without whose help, co-operation and assistance the position of this camp would have been far from satisfactory. Last but not least may I take this opportunity of thanking on behalf of the members of the Rani of Jhansi Regiment and of myself our worthy Chairman of the Syonan Branch and his able friends and assistants. Our special thanks are also due to Sjt. Sithambaram Chettiar for his personal supervision in completing the work of the Camp in such a short time.

Finally to you our beloved Netaji, on behaf of every one of us I give you this our most solemn assurance. We have forsaken and forgotten our old lives of comfort and security and we are ready to follow you. We shall never betray the trust and confidence you have placed in us. Night and day we shall prepare ourselves for the task ahead—never even once faltering however long and perilous the journey may be, for we are all absolutely confident and certain that you will lead us to victory.

Declaring the camp open Netaji said :

Sisters and Brothers.—The opening of the Rani of Jhansi Regiment Training Camp is an important and significant function ; it is a very important landmark in the progress of our Movement in East Asia.

To realise its importance, you should bear in mind that ours is not a merely political movement. We are, on the other hand, engaged in the great task of regenerating our Nation. We are, in fact, ushering a New Life for the Indian Nation, and it is necessary that our New Life should be built on sound foundations. Remember that ours is not a propaganda stunt ; we are in fact witnessing the re-birth of India. And it is only in the fitness of things that there should be a stir of New Life among our womenfolk.

Our past has been a great and glorious one. India could not have produced a heroine like the Rani of Jhansi if she did not have a glorious tradition. The history of the great women in India is as ancient as the Vedic Period. The greatness of Indian womanhood had its roots in those early days when India had its Sanskrit culture. The same India which produced great women in the past also produced the Rani of Jhansi at a grave hour in India's history. And to-day while we are facing the gravest hour in our history, I have confidence that Indian womanhood will not fail to rise to the occasion. If for the war of independence of Jhansi, India had to produce and it did produce a Lakshmi Bai, to-day for the war of Independence of the whole of India, to liberate 38 crores of Indians, India has to produce and shall produce thousands of Ranis of Jhansi.

In the same way as we have figures like Maitreyi in India's ancient days, we have the inspiring examples of Ahalyabai of Maharashtra, Rani Bhawani of Bengal, Razya Begum and Noor Jehan, who were shining administrator in recent historic times prior to British rule in India. I have every confidence in the fertility of the Indian soil. I am confident that India, as in the past, will also produce the best flowers of Indian womanhood.

When in 1921 a new political life started in India, thousands, nay lakhs, of our sisters also joined the movement and came forward to make sacrifices. In those days it was a great thing to go to prisons. Our Indian brothers and sisters got ready to undergo the ordeal of prison life and I remember still how in December 1921 at Calcutta the two jails were full. The Britishers built two more jails and these two were also packed in a few days.

When the Britishers found that the Indians were not restrained by fear of prison life, they changed their tactics. They resorted to the method of throwing leaders into prison and using lathis and bullets against the masses. Joining the Civil Disobedience Movement then meant willingness to face lathi charges and gun-fire and the Indians—not only men but also women—got ready to face lathi charges and gun-fire. I cannot forget an incident in Calcutta when we held a procession against the orders of the Government and when the police tried to break the procession by lathi charge, some of our sisters made a cordon around us (coming between us and the police), without flinching to face lathi charges. Thus, I have witnessed while in India how the spirit and determination our sisters have been growing stage by stage.

Not only in the history of the Passive Resistance Movement but in the history of the Revolutionary Party also we have the examples of our brave sisters who have played a noble part. I know of many sisters who became daring revolutionaries. If one type of courage was necessary for passive resistance, another and more active courage is necessary for revoluntionary efforts, and in this too I found that our sisters were not wanting. In 1931 an English magistrate was shot by two girls; the age of one was 16, the age of the other was 17. In India even ordinary men will shudder before magistrates, but then two young sisters bravely went to the house of the magistrate and fired at him. You can easily imagine what wonderful courage those young sisters might have had. Such courage does not descend from the skies; it comes from the soil of India; it has its roots in the age-old traditions of India's past.

Since 1928 I have been taking interest in women's organisations in India and I found that, given the opportunity, our sisters could rise to any occasion. There was one Rastra Mahila Sangh of ladies in Bengal which did splendid work. In December 1928 a volunteer corps of 500 women was formed which was not only run on sound lines but their parades and their discipline gave us great hopes and confirmed my belief in the fact that, given the impetus and opportunity, Indian women could perform duties entrusted to them in a befitting manner. I have also seen women's organisations in India giving training in arms available in a slave country, like lathis and daggers and the way our sisters were progressing was remarkable.

Rani of Jhansi Regiment

Netaji inspecting the Gaurd of Honour presented by the Rani of Jhansi Regiment on the occasion of opening of the Camp (22-10-43)

Route March of the Rani of Jhansi Regiment in Burma

And so when I began to undertake the task of guiding the Indian Independence Movement, I felt that our sisters should also be given the opportunity to serve India at this grave emergency, I consulted many and I was told by some that though to raise a women's regiment might be possible in India, it would be an impossible task in East Asia. What they said did not affect my conviction and my determination. And to-day you have before your own eyes what our sisters have accomplished. Their work was started in July and if only now the Training Camp for them is being opened, the delay is not due to any shortcoming on their part. The delay was due to our difficulties in finding the accommodation and making the necessary arrangements. Meanwhile, I know that our sisters were getting impatient and anxious. I heard that they were intending to lead a deputation to me to ask me whether I have forgotton them. I feel happy to-day that the camp is ready and the camp is being opened to-day on the anniversary of the birthday of the Rani of Jhansi.

I may at this juncture say a few words about the Rani of Jhansi. When the Rani of Jhansi started her fight, her age was only twenty. You can easily imagine what it would have been for a girl of twenty, riding a horse, and wielding her sword in open battle. You can easily realize what courage and spirit she must have had. The English Commander who fought against her said that "she was the best and bravest of the rebels." He made this admission because Jhansi Rani's bravery was something which he could not hide, for he himself had to fight against her. First she fought from the Jhansi Fort and when the fort was besieged, she escaped with a party to Kalpi from where she put up a fight. Then she had to retreat from this battlefront, she made an alliance with Tantia Topi, attacked and captured Gwalior Fort and using that Fort as the base continued the battle and in this last and great battle she died fighting.

Imagine what amount of courage would have been necessary to carry on the fight inspite of more than one defeat. Yet this 20 year old Rani had the courage and showed a valour which shall be a source of inspiration to Indians for generations to come.

Unfortunately, Jhansi Rani was defeated ; it was not her defeat ; it was the defeat of India. She died but her spirit can never die India can once again produce Jhansi Ranis and march on to victory.

156 of our sisters are going to start their training in the Camp which is being opened to day. But I hope that their number at Syonan will reach 1,000 very soon. Training Camps for women have also been started in Thailand and Burma but at Syonan we have the Central Camp and I feel that in this Central Camp we should at least have one thousand potential Ranis of Jhansi.

You have just now heard the brave words of the Commandant of the Rani of Jhansi Unit at Syonan. She expressed their determination to work ceaselessly day and night, to get prepared for the onward March to Delhi. I feel joyous at hearing that slogan " On to Delhi" from our sisters as I have been hearing it from our brothers.

With these words, I declare the Training Camp open. And I would appeal to all the delegates present to carry my message to their localities and to make every effort to realise the programme I have now laid before you.

The name of Rani Lakshmi Bai, Rani of Jhansi the heroine of 1857—and the tale of her heroic death in battle roused the patriotism of the Indian women and they anxiously awaited the day, when they would be fighting in the front side by side with their brothers. It was rightly thought that apart from the fighting value of their presence right in the front line would be very great and the presence of Indian women. armed for the freedom fight, would have a great effect on the mentality of the men in the British Indian Army on the other side, when they came into contact with them.

At a later stage, we shall have to refer briefly to the noble part played by the brave soldiers and nurses of the Rani of Jhansi Regiment and their heroic deeds at the Burma front issued after some time. But before closing this chapter, it shall not be out of place to narrate some incidents of the training period, which show how enthusiastic the women were to join the camp and serve their motherland. In a brief statement Captain (Mrs.) M. S. Thavar, the commandant of the Rani of Jhansi Camp said :—

The Rani of Jhansi Regiment Training Camp was officially opened on 22nd Oct. 1943 in Syonan by our Netaji Subhash Chandra Bose. One hundred women patriots promptly responded to the call of their noble leader. At this call for service and sacrifice both the rich and the poor, the literate and illiterate, the old and young forsook their luxuries and comforts and walked into a life—full of hardships, Thus this Rani of Jhansi Regiment started with 100 Volunteers. In a short period we have increased tremendously in number and improved ourselves physically, mentally and spiritually. Some of us who joined as mere school girls are proud today to hold responsible posts as Officers of the Azad Hind Fauj (Indian National Army). It would be interesting to note how keen our sisters are to join this camp.

One dark night in January 1944 at 2 o'clock in the morning a young girl of 16 years, Kantha Lakshmi by name, rushed to the gate of the Rani of Jhansi Regiment camp only to be stopped at the point of the sentry's bayonet with "Ruk Jao". Standing like a ghost she shouted at the sentry, "Open the gate, I have come to join the camp, please let me get in quickly." Hearing this the guards inside the camp opened the gate and let her in and to her surprise the guard found the enthusiastic recruit's hands and feet bleeding and when questioned she narrated her story thus.—"I was very anxious to join the camp from the very moment Netaji opened it. Many a time I expressed my desire to my parents but they scolded me and threatened me. One day I told them that I would run away to the camp if they would not willingly consent and grant my only desire. Then they beat me and put a watch over me during the day. So my only hope of escape was by night. I took a strong rope and hid it under my bed upstairs. I waited till all went off to sleep. As soon as I was convinced that no one would watch my movements, I got up and tied one end of the rope to the window and let down the other end to the road. Then I caught hold of the top end of the rope and slowly climbed down to the road and from there I ran two miles to reach here. While I was running my only prayer was that my parents should not get up and search for me. I did not realise till I reached here that my hands and feet were bleeding due to the rough rope. Had it not been for this initial spilling of blood I would not have got a chance to shed more blood for my country. Please take me to your Commanding Officer and let me explain to her.'

It took about one and a half months for her hands and feet to heal. Today she is one of the N.C.O's (Non Commissioned Officers) sent to the Indo-Burma front. She is a smart girl with cheerful countenance.

Another striking incident which I shall never forget is about a Mohamedan girl of 15 years. One afternoon she rushed through the gate and walked in straight into the office. I asked her the reason for this unmannerly behaviour. She came close to me with tears in her eyes and said. "Please do not send me out, I wish to stay in this camp." "Why do you wish to stay in the camp ?" I asked her. "I have a great desire to serve my country like the other sisters who have already joined," she said. "Do you know that the life of a recruit is full of hardships," I asked to test her. "I know we ought to be prepared to give our lives and I am not afraid to die," she said. She was allowed to stay in the camp that night.

The next morning her parents were sent for. At about 11 o'clock her elder brother and her father came and they wanted to take her back. They tried to argue with her in every possible wav asking her to return but her determination was firm ; she caught hold of the handle of my chair and refused to move even an inch from there. After a short while her mother with her three elder daughters came with tearful eyes pleading with her to return, but she obstinately refused to move from the office. Failing to win her by kindness one of her sisters abused her and asked her to return all the jewellery that she was using. One by one she took off and handed over to her sister all the ornaments that she happened to wear, Then her sister asked for the clothes that she was wearing, This little girl seeing that she had none to spare ran immediately to the barrack to one of her comrades, borrowed some clothes and brought a bundle of clothes to sister. It brought tears into the eyes of her sisters and they all cried, "You are such a hard-hearted girl, how can you run away from home leaving your old parents and all three of us. What have they done to you ?" They have done no harm to me and neither have I done any harm to them, I came here to join the camp and serve my country," she explained. The eldest sister was so annoyed at this that she took the bundle of clothes and the jewellery and said, "We shall take these things and perform a cremation ceremony in your name." To this our new young recruit replied "Yes, it is true from today I am dead to you. From now on I am reborn to serve Mother India."

In the month of April 1944 a married woman came to me and handed a small note containing the address of her husband and requested me to send for her husband. She would not answer any of my questions unless her husband was sent for.

On the arrival of her husband she said, "We were married for three years and we had no children. When the call for 1000 women Volunteers came from Netaji I requested my husband to allow me to join the camp and himself to join the Seletar Training Camp. He flatly refused and abused me. He asked me to stay in the kitchen and cook his food. I told him that I felt within me it is wise to serve my mother-country and that I had taken my decision to join the camp. If he wishes to emulate my example he should join the Seletar camp.

Her husband was very annoyed. He asked her to return immediately threatening to take necessary action if she persisted. She replied, "You can never see me alive outside the gate of the camp if you force me to return." On this I had to interfere and send the woman to the barracks. I spoke to her husband for about half an hour and I succeeded in convincing him to such an extent that he agreed to join the Seletar Training camp himself.

These are few of the episodes clearly distinguishing the spirit, courage and determination of our would be soldiers. There are many such daughters of India who are eager to serve their country only awaiting their parents' permission. But it is clear that one day a thirsting soul will find a place to quench its thirst somewhere. Such are the patriotic daughters of India thirsting to serve their country's cause despite all obstacles.

It gives me great pleasure to see three or four recruits from the same family and my thoughts go straight to their parents. What a sacrifice they make in sending all their daughters and in some cases their only child, a daughter, and if they possess more would willingly sacrifice them also. Those are the worthy few who have paid any heed to the pathetic cry of their 400 million poverty-striken, starving and enslaved brothers and sisters and those are the patriotic few who can be really said to have responded to call of Netaji Subhash Chandra Bose.

Captain (Mrs.) M. S. Thavar, the Commandant of the Rani of Jhansi Training Camp in Singapore in a spirited address at the impressive Passing-Out Ceremony of the Second Batch of Volunteers held on Wednesday, 25th October, 1944, declared :—

It is exactly a year since our Regiment was first started. A fighting Regiment of women is a unique and unparalled feat in the history of the world. The fact that our revered Netaji struck quite a different note in originating the Regiment in spite of all odds, is proof enough of the unbounded confidence that he has in the capabilities of Indian women.

During this short period of a year, we have already sent one batch to Burma, who are now at the front fighting shoulder to shoulder with their brothers. Another batch is awaiting transport to join their predecessors in Burma. Today we are not only celebrating the first anniversary of our Regiment, but we are also simultaneously holding our second Passing-out Parade.

Our Regiment consists of two Sections, namely, the fighting and the nursing sections. It depends on the choice of the new volunteer whether serve our cause, in wounding the enemy, or healing the friend—I mean, whether to serve as a soldier or a nurse. I must however make it clear here, that even our nurses are fully trained in the art of self-defence, ready to meet any eventuality. In their discipline and training they are in no way inferior to our soldiers, because we have firm belief in one principle, that to be an honourable citizen of the future in a free and ideal India, every Indian, whether man or women or child must be thoroughly disciplined and trained to defend oneself and one's nation. After this preliminary ground work is prepared, it is left to the choice of the volunteer, to choose one of these two ways of serving our cause, either to kill the foe or revive the comrade. To take a simile from philosophy, it matters little whether one chooses the Bhakti Margam or Karma Margam, as both lead to the same goal so long as devotedness is there.

Rani of Jhansi Regiment

A group photograph of the Singapore Staff
Miss Janki Thaver-Commander of the Rangoon Camp
sitting fourth from the left

Major Mrs. Manoranjita Thaver
Commandant of the Training
Camp Singapore

Col. Lakhshmi
Commander of the Regiment
and Minister of Women's
Organization

We enlist only those who have completed their 15th year, but in a few cases the uncompromising enthusiasm of some young recruits, got the better of our strictness and we had to admit them as exceptions. As such we have volunteers in our Regiment, who are below the minimum age limit, but they happen to be some of our most efficient members. Their spirit overcomes the disadvantage of their age They are a living proof of a perfect warrior at the age of twenty two and there is no reason why amateur warriors should not start their lessons at the age of eleven.

We also trained a Balak Sena batch, who after completing their two months course in drill, physical training, use of arms and Hindustani have now been posted at different centres in Malai and we are training similar batches here.

According to the modern conception, a girl must either marry and work in the kitchen or pass her Senior Cambridge and serve in some convent. But we are gratefnl to our leader, to have given us the opportunity to show to the world that there is a third, more glorious course, open for Indian women and that is of fighting for their country, not with hotly worded resolutions in cosy corners, but with cold steel in tight corners.

It would not be out of place to give you a rough idea of the training of volunteers in this Camp In the morning from 8.30 to 9 a.m. we have physical training and breakfast at 9 a.m. From 9-45 to 11-45 a m. we have military training. Lunch is served at 1 p.m. From 2 to 3 p.m. we rest in bed, from 3 to 4.30 p.m. Hindustani is taught. Then at 4-30 p.m. tea is served either with fruits, ground nuts or ragi porridge. From 5 to 7 p.m. we have again military training which completes with games for half an hour. Dinner is served at 8-30 p,m. Lectures are given between 9-30 p.m. on alternate nights, and at 11 p.m. the lights are off.

Nurses are sent to the Bidaderi Hospital for training in the morning and on their return at 1-30 p.m. they join with the others in the afternoon training programme.

We have a hospital of our own in the camp and a Lady Medical Officer in charge of it, We have formed a band of our own which I hope will be seen ready to take part in our future programme. Twice a month the volunteers are sent to picture shows, once a month they are taken to a picnic and those recruits who have come from Syonan, are sent home once a month on a Sunday and the others are taken for walks or shopping etc. No visitors are allowed except a blood relative to visit the recruits. To safeguard the reputation of your daughters, sisters and wives we have the discipline of this camp quite strict.

CHAPTER X

NETAJI AT THE ASSEMBLY OF GREATER EAST ASIA NATIONS

After the formation of Povisional Govt. of India and the Rani of Jhansi Regiment, Netaji addressed a meeting of the Indian merchants at Singapore on the 25th October 1943. This was his first address for Total Mobilization. On the 26th October he left for Bangkok by air. There he was the guest of honour of the Thai Government. From there he left for an undisclosed place with his Ministerial staff.

The Japanese Board of Information in a communique on the afternoon of October 31, announced that Syt. Subhash Chandra Bose had arrived at Tokyo. It was understood that during his stay in Japan, Netaji would exchange views with Premier Tojo and other Japan Government leaders on various problems, including future cooperation between Japan Government and the Provisional Government of Free India.

Netaji was accompanied by his Excellency Lt. Col. J. K. Bhonsle Chief of Staff of the Supreme Command (Minister without Portfolio) H. E. Mr. A. M. Sahay (Minister without Portfolio) chief of the Cabinet Secretriate, H. E. Lt. Col. D. S. Raju attached to the Supreme Command and Mr. A. Hassan Private Secretary to H. E. Sri Subhash Chandra Bose. On his arrival he was warmly welcomed by the Japanese Foreign Minister and other prominent officials and members of the Indian Independence League Tokyo. Netaji made an official call on Premier General Tojo on November 1 and was closeted with him for forty minutes. The Foreign Minister of Japan gave a dinner in honour of Syt. Bose at his official residence on November 2.

On the 5th and 6th November Netaji attended the historic Assembly of Great East Asia Nations as a visitor along with his Ministerial Staff. In this Assembly representatives of six Asiatic Nations had gathered to confer upon various problems of mutual interest. They were :—

(1) General Tojo, Prime Minister of Japan (2) Wang Chingwei, President China (3) Prince Wan Weithayakon, Representative of the President of the Council Thailand. (4) Chang Chinghui, Prime Minister Manchoukuo (5) Dr, Jose P. Laurel, President Phillippines (6) Dr. Ba Maw, Prime Minister Burma.

On the opening day were delivered speeches by the delegates of the six participating Nations. On the 6th November, the Assembly, first of all, adopted the following Joint Declaration:—

"It is the basic principle for the establishment of world peace that the nations of the world have each its proper place, and enjoy prosperity in common through mutual aid and assistance.

"The United States of America and the British Empire have in seeking their own prosperity oppressed other nations and peoples. Especially in East Asia, they indulged insatiable aggression and exploitation, and sought to satisfy their inordinate ambition of enslaving the entire region, and finally they came to menace seriously the stability of East Asia. Herein lies the cause of the present war.

"The countries of Greater East Asia with a view to contributing to the cause of world peace, undertake to co-operate toward prosecuting the War of Greater East Asia to a successful conclusion, liberating their region from the yoke of British-American domination, and assuring their self-existence and self-defence, and in constructing a Greater East Asia in accordance with the following principles :—

"1. The countries of Greater East Asia through mutual co-operation will ensure the stability of their region and construct an order of common prosperity and well-being based upon justice.

"2. The countries of Greater East Asia will ensure the fraternity of nations in their region, by respecting one another's sovereignty and independence and practising mutual assistance and amity.

"3. The countries of Greater East Asia by respeting one another's traditions and developing the creative faculties of each race, will enhance the culture and civilization of Greater East Asia.

"4. The countries of Greater East Asia will endeavor to accelerate their economic development through close co-operation upon a basis of reciprocity and to promote thereby the general prosperity of their region.

"5. The countries of Greater East Asia will cultivate friendly relation with all the countries of the world, and work for the abolition of racial discriminations, the promotions, of cultural intercourse and the opening of mankind."

After the main business of the Assembly was concluded, Dr. Ba Maw made the following brief address by way of introducing Syt. Bose. Drawing the attention of the gathering to the Indian problem he said :—

Mr. Chairman, Your Excellencies :

Now that the main business of the Greater East Asia Assembly has concluded, I wish to draw your attention to a collateral question which follows us constantly like a shadow. That question is nothing less than the Indian question. His Excellency, the Head of the Indian Provisional Government, is present among us as a guest. His presence is sufficient to endorse whatever statement I may make on this great Indian question.

Yesterday in the course of my observations, I made a categorical statement that in my view Asia cannot be free unless India is free. Having made that observation, it is my duty to pursue it logically, Mr. Chairman, your Excellencies. As the Representative of Burma, I am in a peculiarly fit position to pursue the Indian question as I have not yet exhausted it and because I understand that my friend Mr. Bose will also have an opportunity to address Your Excellencies. All that I wish to say will be in the nature of preparatory observations, preparing the way for the Indian leader.

Burma is in a peculiar position to speak on the Indian question. For a generation, as the world knows, by the forces of historical circumstances, Burma and India had to travel the same hard, bitter road. Linked in every way, we had to pursue the same struggle against the same enemy. We had to act in unity of purpose of action, of objective. I am proud to admit that much of the political philosophy that the Burmese learned, much of the political techniques that Burma learned, were learned from India. Burma derived from the past her religious philosophy from India. In the present, I, as a leader of my people, cheerfully acknowledge that we learned much of our political philosophy also from India.

For generations the Burmese and Indians had to carry on the same struggle. Most of you will not understand the real meaning of my words. It was a struggle against the most powerful, the most merciless, the most predatory power in the world. It was a struggle between men and guns. Needless to say, every time the guns won. The men every time rose, but the guns crushed them every time. And it was in those battles—it was at the time of bitter struggle against odds of the most overwhelming character—that I learned my present realism, that whatever we may say of our philosophy, of this, of that, the ultimate decisive victor is force. But, we still carried on.

I am not ashamed to say that my country rose at every turn. Every revolt was crushed with guns. As I happened to tell an Englishman in England, it is easy to keep 16 million people down with guns, if they gave me the guns, if they gave me a force of 100,000 armed with guns, I can keep the whole of Britain down. Only the guns were in their hands and not in ours.

That, in short, is the substance of the common struggle that India and Burma had to carry on. And out of this struggle, out of the fires of these constant revolutions rose men, great men, selfless men, men of light and leading, who gave their lives and careers, everything they possessed, to the cause of their motherland. Among these great patriots, patriots of international reputation is, as we now have as guest here, Mr. Subhash Chandra Bose.

I am perfectly certain that the story of Subhash Chandra Bose is known to all of us, that he symbolizes the resurgent, the revolutionary spirit of India—India, although divided, yet remaining unbroken. And we must all be glad to know that Mr. Subhash Chandra Bose is now with us prepared to carry on the same struggle, and now not isolated but with a thousand million East Asiatics behind him. I will empahsize the fact that there cannot be a Free Asia without a Free India. I am speaking quite literally. For a hundred years Great Britain pursued her colonial policy in Asia with Indian strength, with Indian resources from even in the West right down through Singapore and Hongkong in theEast. It was with Indian manpower, Indian resources, Indian wealth that Great Britain built her great, her vast predatory empire.

I am speaking from personal experience that my own country collapsed before the British, because the British, according to their traditional policy, never fought themselves. They fought and won Burma with Indians just as they fought every war with every other person except themselves. This war they will fight to the last Russian ; they will fight to the last American ;

fight to the last Indian, but Britain according to her traditional policy will never use her own self and resources.

And the following her traditional policy, she came to Burma, saw Burma, she conquered Burma with Indian manpower and Indian wealth. That is why she pursued the same policy downward to the right and from India upward to the left across Asia. It was Indian wealth that maintained British power, and it was Indian manpower that made Britain the instrument of a colonial policy.

That is why you will understand me when I say that if we wish to destroy that predatory empire, if we wish to destroy anti-Asiatic powers, we must turn them out, drive them out of their Asiatic stronghold, and that stronghold is India. The British Empire cannot be goaded until and unless British power, British domination of India, is destroyed.

I will not say more—this is not an occasion for words. The great Indian leader who will follow me will, I am sure, state the Indian case. He will state it with his usual clarity and force, and so, as I have said, these remarks of mine are just preliminary, just to propose before this Assembly that we do here solemnly declare that we give our complete support to the cause of India's Independence, to His Excellency Mr. Subhas Chandra Bose, who as the head of the Indian Provisional Government is pursuing the struggle, preparing for the day when he and his Indian Independence Army will march into Delhi and redeem India,

After this address in a stirring 20 minute address before the Assembly, Netaji Sahhash Channra Bose voiced aeep gratitude for the unanimous pledge of sympathetic assistance by East Asiatic natioes to the Indian Independence movement, and declared that this support had provided a tremendous stimulus to all Indians. He promised that a decisive battle against Britain to free India would be launched in the near future.

Netaji then pointed out the marked difference between the current assembly and international conferences held in the past. He emphasized that the Assembly of Greater East Asiatic Nations represented a spectacularly marked departure from other conferences in that it was based on mutual aid and respect for the independence and sovereignty of all participating member nations.

He asserted it was only natural that Japan should have convened the Assembly in as much as Nippon was the pivotal influence in East Asia, and pointed out that other Asiatic races had looked to Nippon as liberator ever since the days of the Russo-Nippones War.

Turning to India's present plight, Netaji stated that India's subjugation by Europeans was originally started by errors made centuries ago. He stressed that Indians to-day realized this fact and they also realized that there was no room for a compromise with Britain. H declared the only way India could win its independence was to fight Britain and come out victorious.

Netaji spoke of the thousands of Indians who were dying to-day of starvation. With sudden emphasis he disclosed that the Indian National Army was to-day poised for its advance to Delhi.

Netaji next expressed his deepest wishes for the successful establishment of Greater East Asia and for the completion of Japan's great work of construction. He pointed out that the Greater East Asia joint declaration was a declaration of liberation of East Asia—the Magna Charta of 1943 which would live forever in world history.

He concluded by reiterating his determination to exert his utmost efforts to drive out Britain from India and bring about early materialization of the establishment of Free India.

Japan was ready shortly to transfer the Andaman and Nicobar Islands to the Provisional Government of Free India headed by Subhash Chandra Bose declared Premier General Hideki Tojo in response to the speech delivered by Netaji at the Assembly.

Netaji also delivered a stirring speech in Hindustani at the mass meeting held in Tokyo on 7th November 1943.

Netaji Subhash Chandra Bose was granted audience at the Phoenix Hall in the Imperial Palace at 10-30 a. m. on November 10 by Tenno Heika (Emperor of Japan).

In the audience Tenno Heika was pleased to honour Netaji Bose with words of sympathetic appreciation for the latter's efforts to attain Indian Independence.

Following Imperial audience Netaji Subhash Chandra Bose issued the following statement :—

"Tenno Heika was gracious enough to receive me in audience this morning as Head of the Provisional Government of Azad Hind. That was the highest honour that India and I personally, could receive. I have renewed my determination to fight shoulder to shoulder with Tenno Heika's Government, Army and Navy, till the bitter end, until our common victory is achieved. The memory of this reception in audience by Tenno Heika will remain engraved in my memory for all time."

Netaji Subhash Bose and his party were honoured at a luncheon party on November 15 given by Mitsuru Toyama, noted Nippon patriot.

Rash Behari Bose, Supreme Adviser to the Provisional Government, was also a guest at the function. The party was attended by more than 44 notables including General Shigeru Honjo, President of the Military Welfare Board of the Welfare Ministry, and Yoshihisa Kuzuu, Director of the Imperial Rule Assistance Association.

On November 18 Netaji Subhash Chandra Bose arrived at Nanking on his return journey. As soon as he arrived in the morning he worshipped at the Chungshan Mausoleum where the ashes of the late Dr. Sun Yat sen; "Father of Modern China," repose. Later he made a courtesy call on President Wang Ching wei. At noon he was guest of honour at a luncheon given by President Wang and attended by other high officials of the National Government of China. In the afternoon, Netaji paid a courtesy call on General Shunroku Hata, Commander in-Chief of the Nippon forces in China, at the latter's headquarter and also on Nippon Ambassador Masayuki Tani at the

Nippon Embassy. After calling on the German as well as Manchoukuo Embassies, Netaji Bose received return calls by General Hata and Ambassador Tani at the Government's Guest Hall.

At 8-30 p.m. Netaji was guest at a banquet given by Foreign Minister Chn Min-yi.

Netaji Subhash Chandra Bose, at 10-00 a. m. on Nov. 19, received return visits from Dr. Ernest Woermann German Ambassador to Nanking, and Lu Yung-huan, Manchoukuo Ambassador to Nanking, at the Guest Hall.

At 11-00 Netaji attended the Nanking citizens' welcome meeting held in his honour at the National Public Hall.

China and India should join hands for crushing Britain and the United States in order to attain complete Greater East Asiatic freedom, declared Netaji, at the welcome rally. He called on Chiang Kai-shek and other leaders to shake off Anglo.American influence and do their utmost for the unification of China, the gaining of Indian independence and the complete emancipation of Greater East Asia.

Referring to the visit of Madam Chiang to India last year to ask Indian leaders to co-operate with the Indian Government, Netaji Bose declared that if Chiang Kai Shek actually desired the independence of China he should not have asked Indians to co-operate with their oppressors, who had enslaved 388 million Indians. Netaji stressed that China and India should both fight for the freedom and liberation of Greater East Asia.

Netaji Bose recalled that in 1939, when he was the President of the Indian National Congress, he sent a medical mission to Chungking as an expression of India's sympathy and goodwill.

Netaji Bose added, "Chungking should not take up arms against Indians, but should fight side by side with India against the common enemy, because China will never prosper under Anglo-American control." He recalled that Dr. Sun Yat-sen was an ardent supporter of India and a torch-bearer for a United East Asia

Following the mass meeting, he was guest of honour at a luncheon party given by Massayuki Tani, Nippon Ambassador to China.

At 3-0 p.m Netaji conferred with President Wang Ching-wei at the latter's official residence and at 4.30 with Dr. Ernst Woermann. In the evening, he was guest of honour at a dinner party tendered by General Shunroku Hata, Commander-in-Chief of the Nippon forces in China.

Netaji Subhash Chandra Bose, who visited Nanking and Shanghai after attending the Assembly of Greater East Asiatic Nations in Tokyo, arrived at Manila by air at 3 1 p m. on November 22 He was greeted at the airport by President José P. Laurel, Ambassador Shozo Murata, Lieut.-General Shigenori Kuroda, C-in-C. of the Nippon forces in the Philippines, and other high officials of the Philippine Government.

Netaji Subhash Chandra Bose called on President Jose P. Laurel at the Malacanan expressing congratulations on the birth of the new Republic of the Philippines. In the evening Netaji received representatives of the Indian residents at the Malacanan where he stayed during his visit.

He was guest at a dinner given in his honour by President Laurel at Malacanan in the evening. The dinner was attended by Ministers of State, Nippon Ambassador Shozo Murata and other distinguished Filipino Nippon and Indian leaders

" British imperialism is dead ; however, the United States is succeeding and replacing it in all its mercilessness and injustice," warned Netaji Subhash Chandra Bose in an address delivered at the dinner.

"The world must choose between the perpetuation of this imperialism or establishment of a new world based on justice and equality," Netaji declared. "To compromise with British imperialism is to compromise with slavery because it always oppressed peoples economically, politically and socially." Regarding the rise of American imperialism, Netaji asserted, " We must be aware of this new menace and prevent its tentacles from spreading."

Recalling that in the past Asiatic peoples, including Indians, had looked up to the United States, He said, " But now we know the American colonial policy is actually a menace to smaller nations."

Urging total sacrifice on the part of all East Asians, he declared, " I have always been a determined and consistent fighter against oppression. As individuals we do not matter. We will die soon enough. We must die but we must strive to make our nation live forever."

He recalled that the United States imperialism formerly only covered the political field ; however, it has expanded to include social and economic fields as well.

Hailing the convention of the Assembly of Greater East Asiatic Nations in Tokyo recently, Netaji said, "It marked the realization of my dream to see East Asiatic nations together "

Stressing the Indian determination to fight to the last, Netaji said, "Indians are fully prepared to die in order to salvage our country. We must die because he who lives for India is he who dies for India. We are prepared for a long and bitter struggle."

Expressing profound thanks to his host, Netaji said, " I am grateful to Your Excellency, the Government and people of the Philippines and wish everlasting freedom and prosperity to your Republic "

Netaji Subhash Chandra Bose on his way back to Syonan from Nippon arrived at Saigon at 1-30 p. m. on November, 24 from Manila. After a brief rest at the Nippon Hotel, Netaji paid courtesy visits to local commanders of the Nippon Army and Naval Forces.

In the evening, he attended a banquet given in his honour by the Nippon Minister, Shigenori Tashiro. Later Netaji Bose addressed a mass rally of local Indian residents at which he exhorted his compatriots to join in the crusade to liberate their motherland from British shackles.

Netaji Subhash Chandra Bose returned to the Headquarters of the Provisional Government at Singapore on November, 25.

CHAPTER XI

TOTAL MOBILIZATION

After his return from Tokyo, hurried preparations were made for the move of the Indian National Army to Burma. The stage was set for the *action—to strike the last below. All the* resources of the Indians in East Asia, in men, money and material were required for the successful prosecution of this purpose. From the very beginning Netaji had called for Total Mobilization. The poor had *splendidly responded to the call. Thousands of them* had offered, all they possessed, at the feet of Netaji. They gave all their property and cash for the furtherance of the cause of India's Freedom and enlisted themselves and their children (sons and daughters) in the Indian National Army. They sacrificed their lives at the altar of Liberty. The stories of these sacrifices make a book in themselves, so a few examples chosen at random will suffice to show how enthusiastic the people were for the cause.

Mr. Sharma of Alor Star enlisted himself in the Army. His wife and daughter joined the Rani of Jhansi Regiment. One of his sons was trained in Japan as Tokyo Cadet, the other joined the officer's training school at Singapore, while the third was in the Field Propaganda Unit in Burma. He gave his all to the movement. Similar was the case of Dr. Ponniah of Perak. He offered his services as a doctor to the biggest Civilian Training Centre in East Asia at Tanjong Rambutan (Perak) and gave all his medical equipment and medicines to the hospital. The stock of medicines was so big, that it did not exhaust even long after the surrender in 1945 movement. The doctor died, while in the service of the motherland. His wife worked as a nurse in the Maymyo hospital of the Advanced Headquarters of I. N. A. His daughter joined the Rani of Jhansi Regiment, while his son after passing the course from Officer's Training School joined as 2nd Lt. in the I. N. A. Examples of this sort can be multiplied immensely.

Seeing that the rich were not doing their duty, Netaji called a conference of All Malai Chettiars and other Indian Merchants at Singapore on the 25th Oct. 1943 and addressed them as follows :—

Friends ! I would first give my hearty welcome to our sisters and brothers who have come to attend this conference from all parts of Malai You have come here to take part in a conference, which, I am confident, will prove to be of great significance and importance. We have heard considerable assurances of loyalty toward our great cause and this conference is going to put that loyalty to the test.

I do not propose to deliver a long speech because long speeches are not necessary. Firstly, I would appeal to you to realise what each one of you would do if the responsibility of liberating India was on your shoulders ; to free India is a responsibility which lies on the shoulders of every Indian in East Asia, and I hope that you will realise this great responsibility which has devolved upon you.

When an army goes to the battlefield, the responsibility of fighting and winning rests equally on every individual of the army, whether he is an officer, an N. C. O. or an ordinary soldier. Only that army will win, every soldier of which is ready to do his duty. You must realise that the Indians in East Asia have to-day become an army which has to fight and win. As in the case of every soldier at the front, so also on every Indian in East Asia a great responsibility has fallen. I know that some of you are rich and some of you are poor. I know that some of you are educated while others are not. Whatever be your differences, I want you to bear in mind that all of you are equal as far as your duty is concerned. I want every Indian in East Asia to do his duty.

Whan in an army some one is appointed as an officer, it becomes his duty to go forward himself and to lead others to go forward. Syonan has assumed a great importance in our fight in East Asia ; the Headquarters of the Indian Independence League is here ; the Headquarters of the I. N. A. is here ; and only recently the Provisional Government of Azad Hind has also been established here. Syonan was once a fortress of Britain, but to-day it has become the Headquarters of the Indian Independence Movement in East Asia.

Syonan's relation to other places in East Asia is the same as the relation of a commander to the troops of his regiment. The success of a battle not only depends upon the way every soldier performs his duty but it also depends on the correct lead and right example given by the officer commanding the army.

You will thus realise that any voice which rises from Syonan will have its echoes all over East Asia ; that any action which you take here will have its repercussions all over East Asia. The part which Indians in various parts of East Asia are going to play will greatly depend on the example which you are going to give from Syonan. I want you to remember that your responsibilities are great because you have to give the lead, you have to provide the inspiration for Indians in other parts of East Asia.

I want you to think for yourselves and visualise what a Free Indian Government would have done when faced with a grave emergency like a foreign invasion. Supposing India was a free country and supposing there was the danger of an attack by a foreign enemy, what would the Government of Free India do ? Would they not have started Total Mobilisation then ? You could easily understand that this is the normal duty of any free government. Keeping this fact in mind I want you to realise what your duties are in our great attempt to get our independence and maintain it.

Think also of what the procedure would be in a free country when it is in a state of war. Would there be meetings and appeals as is the case with us so far ? No ! A free government, on the other hand, would issue only a call for all able-bodied men between specific ages to assemble at a certain place on a certain day, at a certain hour. Voluntarily and without any grumbling people will respond to the call. Why, because people of independent countries know that they have to make sacrifices for their liberty. And when a free Government needs money to defend its independence, it does not proceed to hold meetings and start begging campaigns.

On the contrary, free governments would prepare budgets of their war requirements, think of ways and means to collect that money, keeping in view the financial conditions of the people, and straight-away proceed to levy the necessary taxation. I would ask you whether any man can refuse to become a soldier or to contribute war taxes in a free country ? India is not yet free but we are free in heart and spirit. And by the establishment of the Provisional Government we have become a free people.

Now it is our responsibility to liberate India and to establish a free Government of India. If we feel that we are fit for independence, if we really desire independence, we should straightaway live and act as we would do if we lived in free India under the aegis of our Free Government at a time of a grave national emergency. Whatever we would have done in a free India in response to the call of the Free Indian Government, it has become our solemn duty to do forthwith. Look at the people of Germany and Nippon and how in those countries all the resources of the people have been mobilised by the governments. When it is the duty of a government to defend its own independence, they have to do it at any cost and they have to pool all the resources of their countries.

Legally speaking there is no private property when a country is in a state of war. The government has absolute right over the lives and properties of its people during such emergencies. We too are a free people with a free government. If you think that your wealth and possessions are your own, you are living in delusion. Every life and every property belongs to the nation when it is involved in a war. Your lives and your properties do not now belong to you ; they belong to India and India alone.

I have every confidence that if you realise this simple truth that we have to achieve Independence by any means and at any cost, and that we are now a free people in a state of war, you will realise that nothing belongs to you, that your lives, properties and everything are no more your own.

If you do not want to realise this simple truth then you have another path clearly chalked out for you. If you do not want to be, and shoulder your duties as a free Indian living under a free government, if you do not want independence and if you are not ready to pay the price of independence, you have only one course before you and that is the path taken by the Englishmen.

They lived as rulers once here, but now they have only one place left here and that is the prison. If you choose, you can go to prisons and keep company with the Englishmen. But remember this : when the war is over and India becomes independent, you shall have no room in Free India. If the Indian Government condescends to take pity on you the highest act of mercy which the Free Indian Government can do is to provide you with third class tickets to leave the holy soil of India and to go to England.

I have heard that some of the rich Indians in Malai are murmuring that I am harassing them. I want to have a straight talk with them so that they can take a straight path hereafter. I have heard that some rich Indians are thinking of changing their nationality to save themselves from making contributions towards the cause of Indian Independence. I have also heard that some are thinking of handing over their properties to the custodians and of claiming them back after the war is over.

Then again I have heard of people who are thinking of adopting a ruse of promising, say a lakh of Rupees, and trying to gain time by paying that amount in small instalments hoping that sooner or later we will be going away to Burma and then to India and thus they would be able to evade payments.

But they are miserably in the wrong and it is not going to be so easy for them to deceive us, and to shrink performing their duties. Whether we are here in Syonan, whether we are in Burma or in India itself, our organisation shall remain here because it has to remain here to carry on its work till India becomes completely independent and the last Englishman is driven out of India.

I would appeal to every Indian whether he is a Hindu, Sikh, Muslim or a Christian not to fail in performing his duties. I know who are doing their duties and who are shirking them.

I have to liberate India and I shall make India independent by all means and at any cost and I would appeal to you to realise that it is your duty too to shoulder the burden whether it pleases you or not. If you want to evade the issue, say plainly that you do not want independence, then as I have already told you, a different path lies ahead of you.

So long as you say you are Indians and you want to claim and make money in East Asia as Indians you cannot shirk performing the duties which devolve on you as free Indians. Do not think that it is left to your option to perform your duty or not.

I have already said in my last speech in Syonan that I am making my last appeal. Today I am standing here not to make another appeal and I am not standing here as a beggar with outstretched hands. I stand here today representing the Provisional Government of Azad Hind which has absolute rights over your lives and properties.

I assure you, friends, I am not one who is accustomed to tall talking or making empty threats. Whatever I say, I say after the fullest consideration and I mean what I say. Even my enemies know that I seldom say what I do not mean. I have said that we have to get Indian Independence by all means and at any cost and that we have to carry out Total Mobilisation voluntarily if possible, by compulsion if necessary. And I would reiterate to you that I mean what I said.

I am speaking at length to you to-day so that you shall not be under any delusion, so that you may not say afterwards that you were not given the fullest opportunity to come forward on a voluntary basis. It will be an honourable course for you and I would feel proud of you if you come forward voluntarily. But if you do not choose to come forward voluntarily, then we are not going to remain slaves on that account.

I am really surprised to hear that there are a few people who say that it took years for them to amass their money and that they have many children to provide for If on this account, they had refused to make sacrifices, in a Free India under a Free Government, I would ask you to imagine, what would have happened to them. Surely they would have been regarded and treated as enemies.

You could either be a friend or a foe. Do not think that only the Britishers are our enemies Every ne who helps the Britishers, everyone who refuses to help our cause, is also our enemy because we are engaged in a life and death struggle to-day.

Look at those who have volunteered to join the Indian National Army and who are now getting the necessary training. They do not know how many of them would live to see India free. They are getting ready with the one thought of shedding their last drop of blood. They are getting ready to go to a free India or to die on the way. There is no programme of retreat for them. Let the programme of retreat be reserved only for Wavell and his army.

The British Government has given him promotions and have now made him the Viceroy of India because he has proved himself to be a past-master in the art of saving his own life by retreat after retreat. The I. N. A. has no plan of saving its life by retreat. When the I.N.A. is getting trained either to march to victory or to spill its last drop of blood on the way, the rich people are asking me whether total mobilisation means .0 per cent. or 5 per cent. I would ask these people who are speaking of percentages whether we can tell our soldiers to fight and spill only 10 per cent. of their blood and save the rest.

You could see with your own eyes the spirit which is permeating our young men who have become recruits and our sisters who have rallied to the Colours. Fortunately, we are not short of men. The response has been so great that we have enough recruits to get prepared even for a long war.

What we are wanting is similar response in money and materials. If we are all poor then we would be justified in seeking foreign help, but there are also rich people amongst us and our foreign friends also know it. When our own people have ample resources, it is sheer disgrace for us to stretch our hands to others for help.

When there are brothers and sisters coming forward in large numbers offering their lives, I cannot understand why those who do not want to give their lives are even grumbling to part with their possessions. What is money after all ; compared with life, money is nothing. Supposing a foreign government tells you that either you have to give the crore you possess or your life, surely you would rather choose to part with your crore than your life.

In the same way as youngmen have come forward to offer their lives, the poor classes have been coming forward voluntarily and with enthusiastic spirit to offer everything that they have. Poorer classes of Indians like watchmen, washermen, barbers, petty shopkeepers and *gowalas* have come forward with all that they have.

And in addition to that some of them have also offered to become volunteers. Some friends ask me what I mean by the word "Total Mobilisation". These poor men who have volunteered not only their possessions but also their lives, have demonstrated by their own example the exact meaning of the word " Total Mobilisation."

Some of these poor people came to me, and not only did they give all the cash they had in their pockets but went further and gave me their 'savings bank books" which represent their live's savings. Is there not one rich man among the Indians in Malai who can come forward and say in the same spirit "here is my bank book" for the cause of Indian Independence ?

The Indians as a nation believe in the ideal of self-sacrifice. Among the Hindus we have the ideal of the Sanyasins and the Muslims have the way of the Faqirs. In our history we have instances of numerous kings who chose to become Faqirs for the sake of faith, justice and truth.

Can there be a greater cause, a nobler cause and holier cause than that of liberating 38 crores of human souls and is there not one rich man who could come and say "here is my bank book" for such a great cause ?

If you are not self-sacrificing enough to offer your lives, I cannot understand why there should not be even a few among you who could say " Spare only our lives, but we give everything else."

I shall now proceed to place before you the programme of the Provisional Government of Azad Hind. In carrying out this programme we have to proceed slowly, steadily, and systematically as any government would do. The wealth of Indians in Malai according to pre-war estimates was 100 crores and as you know, values have increased since then. Usually a Government makes a yearly budget and, when it is necessary, supplementary budgets also during the year. I also propose to do the same thing.

It is up to you either to come forward voluntarily in the spirit of Total Mobilisation or you shall have to meet the demands made by us from time to time till the war is over.

My first demand from Malai is for 10 crores of Rupees, which would be approximately 10 per cent. of the value of Indian possessions in Malai. And as in this conference many rich people of Malai are present. I would expect at least one crore of Rupees straightaway and I hope within a month the 10 crores would be forthcoming from Malai.

This speech had the desired effect. As a result of this appeal many came pouring in from all directions. About Rs. one crore and 30 lakhs were promised on the spot. The report of the I. I. L. Malaya Branch published at the end of 1943, reveals that collections from Malya only amounted to 77,27,917 dollars in cash, besides 86,810 dollar's worth articles of gold jewellery. In July 1944 this amount had gone up to 1,53,54, 104 dollars. Total contributions from Malaya were about Rs. 5 crores, from Burma 15 crores and from Thailand 1½ crores.

Some individual contributions need mention here. These are a few examples out of hundreds and thousands to show how Netaji had inspired the Indians in Far East.

1. Mr. Habib—a Muslim millionaire of Rangoon—all his property, estate and wealth amounting to more than one Crore of rupees. He was presented ' Sevak-i-Hind' medal by Netaji on 9.7.44.

2. Srimati Betai of Rangoon gave all her cash and ornaments worth about Rs. 50 lakhs. She was also awarded 'Sewak-i-Hind' medal on 21.8.44.

3. Mr. B. Ghosh Rangoon—Rs. 5 lakhs.

4. Mr. Kiamal Saigaon—7 lakhs Piasters.

Total Mobilization

Netaji collecting funds at a Conference of the Malai Indian Merchants Singapore (25-10-43)

L. Jagat Ram of Bangkok who donated $22\frac{1}{2}$ lakhs tickles

S. Boor Singh of Messrs. Boor Singh Indar Singh, Bangkok offering a purse of one lakh to Netaji

S. Bhagwan Singh of Messrs. Gian Singh & Co. Kuala Lumpur

TOTAL MOBILIZATION
THE WHOLE FAMILY IN NATIONAL SERVICE

Dr. Ponniah of Perak

Sub Officer
Mrs. Ponniah
of the Rani of
Jhansi Regiment

2/Lt. Master Ponniah
of the I.N.A.

THE RICH GAVE LAKHs BUT THE POOR GAVE ALL THEY HAD

S. Iqbal Singh Narula who gave 200 lbs. of silver (equal to Netaji's weight) for the Azad Hind Fund

A hawker of Bangkok who gave all his daily earnings

S. Mahan Singh, who donated all his property (cash and cattle) to I.N.A. and gave also his daily earnings

5. Messrs. Gian Singh and Co. Singapore—10 lakhs dollars.

6. S. Bhagwan Singh of Messrs. Gian Singh and Co. Kuala Lampur—10 lakhs dollars.

7. T. S. Ganpat Ram Penang—3 lakhs dollars.

8. Lala Jagat Ram Bangkok—22½ lakhs Tels.

9. Messrs. Boor Singh Indar Singh Bangkok 12 lakhs Tels.

10. A Maskati (Mr. Kappasi) Bangkok—10 lakhs Tels.

11. Messrs. Gian Singh Nand Singh Bangkok—6½ lakhs Tels.

12. Mr. Mehtani Karachi Stores Bangkok—6 lakhs Tels.

Another huge donation was made by a Punjabi yonngman on the occasion of the Independence Day Celebrations on January 26, 1944 in Rangoon. The story runs: "At the beginning of the meeting Netaji was garlanded. He had wound the garland of flowers round his hand as he spoke. When he finished his stirring speech, enthusiasm was at fever-heat. Then an idea struck him, He asked, if any body was ready to buy the garland; the money he would receive, would go to Fauj Funds.

" The first bid was one lakh of rupees. In a few minutes, the figure swelled. One lakh—one lakh and a half—three lakhs—four—four and a quarter—five—six—seven lakhs!

" A young Punjabi youth had been the first bidder. When the figure reached four and a quarter, he shouted five. When the final bid of seven lakhs was being announced, he looked vexed and intent on an inner struggle. As the garland was about to be declared sold, he jumped up and rushed to the dais. 'I give all my wealth—all that I have—every pie that I own he shouted. Subhash Babu caught the trembling youth by both his hands. He, said ' Done—the garland is yours. Patriotic men like you deserve the crown of glory, our Fauj shall win.' "

As the times passed, more money was required and it was raised by voluntry donations in cash and kind (food stuffs, metalware and all such things that could be of use to the I. N. A.). Thus the Azad Hind Government and the Indian National Army were maintained exclusively by Indians themselves and they received no financial assistance from the Japanese.

To run his Government on sound financial basis, Netaji established The Azad Hind Bank in Rangoon in April 1944. It had an authorised capital of Rs. 50 lakhs and a paid up capital of Rs 25 lakhs. Its head office was situated at 94 York Road. The Bank had a board of seven directors with Mr. S. A. Ayar, Propaganda Minister of the Azad Hind Government as chairman. The Azad Hind Currency bore the signature of Netaji Subhash Chandra Bose on one side and the picture of the Taj Mahal on the other.

Besides the collection of money, elaborate arrangements were made for recruitment of volunteers, who were taken from the civil as well as from the Prisoners of War. More than two lacs offered themselves for recruitment, but it was not possible to train them all. The standing National Army consisted of 1500 officers and 50,000 men. 600 Officers were trained in the Officers, Training Schools. Besides these training was being given to 30000 more recruits.

Besides Military Training, there were Civilian Training Centres at Singapore and Rangoon where training was given in the civil administration for managing the territories liberated by the Indian National Army. The following were the training centres for various purposes :—

(1) Azad Hind Fauj Training Camp Tanjong Rambutan.

(2) ,, ,, ,, ,, Seletar (Singapore).

(3) Azad School Singapore (Civil Administration Training Centre).

(4) Field Propaganda Unit Centre Bauktaw (Rangoon).

(5) Gowshala Civilian Training Camp Rangoon.

(6) Bengali Officers Training Camp Rangoon.

(7) Officers Training School Rangoon.

(8) Rani Jhansi Regiment Camp Rangoon.

(9) Gorkha Training School Camp Kamba (Rangoon).

(10) Bal Saina Camp Rangoon.

(11) Civilian Training Camp Chholpuri (Thailand).

(12) Interpreters' School Singapore.

(13) Cadet's College for Reconstruction Department Singapore.

(14) Training Centre for old men Singapore.

(15) Bal Saina Camps at Singapore and Bangkok.

(16) Rani Jhansi Regiment Camp at Singapore and Maymyo,

Besides this about 50 young men were sent to Tokyo as Cadets to be trained in Navy and Air Force,

The Secretary of the Training Department was Col. Ehsan Qadir, who was later on made the Minister for Man Power.

The training period extended over six months and during this period no one was allowed to leave the training centre, even on Saturdays and Sundays except in groups under the command of instructing officers. Intensive physical and spiritual training was provided. In the Indian National Army all were treated on the same footing irrespective of caste, colour or creed. They ate from one kitchen, in common plates and drank from common mugs—all officers and common soldiers, Hindus, Muslims and Sikhs. Beef and Pork, were prohibited. The troops were dressed in Khaki. They wore a badge on the left side of the forage cap, On the top of the badge were inscribed the words "I. N. A." with a map of India in the centre. At the bottom of the badge were inscribed in Roman script: "Ittifaq, Etmad and Qurbani" meaning Unity, Faith and Sacrifice. They also used to wear another badge on the right side of their uniform. It was marked with the tri-colour map of India. A locket-sized badge bearing a miniature of Netaji was worn on the left side of the uniform. In addition to this the officers used different distinguishing straps on their shoulders.

The Indian National Army was now very well contributed and fully organized as under :—

1. Netaji Subhash Chandra Bose—Supreme Commandar.
2. Col. J. K. Bhonsle—Chief of staff.

Azad School Cadets Singapore

Civilians trained for field propaganda and Civil Administration and sent to liberated area Manipur

Balak Saina Bangkok

Marching in a procession

8. Lt. Col. M. Z. Kiani—Commander I Division (which fought in the front).
4. Lt. Col. S. M. Hussain—I Hind Field Group.
5. Lt. Col. Shah Nawaz Khan—Commander Bose Brigade.
6. Lt. Col. I. J. Kiani—Commander Gandhi Brigade.
7. Lt. Col. Aziz Ahmad Khan (succeeded by Lt Col. G. S. Dhillon) —Commander Nehru Brigade.
8. Major Gulzara Singh—Azad Brigade.
9. Major S. A. Malik—Intelligence Group.
10. Lt. Col. Burhan-ud-din—Bahadur Group.
11. Lt. Col. A. D. Loganadan—Chief Administrator.
12. Major Abdur Rashid—D. P. M.
12. Major P. K. Sehgal—Military Secretary.
14. Captain Krishna Murti—Finance.
15. Col. Habib-ur-Rehman—O. T. S.
16. Legal and Judicial—Captain D. C. Nag.

The following are some of the instructions for the training centre :—

OBJECT

To train the maximum number of able-bodied Indians in East Asia as Revolutionary Soldiers and Free Citizens.

Inception and Necessity

In the History of Wars and Revolutions it has always happened that Battalions composed of unprofessional Soldiers, the free Citizens of a Free State have defeated Battalions composed of regular soldiers twice or thrice their number.

In India of the past, not only was the Army recruited from particular provinces, but it was confined to particular classes, who began to regard it as the monopoly of the professional soldiers. Civilians were kept at arms length, and no citizen was let into the Secrets of the Military profession. The Army was instinctively conservative. Its departmentalism lead it to thought-tight compartments, and whatever Military thought India imbibed during British occupation, was confined to the so-called 'Martial Classes.'

With the establishment of the Provisional Government any such tendency must be removed once and for all.

The part time instruction given in the First Stage of Training is, therefore, intended to lay the foundation of a National Citizen Army. And there is no better place or time to start this, than *Here* and *Now*.

TRAINING.

Before the nation is ready for self-defence, the individual must be capable of defending himself. If the British succeeded in humiliating Indians in the past, it was not because India had no manpower, but because the average citizen neither had the spirit of retaliation nor the capacity for self-defence. Both these qualities essential for freedom have now to be created.

It is obvious that every citizen cannot be armed ; but in the first stage of training he can prepare himself for the struggle by getting strong physically and spiritually.

The mechanical performance of physical jerks is not enough. The mere drafting of Volunteers to the Army is not enough. Every Volunteer in the Azad Hind Fauj has to be backed up by the physical and moral strength of his civilian compatriots. Every Indian should, therefore, enter into the spirit of the Independence movement by undergoing the first stage of training.

RESPONSIBILITY

This training is the entire responsibility of the League branches and can be imparted at small expense. Those who can afford, are expected to meet their own expenses.

Uniforms are not necessary during this stage, but there is no objection to a Territory or Branch providing its Volunteers with Uniforms from local resources.

Local Allowance on the basis of Parades attended by each trainee, may be fixed by the Territories after sanction is obtained from Headquarters.

SYLLABUS

The successful working of this syllabus depends entirely on the initiative of the Chairman coupled with the ability, resourcefulness, and drive of the Member-in-charge Training of the Branch concerned.

With proper co-operation with the Publicity, Recruitment and Education departments of his branch, the Member i/c Training, can overcome the present atmosphere of local inactivity, and the tendency always of awaiting an impulse from above. Unless the office bearers of the League, especially the Members-in-Charge Training, personally take part in this Training as spiritual instructors, recruits, or as both, they cannot convince the public either of the importance or of the necessity of the first stage of Training.

The following Syllabus can be worked, with practically no arms and only by equipment from local resources. Instructors for this stage are trained at the Azad Schools, and can be obtained on application from Headqnarters.

(*i*) **Drill and Field Craft.**

Route Marches. Practice in crawling for Tactical purposes. Use of ground. Camouflage. Tree Climbing. Field-craft both by day and night.

(*ii*) **Weapons Training.**

Rifle and Bayonet (if available, otherwise Dummy or wooden Rifles).

Krishan Lal

Member of Balak Saina who

Krishan Nand

6 years old member of

(iii) Physical Training

Wrestling, Gatka, or other means of un-armed combat, *e.g.* Ju-Jitsu.

Jungle cutting to make tracks. Building small bridges. Swimming. Digging Slit-Trenches, Rowing, Games, Mass P. T.

(iv) Spiritual Training.

Upholding of National Honour and Prestige even at the risk of life. Building of *Character, Initiative, Resourcefulness, Self Reliance.* and *National Discipline.*

Here the word 'Spiritual' has been used not in the Ethical or Religious sense, but in the Military sense. This important part of training needs some explanation.

The true aim of a Nation in *War* is to break the enemy's *Will to War*, with the least possible material and spiritual loss to itself.

Intensive physical training is a safe-guard against material loss, but spiritual loss can only be safeguarded by the development of the Nation's spiritual endurance. To withstand and endure this long war, it is only by spiritual Training that we can strengthen our *Will to War.*

In this connection we can learn a lesson from the present condition in India.

British India's Military weakness does not lie in its armies. In fact it has quite a large Army. It lies in the spiritual weakness of the supporters of British rule. It lies in the extreme vulnerability of their moral, which will crack before a National Army. And once their moral cracks, it will paralyse the Anglo-American Forces.

On the other hand, our spiritual Training imparted during the first stage, will strengthen the patriotic spirit of the masses in East Asia and make them immune to enemy propaganda.

With proper co-operation with the Department of Education and Culture, an unshakable belief can be built up in the Independence of India to be achieved by the Total Mobilization of the Indians themselves, irrespective of what happens in the rest of the world.

(v) Education.

(*a*) Romanized Hindustani (Not Hindi) is compulsory, For the study of Hindustani, daily Hindustani Newspapers can serve as text books.

(*b*) Nippon-go should also be studied by all.. This will bring closer relationship with our Nipponese friends and as such, better understanding and cultural harmony will be created.

(Also see Appendix 8).

(vi) Relief work.

Stretcher-bearing. First Aid, A. R. P. Hygiene, Sanitation. Purification of water. Cooking of food.

(*vii*) **Technical Training.**

(If possible) as Motor Mechanic, Electrician, Telephone operator, Dresser, etc. (Local Talent to be fully exploited).

(*viii*) **Entertainment.**

National and social Dramas and Songs. Bicycle trips to places 30 or 40 miles away.

APPENDIX 2

Hindustani " Words Of Command "

	English		Hindustani	
1.	Parade	1.	Quaid	
2.	Steady	2.	Khabardar	
3.	Words of Command	3.	Hukm	

	Caution in English		*Caution in Hindustani*	
1.	Fall in	1.	Jama Qatar	
2.	Attention	2.	Savdhan	
3.	Right Dress	3.	Dahne se sidhai	"Lo"
4.	Eyes front	4.	Samne	"Dekh"
5.	From the right number	5.	Nafri	"Gin"
6.	As you were	6.		"Wapis"
7.	Stand at ease	7.	Assani se khare	"Ho"
8.	Stand easy	8.	Aram	"Kar"
9.	Open order March	9.	Áge Pichhe khul	"Jao"
10.	Close order March	10.	Pichhe age Wapis	"Jao"
11.	Move to the right or left in threes. Squad right or left turn.	11.	Tin tin men dahine baen murenge. Toli dahine ya baen	"Mur"
12.	Will advance left turn	12.	Tin qatar men baen	"Mur"
13.	Three paces forward march	13.	Tin qadam age	"Barh"
14.	Three paces step back march	14.	Tin qadam piche	"Hat"
15.	Three paces right close march	15.	Tin qadam dahine	"Hat"
16.	Three paces left close march	16.	Tin qadam baen	"Hat"
17.	Quick March	17.	Chatak se	"Kooch"
18.	Quick March while on the Field.	18.	Age	"Barh"
19.	About turn	19.	Piche	"Mur"
20.	Mark Time	20.	Raftar	"Mila"
21.	Forward	21.	Age	"Barh"
22.	Change Step	22.	Qadam	"Badal"

Tokyo Cadets

Civilians of East Asia sent by Netaji to Tokyo for Military Training (Navy and Air Force)

Officer's Training School Singapore

	Caution in English		*Caution in Hindustani*	
23.	Right Wheel	8.	Dahine	"Ghum"
24.	Change direction right or left squad right or left form.	24.	Dahine ya baen rukh badlenge Dahine ya baen rukh	"Badal"
25.	Halt	25.	Ruk	"Jao"
26.	At the halt change direction right. Squad right form	26.	Khare Khare rukh badlenge Dahine rukh	"Badal"
27.	At the halt on the left or right form squad.	27.	Dahine ya baen tin qatar men ruk	"Jao"
28.	Break into slow time, slow march	28.	Dhire chal badlenge, Dhire	"Chal"
29.	Left Right	29.	Sajja-Khabba	
30.	Double March	30.	Dhire	"Daur"
31.	Salute to the right, squad salute.	31.	Dahine salami-Toli	"Salam"
32.	Salute to the left, squad salute.	32.	Baen salami-Toli	"Salam"
33.	Salute to the front with message, squad salute.	33.	Samne salami chithi ke sath	"Salam"
34.	Salute (Dismiss)	34.	"Barkhast",	
35.	Shoulder Arms	35.	Rifle baghal men	"La"
36.	Order Arms	36.	Rifle niche	"La"
37.	Present Arms	37.	Rifle 'Pesh'	
38.	Slope arms	28.	Rifle kandhe par	"La"
39.	Trail Arms	39.	Rifle Tol par	"La"
40.	For inspection port Arms.	40.	Rifle Mulahza par	"La"
41.	Examine Arms	41.	Rifle Muaina par	"La"
42.	Sling Arms.	42.	Rifle	"La"
43.	March at ease	43.	Asani se	"Kooch"
44.	Short Trail	44.	Rifle thora	"Utra"
45.	Pile Arms	45.	Jama	"Rifle"
46.	Ground Arms.	46.	Rifle zamin par	"Rakh"
47.	Fix Bayonet	47.	Sangin	"Charah"
48.	Unfix Bayonet	48.	Sangin	"Utar"
49.	Ease Spring.	49.	Purza	"Hila"
50.	General Direction	50.	Am Rukh	
51.	Action	51.	Action	
52.	Mount Gun or Tripod.	52.	Gun ya Tripod Lagao	
53.	Load	53.	Load	
54.	Un-load	54.	Un-load.	
55.	Dismount	55.	Utaro	
56.	Slightly Right (Left)	56.	Thora Dahine (Baen)	
57.	Half Right (Left)	57.	Adha Dahine (Baen	
58.	¾ Right (Left)	58.	Tin Chauthai Dahine (Baen).	

Cautionn in English	*Caution in Hindustani*
59. Lay	59. Shist Lo
60. Right (Left)	60. Dahine (Baen)
61. One or Two Tap,	61. Ek ya do Tap,
62. D. A. P.	62. Dur Shist ka Nishan.
63. Repeat	63. Dobara
64. O'Clock	64. Baje.
65. Reference points	65. Mashhur Nishan
66. 1st Point.	66. Pehla Nishan.

N. B. These words of command were coined by Hav. Major Partap Singh in the first instance and afterwards improved upon.

APPENDIX 3

List of subjects on which Education Department should be asked to arrange Lectures

(*a*) History of the Indian National Congress and Sacrifices of Congress Leaders.

(*b*) History of Forward Bloc and internal revolution in India.

(*c*) Brief History of India, Proving India's greatness.

(*d*) History of British aggression in Indian.

Note :—In the study of these historical subjects, it is *not* necessary for the lecturer to find texts for long sermons but only to pick up facts for analysis and to draw lessons for the future.

(*e*) Revolutionary History of other Countries.

(*f*) Geography, with special reference to India's Eastern Border.

(*g*) Significances of the War of *Greater East Asia.*

(*h*) Weak points in British War organization and Civil administration in India. (Military Officers on tour can be asked to deliver Military lectures).

(*i*) Youth Organization in Japan.

(*j*) Hitler's youth organization.

APPENDIX 4

List of Stores which can generally be collected locally

Item	Quantity	Remarks
Rifles ...	20 per 100 men.	Can often be obtained by co-operation with Nipponese Garrison.
Wooden Rifles ..	50 per 100 men	For Trench digging.
Pick Axes with handles	20 per 100 men	For Trench digging.
Shovels ...	10 per 100 men	For Trench digging.
Axes Saws ...	10 per 100 men	For wood cutting.
Axes Carpenters...	10 per 100 men	For wood cutting.
Rope 10 yds. long	10 per 100 men	For Bridge Building.
Flanks ...		For Bridge Building.
Beams ...		For Bridge Building.

APPENDIX 6

A simple specimen programme is given below :—

1. **Daily.**

   P. T. 45 mins.

   Drill and Weapon Training 1 hour.

   Instructions for next day and rest 15 mins.

   Total :—2 hours. This is the minimum and not the maximum.

2. **Once a week** : – Route March.

   Distance to be increased from 5 to 15 miles.

3. **Occasionally** :—Relief work.

   Technical Training.

   Camps and Excursions.

   Military Lectures by Military Officers.

4. **Sundays, Holidays** :—or other suitable days, special lectures for spiritual, educational and political training.

   Discussion and suggestions.

CHAPTER XII

INDIAN NATIONAL ARMY IN ACTION

1. The Stage is Set

To put in this 'total mobilization' in action and prepare the Army for the last phase of the struggle for freedom a meeting of the Council of Ministers of the Provisional Government of Azad Hind was held at the official residence of Netaji Subhash Chandra Bose on 9th December, 1943, when the Advisers were also present. The Council of Ministers discussed and adopted, with certain alterations, the reports of two Cabinet Sub-Committees, namely, one on the rewards, decorations, and pensions to be granted to the Azad Hind Fauj warriors who would be taking part in the coming operations, and the other on the plan of National Unification.

The Council of Ministers provided liberally for the families and dependents of the Azad Hind Fauj warriors who might be killed wounded, or disabled in the coming compaign, The Council of Ministers also decided that, in the case of Indian Officers and men serving in the British Indian Army, their previous service should be taken into account for purposes of pension etc., provided they came over to the Azad Hind Fauj during the campaign.

The recommendations of the Cabinet Sub-Committee on National Unification, as adopted by the Council of Ministers, ensured the unification of the Indian Nation, irrespective of difference of caste, creed and religion.

As a prelude to National Unification, Council of Ministers decided that Hindustani shall be the common language of India. "Jai Hind" (Victory for India) shall be the common greeting and salutation between Indians. The present Tricolour shall be the National Flag of India, the song beginning with the words "Sudh Sukh Chai" shall be India's National Song; the Tiger will be India's National Emblem; "Chalo Delhi" will be the National War Cry till the successful conclusion of the Revolution; and "Azad Hind Zindabad," Inqilab Zindabad and "Netaji Ki Jai" will be the National Slogans till the victorious conclusion of the Revolution.

The plan for National Unification in the matter of food, dress, etc., was under the active consideration of the Provisional Government of Azad Hind. This plan for National Unification was to be introduced first among the Indians in East Asia.

Netaji Subhash Chandra Bose visited South Sumatra on December 10, 1943. Acknowledging the Indians' pledge to give unswerving support to the Azad Hind Fauj in men and material, Netaji delivered a stirring address at a mammoth rally held at Palembung by his compatriots living in all parts of South Sumatra.

In the course of his speech, Netaji Bose thanked the Indians for their absolute support and loyalty to the newly formed Government and stressed the imminence of the Indian crusade to rid their Motherland of British influence once and for all.

Netaji Bose

In Shaheed (Andaman) island gazing towards India

Lt. Col. Abid Hassan

Private Secretary to Netaji Subhas Chandra Bose who came with him from Germany

Netaji Bose in Shaheed-Island

Visiting Civilian Gaurd

" With such unflinching determination on the part of my compatriots in every corner of Greater East Asia, and with the help of our Nippon friends, the success of our forthcoming march into Delhi and eventual emancipation of the suffering millions cannot fail," Netaji said.

Netaji Subhash Chandra Bose visited Andaman Islands on December 29 and immediately paid a courtesy-call on the Commander-in-Chief of the Nippon Army forces in Port Blair and expressed thanks for the support of the Nippon Army for the cause of the Indian independence movement as well as the creation of the Provisional Government.

Later Netaji visited the headquarters of the Nippon Military Administration and heard a detailed report on administrative activities in the islands. He also visited Ross Island.

In the evening Netaji was guest at a dinner given by the Commander-in-Chief of the Nippon Army forces and spent the night at the former official residence of the British Governor.

The next morning Netaji attended a grand rally in Port Blair. At the outset of the rally the Indian flag was hoisted personally by Netaji, while the Indian national anthem was being sung. In the course of his address Netaji declared that the Andamans were liberated from the British yoke by Nippon, which was the leader of Asia. " These islands in the near future will become Indian territory. Entry into Delhi at the cost of our blood or to fight our way to death in the present struggle for independence are the only two ways to repay Nippon's sincerity and friendship toward India," Netaji said. Concluding he exhorted all Indians in the Andamans to " follow either of these two courses."

Netaji thanked Mr. Ramakrishna chairman of the Independence League, Mr. Durga Parshad, vice-chairman and Nawab Ali for their loyal support.

Colonel (later Major-General) Loganadan, a Minister of the Provisional Government, was appointed the first Chief Commissioner of the Andamans (re-named Shaheed = Martyrs) and Nicobar (re-named Swaraj) Islands.

After his visit to the Andaman Islands, Netaji Subhash Chandra Bose arrived in Burma on January 7, 1944. The Headquarters of the Provisional Government of Free India and the Supreme Command of the Indian National Army were also shifted to Burma, which was to be the spring-board for the operations of the Army of Liberation.

"Indians at home would be thrilled to hear that Netaji Subash Chandra Bose has moved his Headquarters to within a few hours, flight to Calcutta" This was the comment made by Mr. S.A. Ayer, Minister of Publicity and Propaganda of the Provisional Government of Azad Hind, on the official announcement that the Headquarters of the Free India Government had been moved to Burma. " This is one more decisive step in Netaji's irresistible advance towards India and the British citadel in Delhi," the Minister said.

"Netaji now stands at the eastern gates of India at the head of the Indian National Army. This Army of Liberation impatiently awaits his word of command to fire the shot that will open the campaign ; the report of that shot will echo and re-echo throughout the length and breadth of India ; and that will be the signal for an India-wide uprising against the British ;

only the unimaginative British can be blind to their present perilous position in India," Mr. Ayer asserted.

Continuing, he stressed that the millions of Netaji's followers all over India were fully aware of his hurricane activities since his arrival in East Asia six months ago ; they had heard every one of his momentous utterances over the radio from Tokyo, Syonan Bangkok and Rangoon ; they knew that he had established the Provisional Government of Free India, the Headquarters of which had now moved to Burma : they knew that Netaji had moved nnits of the Indian National Army to within striking distance of the British bases in Eastern India ; thus Netaji's f0llowers in India were fully aware that the stage was now set for the final showdown.

Indomitable and fighting determination to liberate India was the keynote of the fiery one-hour address by Netaji Subhash Chandra Bose given on January, 11 afternoon before troops of the Indian National Army which advanced into Burma along with the Provisional Government of Free India.

With the sweeping march to Delhi imminent, Netaji Bose reminded his soldiers again that 3,000,000 Indians in East Asia as well as the 380,000,000 Indians in India and powerful Axis nations stood firmly and solidly behind them. He pointed in particular to the warm and wholehearted welcome given him by various allied nations of Greater East Asia whom he visited on his way back from the historic Assembly of Greater East Asiatic Nations.

Netaji stressed that the Indian National Army must be prepared to exert its utmost efforts to realize India's independence in order to fulfil the hopes and aspirations of all Indians as well as repay Greater East Asiatic nations for their all-out support and sympathy.

In the morning Netaji Subhash Chandra Bose, accompanied by Capt. Lakshmi, head of the women's organization of the Provisional Government of Free India, inspected the Indian women's corps.

Impressed by the intensive training carried on by the corps, Netaji Bose encouraged women members to continue to fight for the achievement of the ultimate good of liberating India from the Anglo-Americans.

Netaji Subhash Chandra Bose and members of the Provisional Government of Azad Hind were guests at a grand reception accorded to them in Rangoon by the Government of Free Burma on January 23, Speakers at the reception included, besides Netaji himself, the Foreign Minister and the Minister of Defence.

Netaji Subhash Chandra Bose declared, "It is impossible to find words that can give adequate expression to my feelings of gratitude or express my thanks for Burma's official recognition of the Provisional Government and the hospitality so generously offered, and also the unfailing sympathy and support given by Burma to the Indian independence movement." Netaji gave the solemn assurance that Free India would never forget Burma's good deeds.

2.—Preliminary successes of the I. N. A.

The Indian National Army went into action on February 4, 1944. At this time the I. N. A. consisted of three Divisions. The third division commanded by Liet-Colonel G. R. Nagar was stationed at Singapore. The Headquarters of the second division commanded by Col. Aziz Ahmad Khan were

Some Prominent Officers of Azad Hind Fauj

Col. Habib-ul-Rahman

Col, G. R, Nagar

Col. Thakur Singh

Col I. J. Kiani

Col. G. S. Dhillon

Col, P, K. Sehgal

at Rangoon. The first division commanded by Col. M. I. Kiani was put into action in the Assam Front.

The Indian National Army had a very good start. The operations were begun from four places. On the Arakan Front attack was paunched by the first battalion of the Subhash Brigade—the battalion Commandar being Major Rathore. The forces fighting in the Imphal Front comprised of the following Brigades :—

1. Subhash Brigade—Commanded by Col. Shah Nawas Khan (3,200 men) made an attack on Tidum,Hak, Falam and Bishenpur sector.
2. Gandhi Brigade—Commanded by Col. I. J. Kiani (2800 men) attacked Imphal proper *via* Palel.
3. Azad Brigade—Commanded by Col. Gulzara Singh (2800 men) was put into action at Myintha sector.

The following is the official diary of the achievements of the I. N. A. in the first round :—

Feb. 3, 1944—Sri S. A. Ayar, publicity and propaganda Minister announced that preparations had been complete for an attack.

Feb. 4—The I. N. A. in co-ordination with the Japanese Forces attacked the enemy's forces at Buthidang and captured Taung Bazar.

Feb. 5—Enemy's forces retreat from Buthidang—are severely bombed. The I. N. A. and Japanese Forces advance along the Eastern Bank of Mayo river. Vizigapatam bombed.

Feb. 9. Netaji himself visited the front and issued the following Special Order of the Day :—

"The eyes of the whole world are now focussed on the Arakan Front, where events of far-reaching importance are taking place to-day. The glorious and brilliant actions of the brave units of the Azad Hind Fauj working in close concert with the forces of the Imperial Nipponese Army have helped to foil all attempts by the Anglo-American forces to start a counter-offensive in this sector.

"I am sure that the brave deeds of our comrades on the Arakan front will be a source of great inspiration to all the Officers and men of the Azad Hind Fauj wherever they may be stationed at the present moment. Our long-awaited March to Delhi has begun, and with grim determination we shall continue that march until the tri-colour National Flag that is now flying over the Arakan mountains is hoisted over the Viceregal Lodge and until we hold our victory parade at the ancient Red Fortress of Delhi.

"Comrades ! and men of India's Army of Liberation. Let there be but one solemen resolve in your hearts—either liberty or death. And let there be but one slogan on your lips—Onward to Delhi. The road to Delhi is the road to freedom. That is the road along which we must march. Victory will certainly be ours."

Feb. 12—The VII and V Divisions of the 14th British Army were completely routed. The total loss of the VII division amounted to 10,000 killed or made prisoners of war. Many Indian soldiers of the British Army, including a Gwalior Regiment deserted the British Army and came over to the Indian National Army.

Feb. 21—The Headquarters of the Supreme Council of the Azad Hind Fauj issued its first communique as follows :—

"Latest information received from the Arakan front reporting further successess achieved by our units, shows that the Indian National Army participating in the operations in the Akyab district are pushing into enemy positions in co-operation with the main forces of the Niopon Army.

"Meanwhile, advance units of the Indian National Army, who in concert with the Nippon forces are now engaged in cutting off the enemy's retreat near Nyaunggyang, have destroyed bridges in that area and have advanced into the Bawli Bazaar district where they are now operating."

"Another unit of the Indian National Army, which has been pushing forward along the Mayu River since the commencement of operations, has succeeded in bringing over to our side an Indian unit of the British Indian Army. The number of officers and soldiers of this unit will not be disclosed for the time being.

"The same Indian National Army unit has penetrated into the Taung Bazar area, from where it is now pushing forward into the enemy's rear and is steadily gaining the desired war results.

"The main forces of the Azad Hind Fauj in the Akyab sector are preparing for further operations, according to plan."

Advancing with lightning speed, the forces of India's Liberation continued their victorious campaign on all sectors of the Indo-Burma front.

From the northernmost sector of the Burma front down to the coastal plains south of the Arakan range, the combined forces of the Indian National Army and the Imperial Nipponese Army, inflicted further defeats on the British forces.

In the Manipur area, which was the main centre of the Indo-Nipponese campaign, the British suffered terrible losses in men and materials and had been forced to yield considerable ground. In more than one sector the British had been totally routed and, according to the admissions made by the British themselves, they had "taken up new positions" because of "stiff enemy resistance."

The battle for Imphal, important enemy base and capital of the State of Manipur, reached its decisive stage, following the capture by Indian forces of the two vital centres, Ukhrul and Sanghak. These places formed a vital junction in the defence of Imphal and the British loss of these important centres had rendered it virtually impossible for them to hold out at Imphal for any length of time. The frontline despatches stated that Indian forces were within fifteen miles of Imphal.

On March 18, 1944 came the sensational and joyful news that the Indian National Army had captured Tiddum, crossed the Indo-Burma frontier and were now on the Indian soil.

Netaji Subhash Chandra Bose issued the following proclamation on March 21 from an undisclosed quarter on the Front :—

" The Iadian National Army under the leadership of the Provisional Government of Azad Hind and the Imperial Nippon Army, working in the closest co-operation, and fighting shoulder to shoulder, have set out on a sacred mission. At this momentous hour when the allied armies of India and Nippon are crossing the frontier and marching into India, the Provisional Government of Azad Hind makes the following proclamation :—

" Since the bloody war of 1857 when the armies of India were defeated in battle by the invading forces of Britain, the Indian people have never morally surrendered to the British. In spite of inhuman persecusion, and in spite of forcible disarmament, they have continued their resistance to British domination. Through propaganda and agitation, through acts of terrorism and sabotage, through armed revolution, and in recent years through satyagraha or passive resistance initiated by Mahatma Gandhi – they have not only kept up the struggle for independence but have also advanced a long way toward the goal of freedom.

" Since the outbreak of the present war, all attempts have been made by the Indian people and their leaders for the achievement of liberty through peaceful settlement with Britian. But all these attempts have failed. Moreover, Britain has, in the course of this war, strengthened her stranglehold over India through ruthless exploitation and brutal suppression, and has converted India into a gigantic military base for prosecuting her imperialistic war,

" In pursuanee of this policy, foreign troops—namely Australian, American, Chinese and Negro troops—have been imported into India, and owing to the unbearable burden thrown on the shoulders of the already impoverished Indian masses, famine conditions of an unprecedented nature have broken out in large areas of the country.

" In a last desperate attempt to spare India the horrors of war, Mahatma Gandhi advised the British Government to recognize India's demands for independence and quit India. The reply of British Government was to throw him into prison along with hundreds of thousands of India's patriots. The last act of vandalism commiteed by the British Government was the virtual murder of Mrs. Kasturibai Ghandi in British custody.

"Viewing the worsening situation in India, Indians in East Asia numbering about three millions, made a solemn resolve to participate actively in the fight for the Indian people at home and their national liberation. They organized themselves politically under the Azad Hind Sangh or Indian Independence League. They organized an army, and on October, 21, 1943, they set up the Provisional Government of Azad Hind. When the Azad Hind Fauj had completed all its preparations, it launched the last fight for freedom of its sacred Motherland on February 4, 1944, in the Arakan region of Burma.

"The success achieved in this fight by the allied armies of India and Nippon has now enabled the Indian National Army to cross the frontier of India and continue its march to Delhi.

"Since the outbreak of the war in East Asia, the victories achieved by the armed forces of Nippon, which are unparalleled in military history, have rendered it possible for Indians in East Asia to organize themselves for active participation in India's fight for freedom. The Government of Nippon has repeatedly declared before the whole world that Nippon is fighting not only for her own security but also for the destruction of Anglo-Amercan imperialism in East Asia, and further that Nippon stands for the complete and unconditional independence of India.

"In pursuance of this policy, the Government of Nippon has repeatedly expressed its readiness to give all-out aid to India in her struggle for independence, formally recognized the Provisional Government of Azad Hind, and has decided to hand over the Andaman and Nicobar Islands to the Provisional Government.

"Now the Indian National Army has launched its offensive and, with the co operation of the Imperial Nippon Army, is marching shoulder to shoulder in the common fight against the common foe—the Anglo-Americans and their allies. Until these foreign armies of aggression are thrown out of India, there can be no freedom for the Indian people, there can be no freedom and security in East Asia, and there can be no end to the present imperialistic war of the Anglo-Americans.

"Nippon is therefore determined to redeem her pledge to help the Indian people to create an India for Indians.

"The Provisional Government of Azad Hind hereby proclaims its solemn determination to go on fighting in closest brotherhood with Nippon until India is completely liberated. We call upon Indian people who are the bone of our bone, the flesh of our flesh, to render all help—direct or indirect—to our armies of liberation.

"We call upon all patriotic Indians—men, women and children, our brothers and sisters in India, to throw themselves whole-heartedly into this last fight for India's independence. We call upon every Indian to destroy the Anglo-American war effort in India by systematic sabotage, and thereby hasten the successful conclusion of the war for our country's freedom.

"We call upon our brothers, Indian soldiers and officers in Britain's army, to refuse to fight any longer for their despotic rulers, and to come and actively join our ranks. We call upon Indians working in various departments of the British service to render all possible help to us in this sacred fight.

"We solemnly assure the Indian people, our brothers and sisters, that they have nothing whatsoever to fear, so long as they do not help the Anglo-Americans or their allies in India. We assure them, further, that in liberated territory in India, the Provisional Government of Azad Hind will be established and that the Provisional Government will take over the administration of that territory.

"We advise the Indian people, our kith and kin, to keep away from the Anglo-American armies, their aerodromes, their barracks, their munition factories, their harbours and military installations, and their war industries, which may have to be destroyed by us before the enemy can be defeated.

On to Delhi

Mr Kappassi is lead ng a procession of civilians in Bangkok

Indian field Artillery

"Sisters and brothers in India ! This is the golden opportunity for you to fulfil your long-cherished aspirations for freedom. If you rise to the occasion and do your duty, freedom will be yours before long. In this momentous crisis India expects every one to do his or her duty. Jai Hind !

(Sd.) SUBHASH CHANDRA BOSE.

—Head of State of the Provisional Government of Azad Hind and Supreme Commander of the Indian National Army."

March 21—I. N. A. captured Toangzan and Hita Boko Aerodrome at Arakan Front.

March 22—I. N. A. marches to Manipur enroute Tamu in Kaba valley.

March 23—I.N.A. captured Viddak in Kaba valley. 1,000 enemy soldiers killed.

March 24—I. N. A. reached Tamu—Imphal Aerodrome bombed.

March 25—I. N. A. 30 miles off Imphal—Tiddam-Imphal road cut off—I. N. A. gaining ground at Tiddan Tamu and Imphal.

March 26—Tiddam captured—10,000 soldiers of 17th division besieged—15th division in Arakan Front bombed.—The battle of Imphal begins.

March 27—1,000 motor lorries captured in Central sector—I. N. A. crosses Chindwan river.

March 28—Battle for Kohima begins.

March 29—Nikkala Aerodrome captured—Chittagong bombed.

March 30—Sangshal captured—Ukhsal and Palel-Tamu Road cut off.

March 31—Imphal-Kohima road cut off—2,700 enemy soldiers killed and 760 made Prisoners of War at the South Indo-Burma Front.

April 1—fierce fighting near Imphal. I. N. A. captures a ration depot in the west of Mayo river.

April 2—I. N. A. only seven miles off Imphal.

April 3—Imphal Kohima road captured.

April 4—Mavlia, Tamu and Serikung captured. Another Cantonment 30 Kilometers off Imphal captured.

April 7—Assam-Bengal Railway threatened—Sylcher bombed.

April 8—Kohima Fort and a Cantonement over Dimapur-Kohima road captured.

April 9—Fierce battle around Dimapur. Encirclement around Imphal tightens.

April 12—Sebong, Chemol, Tinupur and Chirachanpur forts captured.

April 13—Imphal attached from many sides. Tishanki Cantt on Imphal-Toangyan road captured. I. N. A. reach Moreh.

April 15—Parphema Cantt over Kohima-Dimapur road destroyed—I. N. A. 15 Kilometers off Dimapur—Imphal-Hochang Road cut off—Bishanpur over Imphal-Sylcher road attacked.

April 16—Enemy-forces in Imphal cut off. Nichu Garh situated 10 Kilometers off south-west of Dimapur captured.

April 17—Hill no 8424 aronnd Imphal and hill No. 3449 to the South-East of Pangang Poke captured. Mathingiang Cantt. captured.

April 18—Imphal attacked from all sides. I. N. A. penetrates through north forfications of the enemy.

April 19—Tignali captured.

April 20—The Fourth British Army retreating. I N A. forces swiftly tightening the encirclement around Imphal.

April 22—Battle for Imphal raging fiercely.

April 23—Hill No. 461 on Kohima sector, Palativa, Tignapur and Moirang captured.

April 24—Imphal bombed—Hills to the south of Bishanpur captured.

April 25—28—Shenom and Sebom posts captured.

April 29—Hill no 4080—20 Kilometer south-east off Imphal captured.

April 30—Phalong near Imphal captured. I. N. A. reaches near Kingchop.

May 1—2 –Palel attacked—A post 7 Kilometers off Palel captured.

May 4—Hill no. 3725 near Imphal captured. Langel Post 10 kilometres south-east of Palel captured. On the Boothidaung Front, the main strength of the I N. A. units crossed the Mayu river night and immediately launched a firece offensive completely repulsing the enemy in that sector The enemy forces on the Maungdan front entirely isolated from the Boothidang sector, frantically retreated to rear positions.

May 7—Enemy fortifications south of Imphal bombed.

May 8—Lord Mountbatton's Headquarters announce the capture of Boothidang by I.N.A.

May 12—Imphal and Coxbazar heavily bombed, general attack on Mayu. Many hills in the vicinity of Boothidang captured.

May 13—Imphal bombed. Enemy's tanks and lorries over Kohima-Dimapur road bombed.

May 15—16—Fierce attacks on Bishanpur,

May 17 Hills no 55 and 74 on Mayo Front captured.

May 18—Bishanpur bombed—The enemy defeated in Imal and Limakong valley to the north Imphal.

May 20—Beseige of Imphal tightens.

May 21—Fierce battle over Bishanpur.

May 22—Ukhral road completely in our hands—Enemy's position weak on Palel Front.

May 23—1275 enemy soldiers killed on Boothidang Front.

May 24—Fierce fighting around Imphal—Esham captured.

May 26—Some part of Palel Front destroyed.

May 31—Imphal bombed—I. N. A. penetrates into south-east of Kohima.

June 1—The monsoon rains begin.

June 3—A village to south of Tignapur captured—Fierce battle on Kohima Front.

June 4—I. N. A. captures a cantonement to the south-west of Palel.

June 13—The enemy's 20th division on Palel front forced to retreat.

June 14—I. N. A. reaches Mythin Kanu,

June 16—Kunjala and hill No. 4605 over Palel front captured.

June 17—Khangjol captured.

June 27—The siege of Imphal lifted—enemy begins offensive—I. N. A. on the defensive.

The Monsoon deluge now flooded the communication and supply routes of the I. N: A. on the front. Since it started operations in February 1944, the Indian National Army was halted for the first time in July. Breakdown of transport and supply conditions forced it to fall back. During the five months of fierce fighting; the Indian National Army had given ample proof of their superior fighting qualities, their courage and unshakable devotion to duty. They encountered the ememy's numerically superior and better equipped forces successfully and gave them crushing defeats on various fronts. As the circumstances required temporary postponement of operations, Netaji Subhash Chandra Bose issued the following Special Order of the Day on August 14, 1944.

"My brave compatriots of the Indian National Army!

In the middle of March this year advanced units of the Azad Hind Fauj fighting shoulder to shoulder with their valiant allies, the Imperial Nippon Forces, crossed the Indo-Burma border and the fight for India's liberation thereupon, commenced on Indian soil.

"The British authorities by ruthlessly exploiting India for over a century and bringing foreign soldiers to fight their battles for them, had managed to put up a mighty force against us. After crossing the Indo-Burma border, our forces inspired by the righteousness of our cause, encountered these numerically superior and better equipped, but hetrogenous and disunited forces of the enemy and defeated them in every battle.

"Our units, with their better training and discipline and unshakable determination to do or die on the path of India's freedom, soon established their superiority over the enemy, whose morale deteriorated with each defeat. Fighting under the most trying conditions, our officers and men displayed such courage and heroism that they have earned the praise of every body. With their blood and sacrifice, these heroes have established traditions which the future soldiers of India shall have to uphold,

"All preparations had been completed and the stage had been set for the final assault on Imphal when torrential rains overtook us and to carry Imphal by an assault was rendered a practical impossibility.

"Handicapped by these elements, we were forced to postpone our offensive. After the postponement of the offensive, it was found disadvantageous for our troops to continue to hold the line that we then had. For securing a more favourable defensive position, it was considered advisable to withdraw our troops. In accordance with this decision, our troops have withdrawn to a more favourable defensive position. We shall now utilize the period in full in completing our prepartions, so that with the advent of better weather, we may be in a position to resume our offensive. As we have been successful in defeating our enemy once, our faith in our final victory and complete annihilation of Anglo-Ame ican forces has grown ten fold. As soon as all our preparations are complete, we shall launch a mightly offensive against our enemies once again. With the superior fighting qualities, dauntless courage and unshakable devotion to duty of our officers and men, victory shall surely be ours.

"May the souls of those heroes, who have fallen in this campaign, inspire us to still nobler deeds of heroism and bravery in the next phase of India's War of Liberation ! Jai Hind."

Heroes and Heroic Deeds of I. N. A.

(1)

It was a night of April 1944, when in Kaladan sector, Naik Molar Singh's unit was marching to attack a powerful centre of the enemy on a hill. During the attack, it so happened, that an enemy machine gun started firing from very close quarters.

It was clear as day, that in order to achieve our objective, our unit should invariably check this open-fire. And this hard job necessitated a man's sacrifice. Fortunately time selected its own hero.

Naik Molar Singh, determined as he was to demolish the enemy post, not caring for his own life rushed to charge the post all alone. And he went on till he had stopped the machine-gun ; but his chest was, by then no less than a sieve,—every inch of it pierced by enemy-bullets. The stake of his life got his unit their objective. But he could not survive this victory.

On his expiry he was awarded the much coveted "Shahid-i-Bharat" medal by Netaji.

When Netaji was at Berlin, he organised a "Free India Legion" there in Europe. After the formation of the Indian National Army and Free India Government, this European Legion was affiliated to the I. N. A. The contingents of I. N. A. in collaboration with the German forces, fought to their last the various battles of Europe.

We were always in touch with the valiant deeds that our courgeons men displayed there. Here is one of the many incidents :—

Mohd Rashid, a 19 years young man, was posted with an anti-tank gun on the roadside at a certain place in France. When the American Armoured cars passed by him, he at once opened fire. The enemy retallated with thundering volleys. But despite that, he never budged an inch and rendered many enemy armoured cars uuservicable, which led the enemy to retrace their steps.

(2)

On the 18th of May 1944, a unit of the I. N. A. was picquetting a hill in the central sector of the Indo-Burma frontier Of those on duty, Naik

Kehar Singh was one. On an early morning the enemy made an unprecedented pre-planned attack on our picquet.

One of our comrades, who was working a light machine-gun against the enemy was fatally wounded by enemy fire. He signalled to his comrades to come and occupy his machine-gun. But the man who was to relieve him had already been shot dead by enemy fire. Naik Kehar Singh was witnessing all this from a short distance. He made a spontaneous decision.

The enemy was firing uninterruptedly. But caring not for his own safety, he rushed through the pouring bullets to occupy the machine gun post. By the time he reached the post, the enemy had approached him to as close as ten yards. With a smile, on his lips, Kehar Singh picked up the machine gun and resting it against his hip opened fire on the enemy who were shooting at him with a tommy gun.

Neglecting the enemy fire, Naik Kehar Singh went on working his own machine gun, so much so, that the enemy had to retreat. At this he put the machine gun in position and went on firing to push the enemy back to complete retreat.

This unparallelled bravery and execution of duty was honoured by Netaji with the 'Sher-i- Hind' title.

(3)

Ranjit Singh was a Havildar in No. I Bahadur Group. One day, he was ordered to go from Haka to Falam and there, propogate the cause of I. N. A. by conversion in the British Indian Army.

According to orders, he reached Falam, but the enemy had been preinformed about him and one of their commanders was already aware of all that he was to do. He posted 26 English privates to go and arrest Ranjit Singh.

The patrol of 26 white men, surrounded Ranjit Singh from all the sides and bid him raise his hands. The valiant soldier of I. N. A. laughed at them with a sneer and altogether refused to raise his hands. It was a test for him—one against twenty-six. At once he set his tommy gun and opened fire on them.

He killed most and wounded many others out of them, but the simultaneous fire from 26 guns could not let him save his own life. He died in harness, and never humiliated his conscience for a while, lest he should bring a bad name for his motherland—India. He not only died a valiant's death, but also proved the cause of death for many of his oonntry's enemies.

Netaji, at his brave death for the cause of Freedom, bestowed upon him the honour of "Shahide Bharat" and "Tamghae Shatru Nash Class I."

(4)

It was since March of the same year, that Lt. Kundan Singh had been commanding a certain unit of the I. N. A. During April, the same very unit had displayed various feats of adventure and now it had been ordered to explode a bridge which was extremely vital for the communication of the enemy forces It was thought, this could cut off all their communications.

The bridge was in the enemy's territory—a hundred miles from the firing line. Lt. Kundan Singh, set out for that bridge with his men. Very cautiously, dodging the foe at each step he managed to reach the spot and at once set upon the work for the explosion.

Somehow or other, however, the enemy had come to know of it. They opened fire at once on Lt. Kundan Singh and his men. But those valiant people caring not for the fire, kept on with their own work at last succeeding in their object.

But Lt. Kundan Singh was taken away by enemy fire but while he left his earthly abode, he was bearing a smile on his face—which denoted the great sense of happiness he had of dying while doing his duty.

Netaji bestowed on him the honour of "Shahide Bharat."

(5)

In February, the same year, Hav. Ramlu Naidu of I. N. A. with six other men was sent out on patrol duty in Bishanpore Sector. One night, it so happened that all of them got surrounded by the enemy who had been, for long, lying in ambush. Naidu and his companions got arrested.

While the enemy was busy hand-cuffing them, Hav. Ramlu Naidu was striving to get at some means of escape—and he made an exemplary display of the presence of mind. Despite the enemy pointing tommy gun at him, he shouted out the slogan of "Inqilab Zindabad."

So unprecedented for the enemy was this slogan, that all of them were taken aback. He, who was holding the tommy gun was completely taken over.

The enemy looked sort of stunned for some moments to follow. Hav. Ramlu Naidu realised this to be a golden chance for him. He ran fast, jumping over the shoulders of the enemy soldiers. Creeping along the slope he managed to come to the foot of the hillock—the enemy firing ferociously in the mean time. However, it became clear to the enemy that they had been befooled pretty cleverly.

Hav. Naidu escaped back to our own firing line and hitherto after always displayed great tact and ability in the execution of his duties.

Netaji awarded him "Tamghae Bahaduri."

(6)

Last year, by the end of May. S. O. Gurbachan Singh was going in a boat with some Burmese boatmen to a certain place in Northern Burma,

At some sound in the river, the enemy by chance opened fire and a bullet struck him just below his knee. One of the boatmen was also injured and the other two having lost their senses left rowing.

Thirteen American soldiers fell upon the Sub-officer to arrest him. S. O. Gurbachan Singh plunged into water and lying in concealment behind the boat, began to fire with his pistol. He fatally injured two of the enemy. All his four fingers with which he was resting on the boat got injured, but in spite of that he reloaded his pistol and opened fire again. Just then a bullet crushing his pistol went right through the palm of his right hand injuring further his face and brow.

Still he kept up his courage. With his wounded hand be shifted the boat slightly to the left and with this act saved the life of the two boatmen. After this, when he rowed across to the left bank, he discovered three dead bodies of the enemy soldiers—the rest having fled.

Netaji bestowed upon him the honour of " Vire Hind" and " Tamghae Shatrunash No. 1" for individual valour and execution of duty.

(7)

One day. Sepoy Uttam Singh was sent to explore the defensive position of the enemy and then report about the enemy units in a certain area.

When he reached close to the enemy position, he was spotted out by the enemy. A bullet struck his chest and passed right though. Loss of blood made him too weak to walk easily, yet creeping on his belly he explored the enemy units and gathered all the necessary information.

Having done that he managed to return to our firing line. The information he brought proved very beneficial for our further progress.

Netaji awarded him "Sanade Bahaduri."

(8)

During the war, one day, Hav. L. N. Bose was sent out in Bishanpur Sector to the rear of the enemy's firing line for executing an urgent duty which he successfully fulfilled. While coming back he was entangled by an enemy patrol of four. He bravely saved himself from them and using his hand Grenades suffered them to free. Thus he managed to return safely with such news as subsequently proved vital for a future success. Netaji awarded "Sanade Bahaduri" to Hav. L. N. Bose.

(9)

March 9—This day Nk. Faiz Bakhsh and Sepoy Ghulam Rasul of Intelligence Group were sent out to gather information about some enemy " out-put " near Sikhshi. They were to investigate the strength of the enemy, their armaments and other vital matters.

The Naik and the Sepoy both went far into the enemy outpost and not only returned with full information, but also caught hold of one " white soldier " whom they had made to surrender. He subsequently, furnished them with the requisite information about his men.

Netaji awarded the badge of " Shatru Nash Class II " to Naik Faiz Bakhsh and Sepoy Ghulam Rasul

(10)

On 19th March in connection with some military work Hav. Din Dayal Singh was sent to Central Seetor to map out the position of the enemy, Havildar Din Dyal Singh did his work. While returning, he was fixed on by a Tommy Gun by a patrol of British. He was hit at by a bullet on the knee, but he at once took shelter and called out with great bravery and presence of mind to do "Nippon Charge" and that the enemy was there.

The British patrol thinking that they have been encircled, took to their heels to save their lives.

Hav. Din Dayal Singh opened fire on the fleeing enemy and one British soldier was killed.

Netaji awarded him, the medal of Bravery and Tamaghae Shatru Nash Class I.

(11)

Hav. N. A. Chaudhry was trusted with a special work in Central Sector.

This Havildar, made friendship with soldiers of the British Indian army and some Indian civilians, and did his duties to the best of this capacity.

While doing this work, he remained in a village occupied by the enemy for one and half month. In that village he greatly advanced his movement. After doing his duty, he joined our ranks.

(12)

During military work in the central sector, Naik Sultan Singh preached the British Indian army in a very able way. But one day, he was arrested by the enemy and he was handed over to a British Indian Coy.

He convinced the Indian Commander of that Coy about our I. N. A. and Independence movement in such a way, that next day, when the soldiers of this unit became inclined towards I. N. A. not only Sultan Singh came our rank but he also brought four men, who were placed as gaurds on him. In addition to this, that Coy Commander (Subedar) and his Coy men started propaganda work in British Army for the I. N. A.

Netaji also gave him, "Tamghae Bahaduri".

(13)

In March, in the Central Sector 2/Lt. Durga Bahadur was sent to contact a Gurkha unit of the British army. Durga Bahadur, risking his life, reached the Gurkha unit, through the enemy lines, and talked with them for half an hour.

The Gurkha unit promised to do propaganda for the I. N. A. in other Gurkha units. 2/Lt. Durga Bahadur also told them that I. N. A. wants to capture that position and that is an important point for the I. N. A. from the military standpoint.

The same day, a few hours later another I. N. A. officer met those people and they surrendered that place according to the instructions of the I. N. A. Officers.

Netaji awarded 2/Lt. Dura Bahadur, Sanade Bahaduri.

(14)

Hav. Ahmad Din and Nk. Tara Singh remained in an enemy occupied village war Moising for one month. There they gathered much valuable information ; and then joined our ranks.

In July, these two N. C. O. 12 soldiers of third ruit, one Japanese soldier, and two Indian civilians, who had brought information for us, became the target of enemy bombing at some place.

The hut, in which the Japanese soldier and the two civilians were taking shelter, was bombarded directly. There were two Time-Bombs near that hut.

When the bombardment stopped, these N. C. Os., at once rushed to the spot, to save these Japanese soldiers and the civilians.

While doing this work, they heard some cries at a distance of about two hundred yards down hill. When they reached that spot, they found a Japanese soldier, wounded by a bomb. There, they also came to know that two Indian civilans were hiding in a near trench. Although this spot was close to the enemy lines, and the enemy bombing was in full swing they brought those two comrades to a distance of six hundred feet uphill in a jungle.

Netaji awarded Hav. Ahmad Din and Nk. Tara Singh, the medal of "Sanade Bahaduri.

(15)

On 15th March, a unit of Nipp n army was lying in ambush on the Tiddam Imphal-Road.

A convoy of some British lorries passed that way. When Japanese fired on them, then the enemy drivers leaving their lorries behind, took to their heels. S. O. Hari Singh, who was with the Japsnese, made a good defence line of these lorries on the road, though the enemy was noticing all this. In addition to this S. O. Hari Singh managed to bring one full r tion lorry to our side. although he was being fired on all along heavily.

In April, S. O Hari Singh was entrusted with propaganda work in the Indian army. When he was about three hundred yards away from the enemy lines, he hoisted the Tricolour flag. Along with this, shouts of Inqilab Zindabad—Azad Hind Zindabad and march onward to Delhi were raised and he pierced the enemy lines with great slubbornness.

As soon as he entered the enemy lines, he absorbed the Indian soldiers in a talk about the I. N. A. and gave them a delightful lecture on I. N. A. and the movement of Independence.

The soldiers there, were greatly impressed by his lecture and came to know something about I. N. A. with the result that a unit of Madras Sweepers and Miners joined us.

Afterwards, during military activity, S. O. Hari Singh was sent on a special mission along with five soldiers. But unfortunately his party was encircled by an enemy full unit. This small party of I. N. A. fought to the last with the enemy, when they had no ammunitions then, they ran away very cleverly after breaking the enemy's lines.

In all military activities, S. O. Hari Singh's unit did remarkable work as regards propaganda work, and patrolling of enemy lines.

Netaji awarded him " Shere Hind."

(16)

Lt. Col. Malik was the Commandar of a certain unit of the A. H. F, that displayed great talent in the activities at Tiddam Bishenpur Road. In his command, the unit had been winning great successes.

During the whole period of attack Lt. Col. Malik was always seen in front of his men nearest to the enemy firing line. Following in his steps, his unit displayed great feats of bravery, and dutifulness achieveing many successes at various places.

Netaji conferred upon him the great honour of "Sardare Jang."

(17)

In the central sector, a detatchment of our Army penetrated the enemy positions too far, on May 2. This detachment encircled two piquets of the enemy from all four sides, and with slogans of Chalo Delhi made a charge on them. During the charge on them, when they reached the barbed wire fences, they saw Gorkha soldiers of the Britsh Army on patrol. One of the Gorkha officer shouted, " Oh ! We are your friends !" So saying, he took our men inside the piquet.

Captain Sadhu Singh entered a piquet and said to the Gorkhas, "Brothers ! We are Indians and you are all Indians. Why do you fight us, then ? We are fighting to liberate our mother-land from bondage."

While talking thus, he caught sight of a British Officer, who had a rifle in his hand. Captain Sadhu Singh snatched his rifle and pushed him back. The British officer immediately cried, "I. N. A. kill him at once."

On this a Gorkha soldier attacked Captain Sadhu Singh with a bayonet. The captain repulsed the attack and jumped out. He got wounded in the thigh in this encounter. Rolling down from the Hill, he fell down in a stream. The enemy opened fire on him with a Hand-Grenade. Though wounded, Captain Sadhu Singh managed to join his Unit.

He was awarded "Tamghai Bahaduri" by Netaji.

(18)

It was the night of 1st April when one of our units was attacking a strategic position of the enemy. In this unit, there was a Platoon Commander 2/Lt. Roshan Lal.

A blast of fire from the side of the enemy came to check our advance. 2/Lt. Roshan Lal, with some of his men affected a charge on that enemy Machine-gun-post that was firing, and he pressed the enemy hard enough to leave the post and fly away. This helped our unit to advance and but for the great courage and bravery of Roshan Lal all this would have been impracticable.

Netaji awarded 'Tamghae Bahaduri' to 2/Lt. Roshan Lal.

(19)

4th April—S. O. Ude Ram was sent out to get news about a certain enemy position in Kaladan Sector. A patrol was under his command. As the patrol was returning, having gathered the information, the enemy opened fire from front and the flanks.

S. O. Ude Ram occupied such a position that he totally concealed for the enemy the way by which the patrol could return.

The whole of the patrol passed safe and reached a very safe position— but this became possible only at the stake of his life. When the patrol had gone away the enemy fire became still harder, with holding the way from S. C. Ude Ram to return.

He took his away, therefore through the jungles and next day joined his unit.

Netaji honoured him with "Tamghae Bahaduri."

(20)

During the middle of March one night, Lieut. Lewis, Hav. Nasib Singh and Naik Roshan Lal started for Kyaukchawk, along with a patrol. Going along, they saw some foot-prints on the path and gathered, that a patrol of the enemy had passed that way a little before Lt. Lewis and his party marched on along these foot-prints, until they reached a house. This house was a resting place of the enemy. While reconnoitring, they found there two British soldiers a corporal and a private. Having relieved them of their arms, they took them as prisoners. The main position of the enemy was a few hundred yards off. The enemy came to know of their arrest and opened heavy fire on our patrol with mortars.

Lt. Lewis and his party also opened fire and when the ammunition was nearly exhausted, the patrol was ordered to march back. The British soldiers tried to escape, but were done to death by Hav. Nasib Singh and Naik Roshan Lal. They were awarded, "Tamgha-e-Shatru Nash Class II" by Netaji.

(21)

On the 5th February a small unit of the Azad Hind Fauj in the Arakan sector, penetrated the enemy's lines very far and reached a unit Headquarter. On seeing the soldiers of the I. N. A., a British soldier, who was lying on a bed, got bewildered and tried to take shelter under the cover of the mosquito net, as a drowning man catches at a straw. Two of our soldiers dragged him out of the bed. While trying to escape he was shot by Lt. Partap Singh, who was awarded " Tamgha-e-Shatru Nash Class II" by Netaji.

(22)

In the Arakan sector, Hav. Pir Mohd. and Hav. Hakim Ali, along with some other men, were sent on patrol duty on February 5. On the way they came across a small unit of the 80th Indian cavalry. Our patrol tried hard to persuade this unit to join the Azad Hind Fauj, but as they were under the command of a British N. C. O., they did not respond. Upon this Hav. Pir Mohd. and Hav. Hakim Ali fired at them with Tommy guns and killed a a British officer and soldier. The enemy-unit, who was on patrol took to his heels. Netaji awarded " Tamgha e-Shatru Nash class II " to Hav. Pir Mohd. and Hav. Hakim Ali.

(23)

On April 1, Hav. Ghulab Shah was deputed to go to Kaladan area to bring some news of the enemy. He went there in civilian dress, but detected by some African soldiers, who arrested him and took him to their British Officer. While under detention he escaped from the African guards and ran for his life. He was fired at and got wounded, but was successful in joining his unit. Netaji awarded him 'Sanad-i-Bahaduri."

(24)

In the Central sector one of our piquets was guarding our columns. In this piquet Naik Indar Singh and sepoy Diwan Singh were on duty at one place. On May 4, 15 Punjabi soldiers of the British Army reached this place. They were not made out, until they came very near. Two soldiers of the enemy assaulted Diwan Singh, but he saved himself. He threw one of them down and pierced his bayonet through his body. The other soldier of the enemy wounded Diwan Singh on the right shoulder. Naik Indar Singh opened fire on the enemy with his tommy gun. The enemy took to his heels. One of the soldiers was killed. After this Naik Indar Singh threw a Hand-Grenade and another soldier of the enemy was done to death. Netaji awarded 'Sanad-i-Bahaduri' to Naik Indar Singh and Sepoy. Diwan Singh.

(25)

Major Pritam Singh was commanding one unit of the A. H. F. in Central Sector. This unit had instructions to penetrate the enemy positions and reconnoitre the enemy. He organized his unit and went on his errand early in May.

When Major Pritam Singh and his party reached near their objective, the enemy opened heavy fire on them with machine-guns and mortars. Not caring for the fires, they marched forward and with loud shouts of 'Chalo Delhi' charged the enemy. After fulfilling the duty, with which he was entrusted, he ordered his men to retreat. But it was not an easy job to escape from so heavy fire. With a marvellous strategy, Major Pritam Singh was successful in bringing back his unit, with a very little loss. He also inflicted losses on the enemy. Netaji honoured him with the title of "Sardar-i-Jang" for his personal bravery, his devotion to duty and his excellent cammand.

(26)

In the month of May, a most important piquet of ours was on duty on a hill in the Centre Sector. 2/Lt. Ajaib Singh was its Commander. One evening a Highlander regiment of the enemy attacked our piquet under the cover of fire from artillery, machine guns and mortars. The enemy was numerically ten times stronger. But this brave leader acted as if there was nothing to be afraid of. The piquet retaliated with extraordinary calmness and retaliated back. 2/Lt. Ajaib Singh went from post to post exhorting his men to muster courage. The Highlanders tried to annihtate the whole piquet, but their attempt was foiled by the strategy of S. Ajaib Singh and after a heavy loss, were forced to fall back. This courageous move of S. Ajaib Singh's piquet saved our main force from the attack of the enemy.

2/Lt. Ajaib Sing was honoured with the title of 'Sardar-i-Jang' by Netaji.

(27)

On the night of 2nd May, a detachment of Azad Hind Fauj penetrated the enemy lines in the Central Sector. This detachment was under the Command of Lt. Lal Singh and Lt. Kapoor Singh. Raising slogans of 'Chalo Delhi', it encircled and attacked two piquets of the enemy. Reaching the barbed wire fences of the enemy, they saw a Gorkha guard on duty. On seeing our man, an officer came out and said, "Come on ; we are your friends."

Lt. Lal Singh and Lt. Kapoor Singh entered the piquet. The Gorkha officer asked them, what they wanted. The brave officers, replied. "Blood of the British." Just at that time Lt. Lal Singh, caught sight of two British officers, who were entering in through the piquet-door. He sprang upon them. The Gorkha officer tried to intercept Lt. Lal Singh, but he did not lose a second and pierced his *bhala* through one of the officers. In trying to kill the other, he himself sacrificed his life. During all this time, Lt. Kapoor Singh went on firing with his revolver on the enemy, but he was being fired at by the enemy from all four sides. He also got a martyr's death, after killing a number of enemies. Netaji conferred "Vire-Hind" and "Tamgha e-Shatru Nash" on Lt. Lal Singh and Lt. Kapoor Singh after their death.

(28)

Major L. S. Misra was commanding a unit of the A. H. F. on the Arakan Front in February 1944. Under the command of this Major, the unit not only showed excellent results from military point of view, but was also able to attract many Indian officers and soldiers of the British Army to A. H. F.

At one time he had nothing left except a revolver and feeling helpless, he went into an enemy position. There were stationed some Indian soldiers of the British Army. With great resourcefulness and tact, he was able to win over the whole garrison and bring them to the Indian National Army.

(29)

Captain Mehar Das was commander of a sub-unit of the A. H. F. Once this sub-unit was working in collaboration with a Japanese technical unit. It blasted the bridges on both sides of the enemy positions, and they were cut off from the main force.

On another occasion, Captain Mehar Das, along with his unit attacked a Divisional Headquarter of the enemy. Though the enemy far outnumbered his unit, they were taken by surprise and all killed.

Netaji honoured Captain Mehar Das with the title of " Sardar-i-Jang."

(30)

It was flat stretch of land without any cover either from view or from fire, except a shallow dry pond, near which three roads of great importance met. Four miles North-West of this point was a Hill 1428 feet high, beyond which the enemy Artillery was located so as to cover the road junction and the area south of it, the occupation of which would affect the entire plan of operations.

At a key point like this, was placed a Company of the Azad Hind Fauj, under the command of 2/Lt. Gian Singh Bisht trained at the Officers Training School, A. H. F. The company was only 98 strong. They had no machine-guns or even light machine-guns. Good old rifles were their only weapons of defence or offence, apart from two A/TK mines. Their orders were to check any enemy advance at all costs.

They remained in that position for two days, but the enemy dared not advance. Then on 16th of March 1945, starting early morning, hostile Fighting Planes bombed and machine gunned their positions, until about 11 a. m. Having got rid of all the load they had, the aeroplanes went away.

Then enemy guns from behind the Hill started registering, and behind this barrage of artillery-fire advanced a column of motorised infantry consisting of 18 tanks, 11 armoured cars and 70 trucks. Half of this column made its way, straight towards the pond, where two Forward Platoons of the Company were being thrown out of the armoured fighting vehicles, but this would not frighten our boys. They waited in their trenches for the infantry to debuss. Tanks and armoured cars like steel monsters, creating hell with their fire-power, approached so close, that they started charging on to our trenches, so as to crush and cripple our men under this heavy weight. Two mines were thrown in their way, which unluckily did not burst, but they caused monsters to stop, which having stopped, became stationary pill boxes, oozing out most inhuman forms of killing materials.

There was no communication between this post and Battalian Headquarters. When 2/Lt. Gian Singh appreciated that their rifle-fire was no match to the enemy's mortars, machine-guns, light automatics and hand-grenades, and their stay in trenches meant certain death or captivity with no loss to the enemy, he ordered "charge." Leading the assault, he shouted slogans of "*Netaji Ki Jai*", "*Inqilab Zindabad*," "*Azad Hindostan Zindabad*," and "*Chalo Delhi*." All the men responded to the slogans, which echoed above the enemy-fire. This was the only support, which these heroes had against the superior armament of the enemy. In the name of India and Indian Independence, they charged into the enemy trucks. The enemy immediately debussed. Hand to hand fighting ensued, which lasted for full two hours. But our heroes would not give in. Forty of them sacrificed their lives after killing more than their equal number of the enemy. Their unconquerable spirit harassed the enemy so much that he started retreating.

Just then, 2/Lt. Gian Singh called forward his 3rd. Palatoon commander, 2/Lt. Ram Singh and was giving out orders, when a bullet struck on his head and he fell down, never to give out orders again. 2/Lt. Ram Singh then collected the remmants of the company and reorganized.

2/Lieut. Gian Singh Bisht used to tell his men that he would die with them ; he fulfilled his promise and remained their comrade in life and death. This was a glorious deed, of which the history will remain witness as long as there is world. 2/Lt. Gian Singh and his men lived up to the ideals of our Great Leader—the Netaji—and have laid down their lives, fighting by their posts to build up a tradition for us to follow. In free India, the spirit of these heroes, who knew no defeat will be worshipped for generations to come and will inspire the future sons of India to live up to such high ideals.

4—Netaji restores confidence

The advance of the Indian National Army was so rapid and its initial successes were so prominent that the fall of Imphal was taken for granted. In fact the Anglo-American Military High Command had at one time decided to vacate Imphal, but rains came to their rescue. When the capture of Imphal was delayed, the people became impatient and finally when the I. N. A. decided to postpone operations, the enthusiasm and revolutionary spirit seemed to be fading.

But the Indian National Army and the Provisional Government of India did not lose heart. Netaji's indomitable spirit, his optimism and faith in final victory and his burning passion for the freedom of his country had steeled their hearts. They resolved to carry on their freedom struggle with renewed vigour and redoubled energy.

The first anniversary of the establishment of the Provisional Government of Free India, which fell on Oct. 21. was celebrated througout East Asia by the freedom-loving Indians. Fitting ceremonies were observed for a week. One of the features of the celebration in Burma was a parade by the crack units of the Azad Hind Fauj and the Rani of Jhansi Regiments in the presence of Netaji Subhash Chandra Bose.

Expressing his determination to launch as many offensives as necessary until the enemy was smashed, Netaji said, " The war-cry of the coming year would be, 'Blood, blood, blood. To take the enemy's blood, Indians must be prepared to shed their own."

Before proceeding further. it would be advisable to enumerate, some other activities of the Provisional Government of Azad Hind and the Indian Independence League in addition to military operations, during the period.

As announced by the Japanese Premier, General Tojo, at the Assembly of the Greater East-Asiatic Nations, the Japanese Government formally ceded the Andamans and Nicobar Islands to the Provisional Government of Aza : Hind on 17th February 1944. Accordingly Netaji sent Col. Loganadan as Chief Commissioner of the islands, (renamed Shahid and Swaraj) where with due ceremony held at the Indian Independence League Headqarters at Port Blair, the islands were formally handed over to him.

The Japanese Government also ceded to the Azad Hind Government theZiawadi territory. It was a property about 50 square miles in area and had the biggest sugar mill, a jute mill and a cotton mill over it. It belonged to an Indian Raja Sir Annamal and had been declared enemy property and taken over by the Japaneses. It was later on transferred to the Provisional Government of India. The Government started here some training centres and carried on the administeration through men of the Azad Hind Fauj and Civil administrators, who had now been organized as Azad Hind Dal.

As soon as the I. N. A. crossed the borders of Burma into India a pact was signed between the Japanese and Provisional Government of Azad Hind. It was clearly stated in the Pact that any post of the Indian Territory aequired by conquest or otherwise by the Japanese army will be handed over to the I. N. A. for the purpose of forming part of the liberated territory and to be administered by them.

Immediately after the Indian National Army set foot on the Indian soil, a contingent of Azad Hind Dal—a group of selected people specially trained for the civil administration was despatched there. Col. A. C. Chatterji was appointed the Governor of the Liberated area (Manipur and Vishnupur) Sri Anand Mohan Sahay, Secretary to the Provisional Government of Azad Hind and Col. Allagapan Minister of Supplies also visited this area. Mr. A. N. Sircar was appointed Revenue Minister for Ziawaddi and other areas. The people of Naga, Kuki and Chin races inhabiting Assam frontier were very sympathetic and co-operated whole heartedly with the I. N. A. They gave very useful information to them. After the postponement of operations they were reported to be severely dealt with and persecuted by the British Government. It was said that heads of some of them were cut off and hung on the trees.

The Advance Headquarter of the Provisional Government of Azad Hind in Burma announced the appointment of five new Ministers of state in a special communique on April 18, 1944. They were Mr. N. Raghwan, Mr. A Yellapa, S. Ishar Singh, Lt. Col. G. R. Nagar and Lt. Col. Habib-ur-Rahman. The communique also said that Mr. S. M. Bashir of Rangoon was appointed Adviser to the Provisional Government of Azad Hind and Lt. Col. S. C. Allagapan, Minister without Portfolio, would be Minister-in-charge of Supplies, in addition to his other duties.

In another Communique of the Provisional Government of Azad Hind issued on July 29, 1944, it was announced that Mr. A. N. Sircar was appointed Minister of Man-power. Mr. N. Raghwan was appointed Minister of Finance in place of Col. A. C. Chatterji. In addition to this he would also hold the Department of National Planning. Col. A. C. Chatterji would continue to be the Minister of state. The communique also stated that Mr. Karim Ghani was appointed a Minister of State and Srimati Chidambaram Deputy Minister of Women's Department.

During this period, the Headquarters of the Provisional Government of Azad Hind and Supreme Headquarters of the I. N. A. were at Rangoon. The Rear Headquarters situated at Singapore consisted of two sections while the Indian National Army Headquarters under the chief of staff—Maj. Gen. J. K. Bhonsle—carried on the work of recruitment and training, the Indian Independence League with its energetic General Secretary, Dr. M. K. Lukshumeyah did other work in connection with collection of money, publicity and propaganda. It was also doing the relief work among the Indian Community. It had now 24 branches in Thailand, 70 in Malaya, 100 in Burma and several others in Java, Sumatra, Japan, China, Philippines, Borneo, Manchuko and Andamans etc. It opened relief camps hospitals and free dispensaries in various places, where hundreds of diseased, decript and destitute people were looked after. It supplied free food, medicines and clothes to the deserving people and helped the distressed Indian labourers, who had been badly hit by war. The magnitude of this work can be guessed by the work done by the Indian Welfare Centre at Kaula Lampur, where the strength of the inmates was over 700 and the expenditure amounted to 70,000 dollars per month.

One of the new activities of the League, was starting of an organization known as 'Balak Saina.' Children of all ages between 5 and 17 were recruited in this Saina and trained as Boy Scouts. This Saina did propaganda work by organizing processions, demonstration and dramas etc. and otherwise rendered help to the Independence Movement. After the surrender of Singapore, the Balak Saina, rendered great assistanee to the I. N. A. prisoners of war and circulated leaflets in the British Indian Army, whom they nick-named "Ghulam Hind Fauj'. One of the members of the 'Balak Saina'—Mr. Krishan Lal was detained for 24 hours by the Field security service and released after a demonstration by the Saina. 'Balak Saina Camps' were organized at Kambe (Rangoon) Singapur, Ziawaddi and Bangkok.

Similar relief and other work was taken in hand by the Indian Independence League Headquarters at Rangoon and Advance Headquarters Mandalay, The General Secretary of the Rangoon Headquarters was Mr. Deb Nath Das and that of Mandalay S. Gopal Singh who collected more than Rupees two crores for the movement from North Burma, These Headquarters opened hospitals in Burma for the wounded I. N. A. soldiers at Rangoon, Mandalay, Maymyo, Kalewa. Yeu, Endanai, Menowa, Taunggyi and Ziabaddi. The nurses of the Rani of Jhansi Regiment rendered marvellous services in these hospitals.

Prior to starting the second campaign Netaji Subhash Chandra Bose visited Japan at the invitation of the Japanese Government to confer with the Government and military authorities on various matters and to secure closer co-operation between his Government and the Government of Japan. Netaji accompanied by Col. A. C. Chatterji State Minister, Col. M. Z. Kiani, Commandar of the first division of the I. N. A. and Lt. Col. Habib-ul-Rahman Deputy Chief of Staff arrived at Tokyo on November 1944 by air. He was accorded a right royal reception at the aerodrome by the Foreign Minister, high military officials and Indian residents. After conferring with the Premier and Foreign Minister, he returned to Singapore.

On December, 17, 1944 he addressed a mammoth gathering of Indians in Singapore. In his fiery address of over two hours he referred to the events of the past year and I. N. A. reverses and giving general survey of the first compaign, renewed their enthusism. He said :—

"We have achieved a lot during the past one year. The establishment of the Provisional Government last year in the month of October was the stepping stone for our success. When our Army of Liberation started from Syonan on their march to Delhi, Indians were thinking under what government we are going to fight and to whom our victories can be attributed. History records many instances of establishment of similar Provisional Governments. But the establishment of our Provisional Government was unique in that it was recognised by nine world Powers. No other revolutionary govern ment has received so much esteem and respect as ours. India is no longer a slave country in the eyes of these nations. In the history of the world we have witnessed many revolutions. Let us take, for instance, Ireland. The Irish people established their Provisional Government. But the respect that our Provisional Government commands to-day was never commanded by Ireland. America had sympathies with the Irish cause. De Valera went to America to seek American assistance. He managed to get money, but not respect. He returned disappointed. The secret of respect commaded by us lies in the recognition of our Government by nine world powers. The Indian sisters and brothers in Malaya will have their honourable place in the history of India. It is here in Syonan that the Azad Hind Fauj was organised. It was here in Syonan that the Provisional Government of Azad Hind was established. And it was from Syonan that the Azad Hind Fauj began its march to India. We expect ceaseless help and assistance from Syonan.

While I was in Rangoon I learnt that the revolutionary spirit and enthusiasm of the people in Malai and Syonan is coming down. I have come here to see it for myself, If it is really true, I am sorry to say that it is a matter for regret. The war of independence for India is not a child's play. It is a matter of life and death for 38 crores of Indians. Either we will live like free men or we will embrace death.

I know there are British agents in Syonan, left by them when they retreated to spread false rumours and propaganda. But it does not concern us Indians. There is only one way left to us and that is the way to Delhi. There is no room for compromise. These enemy agents may be able to put obstacles in our path, but we have only one thought branded in our heart and soul and that is India and her independence.

I have brought with me Divisional Commander Colonel M. Z. Kiani to furnish you with up-to-date information about the battles in the Arakan and Imphal. I could have brought other Commanders also with me. But it was not possible to bring all of them here.

Before I came here I went to Tokyo. My object in visiting Tokyo was to establish personal contact with the members of the new Cabinet and to discuss with the members of the Imperial Government and leaders of Army and Navy concerning future programme, both political, and military. We have settled all questi ns, both military and political amicably. As regards military questions, I cannot disclose them as they are military secrets. As regards political questions, diplomatic relations will be established very soon which will strengthen our position. That will enable us to work with close co-operation and prosecute the war successfully.

At the end of December last year I toured the Andamans On the 30th December we hoisted our National Flag on the British Chief Commissioner's residence. I had talks with Nipponese authorities and it was agreed that the Provisional Government of Azad Hind should send a Commissioner there. So Colonal A. D. Loganathan was sent to Andamans as Chief Commissioner. In January I went to Rangoon and along with me Army and League Headquarters were shifted to Rangoon. On the 4th February, an offensive was launched in Arakan against the Anglo Americans. The Arakan fight was a minor struggle, but great importance was attached to it. It was the first test to our Army of Liberation. Hitherto no one knew much about the Azad Hind Fauj. The world was amazed at the bravery and courage displayed by the Azad Hind Fauj. It was a wonder not for us but for those who had shades of doubt in the core of their heart. Before we began the offensive Nipponese Army authorities asked a question whether the Azad Hind Fauj will be able to undergo all hardships with Nippon forces. The commanders were instructed to ensure from their officers and men, before giving any definite answer. When the soldiers of the Azad Hind Fauj were questioned they all with one voice replied that they are capable of enduring as many hardships as the Nippon soldiers can endure and even more. They knew they were fighting the battle of India's independence. But in spite of this assurance, the Nipponese still had some doubts. But when it was proved that the Azad Hind Fauj is giving a bold show to the enemy, they were very much surprised.

This war is not waged by Nippon alone. It is a national war for India's liberation. We have to go to India and therefore will have to suffer more and more difficulties. Although the battle of Arakan was a minor struggle it was very important to us because it was the first test of our forces. On the 18th March the Provisional Government proclaimed that the Azad Hind Fauj crossed the Indo-Burma border and were fighting on Indian soil. In March our advance was so rapid that when our thrust into Imphal was delayed there were inquiries why Imphal was still standing against our assault. I was annoyed at persons asking such questions. These were persons who were not actually on the front line, but far behind in their homes. Those who know anything about fighting will not ask such questions. Only military observers realise the strategical importance of Imphal and Chittagong. If these cities had no military importance we wonld have captured them earlier. The fortifications on the Eastern Front of India are like that of Maginot Line in France. So long as these fortifications are safe, the British are secure. When these fortifications are pierced through, our forces will easily make rapid advance towards Delhi.

In each and every battle there is a certain strategic point which will decide the course of the war. Those who are aware of the past history of India know well that Panipat always settled the fate of India. But in this war the fate of India will be settled somewhere in the jungles between Imphal and Chittagong. When once we smash enemy fortifications on the Eastern Frontier and reach the plains of Bengal and Assam then our road to Delhi will be clear. So the enemy will strive hard to hold these fortifications. In this war when the Maginot Line was pierced, France collapsed in a few weeks. So when the fate of Chittagong and Imphal is sealed there will be no war in the Bengal Province and our advance to Calcutta will be only a route march.

I have just now told you the battle of Imphal and Chittagong will settle the fate of India. We will get hold of these important strategic points at all cost even if we have to attempt ten times or more. When we withdrew from Imphal people were disappointed. They asked for my opinion and I replied that there is no doubt for any such ground. We know our path and we will never waver until we reach our goal.

Friends, we should realise the importance of Imphal and Chittagong and be ready to make any sacrifice to occupy these cities. Once we take these strategical centres, our task will become easier for it will have wide repercussions throughout India. There is no Indian who likes the British. Every Indian hates the British and if a handful of them side with the British it is not out of love for the British but to achieve their self-interests. If the three hundred and eighty million Indians rose in revolt they could have annihilated the British with sticks and stones. Then there would have been no necessity for the Azad Hind Fauj. It is regrettable that they have not seen the destruction of the British with their own eyes as we Indians in East Asia have experienced. You are confident that the British Empire will be shattered. Now it is our duty to go into India and defeat the British so that the 380 million Indians could see the destruction of the British with their own eyes. When they see it for themselves they will get courage and self-confidence and revolution will break out in every nook and corner of India and our task will become easier.

Friends, you perhaps remember that in August last year in the course of a speech at the Farrer Park I said that before the end of this year we will cross the Indo Burma border and will stand on Indian soil. When I spoke I thought we will be able to commence fighting in the month of December. But we were delayed on account of necessary military preparations. Our forces entered India in March and we were fighting on a broad front from Akyab to Kohima. We defeated the enemy in every battle but due to transport difficulties we could not continue our advance. In the heavy rain we had only two courses open to us : either to stay in these jungles or to withdraw. The Nippon Commander and our Commanders considered over the matter and it was decided to withdraw because to stay in these jungles meant disaster to the army. When the enemy saw that we have withdrawn and the road was clear they occupied the place without resistance and proclaimed to the whole world by every weapon of propaganda that they have won a great victory. But our officers and men know the real reason for our withdrawal. We are confident that we can occupy all the lost ground in no time. I would once again stress the importance of Imphal and Chittagong and we will have to occupy thase places at any cost. After six months of battle we have judged correctly our strength and the strength of our enemy.

When the Azad Hind Fauj was organised the enemy began to make propaganda that the Azad Hind Fauj was not an army but only a propaganda stunt. But when our army went into action the British propagandists changed their tune and began to give out that the Azad Hind Fauj was very poorly equipped. In reply I said that our army possessed everything except meat, rum, beer and whisky which were abundantly supplied to the British forces. Our army will fight in the face of hunger and thirst. There have been many revolutions in the world history, but you can never find a single example where the revolutionary army was better equipped than their opponents. They have succeeded not because of the strength of their weapon or of numbers but by the strength of their conviction that they are fighting for a sacred cause. Take the case of Ireland. She had 5,000 revolutionaries who had dedicated their lives for their country. The British sent 50,000 troops well equipped to crush the revolution. But they miserably failed in spite of their superiority in number and weapons. I know very well the strength of our enemies and I know what we are capable of doing. We will have to make great sacrifices. Even if every soldier and officer of the Azad Hind Fauj has to lay down his life for the liberation of 380 million Indians, we are prepared for that Even if the three million Indians in East Asia turn destitutes, that is nothing. We are proud that we are given such a golden opportunity to serve our Motherland. We are thankful to God that we have got men and material needed for the liberation of India. Three million Indians have been united Now we have to pay the price of our independence with our blood which is not a big price Now the responsibility that lies on our shoulders is to strengthen our army and march across into India. There is only one way for us. We have to shed our blood. So many of our comrades laid down their lives in the first campaign ; nobody can say how many of us will remain alive until the war of liberation comes to a successful conclusion. Officers and men who hesitate to lay down their lives have no place in this army. Side by side with the Army the nation has to make total sacrifices. The nation must be prepared for such a sacrifice.

Last year in Bengal Province alone 20 lakhs of Indians perished due to starvation. 5 lakhs of Indians retreated along with the British from Burma and out of these more than one lakh lost their lives. If so many Indians had given up their lives for the independence of our Motherland, India to-day would have been a free country. If you are not willing to face death for the liberation of your country you have no right to call yourself an Indian. Some so-called Indians think that if India is freed they can go to India and if the British came back then also they can go back to India. I can assure these traitors that they will not go to India. We are not liberating India for them. They will have no place in a free India. We will pick up all those traitors and they will be at the mercy of the Free Government. The only favour they may expect from us will be a third class ticket to Britian.

Friends, we have to enhance our programme of total mobilisation. Preparations are being made for the next offensive and we are collecting materials for this campaign. Our well-to-do brothers who are lagging behind will have to come forward and make sacrifices. Those wealthy Indians who have amassed a great fortune and are afraid to lay down their lives will have to take a Habeeb mixture. Janab Habeeb is the first patriot who has sacrificed all his property, amounting to ten million and three thousand rupees. Those people who do not enjoy sleep thinking of their money may better take a dose of Habeeb mixture and cure themselves by contributing all their money for our funds. I tell you as long as the entire nation is not fully prepared to sacrifice everything. our victory cannot be achieved. We must inspire and set an example to those who are obstructing our way. Fortunately their number is very small. Still they are doing harm to our movement. They think that we can only prattle and that we cannot suppress them. Now the entire nation has to come under military discipline. Those who are weak we will make them strong. And if we are forced to suppress these enemy agents disguised as Indians I know the whole nation will support us. Up to this time we entreated you with folded hands. In Nippon, Germany or in England, the Governments never request but order. I can ssure you that not only Syonan but the whole world, except perhaps America, is suffering from food shortage. The reason for America not suffering from such food shortage is that war has not gone to American soil. If you are prepared to sacrifice everything then the food problem will not exist at all. We also need more volunteers for the Rani of Jhansi Regiment ; so I have to appeal to our sisters to come forward and join the Regiment.

I would like to ask you a question. I want you to answer honestly. When I was in Rangoon I received a report that the revolutionary spirit and enthusiasm of Indians in Syonan are fading. Now tell me how many of you are willing to work with us, prepared to make any sacrifice and to fight shoulder to shoulder with us and, if need be, to die with us ?"

Immediately the whole audience got up and expressed their willingness to lay down their lives or make any sacrifice for the liberation of India. They shouted " Inqilab Zindabad," " Netaji ki Jai " and " Chalo Delhi."

Netaji Subhash Chandra Bose then toured North Malaya. On December 22 he visited Kuala Lumpur and addressed a mass meeting of Indians. The following day he inspected the Indian Welfare Centre conducted by the Selangor Branch of the Indian Independence League at Kuala Lumpur for the care of sick and destitute Indians.

After having toured North Malaya, Netaji visited Summatra and received donations amounting to one million dollars. During his tour in

Malaya and Summatra in three weeks, Netaji received over one crore dollars contribution to the Indian Independence fund. Before returning to Burma, Netaji addressed a big meeting of Indians at Singapore on January 7, 1945 and exhorted them to make virgorous efforts for more men, more money and more material for the successful prosecution of War.

CHAPTER XIII

THE FINAL PHASE

1. The Second Campaign

The second campaign of the I. N. A. began in January 1945, immediately after the return of Netaji Subhash Chandra Bose from Singapore to Rangoon. Circumstances had undergone a considerable change since the last campaign. After the I. N. A. had withdrawn from Imphal, the Anglo-American forces had been able to advance into Burma. The advanced mechanized units, consisting of tanks, armoured cars etc., of the enemy, were able to break through defences of the I. N. A. and Japanese Army. The crisis in Europe was nearing. The Allied Forces had gained a round of successes in Europe over Germany. This had also affected Japan, who were experiencing a series of reverses in the Pacific islands. It was not possible for the Japanese to spare any effective force or aeroplanes to resist the Anglo-American onslaught in Burma. The I. N. A. had to encounter the enemy single handed. And the enemy was decidedly stronger, not only numerically, but was also better equipped.

But the indomitable spirit of Netaji knew no defeat. Starting the campaign, he addressed the fighting forces at Mingaldan Camp as follows :—

Last year the I. N. A. faced the enemy on the battle-field for the first time. The deeds of the I N. A. were glorious ; they were beyond any expectations and won the praise of both friends and foe. We dealt the enemy a crushing defeat, wherever we fought him. Without being defeated, we had, as a tactical move, to bring back our forces from the Imphal Front due to bad weather and other handicaps.

"Now we have tried to overcome these difficulties. But every one should remember that our army is a revolutionary army. We are not so well-equipped in man-power as our enemies are. Our enemies have decided that they will fight their first battle for the defence of India in Assam and they have made this area India's Stalingrad.

"This year will be the decisive year of the war. The fate of India's freedom will be decided near the hills of Imphal and on the plains of Chittagong. Last year some of our men joined the enemy. I do not want even a single man to go over to the enemy this time, when we go to the Front. Therefore, if any one thinks that he is incapable of going to the Front, due to weakness or cowardice or for any other reason, he should report to his regimental Commander and arrangements will be made to keep him at the base.

"I do not wish to point a very rosy picture to you. You will have to face hunger, thirst and other hardships and even death, when you go to the Front. Because the enemy has made the utmost preparations, we too shall have to mobilize all our resources.

"In addition to the present slogan of the I. N. A., namely 'Chalo Delhi', another slogan will be added from to-day, and that will be "Khoon, Khoon, Khoon (Blood, Blood, Blood.") This means that we shall shed onr blood for the freedom of 40 crores of people in India. Similarly, we shall shed the blood of the enemy for the same cause—The slogan for the Indian civilians, who are in the south will be: "Karo sab nichhawar, bano sab faqir' (sacrifice every thing, become all paupers)."

The Indian National Army had to launch the offensive under most trying circumstances. But it did not lose heart. The second division under Col. Shah Nawaz Khan started the operations. It consisted of fourth (Nehru) Guerilla Brigade under Lt. Col. G. S. Dhillon, fifth Guerilla Brigade under Lt. Col. P. K. Sehgal and second Infantry Regiment under Lt. Col. Hussain. They encounterd the enemy between Pyinmana and Mandalay, along the Irrawaddi river. Fierce fighting also raged between Myingyan and Maugwe. Netaji visited Pyinmana (which was now the Divisional Headquarter of the fighting forces) on the 21st February 1945 and addressed the forces for over an hour He paid glowing tributes to the courage of the I. N. A., especially the Nehru Brigade commanded by Lt. Col. G. S. Dhillon. He remained on the Front up to the 28th February. The I. N. A, showed unprecedented bravery and courage on the battle field, but it was not possible to check the advance of the 14th British Army, without heavy reinforcements, supplies and air support. The Japanese air-power gave no assistance for obvious reasons, and the supply lines were cut off. The result was starvation, death and devastation.

The result was a series of defeats, By the first week of March, the Anglo American Forces had captured Akyab Island, Shwebo, Myebon Peninsula, Ramree, Meiktila and Mandalay. To make the matters worse, increased difficulties and privations on the front, led some officers and men of the I. N. A. to desert and go over to the British. To keep up the morale of the I. N. A., Netaji issued another Special Order of the Day on March 13, 1945 as follows :—

"Comrades! As you all know, the positive achievement of the officers and men of the Azad Hind Fauj last year on the field of battle and victories, that they scored over the enemy, through their patriotism, bravery and self-sacrifice, were marred to some extent by the cowardice and treachery of a few officers and men. We were hoping that with the advent of the new year, all traces of cowardice and treachery would be wiped out and that in this year's operations, the Azad Hind Fauj would be able to put up an unsullied record of heroism and self-sacrifice. But that was not to be. The recent treachery of five officers of the Headquarter of the second division has come as an eye-opener to us, that all is not well, within our ranks and that the seeds of cowardice and treachery have yet to be wiped out. If we now succeed in exterminating cowardice and treachery once for all, this shameful and despicable incident may, through God's Grace, ultimately prove to be a blessing in disguise. I am, therefore, determined to take all possible measures, necessary for the purification of our Army. I am confident, that in this I shall have your full and unstinted support.

"In order to destroy completely the germs of cowardice and treachery, the following measures will have to be adopted :—

1. Every member of the Azad Hind Fauj, officers, N. C. O. or sepoy will, in future be entitled to arrest any other member of the A. H. F., no matter what his rank may be, if he leaves in a cowardly manner or to shoot him, if he acts in a treacherous manner.

2. I am giving an opportunity to all members of the A. H. F., who may not feel inclined to work dutifully, or fight courageously in future, to leave the rank of the A. H. F. This offer will be open for one week from the time of its communication.

3. In addition to giving an opportunity to unwilling elements, to leave voluntarily the ranks of the A. H. F., I want to carry out thorough purge of our Army. During the course of this purge, all those will be removed against whom there is suspicion that they may fail us or betray us, at the critical moment. In order to carry out this purge successfully, I want your fullest co-operation and I want you therefore, to give me and my trusted officers all available information about any cowardly or treacherous elements, that may still exist in our Army.

4. It will not be enough to carry out a thorough purge now. In future also, vigilance will have to continue. It will, therefore, be the duty of every member of the A. H. F. in future, to keep his eyes and ears open in order to detect in good time any tendency towards cowardice or treachery. In future, if any member of the A. H. F. detects any tendency towards cowardice or treachery, he should report atonce, either orally or in writing, either to me or to the officers who may be within reach. In other words, from now onwards and for all times, every member of the A. H. F. should regard himself as the custodian of the honour and reputation of the A. H. F. and the Indian Nation.

5. After the purge has been carried out and unwilling elements have been given an opportunity of leaving our Army, if there is any case of cowardice or treachery, the punishment will be death.

6. In order to create within our Army, a moral bulwark against cowardice and treachery, we have to create an intense hatred against cowardice and treachery in any form. A strong feeling has to be created in the mind of every member of this Army, that for a member of a Revolutionary Army, there is no crime more heinous and despicable than to be a coward or a traitor. Instructions are being issued separately, as to how we can create such an intense hatred against cowardice and treachery, so that there will be no more cowards or traitors within our ranks.

7. After the purge has been carried out, every member of the A. H. F. will be required to renew his oath to fight on bravely and courageously, until the emancipation of our dear Motherland is achieved. Instructions regarding the form and manner of this oath will be issued separately.

8. Special rewards will be given to those, who give information regarding cowardly and treacherous elements or who arrest or shoot at the front cowardly and treacherous elements."

The five officers, who are referred to in the above communique as deserters, were Major Riaz, Major Madan, Major Dey, Major Sarwar and Lt. Mohd. Bakhsh. In addition to these the following officers also deserted on different occasions in the Imphal Front and later in the Central Burma Front:—

1. Major Mahabir Singh Dhillon (*who escaped* to India from I. N. A. of General Mohan Singh).

2. Major Prabhu Dayal 2nd. in command of Col. Gulzara Singh (Azad Brigade).

3. Lt. Pars Ram of Azad Brigade.

4. Major Grewal of First Division Headquarter.

5. Lt. Khazin Shah.

6. Lt. Yasin Khan.

7. Lt. Ganga Singh.

8. 2nd. Lt. Chain Singh.

9. 2nd. Lt. Balwant Singh.

10. Sub-Officer Barfi Ram.

11. Sub-officer Abdul Hakim.

12 Havildar Baldev Singh etc

To further intensify the campaign against treachery and cowardice, a Traitor Day was observed and a drama entitled "Traitor" was played in all the Military and Training camps at Rangoon. The civilians were not allowed to see this play. Effigies of the traitors were burnt. A couplet composed at the time, was on the lips of every member of the Balak Saina in Rangoon :

Dey ko lagao dande, Sarwar ka sar ura do.
Maro Riaz Todi, zinda Madan Jala do.

... ...

Col. P. K. Sehgal traces the cause of treachery to a lack of faith in final victory. Most people had begun to believe that Anglo-Americans. superior in numbers and armaments, were going to win the war and it was futile to carry on the struggle," He points out that none of the officers, who went over had ever shown cowardice and right up to the time they went over, they fought most courageously. They attacked the enemy much superior in numbers and armaments, and not a single soldier ever wavered.

The Indian National Army continued its fight against heavy odds undeterred, even when it admitted the superiority of the enemy and clearly saw that the end was not far off. They kept their morale up to the last. Col. G. S. Dhillon in a letter to Col. Shah Niwaz Khan wrote. "We are prepared to continue fighting in the front line. We will sacrifice our lives to maintain the honour of the A. H. F. Water, or no water, rations or no rations, will not affect our fighting capacity—assuring you that we will fight up to the last."

Netaji congratulated Col. Dhillon on the manner, he had stood up to face bravely that difficalt situation and his complete confidence in him and his companions. In the same letter Netaji expressed his firm conviction that no power on earth could keep India enslaved any longer.

Early in April 1945, the Burmese Defence Army under Major General Aung San turned against Japanese. The Soviet-Jap Neutrality Pact also broke down. These factors further made the position critical. Out of the able-bodied soldiers of the first division, X Regiment was formed under Col. Thakar Singh. This regiment fought at Pynmana, but had to surrender on the 24th April 1945 in small batches. The main force of this regiment managed to retreat to Bangkok. By this time the enemy had also captured Taunggy and Maymyo. The fourteenth British Army was nearing Rangoon. Col. P. K. Sehgal surrendered on the 28th April, Pegu was captured on the 2nd May and two days later the Anglo-American Forces entered Rangoon. Many batches of the I. N. A. were taken as prisoners of war. Finally Col. Shah Niwaz and Col. Dhillon laid down arms on the 18th May 1915 and were taken as prisoners of war. Thus the hostilities came to an end.

Three months later, at the time of Wavell Conference, Netaji broadcasting from Singapore to the Indian revolutionaries at home, described how the Indian National Army had suffered great losses by the British bombardment He said :—

Comrades ! I would never have opened my mouth and said one word to you, if I had been sitting as an armchair politician here. But I and my comrades here are engaged in a grim struggle. Our comrades at the front have to play with death. Even those who are not at the front have to face danger every moment of their existence. When we were in Burma, bombing and machine-gunning was our daily entertainment. I have seen many of my comrades killed, maimed and injured from the enemy's ruthless bombing and machine-gunning. I have seen the entire hospital of the Azad Hind Fauj in Rangoon razed to the ground, with our helpless patients suffering heavy casualties.

That I and many others with me are still alive today, is only through God's grace. It is because we are living, working and fighting in the presence of death that I have a right to speak to you and to advise you. Most of you do not know what carpet-bombing is. Most of you do not know what is to be machine-gunned by low-flying bombers and fighters. Most of you have had no experience of bullets whistling past you, to your right and to your left. Those who have gone through this experience and have nevertheless kept up their morale, cannot even look at Lord Wavell's offer."

2. – Netaji back to Thailand and Malaya

Towards the end of April, 1945, when the British forces were advancing towards Rangoon, Netaji was still there, determined to stay with his army and face the enemy. Night and day for a week his Ministers and high-ranking officers pleaded with him to leave Rangoon and carry on the war from elsewhere. Netaji did not budge. The British spearhead was heading towards Rangoon, and only a few hours left, then it would be too late. With tears in their eyes the Ministers and Officers begged him to leave even at the last hour. At last Netaji had to give in.

Before leaving Rangoon, Netaji settled all the account with Burmese and Japanese Governments. The members of the Rani of Jhansi Regiment Rangoon Branch had already been disbanded and sent back to their homes. A batch of 50 Jhansis belonging to Malaya and Thailand had also been sent back by train. A tragic incident happened in the way, when on Tiffli Railway

Station (between Sittang and Martban) the train was fired at by the Burmese Defence Army and two members of the Regiment Miss Stella and Miss Jozephine were killed and some others wounded.

About 7,000 men and officers of the I. N. A. were left in Rangoon under the command of Major General A. D. Loganadan to protect life and property of the Indians. Lt. Col. Arshad was appointed as Chief of Staff and Lt. Col. Mehbub acted as Military Secretary. Mr. J. N. Bahaduri was appointed President and Mr. Kananpilly as Secretary of Indian Independence League Headquarters. They had instructions to cease hostilities. The I. N. A. personnel was arrested on the 28th May 1945. The Azad Hind Bank was also taken over by the British.

Netaji left Rangoon on the evening of 24th April 1945, by road for Bangkok. The Ministers of Provisional Government of Azad Hind, the staff of Indian Independence League Headquarter, about 100 Rani Jhansis, 100 civilians and 800 I. N. A. men went with him. It took him three weeks to cover the 300 odd miles to Bangkok Holding his life in his hand and undergoing indescribable physical hardships, he reached Bangkok on May 14.

Mr. Ishiyama, chief correspondent of the "Asahi Shimbun" in the Southern Regions, who had come into close contact with Netaji at Rangoon, narrated to a select gathering of high officers of the I.N.A. and the League at Singapore later some striking incidents as revealing Netaji's sense of duty and concern for the I. N. A. and the Rani of Jhansi Regiment and his bravery in the face of great danger.

Mr. Ishiyama said that when the I.N.A. troops were in Pegu they were within striking distance of the enemy. They should have hurried to get away but Netaji would not get away but until the arrival of other detachments of the I.N A. who were still on the move. It was only after their arrival Netaji left Pegu.

At Sittang there was need for transport for the removal of a number of patients and weak people. There was some transport but as these were required for the use of the patients, Netaji undertook to march from Sittang to Noulmein—a distance of about 70 miles—walking five days.

At Tambuzee, a railway junction south of Moulmein, an enemy tank force was operating and it was expected that there might be bombing and shelling at any time. There was every danger but Netaji waited there till all the I. N. A. troops had left.

The last time he saw Netaji, said Mr. Ishiyama, was at a wayside between Rangoon and Moulmein, some time at the end of April. It was somewhat of a dramatic scene. He was tired and sitting on the side of the road. It was a moonlight night and he could see Netaji leading 200 or 300 I.N.A. troops and Jhansi volunteers in a very orderly manner.

Owing to Netaji's reluctance to leave Burma in spite of the Nippon military authorities' advice to leave the place as quickly as possible, his departure from Rangoon was delayed for a few days. Netaji had insisted to remain in Burma and continue the fight against the British but he had to accede to the request of his Cabinet Ministers.

Another notable incident which shows Netaji's bravery was provided in the dangerous crossing of the river at Sittang. The crossing was not an easy affair and at the same time Netaji had to do it during enemy's bombing and machine-gunning. Netaji could agree to cross the river only after all the I.N.A. and the Jhansi Regiment volunteers had completed the crossing.

"Netaji Bose had not only impressed him with his solicitude for the Jhansi and the I.N.A. members, said Mr. Ishiyama, "but he had also impressed the Nippon Military authoriries very deeply. Netaji's concern and anxiety for the safety of the members of the Jhansi Regiment and the I.N.A. was remarkable."

After his arrival in Bangkok, Netaji issued the following special order of the Day to the officers and men of the Azad Hind Fauj on May 21, 1945:—

Brave Officers and men of the Azad Hind Fauj :

It is with a very heavy heart that I am leaving Burma—the scene of the many heroic battles that you have fought since February, 1944 and are still fighting. In Imphal and Burma, we have suffered a reverse in the first round in our fight for independence. But it is only the first round. We have many more rounds to fight for independence. I am a born optimist and I shall not admit defeat under any circumstances. Your brave deeds in the battles against the enemy on the plains of Imphal, the hills and jungles of Arakan and the oil-field area and other localities in Burma will live in the history of our struggle for Independence for all time.

Comrades : At this critical hour, I have only one word of command to give you, and that is, that if you have to go down temporarily, then go down fighting with the National Tri-colour held aloft ; go down as heroes ; go down upholding the highest code of honour and discipline. The future generations of Indians, who will be born, not as slaves but as free men because of your colossal sacrifice, will bless your names and proudly proclaim to the world that you, their forebears, fought and suffered reverses in the battle in Manipur, Assam, and Burma, but through temporary failure you paved the way to ultimate success and glory.

My unshakable faith in India's liberation remains unaltered. I am leaving in your safe hands our national Tricolour, our national honour and the best traditions of Indian Warriors. I have no doubt whatsoever that you, the vanguard of India's Army of Liberation, will sacrifice everything, even life itself, to uphold India's National Honour, so that your comrades who will continue the fight elsewhere may have before them your shining example to inspire them at all times.

If I had my own way, I would have preferred to stay with you in adversity and share with you the sorrow of temporary defeat. But on advice of my Ministers and high ranking officers I have to leave Burma in order to continue the struggle for emancipation. Knowing my countrymen in East Asia and inside India, I can assure you that they will continue the fight under all circumstances and that all your suffering and sacrifices will not be in vain. So far as I am concerned, I shall steadfastly adhere to the pledge that I took on the 21st of October 1943, to do all in my power to serve the interests of 38 crores of my countrymen and fight for their liberation. I appeal to you, in conclusion, to cherish the same optimism as myself and to believe, like myself, that the darkest hour always precedes the dawn. India shall be free—and before long.

May God Bless You !

Inquilab Zindabad ! Azad Hind Zindabad ! Jai Hind. !

(Sd.) Subhash Chandra Bose
Supreme Commander Azad Hind Fauj.

Netaji Subhash Chandra Bose gave the following message to his Indian and Burmese Friends in Burma on the some day : —

Brothers and Sisters : I am leaving Burma with a very heavy heart. We have lost the first round of our fight for Independence. But we have lost only the first round There are many more rounds to fight. In spite of our losing the first round, I see no reason for losing heart.

You, my countrymen in Burma, have done your duty to your Motherland in a way that evoked the admiration of the world You have given liberally of your men, money and materials You set, the first example of Total Mobilisation. But the odds against us were overwhelming, and we have temporarily lost the battle in Burma.

The spirit of selfless sacrifice that you have shown, particularly since I shifted my Headquarters to Burma, is something that I shall never forget, so long as I live.

I have the fullest confidence that that spirit can never be crushed. For the sake of India's Freedom, I beseech you to keep up that spirit, I beseech you to hold your heads erect, and wait for that Bleseed Day when once again you will have an opportunity of waging the War for India's Independence.

When the History of India's Last War of Independence comes to be written, Indians in Burma will have an honoured place in that History.

I do not leave Burma of my own free will. I would have preferred to stay on here and share with you the sorrow of temporary defeat. But on the pressing advice of my Ministers and High ranking Officers, I have to leave Burma in order to continue the struggle for India's liberation. Being a born optimist, my unshakable faith in India's early emancipation remains unimpaired and I appeal to you to cherish the same optimism.

I have always said that the darkest hour precedes the dawn. We are now passing through the darkest hour ; therefore, the dawn is not far off.

INDIA SHALL BE FREE.

I cannot conclude this message without publicly acknowledging once again my heartful gratitude to the Government and people of Burma for all the help that I have received at their hands in carrying on this struggle. The day will come when Free India will repay that debt of gratitude in a generous manner.

Inquilab Zindabad ! Azad Hind Zindabad ! Jai Hind !

(Sd.) Subhash Chandra Bose.

The Headquarters of the Provisional Government of Azad Hind issued the following Communique on 5th June 1945, from Thailand :

All the Ministers of the Provisional Government of Azad Hind who were not engaged in war operations in Burma, have arrived in Bangkok along with Netaji Subhash Chandra Bose, with the exception of Lieutenant-Colonel Ehsan Qadir who was engaged on special duty.

Lieutenant-Colonel Ehsan Qadir, Minister of Manpower, is relieved of the portfolio of Manpower.

Sri A. M. Sahay. Minister of State is appointed Minister of Manpower.

Sri. Parmanand, Deputy Minister of Supplies, is appointed Minister of Supplies.

Sri. S. A. Ayer, Minister of Publicity and Propaganda, relinquishes the office of Secretary to the Provisional Government of Azad Hind.

Sri. J. A. Thivy, Adviser to the Provisional Government is appointed Minister of State and Secretary to the Provisional Government.

Netaji Subhash Chandra Bose gave a soul-stirring broadcast to the Indian people on June 14, 1945 from the Bangkok radio. He reviewed the situation in Europe and expressed his strong belief that an acute conflict would soon develop between Russians and Anglo-Americans. In Burma, the British will not have easy way and Japan also could hold out successfully.

Then he went on to discuss the Indian problem and said :—

Coming now to India, I want to say, first of all, that India's case is a unique one. Whatever happens during the course of this war, there is nothing that can stand between the Indian people and their cherished goal, liberty. Even a flunkey of British Imperialism like Sir Feroze Khan Noon had to admit the other day that the forces of nationalism working inside India, and world-forces working outside, are irresistible. We Indians who are working outside India have endeavoured, up till now, to take the fullest advantage of the international situation and we shall go on doing so in future. The situation for us may appear outwardly to be very gloomy today. In fact, it may be called our darkest hour. But that is true only superficially. In reality, India is every day moving nearer to her objective of freedom. Bigger opportunities still lie ahead of us, than what we have hitherto obtained and we are determined to seize them when they do arrive.

We have recently suffered a serious reverse in Burma. Our losses in men and materials have been heavy indeed. But this reverse—and the accompanying losses—will prove to be a blessing in disguise. This is not rhetoric—nor is it propaganda. It is the plain and unvarnished truth. And those who doubt the truth of this statement have only to wait and see. The ways of history—like the ways of Providence—are often mysterious. "God fulfils himself in many ways"—as the poet said. For the fulfilment of our objective, it was perhaps necessary that the British Indian Army should come into Burma and see the Indian National Army—the Azad Hind Fauj—with their own eyes. Those who came to scoff will now remain to pray. The

British Indian Army have now seen us with their own eyes. What is the result ? There is no longer any talk of a puppet Army—of a Japanese Indian Force or "JIF." Even enemy propagandists now talk, at last, of an Indian National Army. That Indian National Army still exists *outside* Burma—in spite of the heavy losses that it has sustained *inside* Burma. That I. N A. will go on fighting as long as there is an enslaved India. And that I. N. A. will go on fighting to the last man and the last round.

Nobody is grieved more than we are that we could not take Imphal last year. Nobody is more grieved than we are that we suffered a serious reverse in Burma this year. But when we started our campaign in February 1944, in the Arakan region of Burma, I wanted at least two years' time for the fulfilment of our programme. February 1946, is still a long way off. The road to Delhi is a long and difficult one and we have still to fight on, before we can reach our goal. But Delhi remains our one and only destination. "Chalo Delhi" remains our slogan. We may not travel to Delhi *via* Imphal—but we shall get there all right. The roads to Delhi are many—like the roads to Rome.

Sisters and brothers at home !

To those who have suffered and are suffering—and to those who are languishing in prison—at home, we send, through you a word of good cheer. In spite of what has recently happened, our faith in final victory and freedom remains undiminished. We know the strength of our enemies—but we are also conscious of our own strength. The allied supreme commander in the last European War, Marshal Foch, once said, "That army is beaten which considers itself to be beaten." No one here considers himself to be beaten. We are invincible, because our cause is just and because we are prepared to pay the full price of Liberty. I beg you to cherish the same optimism about our final triumph that we do here. But I warn you also that your task inside India has become harder than it was hitherto. Greater sacrifice and tenacity is needed on the part of the revolutionaries working at home. Above all, do not be deceived or demoralised by the superficial—or pyrrhic—victories of our enemies. Remember, that Turkey lost the war in 1918 when her allies were winning—but she triumphed in 1921 after her enemies were victorious. The Irish Easter Rebellion was crushed in 1916 when England was in peril. But after England's victory, the Irish Sinn Feiners came out triumphant. So shall it be with India. We have lost the first round in the Battle of Burma in 1945. But, believe me, we shall win the last round in the battle of India in 1946. Jai Hind !

... ...

While Netaji Subhash Chandra Bose was engaged in drawing up plans for future action, Lord Wavell, Viceroy of India, made an offer to India on the 14th June 1945, to Indianise his Executive Council in return for the active co-operation of the Indian National Congress in Britain's war against Japan. Netaji was much worried over this. A meeting of the Council of Ministers of the Provisional Government of Azad Hind, was held in Bangkok on the 16th June to consider the Indian situation. It unanimously arrived at the conclusion that the British proposals were reactionary and suicidal to India's aspirations and by accepting them, the Indian National Congress would be voluntarily giving up its position as the representative of the Indian masses. The Council of Ministers appealed to Mahatma Gandhi and the

Working Committee of the Congress to reject the offer and authorised Netaji to issue any further statements that might be necessary to expose the other obnoxious features of Lord Wavell's offer.

Consequently Netaji issued a detailed statement on the offe on June 18 from Bangkok in which he comprehensively dealt with the pros and cons of the Viceroy's offer and concluded that Indians had nothing to gain, but much to lose by the British Proposals.

When Netaji learnt that the Congress Working Committee had decided to attend the Simla Conference, he immediately flew to Singapore on June 18, and from that night onwards he broadcast to his countrymen in India, night after night for one month, pleading with them, not to bring about a compromise on the issue of independence, through accepting Lord Wavell's offer.

The gist of his broadcasts was that, as a result of the present war, the Indian issue had become a live issue in international affairs and whatever the ultimate result of the war, India was bound to get independence after war.

The acceptance of the British proposals, will convert the Indian issue into a domestic issue of the British Empire and thereby forestall and preclude all help to India in the international field from all friendly powers, including Soviet Russia.

Netaji asserted, " The more I think. the more I am convinced that incalculable harm will be done to the Congress and to India by accepting this offer. We shall be putting back the clock by at least 25 years. All that we shall gain in return, will be a few jobs in the Executive Council for some ambitious Congressmen."

Netaji also maintained that the Congress Working Committee was not justified in making a final decision on such an all-important issue, specially, when the left wing of the Congress was not represented on the working Committee and most of the revolutionary element was behind the prison bars. From a purely moral point of view, it was wrong and unfair for the Working Committee to make any decision behind the back of the Congress. He appealed to the general public and Left Wingers to assert themselves and carry on a country-wide agitation against this sinister offer.

Analysing the implications of the offer, Netaji said that Wavell's offer was just like the Cripp's Scheme. It offered (1) a promise of self-Government —not independence (2) a few more seats on the Executive Council and (3) re-establishment of Congress Ministeries in the Provinces. All there things were offered to us long before. On the other hand Viceroy's veto was there ; Muslim League had been given representation out of all proportion to their number and there was an unfortunate implication that the Congress was a body of Caste Hindus.

In conclusion he appealed to Mahatma Gandhi to extricate the Congress from an exceedingly difficult and embarrassing position and save the Congrss and the Country from impending danger.

When he heard that the Congress was going to accept Lord Wavell as arbitrator, he warned the Congress not to do so, as Lord Wavell was sure to give his award in favour of Muslim League ; Mr. Jinnah will not accept Lord Wavell as arbitrator unless he was sure that the award would he in his favour. Netaji had a real apprehension that the Muslim League and the

British Government were outwitting the Congress and the Congress was falling into the trap due to its eagerness for a compromise.

Netaji was mush relieved, when he heard of the failure of the Simla Conference Even then he gave four broadcasts on the losses and results of the Conference. His view was that as a result of the Simla Conference, prestige of the Congress had been badly damaged. The Congress had shown diplomatic inefficiency and political shortsightedness in rushing headlong along the path of compromise, throwing to the winds all caution and resrve. It went on making commitment after commitment, but did not secure any commitment. It had made its position weak on the bar of the world-opinion as (1) it did not expose the hollowness of the British proposals (2) It did not point out that a National Cabinet could not possibly be formed on a communal basis and (3)It went out of its way to praise Lord Wavell.

One of the most luminous and all-comprehensive broadcasts on this subject was given on July 15, 1945. It ran as follows :—

Sisters and Brothers in India !

Today I am going to speak to you, first of all, about the lessons of the Simla Conference. What I shall say on this topic will be based on the reports from India. Though I have the impression that the reports which came to us from India over the radio and through various news agencies were generally reliable, nevertheless, there is a possibility that some of them were not wholly correct. Therefore, if any of my conclusions is based on a wrong premise, I should like to apologise in advance.

To an outside observer, it was apparent that some of the Congress leaders were showing excessive eagerness for a compromise with the British Government. This eagerness was, in some cases, not only unseemly and undignified, but even indecent. As against this, Mr. Jinnah's attitude, throughout, was dignified and reserved. It should be clear to every politician that in negotiating with such a shrewd enemy as the British, we have to couduct ourselves with proper dignity and reserve. If we do not do so, and if we exhibit any weakness, British politicians are bound to take advantage of it and get the better of us in any negotiations or political bargaining. As it is something difficult for us to see ourselves objectively, it is necessary for others to point out our mistakes. That is why the lessons of the Simla Cenference should be studied objectively so that in any future negotations with the British Government, the Congress leaders may show greater dignity, political sagacity and diplomatic skill.

Excessive eagerness for a compromise, to which I have referred above, was exhibited by some Congress leaders in various ways. For instance, certain statements were made to the effect that the Congress must come to an agreement with Lord Wavell Further, it was reported that Pandit Jawahar lal Nehru said in one of his statements, that he was prepared to work under Lord Wavell's leadership. If this report was correct, then it must have come as a rude shock to the Indian people. I am reminded that on a previous occasion, when there was a dispute between Pandit Nehru and a British district magistrate, Pandit Nehru declared that he would not take orders from the British Government. Now the same Pandit Nehru could agree to accept Lord Wavell's leadership passes my comprehension.

Lord Wavell has let the Congress leaders down very badly. First of all, in preparing his list of members, for the Executive Council, Lord Wavell did not include the name of any Congress Muslims. While the Congress Working Committee suggested only three Muslim Leaguers for the Executive Council, Lord Wavell proposed four Muslim Leaguers and he gave the fifth seat not to a Congress Muslim, but to a member of the Punjab Unionist Party. Even that did not placate Mr. Jinnah. The Congress leaders, more-over, went so far as to accept Lord Wavell's leadership and to agree to co-operating with him even if the Muslim League did not do so. But Lord Wavell insultingly declined to accept the hand of co-operation offered by the Congress Working Committee.

The net result, therefore, is that the Muslim League administered one slap on the face of the Congress, while Lord Wavell administered another slap. There can be no doubt that the Congress Working Committee has come out of the Simla Conference with its prestige considerably impaired. The prestige of the Congress might have been saved, if the Working Committee had declined to accept Lord Wavell's list, just as the Muslim League did I fail to understand why the Congress Working Committee did not do so. The only explanation I can find is that there was excessive zeal on the part of the Congress to arrive at a compromise by any means.

While making the above remarks, I should thankfully admit that what saved the prestige of the Congress, to a certain extent, was the attitude of reserve adopted by Mahatma Gandhi after his interview with the Viceroy at Simla. In fact, I have the impression that Mahatmaji was personally not enthusiastic about Lord Wavell's offer, but that he was carried away by the enthusiasm of some prominent members of the Congress Working Committee.

To an outside observer, it appeared that one of the reasons why some of the members of the Congress Working Committee were so enthusiastic about Lord Wavell. They thought that he would back the Congress, even if the Muslim League did not come forward to co-operate. At that time, I told many of my friends here that these Congress leaders were misjudging Lord Wavell altogether. I also told them that however friendly Lord Wavell might outwardly appear to be, he would ultimately have to execute the policy of the British Government That policy clearly is to back the Muslim League, under all circumstances.

What I anticipated has now come out to be true, I am told that the Congress Working Committee in its last sitting, assessed the gains and losses arising out of the Congress Party's participation in the Simla Conference. Though the report does not say what conclusions were reached on this point, the All-India Radio Special Correspondent says that, in the opinion of some leading Congressmen, the positive gain that has resulted is the creation of mutual esteem and friendship between the Viceroy and top-ranking Congress leaders. If correct, this is strange news. So long as India rmains morally in a state of war with the British Government, it is not the duty of the Congress leaders to cultivate friendship with the arch-champion of British Imperialism in India.

To sum up, I should like to say, that if we desire to learn from our mistakes, we should recognise the fact that out of the Simla Conference Mr. Jinnah has emerged with added prestige, while the prestige of the Congress has been greatly impaired. It is no use blaming either the Muslim League or the British Government for the failure of the Simla Conference, as the Congress President has done. Both the Muslim League and the British Government, represented by Lord Wavell, have done what was anticipated of them. In fact, if either of them had acted otherwise, it would have come as a surprise to us. The Congress President and other members of the Congress Working Committee should blame themselves for not being clever or shrewd enough to foresee what the Muslim League and Lord Wavell would do. Did the Congress Working Committee anticipate that Mr. Jinnah would go into the Executive Council unless he was absolutely sure that by doing so he would realise his dream of Pakistan ? Did the Congress Working Committee also anticipate that Lord Wavell would give up the Muslim League and support the Congress ?

If anybody in the Congress anticipated either of these two things, then he certainly lacks political wisdom and does not deserve to be called a leader Two things should have been crystal clear to every Congressman at the very outset – firstly, that Mr. Jinnah would not aceept any ad interim arrangement which did not ensure the realisation of Pakistan, and secondly, that the British Government, will never let down the Muslim League.

To me, the most tragic thing is that the Congress Working Committee bungled the whole affair, when it was strategically in the strongest position. The Congress is the only party in the country that is fighting the British Government and is therefore, the only party that is entitled to sit at a round table conference with that Government and to dictate terms of peace. Therefore, in my view, the most important lesson to be learnt from the Simla Conference is that the Congress should never, in future, sit at a round table conference with the British Government along with other party.

A peace conference is always a conference of the belligerent parties. Who, may I ask, are the belligerents on the Indian side ? Certainly, not the Muslim League. The importance of the Muslim League is largely of an artificial nature—created, on the one hand, by the British Government, and by the Congress on the other by giving so much attention and importance to the Muslim League. If the Muslim League goes through one campaign of Civil Disobedience against the British Government, inviting the ruthless oppression of the latter, I should like to see what would then remain of the Muslim League. A movement led by millionaires, landlords and capitalists is not a mass movement.

In this connection, I should like to repeat what I so often said in the past. Let us resolve to do in future what the Sinn Fein Party in Ireland did in the past when it was faced with a similar situation. When Prime Minister Lloyd George, wanted to confound the Irish politicans by sponsoring an Irish Convention—similar to our All Parties' Conference—the Sinn Fein leaders refused to walk into his trap. They claimed and rightly too, that they alone were entitled to represent Ireland who fought for Irish Freedom.

The Sinn Fein Party, accordingly, boycotted the Irish Convention and thereby turned it into a fiasco. Thereafter, the Sein Party continued the struggle until the day arrived when the British Government had to recognise that party as the sole representative of the Irish nation. Let us, similarly, carry on our struggle till the day arrives when we and we alone shall be entitled to speak in the name of the Indian nation.

It is useless to think of peace until we reach that stage. If we try to make peace with the British Government before the Congress reaches that stage, we shall land ourselves, not in peace but in civil war. I earnestly request all Left Wingers and Left Wing organisations in the country to popularise this idea among the masses that only those who fight for India's freedom are entitled to speak in the name of the Indian people and to sit at a round table conference with the British Government. And, by doing so, let us once for all, knock the bottom out of the religious divisions artfully created and carefully fostered by our enemies.

In spite of recent setbacks the three million Indians in East Asia celebrated on July 4, 1945 the second anniversary of the historic day on which Netaji Subhash Chandra Bose assumed the leadership of the Indian Independence Movement in East Asia. The day was celebrated with mass meetings and demonstrations and Indians in East Asia renewed their pledge of the loyalty to the Provisional Government of Azad Hind and to their leader, Netaji Subhash Chandra Bose. They also reaffirmed their grim resolve to wage the war of India's liberation until victory was achieved. These observances in connection with Netaji Week lasted for the entire week and concluded on July 10th.

In Syonan on July 4 prayers were held in all mosques, churches and temples for the long life of Netaji Subhash Chandra Bose and the complete success of his mission in life, *i.e.*. the complete liberation of India from the British yoke. The day's octivities commenced with the singing of the National Anthem. The climax was reached in the evening when tens of thousands of Indians rallied at a huge mass meeting which was addressed by their beloved leader Netaji Subhas Chandra Bose.

Before the proceedings commenced Netaji stressed the importance of the new National Anthem for India that had been in vogue in East Asia since 21st October, 1948—the day on which the Provisional Government of Azad Hind was formed. Netaji stated that the new National Anthem had been composed by Janab Syed Mumtaz Hussain of the Publicity Department of the Indian Independence League Headquarters in East Asia. Netaji appreciated the composition and adopted it as the future National Anthem of Free India acceptable to all Indians without any distinction of caste or creed. In appreciation of Janab Hussain's services for the cause of Mother India Netaji presented him with a beautiful silver casket containing a cheque for ten thousand dollars.

Then Netaji addressed the meeting in Hindustani for well over two hours. Netaji asked the gathering whether they were prepared to continue the armed struggle against the Anglo-Americans until India was completely free. For a couple of seconds the whole atmosphere was tense and then the whole gathering stood up as one man and signified their willingness to follow their leader to freedom or death.

An event of great importance in the history of the Indian independence movement in East Asia took place on July 8 when the foundation stone for a memorial to the Indian martyrs who laid down their lives in the cause of India's battle for freedom was laid by His Excellency Netaji Subhash Chandra Bose, Head for the Provisional Government of Azad Hind and Supreme Commander of the Azad Hind Fauj on the waterfront in Connaught Drive, Syonan. The function was attended by the Azad Hind Fauj and the Volunteers of the Rani of Jhansi Regiment, who were drawn up to form three sides of the square, while a number of others were lined up on the road. The Balak Sena unit and girls of the Indian National School also took part in the ceremony. High ranking Nippon officials, high officials of the Provisional Government of Azad Hind of the I. N. A. and of the Indian Independence League, and prominent members of various communities were present.

The ceremony began punctually at 11 o'clock with the arrival of Netaji Bose followed by the hoisting of the national flag, the band playing the National Anthem. Netaji then gave an address in Hindustani extolling the supreme sacrifice made by the martyrs.

Addressing the gathering Netaji said : "To-day is for us Indians a memorable day—a day that will live in our history for all time. We have assembled here to-day in a solemn ceremony to pay our respectful homage to all those who have given their lives for the freedom of our Motherland under the leadership of the Provisional Government. As you know, the Provisional Government of Azad Hind declared war on Britain and America on the 23rd of October, 1943, and the armed struggle for India's liberty was actually launched on the 4th of February, 1944.

"Since then, we have, on several occasions, paid our homage to those heroes who died for the freedom of India. But this is the first occasion when we are erecting a memorial to our Glorious Dead. It is, I believe, in the fitness of things, that our first War Memorial should be put in this city. Syonan is also the birthplace of the Azad Hind Fauj. Syonan is also the birthplace of the Provisional Government of Azad Hind.

"It is from Syonan that the troops of the members of other auxiliary organisations like the Azad Hind Fauj Dal marched to Burma, on their way to India. Furthermore, Syonan and Malai have contributed a large number of recruits for our Army and large number workers for our independence movement. That is why the Provisional Government of Azad Hind decided to erect the first memorial to the heroes of Azad Hind in this city, which was once the bulwark of the British Empire in the East and which became later the starting-point of India s last War of Independence.

"There are occasions when thoughts lie too deep for words and this is one of those solemn and sacred occasions. Let us therefore, pay our respectful homage to the immortal dead in solemn silence. And, while paying our homage, let us pray to the Almighty Father to give us strength to continue and complete the work that our heroes left unfinished. Their immortal souls are with us to-day to inspire us to greater deeds of heroism and valour. With God's blessings and with the inspiration given us by heroes, let us continue the struggle without faltering and without compromising, until the complete independence of India is achieved. And let us have unshakable confidence in our final victory, as well as unflinching determination to achieve that victory in spite of all difficulties and tribuialions."

Netaji then laid the foundation stone by placing a marble plaque bearing an inscription in Hindustani with flag standing at half mast. The whole parade was brought to attention and two minutes silence was observed with the guard of honour standing with arms reversed. Wreaths were placed by Netaji, high-ranking officers of the Provisional Government of Azad Hind and of the Nippon Administration and leaders of various communities.

With three salvoes of fen de joie by the guard of honour, followed by the singing of the National Anthem, and with the flag flying full mast the ceremony came to an end amid shouts of 'Azad Hind ke shahidon ki jai.

While Netaji was touring Malaya, engaged in working up to white heat the enthusiasm of the people for total mobilisation with a view to the renewal of military operations, the news of the unconditional surrender of Japan came on August 15 like a bolt from the blue. Instruction was at once given for the winding up of the Indian Independence League in Malaya and other parts of East Asia.

The following Special Order of the Day was issued by Netaji Subhas Chandra Bose, Supreme Commander, to Officers and Men of the Azad Hind Fauj on the eve of his departure from Malaya.

To Officers and Men of the Azad Hind Fauj:

Comrades,—In our struggle for the independence of our Motherland we have now been overwhelmed by an undreamt of crisis, You may perhaps feel that you have failed in your mission to liberate India. But let me tell you that this failure is only of a temporary nature. No setback and no *defeat* can undo your positive achievements of the past. Many of you have participated in the fight along the Indo-Burma frontier and inside India and have gone through hardship and suffering of every sort. Many of your comrades have laid down their lives on the battlefield and have become the immortal heroes of Azad Hind. The glorious sacrifice can never go in vain.

Comrades, in the dark hour I call upon you to conduct yourselves with the discipline, dignity and strength befitting a truly Revolutionary Army. You have already given proofs of your valour and self-sacrifice on the field of battle. It is now your duty to demonstrate your undying optimism and unshakable will-power in hour of temporary defeat. Knowing you, as I do, I have not the slightest doubt that even in this dire adversity you will hold your heads erect and face the future with unending hope and confidence.

Comrades, I feel that in this critical hour, thirty-eight crores of our *countrymen at home are looking at us, the Members of India's Army of* Liberation. Therefore remain true to India and do not for a moment waver in your faith in India'a destiny. The roads to Delhi are many and Delhi still remains our goal. The sacrifices of your immortal comrades and of yourselves will certainly achieve their fulfilment. There is no power on earth that can keep India enslaved. India shall be free and before long.

"Jai Hind"

Subhash Chandra Bose,
By Order, J. A. Thivy, Secretary,
Provisional Government of Azad Hind.

17th August, 1945.

Netaji Subash Chandra Bose addressed the following special message to Indians in Malaya, Thailand, Indo-China, Java, Sumatra, Borneo, Philippines, Japan and other parts of East Asia :—

Sisters and Brothers— A gloriuos chapter in the history of India's Struggle for Freedom has just come to a close and, in that chapter, the sons and daughters of India in East Asia will have an undying place.

You set a shining example of patriotism and self-sacrifice by pouring out men, money and materials into the struggle for India's Independence. I shall never forget the spontaneity and enthusiasm with which you responded to my call for "total Mobilisation." You sent an unending stream of your sons and daughters to the camps to be trained as soldiers of the Azad Hind Fauj and of the Rani of Jhansi Regiment. Money aud materials you poured lavishly into the war chest of the Provisional Government of Azad Hind. In short, you did your duty as true sons and daughters of India. I regret more than you do, that your sufferings and sacrifices have not borne immediate fruit. But they have not gone in vain because they have ensured the emancipation of our Motherland and will serve as an undying inspiration to Indians all over the world, Posterity will bless your name, and will talk with pride about your offerings at the altar of India's Freedom and about your positive achievements as well.

In this unprecedented crisis in our history, I have only one word to say. Do not be depressed at our temporary failure. Be of good cheer and keep up your spirits. Above all, never for a moment falter in your faith in India's destiny. There is no power on earth that can keep India enslaved. India shall be free and before long.

"Jai Hind"

Subhash Chandra Bose,
By Order, J. A. Thivy, Secretary,
Provisional Government of Azad Hind.

17th August, 1945.

Netaji had been advised by the Japanese Government to come over to Japan. Accordingly he left Singapore on the 15 August by air, with the Deputy Chief of Staff-Col. Habib-ur-Rahman. The plane reached Bangkok early in the morning—August 17. From thence it flew to Saigaon. It left Saigaon on the afternoon of August 17, on its way to Tokyo. It reached Taihoku in Taiwan the following day August 18, and took off from the airport at 2 p.m. It had been hardly two or three minutes in the air when the passengers heard a loud report. They thought it was gun fire. It turned out later that one of the propellers had broken. Immediately the plane started wobbling and the pilot could not steady it. In less than two minutes the plane crashed to the ground. The petrol tank burst open and Netaji and other passengers were splashed with petrol. Fire broke out inside the wreckage and Netaji staggered out of the plane followed by Col. Rahman. Meanwhile Netaji's clothes had caught fire extensively as he was wearing cotton uniform. Col. Rahman was wearing woollen uniform and he got less petrol on his clothes. He suffered from less injuries and burns than Netaji. Within a few minutes ambulance was rushed to the scene of the accident and Netaji and other passengers were taken to the military hospital where first aid was given within fifteen minutes of the crash. Two or three of the Japanese passengers died on the spot while others were more or less seriously injured. In spite of the best available medical attention Netaji breathed his last at 9 p.m. on the 18th August, 1945.

Netaji's parting message to his countrymen was : "Col. Habib ! Give this message to my countrymen. Tell them that Subhash Bose till the last moment of his life fought for the freedom of India."

The tagic news of the death of our beloved Netaji, was first communicated by a news-agency. It was confirmed later on by Col. Habib-ur-Rahman, the only fellow Indian passenger on the aeroplane and he supplied the details of the sorrowful accident. Since then, his report obviously based on personal knowledge has been contradicted by various sources. It has been said by responsible and reliable persons, including the leaders of the Forward Bloc that Netaji is still alive, and has been seen by various persons in Malaya and India and some people have also received his letters It is authoritatively stated that he has disappeared and will come out at the opportune moment. The controversy is growing more and more complicated every day by statements and counter statements.

But whether Netaji is alive or gone to his Eternal Abode, his spirit lives in the hearts of all Indians, for ever. His burning love for his motherland, his passionate zeal for sacrifice, his high ambition, his lofty spirit and above all his marvellous ability for leadership and capacity for work have made him immortal.

CHAPTER XIV

THE AFTER EFFECTS

The fighting programme of the Indian Independence League ended with the surrender of Japan and occupation of Malaya by the British.

The Movement had failed in achieving its immediate object, but all this struggle had not been in vain. It left an everlasting impression on the minds of three million Indians living in East Asia. Three years of grim fight, hardships and sacrifices and above all a sense of pride, honour and self-respect, which they enjoyed due to liberty, had infused in them a new spirit. The courage and confidence, with which they carried on their struggle and the charming personality of Netaji Subhash Chandra Bose revealed to them their capabilities. The Indians in East Asia, showed to the world at large, what Indians were capable of. In spite of the ordinary human weaknesses desertions were negligible, quislings and British agents could be counted on fingers and communal differences were an exception. The Indians generally reacted most favourably to the Movement.

This high spirit did not die with the surrender. There were wholesale arrests in Malaya, Thailand and Burma, after the occupation of these countries by the British. Even ordinary Civilians, not to speak of those who

Muslim Nationalist did their duty in the War of Independence

Sri S. T. Seeniketty

State Branch Chairman of Perak

Hafiz Mohd. Khalif-ur-Rehman

Maulana of Saigaon Mosque

Maulana Ali Akbar

Secretary of the branches department I.I.L. Thailand

Babu Buchan Singh

Enthusiastic worker of Thailand

Swami Atma Ram

A labour leader of Malaya

had actively participated in the Indian National Army and Indian Independence League, were taken into custody. Many persons preferred to go to lockups. The cadets of the Officer's Training School undergoing training were also arrested. The treatment meted out to them in lockups was most inhuman and barbaric But no amount of savagery could now deter them from asserting their free will. At last there was country-wide agitation in India. Pandit Jawahar Lal Nehru went to Malaya and Thailand on a short visit and saw the higher authorities. His intervention ultimately brought about their release after seven or eight months, It is interesting to note that the people of Malaya, Thailand and Burma served the I. N. A. prisoners whole-heartedly during this period.

The following communiques of the Vice-President Indian Independence League will show, how admirably the general public behaved during the darkest hours :—

Comrades,

At this turning point, I offer you from the bottom of my heart my warmest appreciation for the magnanimous way you responded to your country's call. Rich and poor, young and old, Indians in Thailand, contributed their mite in the historic struggle for the liberation of India. What does it matter if we did not completely succeed in our attempt ? The fact that the Indians in East Asia did not leave a single stone unturned in their efforts to free India when International situation presented them an opportunity will, I am sure, give inspiration to the Indian nation for generations to come. I admit that we have been defeated today but remember there is something to be proud of even in our defeat. We have set up a glorious tradition. We have shown to the world that India too can produce revolutionary fighters. Let the enemy of India's freedom say anything. We know what we were fighting for and under what circumstances we carried out that fight. Who amongst us did not know that the pact we had made with Japan was entirely a diplomatic one necessitated by circumstances ? Who knew better than us that the menace of European Fascism and Japanese militarism was detrimental to human civilisation ? But when we found a little chance to do something to help the freedom fighters inside the country, we did not let that opportunity pass. Our concern was nothing but India's freedom. If that is a crime we emphatically plead guilty and are happy to pay the price. But let not our enemies forget that the fire for freedom that burns in the hearts of a nation can never be put out by the blood of patriots. Comrades, I want you to know one thing. There is no royal road to freedom other than through the process of 'Blood-Bath'. We have to struggle and we have to die if we want our nation to regain its lost liberty. And so long as blood runs through our veins we shall strive to make India free.

When I say this I want to make one point clear. We have no hatred for individual Briton. He is as much a victim of the capitalist order of society as we ourselves are. India's mission will not be over just by regaining her independence. So long as exploitation of nation by nation and man by man is not obliterated completely from the face of this earth, India's heart will continue to throb.

Now I would like to touch another point—the death of our beloved leader Netaji which we all mourn. We have been receiving blows from everyside for sometime. But that has been the greatest blow so far. He was the embodiment of Indian revolutionary spirit. He organised us, he led us to the battle-field and now he is no more. Is it credible ? Still, comrades, that is the unfortunate fact. We have to continue our struggle without the leadership of Netaji. But the fact remains that there is a little part of Netaji in every one of us and that is the best part of all of us. Let us try to develop that part as much as we can.

At this critical moment I must lay stress on another fact. We have to behave as a well-disciplined body. With malice towards none let us work for India's independence. Our motto is 'Unity, Faith and Sacrifice.' Let us remain true to it.

We have now to discontinue our armed struggle. When the army of occupation comes to this country let us behave as law-abiding citizens. We should not make any clash with them. This is my request to you.

Our present task is to follow the course that events take inside India today, When the Congress acts, as it will, it should not see us lagging behind. For that pupose we must cast away all depression from our minds. India is much nearer to her goal today than she was ever before and she will be independent before long.

Therefore, Comrades, "with full confidence in the people and devotion to the cause let us march ahead. Let our steps be firm, our hearts resolute and our vision undimmed. The sun of India's freedom has arisen above the horizon. Let not the clouds of our doubts and disputes, inaction and faithlessness obscure that sun and drown in darkness created by ourselves.

"In the end, Comrades, I should like to say that I had been inexpressibly happy that I had been able to place my services at your disposal so far. In serving you, the words of our leader 'Do or Die' have been and shall be my guiding star, your co-operation my strength and your command my pleasure."

Jai Hind.

(Sd.) Parmanand
Vice President, and Officer-in-Charge,
Indian Independence League
Headquarters, East Asia.

Bangkok, September 3rd, 1945.

To all Members of the Indian Independence League in Thailand,

Comrades,

Jai Hind,

I have the melancholy privilege to inform you that your Azad Hind Fauj has been compelled to lay down its arms before the victorious army of occupation—superior in number and superior in equipment. The Azad Hind Fauj has had to take this painful decision under the force of circumstances. This army of liberation has never thought of sparing its blood and as you all are aware, the Azad Hind Fauj has merited records of sacrifice, gallantry and chivalry second to none. Our fight was meant for liberation of India and on Indian frontiers and not abroad. Hence the decision to lay down arms and avoid unnecessary blood-shed and disturbance of public peace. At this fateful moment, I like to give you a few points of warning :

1. With the laying down of arms by the Azad Hind Fauj our armed struggle discontinues.
2. We must take our defeat in the coolest and most sporting manner.
3. Do not harbour any malice or hatred towards the Army of occupation, because we are vanquished today.
4. Be perfectly law-abiding, strictly disciplined and dignified in all your behaviour.
5. Avoid all possibilities of clashes with troops and one of the best means is to avoid trespassing the army camps and vicinity. Do not enter into unnecessary discussions or say or do anything likely to result in unpleasantness.
6. Remember : (a) Your goal : "Independence of India"
   (b) Your motto : "Unity, Faith and Sacrifice."

Remember always that with the discontinuance of armed struggle, the fight for India's freedom does not cease. We must and will continue our struggle till our goal of complete independence is achieved. Our countrymen inside India under the lead of the Indian National Congress are working with full determination to liberate India. We must be ready to do our mite in that struggle and for the sacrifices that will free India, when the call comes.

India is bound to be free and before long.

Jai Hind,

(Sd.) Parmanand,

Officer-in-Charge, Indian Independence League

Bangkok, 6th September, 1945. Headquarters, East Asia.

It is gratifying to note that All Malayan Indian National Congress has now been formed in Singapore under the Presidentship of Mr. J. A. Thivy and is doing excellent work in following up the movement and is safegaurding the interests of Indians.

CHAPTER XV

THE TRIAL OF THE I.N.A.

The personnel of the Indian National Army, belonging previously to the British Indian Army were brought to India and detained in Red Fort at Delhi and various other places. They numbered about ten thousand. Immediately the public came to know of the true facts about I.N.A. there was a country-wide agitation for their release. As early as August, 20, 1945, Pandit Nehru warned the Government that harsh or vindictive treatment to them would create a deep wound in the hearts of milllons of Indians, and would widen the gulf between England and India.

The Government of India had to yield before strong public opinion. On August. 27, it issued a commuique in which it declared that " the offence of going over to the enemy and fighting against his former comrades is the most serious that a soldier can commit. It is punishable with death by the laws of all countries... The Government of India feel, however, that allowance must be made for the circumstances, in which the rank and file found themselves placed after their capture...They will be treated with elemency.... But there remains a number—who are alleged to have killed their former comrades or to have been responsible for the capture or torture of Allied soldiers and some leaders, who appear to have consciously embraced the Japanese or German cause... These men will be tried by court martial."

The first Court Martial of the I. N. A. men tried Captain Shah Niwaz, Captain P. K. Sehgal and Lt. G. S. Dhilion. It commenced its sitting on Nov. 5, 1945 in the Red Fort, The Congress Working Committee had appointed a Committee for their defence. It consisted of nine senior counsels, namely, Pandit Jawahar Lal Nehru, Sir Tej Bahadur Sapru, Sri Bhulabhai Desai, Dr. K. N. Katju, R. B. Badri Das, Mr. Asaf Ali, Kanwar Sir Dalip Singh, Bakhshi Sir Tek Chand and Mr. P. K. Sen.

The case of the Prosecution was that these three officers were in the Indian army, that while prisoners of war they joined the I. N. A. and as its officers waged war against the King by invading India and that they ordered the execution of five sepoys. The Prosecution produced 31 witnesses and several documents to prove their case.

The Chief Counsel for the Defence, Mr. Desai, brought out in his Cross-examination that the predominant motive of the Azad Hind Government and the I. N. A. was to free India for the sake of Indians and that they were acting as Allies of Japan as equal partners, and in no way subordinate to the Japanese Government.

On December 7, 1945, the statements of the accused were recorded. Captain Shah Niwaz stated that in joining the I. N. A. he had been prompted only by motives of patriotism. He had fought a straightforward and honourable fight on the battle-field. He further said that he did not deny having taken part in the fight, but he had done so as a member of regular forces of the Provisional Government of Free India, who waged war for the liberation of their country according to the rules of civilized warfare.

In his statement Captain Sehgal denied being guilty of any offence, with which he had been charged and claimed further that he was entitled to all the previleges of a prisoner of war.

In his brief statement Lt. Dhillon said, "It was at the Indian Military Acadany, Dehra Dun, that I learnt to serve my country above everything else. I read in Ghetwood Hall in block letters in gold ; 'The hononr, welfare and safety of your country comes first, always and every time. The comfort, safety and welfare of the men you command comes next. Your own safety and comfort comes last, always and every time.'

" Ever since I read this motto, the sense of duty towards my country and my men had under all circumstances reigned supreme in my thoughts. It was with this motto in front of me that I served my country as an officer of the Indian Army.

" I am further advised that in point of law my trial by the Court Martial is illegel. I joined the I. N, A with the best and purest of motives. As a member of the I. N. A. I was able to help a number of prisoners of war with money and materials. The I.N.A. was able to protect life, property and honour of Indians in Far East."

From December 8 to 18, the Court Martial examined the Defence witnesses. The prominent witnesses were Mr. S. A. Ayar the Propaganda Minister of the Azad Hind Government, Lt. Col. Loganada, the Chief Commissioner of Andaman Islands, appointed by the Azad Hind Government and some Japanese officials. They all deposed that the Provisional Government of Azad Hind was an organised Government, recognized by nine foreign powers ; three million Indian residents of East Asia owed allegiance to it and it had ample resources of its own to maintain the Civil Government and the army. They further submitted that this Government had an Army, which was properly organised, having its own destructive badges and emblams. The Japanese witnesses made it clear that the freedom of India was one of the war aims of the Japanese.

During his closing address Mr. Desai maintained that the Indian National Army was formed with two purposes—the securing of the liberation of India and affording protection to the Indian inhabitants of Burma, Malaya and Thailand, particularly during the days, when their life and property was in danger and law and order was poorly looked after.

Mr. Desai argued at length that the Indian National Army had waged war for the purpose of liberation of the country and any war made for the purpose of liberating one's self from a foreign yoke was completely justified by moral law. He also proved that the I.N.A. was not an instrument in the hands of the Japanese. The Japanese undertook to assist in liberating India and hand over all liberated areas to the Provisional Government. It was a genuine war of Independence for the I. N. A., as a result of the successful termination of which, they expected their freedom.

The Prosecution counsel gave his concluding address on the 22nd December 1945 and after the Judge-Advocate had summed up case on December 29, the Court Martial adjourned to record its findings.

In the meantime the agitation for the release of I. N. A. had increased. There had been violent demonstrations in Calcutta, Bombay, Delhi and other towns, in consequence of which the Government had to open fire at some places. The goal of the I.N.A. was Red Fort, Delhi. The Government, therefore, in order to teach them a lesson and inspire awe detained and tried the I.N.A. officers in the Red Fort and proposed to hang them in front of this Fort, as it had done after the failure of Freedom fight in 1857. But the strong public opinion thwarted its move. Consequently by a Press communique issued on January, 3, 1946, the Government announced that though the Court Martial had found all the accused guilty of the charge of waging war against the King, the confirming officer—the Commander-in-Chief had decided to remit the sentence of transportation for life against all the three accused. He, however, confirmed the sentences of cashiering and forfeiture of arrears of pay and allowances. On the same evening they were set free from the Red Fort.

Immediately on their release they issued a joint statement saying that their release was a victory for India. It was a source of pride and joy to them that the Indian people had appreciated their work in the Far East. They further said that they had taken a pledge before Netaji, their Supreme Commander to fight for their country's freedom...and they would carry on their struggle for Indian Independence under the leadership of the Congress.

After these trials of the I.N.A. Officers by the Court Martial, Captain Abdul Rashid, Captain Burhan-ud-Din were sentenced to seven years' imprisonment and it was also cofirmed by Commander-in-Chief. The international situation, however, forced the Government to discontinue the trials and all the officers and men of the Azad Hind Fauj in India, Burma, Malaya and Thailand, including General Mohan Singh, the Founder of the I.N.A. were released.

The Future of I. N. A.

The Indian National Army has secured a firm place in the body-politic of India. It has revolutionized the whole outlook. It has given further prominence to the Socialist Party, the Forward Bloc and other Left-wing Organizations. In fact the Right wing has swung to the Left. In our future struggle for Freedom, the I. N. A. is expected to play a great part. By virtue of its decision not to take part in party-politics it will be most suited to serve the motherland in its fight for independence. The I. N. A. Volunteer Corps scheme prepared by Col. Shah Niwaz has been approved and the Col. is now busy touring different places, in order to organize the Corps. The I. N. A. Central Committee has taken in hand the work of providing the unemployed young men of the Azad Hind Fauj with work and establishing a permanent organization for social and political work.

The moral and political effect of the I. N. A. on the British Indian Army has been marvellous and of far-reachiug consequences. It has inculcated in them a National Spirit. It is said that during the trial of Captain Shah Niwaz and others the Commander-in-Chief took a referendum from the Indian Forces about the I.N.A. and 60 percent of them said that they wanted the I. N. A. Officers to be released. The British Government now realises that they will not be able to use the Indian Forces for supperssion of the Indian Independence Movement. What is true of the Army, is also true about the Indian Police and other services. In our future struggle for independence, the Army and Police is expected to espouse the National cause. And in the present changed outlook, it can be safely asserted that *India shall be free and before long !*